RECONSTRUCTING AMERICA
Andrew L. Slap, series editor

Embracing Emancipation

A Transatlantic History of Irish Americans, Slavery, and the American Union, 1840–1865

Ian Delahanty

Fordham University Press
New York 2024

Copyright © 2024 Fordham University Press

All rights reserved. No part of this publication may be reproduced, stored in a retrieval system, or transmitted in any form or by any means—electronic, mechanical, photocopy, recording, or any other—except for brief quotations in printed reviews, without the prior permission of the publisher.

Fordham University Press has no responsibility for the persistence or accuracy of URLs for external or third-party Internet websites referred to in this publication and does not guarantee that any content on such websites is, or will remain, accurate or appropriate.

Fordham University Press also publishes its books in a variety of electronic formats. Some content that appears in print may not be available in electronic books.

Visit us online at www.fordhampress.com.

Library of Congress Cataloging-in-Publication Data available online at https://catalog.loc.gov.

Printed in the United States of America

26 25 24   5 4 3 2 1

First edition

Contents

Introduction | 1

1. "We want no slave lecturing here": The Irish Critique of Abolitionism | 15
2. "Over the broad Atlantic": Abolitionist Appeals to Emigrants and Immigrants | 42
3. Irish-American Unionism and Slavery | 65
4. "As if I was a common Irishman": The Irish-American Critique of Antislavery | 99
5. Irish Americans and the Union War | 134
6. Unionism and Emancipation on the Home Front and Battlefield | 168
7. "All true Republicans": Irish-American Leaders and Emancipation | 203

Conclusion: Irish America and Ireland after the Civil War | 237

Acknowledgments   251
Notes   253
Bibliography   293
Index   313

EMBRACING
EMANCIPATION

Introduction

On an early April night in 1863, seven thousand New Yorkers, the great majority of them Irish-born, crowded into New York City's Academy of Music to attend a fundraiser sponsored by the Knights of St. Patrick. Their fifty-cent admission charge, in addition to donations made by the city's leading Irish-born and second-generation Irish-American residents, contributed to a fund established by the Irish Relief Society to send financial relief to Irish farmers who, for the second time in two decades, stared down the grim prospect of famine. Speeches from Irish-American officers in the Union army, prominent Irish-American nationalists, and distinguished Irish-American jurists—not to mention an impromptu speech by the famed former commander of the Union's Army of the Potomac, General George B. McClellan—extolled the generous spirit of the United States and its singular capacity to uplift the people of Ireland and advance the cause of Irish nationhood, even amid a civil war.

The idea that the United States was destined to help Irish people on both sides of the Atlantic realize their socioeconomic and political aspirations was a rare point of agreement within the motley assemblage. It allowed anti-war Peace Democrats and steely Union veterans momentarily to set aside their differences over the war. It crossed class lines between genteel second-generation Irish Americans and Irish-born wage laborers. It even allowed native-born, Protestant New Yorkers who harbored deep suspicions about the city's Irish-born population to clap themselves on the back for their philanthropic spirit. Fittingly, it was a line from Richard O'Gorman, an exiled Irish rebel who now lived the comfortable life of a successful New York attorney in between delivering blistering attacks on the Lincoln administration, that best captured the dominant theme of the evening's speeches. "The union between Ireland and America," O'Gorman rhapsodized, "increases day by day; there is not a ship that crosses the ocean from an Irish to an American port, but is as the shuttle weaving in closer and firmer ties the destinies of these two nations, now and forever united."[1]

Between 1840 and 1865, that union between Ireland and America entangled Irish people on both sides of the Atlantic in a debate over the future of American slavery, one that ultimately provoked a civil war that imperiled the future of the United States itself. Over these two and a half decades, Irish Americans' involvement in the contest over the future of American slavery was influenced by their backgrounds in and continuously renewed connections with Ireland. Moreover, and more to the point in terms of how this book aims to change our understanding of the Civil War era, Irish Americans' views on slavery and emancipation changed during the war. Before 1861, the vast majority of Irish Americans in the free states vehemently opposed all types of antislavery reform and politics, and they acted in the streets and at the polls in the interests of proslavery Southerners. But this dynamic changed during the Civil War. Growing numbers of Irish-born soldiers in the Union army and an influential coterie of Irish-American leaders accepted the necessity of emancipation and, in the case of soldiers, aided enslaved peoples' acts of self-liberation. Understanding both how the Irish in America came to oppose all forms of antislavery before 1861 and why many of them embraced emancipation between 1861 and 1865 requires the type of transatlantic perspective on the relationship between Ireland and the United States that Richard O'Gorman evinced in his speech at New York City's Academy of Music in April 1863.

While O'Gorman's vision of the transatlantic ties that bound Ireland and America focused on emigrant vessels crossing from east to west, those ties were just as much the products of ships carrying news, money, and people in the other direction. Before, during, and after the Great Irish Potato Famine (1845–54), Irish society—including not only the island's stratified classes of rural dwellers but also its urban, middle-class reformers, would-be revolutionary nationalists, and the 100 Irish Members of Parliament in London—consumed American news, accepted American money, and welcomed American guests. Prospective emigrants read or listened to others read aloud newspaper reports of economic conditions and political jockeying in the United States; some received personal accounts of such matters in letters from loved ones or close acquaintances in America. Myriad Irish families awaited envelopes carrying cash remittances or prepaid ship fares from family members in America, while Irish nationalists and Irish famine relief overseers courted donations from native- and Irish-born Americans alike. During the 1840s, especially, American abolitionists—none more famous than the escaped slave Frederick Douglass—delivered lectures in Dublin, Cork, Limerick, Galway, and Belfast to crowds that included prospective emigrants. Irish newspapers gave extensive coverage to these lectures, just as they did for Congressional debates over slavery's expansion during the 1850s and for the proliferation of revolutionary Irish-American nationalist organizations during the Civil War era.

All sorts of Irish people were on the receiving end of news, money, and visits from the United States because Irish Americans in the Civil War era never allowed the Atlantic Ocean to act as a barrier to their continued involvement in the affairs of their or their family's native land. Irish-American newspapers, which proliferated in number during and after the famine migration, featured regular columns with news of crop yields, emigrant vessel departures, and nationalist politics in Ireland. Such coverage allowed Irish Americans to respond rapidly to reports of food shortages in Ireland by organizing relief campaigns that yielded vast sums of money and foodstuffs. It also enabled Irish nationalists in America, including exiled rebels, to organize many associations, societies, and brotherhoods whose aims amounted to one form or another of Irish independence from Great Britain. From New York to Chicago to San Francisco and virtually every city and industrial town in between, Irish immigrants sent letters to family and friends in Ireland, sometimes including in the same packet the most recent edition of an Irish-American newspaper or, more often, hard-earned money that might allow a parent to pay rent or finance the transatlantic passage of a sibling. In these ways, Irish immigrants in the Civil War era lent credence to their characterization, as proffered by another speaker at the Academy of Music fundraiser, General Thomas Francis Meagher. Even while serving his adopted country in its greatest hour of need, Meagher declared, the Irish soldier "never ceases to think of the land that bore him, and the claims which her misfortunes, as well as her grand aspirations, have sacredly and eternally imposed upon him." Six years earlier, upon sentencing twelve Irish-American naturalized citizens in Cincinnati for having violated American neutrality law by dint of their involvement in a revolutionary Irish nationalist society, a judge had lectured the men that there "can be no such thing as a divided national allegiance." Meagher and tens of thousands more Irish-American Union soldiers, along with many of their families and supporters in Northern cities, no doubt begged to disagree.[2]

In this constellation of nodes between Irish society and the Irish in the United States during the Civil War era, the question of slavery's future in the United States cropped up incessantly. It first materialized early in the 1840s when the Irish nationalist politician Daniel O'Connell, propelled by a lesser-known group of Irish abolitionists in the Hibernian Anti-Slavery Society (HASS), injected antislavery rhetoric and direct attacks against Irish-American opponents of abolitionism into a mass political movement for Irish domestic sovereignty. It resurfaced in the mid-1840s when famine relief overseers in Ireland objected to receiving donations from the United States that might have originated in the labor of enslaved African Americans. The same American newspapers that carried news of would-be emigrants' economic prospects included coverage of the divisive debate over the future of American slavery during the 1840s and 1850s. And during the early to mid-1850s, no sooner did the fanfare surrounding exiled Irish rebels' arrival in the United States subside than came calls from abolitionists in Ireland and the United States for those exiles to use their influence over the Irish in America to recruit them into the antislavery movement. Even something as intimate as a letter between brothers now living on opposite sides of the Atlantic Ocean could provoke a disagreement over American slavery, its supporters, or its foes. The economic prospects of current and future immigrants, the constitutional privileges afforded to American citizens regardless of creed or nationality, the potential for the United States to act as an incubator for republican government the world over—all of these were matters of concern to Irish people on both sides of the Atlantic Ocean, and none of them could be separated from the debate over the future of American slavery.[3]

Historians of both the Civil War era broadly and Irish-American history specifically have long been fascinated by the singularity of Irish Americans' hostility to all forms of antislavery in the antebellum period. Like contemporary abolitionists, they have approached that hostility as a conundrum. Why would Irish immigrants, who had been or at least claimed to have been oppressed in Ireland, join forces with enslavers and their allies in the United States? Answers to that question have pointed to working-class Irish immigrants' fears of competing with formerly enslaved people in the labor market; the influence of an American Catholic hierarchy that opposed most social reform movements, especially abolitionism; and the proslavery Democratic Party's welcoming embrace of Irish immigrants. More recently, so-called whiteness scholars argued that nineteenth-century Irish immigrants supported slavery and readily adopted anti-Black racism to prove their own white racial identity to a skeptical native-born populace. The common thread in these various explanations of Irish-American opposition to antislavery is an exclusive emphasis on circumstances in the United States, be they economic, religious, political, or social. Yet historians of American immigration, including Irish-American history, emphasize the need to balance attention to the host community with attention to the inherently inter- and trans-national experiences and perspectives of migrant communities. Such an approach to Irish-American history has revealed that immigrants' patterns of labor protest, occupational status, and political affiliations in America all had important origins in Ireland. It has also yielded new insights into how Irish migrants around the world constructed an identity that fostered connections not only between Ireland and Irish America but also with communities in England,

Canada, Australia, and other nodes of the Irish diaspora. In fact, several studies of Irish Americans' views on slavery during the early to mid-1840s have shown that antislavery reformers and nationalist politicians in Ireland persistently lobbied their compatriots in the United States to join the abolitionist movement. Based on these approaches, the present work employs a transatlantic lens to question why Irish Americans acted as they did in the slavery debate between 1840 and 1865. It does so by investigating how the abolitionist movement *in Ireland* influenced the views of prospective emigrants and the Irish in America; by evaluating how Irish Americans reconciled their expectation that the United States would aid and uplift Irish people with the internecine strife that threatened to destroy their adopted country; and by focusing on the sustained interchange of people, money, and information between Ireland and the United States that shaped what Irish Americans thought about the major issues of Civil War–era America, not the least of which was the future of African American slavery.[4]

While scholarly explanations of the *origins* of Irish-American views on slavery have varied, there is little disagreement among historians of the Civil War era and the Irish in America over what those views were: Irish Americans opposed all shades of antislavery right through enactment of the Emancipation Proclamation. While general treatments of the Civil War era routinely highlight Irish immigrants' service in the Union army, they almost invariably end their attention to Irish Americans in the master narrative of the Civil War with accounts of the New York City Draft Riots of 1863, in which mobs comprised of New York's Irish working-class acted out their rage over the policies of conscription and emancipation by murdering dozens of Black New Yorkers. More focused works on prominent Irish Americans or Irish-American soldiers also tend to situate the draft riots as a brutal coda to Irish immigrants' consistent support for slavery in the Civil War era. Thus, in bringing to light a substantial body of evidence that reveals support for wartime emancipation among Irish Americans both in the Union army and on the home front, the present work offers a corrective to a relatively small but remarkably durable chapter in the history of the Civil War era. The point here is not to downplay the severity of the draft riots or the deeper histories of Irish-American racism and hostility to antislavery in the nineteenth century. Instead, this study emphasizes the complexities of how Irish Americans understood and took part in the Civil War–era debate over the future of slavery. Even as they rejected, at times violently, the entreaties of abolitionists and cast ballots for a proslavery Democratic Party, most Irish Americans insisted that they detested both slavery in the abstract and African American slavery in particular. And when the circumstances of war forced them to reevaluate their long-standing assumption that deference to proslavery Southerners was a necessary evil for the perpetuity of a robust American republic, many proved willing to embrace emancipation.[5]

In correcting scholarly interpretations of both the origins and nature of Irish-American views on slavery and emancipation, the present work offers historians of the Civil War era a transatlantic vantage point of the antebellum sectional crisis and the Civil War itself. Over the past two decades, transnational analysis has yielded new perspectives on fundamental questions in Civil War scholarship. To understand the war's origins, we must consider how American debates over the future of slavery were shaped by competing interpretations of the consequences of British abolition of slavery in 1834. When we explain how Unionists and Confederates who shared a common political heritage inculcated a distinctive national identity, we must account for how they drew from contemporaneous European revolutionary ideologies to distinguish their causes. And we cannot grasp the full significance of the Union's victory in 1865 without attention to republican thinkers and revolutionaries in Europe, the Caribbean, and Mexico who took inspiration from Unionists' successful prosecution of a war for democratic governance and Black freedom. In these and other examples, a transnational approach to the study of the Civil War era overturns commonly held assumptions not only about the origins, course, and consequences of the war but also about the nature of American politics, the sources of American identity, and the role of the American economy in the nineteenth-century world. Ironically, studies of foreign-born Americans in the Civil War era, whose experiences and views were, in a fundamental sense, transnational, have been slow to adopt such a framework. Instead, they have focused on the quality of immigrants' loyalties to the Union or Confederacy and the domestic or localized circumstances that conditioned those loyalties. Even Susannah J. Ural's masterful study of Irish-American soldiers in the Union army, which gives rigorous attention to wartime developments in Ireland, frames its subjects' experiences in the conflict as a contest of loyalties—a choice—between Ireland and America. To be sure, loyalty in a time of civil war matters. But a transatlantic perspective on the Civil War era brings into focus the ways in which loyalty transcended national boundaries.[6]

Following the lead of its subjects, this study incorporates Ireland into its analysis of the debate over the future of American slavery that precipitated the Civil War and the war itself. Most of "the sequence"—the commonly accepted chain of events that led to the Civil War in 1861—will be found in what follows. So, too, will discussion of turning points in the Civil War that effected the mass emancipation of enslaved African Americans and the military victory of the Union's armed forces. However, viewed from Irish Americans' transatlantic perspective, one that assumed what happened in the United States would have reverberations in Ireland and vice versa, these events will look different. Most Americans, including those in the free states, viewed abolitionism as divisive and extreme. But Irish Americans harbored particular grievances over abolitionists having objected to Irish nationalists and Irish famine relief overseers accepting "bloodstained money" from the United States. Many antebellum Americans feared that the rancorous debate over the future of African American slavery jeopardized the perpetuity of the Union and the principles of republican self-government that sustained it. Such fears were more acute to Irish Americans who feared that a weakened American Union would enhance British power and hamstring the United States' capability to back would-be revolutionaries in Ireland. Irish Americans resembled many other white Unionists who came to accept the military logic of emancipation based on events on the battlefield and home front. Yet they added to these factors the urgent needs of prospective emigrants unable to leave Ireland because of the ongoing war and the potential for tens of thousands of Irish-American Union veterans to liberate their native land upon the defeat of the Confederate rebellion. In short, Irish Americans interpreted and took part in the antebellum sectional crisis and Civil War as if Ireland was an extension of the United States and as if they themselves constituted an extension of Ireland. Of course, the Irish were far from the only sizable immigrant population in the United States at this time. During the mid-1800s, many people born in German-speaking lands, England, Scotland, Sweden, Norway, and China brought their own histories and forged various connections with their homelands as they established new communities in the United States. Like the Irish, they interpreted the slavery debate and the Civil War through the prism of their past experiences in and their various connections to their native land. If the history of the Irish in America offers any guidance, historians of the Civil War era must consider the possibility that there were as many antebellum sectional crises and Civil Wars as there were nationalities in Civil War–era America.[7]

Between 1840, when Irish abolitionists founded the HASS, and 1865, when the abolition of American slavery was accomplished, the frequent interchange of people, money, and news between Ireland and the United States produced three intersecting frameworks through which Irish Americans interpreted the major events of the sectional crisis and Civil War. The *Irish critique of abolitionism* coalesced in Ireland during the famine and was transported across the Atlantic to the United States by exiled Irish rebels in the early 1850s. It regarded abolitionism as not only a source of division within Irish nationalist politics but also as a design of British reformers who cared more about the suffering of far-removed African Americans than about the welfare of Irish people in their midst. In the mid-1850s, Irish-American newspaper editors and nationalist exiles adapted the Irish critique of abolitionism to fit the politics of the antebellum sectional crisis, giving rise to the *Irish-American critique of antislavery*. The Irish critique of abolitionism charged that antislavery reformers' meddling had turned Irish nationalist leaders against each other. Likewise, the Irish-American critique of antislavery denounced Know Nothing and later Republican legislators and voters for fanning the flames of sectional animosity as they took increasingly robust steps to prevent the expansion of slavery. The Irish critique of abolitionism had also accused antislavery reformers of ignoring suffering in their own backyard. Similarly, the Irish-American critique of antislavery denounced the purported hypocrisy by which Northern politicians and voters touted their society of "free labor" over the South's slavery-based economy, even as masses of Irish immigrants and other poor white workers in the North toiled for pittances and lived in squalor. By 1860, the Irish critique of abolitionism and the Irish-American critique of antislavery had blended into a transatlantic indictment of all forms of antislavery based on their alleged tendencies to weaken national unity and negate Irish peoples' welfare. *Irish-American Unionism*, the third framework through which Irish Americans interpreted the sectional crisis and Civil War, developed in tandem with but separate from the Irish critique of abolitionism and the Irish-American critique of antislavery. Its central premise was that Irish peoples' socioeconomic and political aspirations hinged on the United States' future as an intact, robust constitutional democracy. On the one hand, Irish-American Unionists argued that the nation's flawed but ultimately uplifting economy and its liberal democratic system offered immigrants and prospective emigrants in Ireland opportunities that did not exist in the land of their birth. On the other hand, Irish-American Unionists believed that Irish independence would not be achieved without assistance from the American Republic, most likely in the form of Irish-American revolutionaries who took advantage of their freedom to organize, speak freely, and train militarily on behalf of their native land. Throughout the Civil War era, Irish-American Unionism was continuously reinforced by the exchange of people, money, and news between Ireland and the United States, the net effect of which was to affirm in most Irish Americans' minds the singular capacity of the American Republic to uplift the Irish people.

In what follows, Chapters 1–4 explain how these three frameworks combined in the 1840s and 1850s to produce an overwhelming Irish-American opposition to all forms of antislavery by the eve of the Civil War. From 1840 until the onset of the Great Irish Potato Famine in 1845, Irish abolitionists were optimistic that they might win sufficient numbers of prospective emigrants in Ireland over to the cause of antislavery and convince enough of their departed compatriots across the Atlantic to unite with the abolitionists to turn the tide of the slavery debate in the United States. But by 1846, prominent nationalist leaders in Ireland labeled abolitionism as a divisive distraction from their efforts to secure Irish sovereignty and chided antislavery reformers' alleged neglect of Irish poverty in speeches and editorials printed in widely read Irish newspapers that were, in turn, reprinted by Irish-American newspaper editors. Over the coming years, the Irish critique of abolitionism was reinforced in the United States by continued efforts on the part of Irish and American antislavery reformers to recruit exiled nationalist leaders into their movement. At the same time, a new source of antagonism between Irish concerns and the antislavery movement seemed to take shape in the United States. In a dramatic escalation of the sectional crisis, antislavery politicians who aimed to halt the expansion of slavery coalesced in a new political movement. Tellingly, in the eyes of Irish Americans, Northern antislavery voters and elected officials aligned themselves in 1854 with anti-immigrant nativists who aimed to curtail "foreign" influences on American society and politics. Heedless of antislavery politicians' moderation in comparison with the abolitionists, the Irish-American critique of antislavery ascribed an anti-Irish animus to all of slavery's foes, especially because the proliferation of antislavery politics in the free states coincided with a growing threat of disunion.

This confluence of the Irish-American critique of antislavery and Irish-American Unionism in the 1850s lay behind the otherwise perplexing tendency of Irish immigrants to do the social and political bidding of proslavery Southerners. Americans' support for the Irish national cause and contributions to Irish famine relief, coupled with expectations of—if not actual socio-economic and political advancement for—the famine immigrants, convinced many Irish Americans that their adopted country was uniquely capable of uplifting downtrodden peoples and poised to aid oppressed nationalities like the Irish. As debate over the future of African American slavery threatened to turn Americans against one another and imperiled the future of the republic, Irish-American Unionism emphasized, above all else, the utter necessity of national unity. With few exceptions, Irish Americans identified antislavery writ large as the chief culprit in the nation's descent into internecine strife. To preserve and perpetuate the nation in which they placed the socioeconomic and political hopes of Irish people in both the United States and Ireland, Irish Americans overwhelmingly spoke, wrote, voted, and acted in the interests of slavery and its proponents through the secession crisis of 1860–61.

Chapters 5–7 explain how, during the Civil War, Irish-American Unionism ultimately overrode the Irish-American critique of antislavery, thereby enabling many Irish Americans to embrace emancipation. Secession and the outbreak of war in 1861 appeared to tear asunder the nation that many Irish Americans had come to see as a haven for immigrants like themselves and an ally to would-be republics like Ireland. Even as they remained suspicious of the Union's Republican-led Congress and the Lincoln administration, especially amid a flurry of antislavery legislation and war policies in 1861–62, most Irish Americans threw their support behind the war to restore the Union. As the Union war effort's antislavery trajectory became clearer and clearer in 1862–63, mounting concerns that emancipation would flood the Northern labor market with formerly enslaved Black men while poor, unskilled white laborers were conscripted into the Union army produced a series of Irish-led attacks on Black communities across Northern states. The most infamous of these were the New York City Draft Riots of July 1863, where the Irish-American critique of antislavery reached its brutal conclusion.

But Irish Americans' involvement in the conflict over the future of American slavery did not come to an end with the draft riots. Instead, a chorus of Irish-American newspaper editors, clerics, and especially soldiers disavowed the grievances and actions of the Irish-born participants in the riots. In so doing, they also reaffirmed their support for the Union war effort, including the policy of emancipation. Indeed, from the war's inception, Irish-American soldiers saw firsthand that their fervent desire to restore the American Union aligned with enslaved men and women's desire for freedom. By the time of the draft riots in July 1863, myriad Irish-American soldiers had either helped enslaved people to secure a tenuous freedom behind Union lines or benefited from the labor and knowledge that formerly enslaved men and women supplied to Union soldiers. Even as these interactions between soldiers and enslaved people undermined the premise of the Irish-American critique of antislavery, developments on the home front and in Ireland served to buttress the tenets of Irish-American Unionism. Anglo-American relations deteriorated to the brink of war in 1861–62, buoying the hopes of Irish nationalists on both sides of the Atlantic who eagerly awaited an opening to strike for Irish independence. Food shortages in Ireland from 1861–63 threatened to give way to famine and served as a reminder that rural Irish society depended on emigration to the United States as a safety valve. And from 1863 until the end of the war in 1865, the Fenian Brotherhood, a revolutionary organization connected to the Irish Republican Brotherhood in Ireland, amassed tens of thousands of members, many of them trained veterans of the

Union army eager to display their martial prowess while leading an armed rising in their native land. Under these circumstances, the perpetuity of the American Union seemed more imperative to the future welfare of Irish people than ever, and a growing number of Irish-American Union soldiers, joined by journalists, nationalist leaders, and clergy in Northern cities and Ireland, embraced emancipation to achieve that end.

Necessarily, a transatlantic study of Irish peoples' involvement in the contest over the future of American slavery relies on evidence of what they said, wrote, or did in relation to that question. Newspapers constitute an invaluable source base for this study. Abolitionist newspapers like William Lloyd Garrison's *Liberator* and the *National Anti-Slavery Standard* carried scores of stories and letters to the editor between 1840 and 1861, many of them from abolitionist colleagues in Ireland and England, concerning efforts to recruit Irish immigrants into the antislavery movement and speculation on why Irish Americans acted in the interests of enslavers. Local newspapers in Boston, New York, Chicago, and Cincinnati, among other Northern cities, provide detailed glimpses of antebellum Irish-American communities that disrupted an abolitionist meeting, aided in the reenslavement of a fugitive from slavery, or attacked Black laborers and their families. Most important to this study are newspapers written by or for Irish people on either side of the Atlantic. In the 1840s, several Irish newspapers published verbatim the speeches and debates from meetings of two Irish nationalist organizations, the Loyal National Repeal Association and the Irish Confederation, in which the subjects of American slavery and abolitionism were raised frequently. The major flash points of the sectional crisis in the 1840s and 1850s were reported on by Irish-American newspapers, which also carried letters to the editor from Irish Americans across the free states. Likewise, the major turning points of the Civil War, including the enactment of antislavery war policies, received extensive coverage and commentary in both Irish and Irish-American newspapers, especially in the form of letters to the editor written by Irish-American Union soldiers that provided a real-time glimpse into changing perspectives on the relationship of American slavery to the future of the American Republic.

To obtain a fine-grained understanding of how developments during the Civil War affected Irish-American views, I surveyed every issue between January 1861 and June 1865 of four periodicals either edited or read in substantial numbers by Irish Americans: the Boston *Pilot*, New York *Irish-American*, New York *Freeman's Journal*, and Cincinnati *Catholic Telegraph and Advocate*. While these publications are far from an exhaustive list of Irish-American newspapers in the Civil War era, they constitute a spectrum of geography, religious inclination, and Irish nationalist thought among the American Irish. Edited by men who left Ireland before the famine, the *Pilot* and *Catholic Telegraph* were official archdiocesan publications. Although the editor of the *Freeman's Journal* was not himself Irish, the newspaper was an explicitly Catholic publication whose name was borrowed from an eponymous Dublin weekly. The *Irish-American* was a product of the famine migration whose editors espoused a militant brand of Irish revolutionary nationalism and, partly as a consequence, clashed with the American Catholic hierarchy. Both the *Pilot* and *Irish-American* reported extensively on Irish nationalist organizations that operated on both sides of the Atlantic, with the *Pilot* assuming a more skeptical view of republican nationalists who often drew the ire of Irish and Irish-American clerics. A focus on two newspapers from New York City is merited by the fact that the Irish-born population there in 1860 exceeded that of every other American city, more than tripled the total number of Irish-born Southerners, and was greater than every city in Ireland, including Dublin. The *Pilot* had many Irish American readers across the United States, especially those who settled in New England. At the same time, the *Catholic Telegraph*'s relatively long pedigree in the trans–Appalachian West and affiliation with the American Catholic hierarchy made it popular with Irish immigrants who settled in the region surrounded by the Great Lakes, the Ohio River, and the Mississippi River.[8]

This book draws from two distinct bodies of correspondence that offer unique vantage points on the origins of and changes in Irish-American views on African American slavery. First, during the Civil War era, Garrisonian abolitionists in the United States produced a voluminous correspondence with members of the HASS in Ireland. In their descriptions of how they planned to bring prospective emigrants and Irish immigrants into the antislavery fold, the transatlantic community of Garrisonian abolitionists revealed some of the very reasons why nationalists in Ireland and virtually all Irish Americans came to see abolitionism as inimical to their interests. Second, like so many of their comrades in arms during the Civil War, Irish-American Union soldiers were prolific letter writers. Much of their official, public, and private correspondence has survived, respectively, in the letterbooks of Irish-American units, letters-to-the-editor columns of Irish-American newspapers, and personal paper collections of archives and historical societies in Ireland and across the Northeast and Midwest. These wartime epistles contain rich descriptions—at times vile or hate-filled but more often curious or even appreciative—of encounters with enslaved African Americans and frank discussions of emancipation. It was a letter from Nicholas Flaherty, an Irish-born soldier in the 9th Massachusetts Volunteer Infantry Regiment, to a close friend back in Boston that first alerted me to the possibility that Irish-American soldiers came to support emancipation during the war. Flaherty was a famine immigrant who came to Boston in 1848. As a sixteen-year-old boy in 1854, he turned out with fellow members of the Columbian Guard, an Irish-American militia unit, to guard against an attempted liberation of Anthony Burns, the escaped Virginia slave captured in the streets of Boston. Writing in September 1863 as a junior officer in the 9th Massachusetts Volunteer Infantry Regiment, Flaherty informed his acquaintance that emancipation was gaining support even within his heavily Democratic and almost exclusively Irish-American unit. Commenting favorably on the valor of Black soldiers in the 54th Massachusetts Regiment at the Battle of Fort Wagner two months earlier, Flaherty asserted that the sacrifices made by Black Union soldiers would convince more and more Irish Americans that "a Negro is a human, and has a right to that freedom for the enjoyment which he has proved himself so willing to sacrifice his life." In the correspondence of Irish-American Union soldiers, indicators of changing views similar to those expressed by Flaherty abound.[9]

It was impossible to conclude precisely how many or what percentage of Irish Americans spoke, wrote, or acted in support of emancipation by 1865. To be sure, the same Irish-American newspapers and regimental letterbooks that furnished evidence of support for emancipation also contained racist screeds and angry denunciations of emancipation, Lincoln, and the Republican Party. Some Irish Americans who came to embrace emancipation continued to describe African Americans in racist terms and showed no inclination to endorse measures of social or political equality in the aftermath of slavery. But historians of the Civil War era and Irish-American history have given ample attention to the many Irish Americans who spoke, wrote, voted, and acted in the interests of enslavers. We can learn something new about the Civil War era by focusing on the experiences of those who, like Nicholas Flaherty, ultimately realized that their transatlantic interests in preserving the American Union were in direct contradiction to a deeply felt animosity toward antislavery. Both the Irish-American critique of antislavery and Irish-American Unionism were borne out of the singular relationship between Ireland and the United States in the mid-nineteenth century, a relationship bound by American money that funded famine relief and nationalists' coffers in Ireland, by Irish and Irish-American newspapers and their readerships, and most of all by the myriad Irish in America who, in various ways, sought to affect the politics, economy, and society of their native land. Secession and the Civil War not only threatened to rupture these transatlantic connections but also confronted Irish Americans with the prospect that the transatlantic bond between the United States and Ireland might never be secured until the bondage of enslaved African Americans was broken. This realization was why the Irish embraced emancipation.

1

"We want no slave lecturing here": The Irish Critique of Abolitionism

The years between 1840 and 1847 witnessed momentous developments in Irish history that bore a lasting influence on how the Irish in America thought and acted with respect to the intertwined issues of slavery and nationhood. The decade dawned at the tail end of a population boom in Ireland that swelled its population to some eight million inhabitants. This population growth not only accelerated the emigration of rural, Catholic Irish—of whom roughly four hundred thousand arrived in the United States between 1835 and 1845—but also strained a fragile landholding system that reduced over half the population to a peasant class of tenants and laborers. Governed by British colonial authorities since the 1801 Act of Union, Ireland was, by 1840, ripe for widespread political agitation. That is precisely what the nationalist politician Daniel O'Connell cultivated through his campaign to repeal the Act of Union, or repeal for short, that dominated Irish politics and society for the first half of the decade. In a sense, O'Connell introduced mass democratic politics to Ireland, just one way modernizing forces increasingly shaped the island over the first half of the nineteenth century. In addition to Irish people's growing, if still fundamentally unequal, involvement in the British Empire, commercialization, trade, and advances in print media that expanded and accelerated communication networks connected Ireland for better or for worse to the broader Atlantic World and beyond.[1]

These intertwined political, social, and communicative transformations thrust abolitionism into Irish life in the 1840s. O'Connell was not only an Irish nationalist but also a British member of parliament (MP) who was instrumental in the abolition of slavery in Britain's colonies in the 1830s. By 1840, even as he launched the repeal campaign in Ireland, he had set his sights on a new foe: American slavery. As a result, the millions of Irish men and women involved in the repeal movement, not to mention the countless Irish- and native-born Americans who backed repeal, were exposed to O'Connell's uncompromising antislavery rhetoric. Simultaneously, a small but dedicated band of Irish reformers who originally coalesced in opposition to the apprenticeship of former slaves in the British West

Indies were inspired by their encounters with British and American abolitionists in 1840. Forming a new Irish abolitionist organization, the Hibernian Anti-Slavery Society (HASS), these reformers aimed to capitalize on the transatlantic popularity of repeal by linking the causes of Irish political autonomy and African American freedom. With prominent abolitionists speaking in person or through the printed word to hundreds of thousands of Irish, the most popular Irishman of the age insisting that the causes of Irish and African American liberty were inseparable, and tens of thousands of Irish leaving for America each year, it seemed that the Irish on both sides of the Atlantic might play a significant part in the campaign to abolish American slavery.[2]

Ultimately, such expectations lay moribund by 1847, as the onset of the Great Irish Potato Famine brought to a boil simmering tensions within the repeal movement and set up a clash between antislavery and nationalism in Ireland. Despite the efforts of HASS members and especially O'Connell to convince repealers that Irish sovereignty must not be purchased at the expense of Black freedom, nationalists in Ireland debated throughout the 1840s whether or not they could accept the rhetorical and financial support—what they often referred to as the "blood-stained money"—of proslavery Americans. With successive failures of the potato crop starting in 1845, the question of whether or not Irish people should accept aid from the slaveholding republic across the Atlantic was extended to the issue of famine relief. Increasingly, a more militant, brash cadre of nationalists known as Young Ireland insisted not only that Irish nationalists and famine relief overseers should accept American support but also that the antislavery reformers who opposed them impeded the cause of Irish sovereignty and jeopardized the welfare of Irish people. Thus emerged from Famine-era Ireland a distinctly Irish critique of abolitionism that rejected antislavery reform as a divisive distraction from the political and social ills that beset the Irish people and championed the United States of America, slavery and all, as an ally in the cause of Irish nationhood.

Abolitionism in Ireland

Antislavery rhetoric and agitation in Ireland during the 1840s typically came from one of two sources. Until his death in 1847, repeal movement leader Daniel O'Connell appealed to Irish immigrants in America to join the antislavery movement and peppered his speeches on Ireland's plight under the Union with condemnations of all forms of oppression, especially African American slavery. O'Connell's antislavery sentiments were genuine, but his political duties in London and his leadership of the Loyal National Repeal Association (LNRA) prevented him from making abolitionism a full-time endeavor. Instead, the men and women of the HASS took up the mantle of antislavery in Ireland. Formed in 1837 around the leadership of two middle-class Dublin Quakers, Richard Davis Webb, a printer, and Richard Allen, a draper, as well as the Unitarian merchant James Haughton, the Irish abolitionists differed substantially in terms of both religion and socioeconomic status from O'Connell's overwhelmingly Catholic, peasant followers. Yet while these confessional and class differences at times led HASS reformers to express frustration with their compatriots, the Society earnestly recruited working-class and even peasant Irish men and women into the antislavery movement. Combined, O'Connell and the HASS brought the issue of American slavery to the attention of the Irish masses.[3]

O'Connell's position as head of the LNRA gave him unrivaled influence over the Irish masses, a circumstance that augured well for abolitionists who aimed to popularize their movement. Founded in 1840, the LNRA sought to annul (or "repeal") the Act of Union that, in 1801, created the United Kingdom of Great Britain and Ireland. Though slow to gain traction, by 1843, repeal was a mass political movement rooted in the Irish countryside, where the rural poor contributed to the cause via a penny-per-month "Repeal Rent." From the LNRA's headquarters in Dublin, O'Connell commanded a vast network of repeal wardens in Ireland and England. In urban and rural parishes, these wardens coordinated between the LNRA and local repeal clubs, filling repeal reading rooms with pamphlets and newspapers that kept interested parties apprised of the movement. The LNRA's ultimate objective remained vague but hinged on the return of an autonomous Irish Parliament to Dublin. The movement captured the support of not only Ireland's rural Catholic population but also an influential group of urban, highly educated, and secular nationalists—the Young Irelanders—whose newspaper, the *Nation*, was the most widely read in Ireland. In 1843, which O'Connell dubbed the "Repeal year," tens of thousands of supporters gathered at "monster meetings" across the island, adding to the campaign an implicit threat of violence to the constitutional, peaceful agitation championed by its leader.[4]

If, on the one hand, repeal's popularity with the Irish masses allowed O'Connell to fuse antislavery reform with nationalist politics in Ireland, on the other hand, repeal's popularity in the United States held out the tantalizing possibility of a joint campaign by Irish nationalists on both sides of the Atlantic to bolster the antislavery movement. Repeal associations made up of both Irish immigrants and native-born Americans flourished after 1840 and sent regular rhetorical and financial support to the LNRA. More than four hundred delegates from over a dozen states attended a National Repeal Convention in New York in September 1843. By then, prominent native-born politicians such as the Whig editor Horace Greeley, the former Whig governor of New York William H. Seward, and the former Democratic president Martin Van Buren counted themselves as repealers. Ganesvoort Melville, brother of the then-whaler Herman, was inspired to stump on behalf of repeal by the sight of bedraggled Irish immigrants arriving in Manhattan. Irish immigrants themselves constituted the backbone of the American repeal associations. Nearly one million Irish, the great majority of them Catholic and most of them unskilled laborers, came to the United States between 1815 and 1845. More likely to find socioeconomic stability and even prosperity than the famine migrants who followed them, many of the pre-famine Irish immigrants took up the political cause of their homeland by joining repeal associations and contributing to the LNRA's coffers.[5]

For O'Connell, such support from American repealers posed a dilemma: could Irish repealers accept support from Americans, whether native- or Irish-born, who condoned or even practiced slavery? It was this very question that led O'Connell and other antislavery repealers to interject the question of American slavery into repeal speeches and debates that were heard or read by hundreds of thousands of Irish men and women. O'Connell never faltered in his belief that opposition to oppression was a pillar of Irish identity. That principle infused his public pronouncements on slavery in the United States and Irish immigrants' seeming indifference to it. In a May 1843 speech to the LNRA at Dublin's Corn Exchange, O'Connell questioned whether Irishmen could "justify, or rather palliate, (for no one could dare attempt to justify)" slavery as it existed in America. "The man who will do so," he concluded, "belongs not to my kind." Addressing a crowd at Dublin's Conciliation Hall two years later, O'Connell again insisted that the Irish people possessed an inborn hatred for slavery. Describing how two decades earlier, West Indies slaveholders tried to recruit him to do their bidding in Parliament, O'Connell proudly recalled his response: "The Irish people sent me here to carry out their principles; their principles are abhorrent of slavery." On occasion, O'Connell or his surrogates made specific criticisms of American laws and policies that advanced American enslavers' interests. In September 1845, O'Connell's son, John, called for the LNRA to condemn the United States' annexation of Texas on the grounds that it would "perpetuate the horrible system of negro slavery." Antislavery rhetoric from the LNRA's leadership reached potentially millions of Irish listeners and readers who could hear it in person or read to them in a repeal reading room or read transcripts in nationalist newspapers like the *Freeman's Journal* or the *Nation*. Thus, repeal leaders introduced the predominantly Catholic, peasant rank and file of the movement to the problem of American slavery and urged them to consider it in relation to their political condition within the Union.[6]

Yet there were considerable hindrances to O'Connell's hopes of conjoining the Irish and Black freedom struggles. For starters, the pitiable circumstances of the Irish peasantry were inopportune for reformers whose chief concern was across an ocean. Ireland remained overwhelmingly rural into the 1840s, with about 6.8 million out of a total population of about 8 million living in towns of less than 2,000 inhabitants. More than half of these rural dwellers were cottiers or laborers who possessed less than two acres of land or none at all and relied almost exclusively on the potato crop for sustenance. Few could have foreseen the catastrophe that resulted from the potato crop's failure in 1845. But as agrarian violence and emigration accelerated during the three decades after Waterloo, the need for land reform was plain to see. Moreover, while O'Connell's Catholicism and deep ancestral roots in County Cork earned him a measure of legitimacy in the eyes of the Irish masses, the vast majority of Irish abolitionists in the HASS were middle-class urbanites and dissenting Protestants who viewed Catholicism with a mixture of bemusement and disdain. One historian alludes to a "curious deafness to suffering at home" on the part of abolitionists in Ireland. Another argues that abolitionists' "middle-class horizons and preoccupations" constrained their efforts to popularize antislavery. With Irish politicians and nationalists agitating for domestic political autonomy to remedy their island's socioeconomic ills, Irish abolitionists' hopes of winning the support of the masses might seem naive.[7]

Yet closer inspection suggests that abolitionists in the HASS were attuned to their compatriots' political and social grievances. Politically, HASS members supported repealers' efforts to secure autonomy from Great Britain. Abolitionists found common cause with repealers frustrated by their island's secondary status in what was theoretically an equal political union between Great Britain and Ireland. But they also had specific complaints about British rule in Ireland. HASS president Richard Davis Webb regarded the Catholic Church's influence on the repeal movement with a mixture of fear and loathing. But he believed that "bad government," above all else, created the conditions that allowed for an undesirable priestly influence. British authorities' response to the famine ultimately convinced Webb that Catholicism alone could not explain Irish poverty. "All Irishmen know what no Englishmen seem disposed to admit," Webb informed an American abolitionist correspondent in 1846, "that nearly all of our misfortunes and faults and miseries . . . are the legitimate result of years of gross tyranny & deliberate misgovernment on the part of England." HASS co-founder Richard

Allen similarly lamented Ireland's political union with Great Britain, noting with satisfaction in 1845 that the repeal movement was "dear to the people's hearts." Like Webb, Allen's political views were hardened by the famine. In 1847, he noted that the "blood is stirred within me when I think of the wholesale wrong that is inflicted on the country by wicked & oppressive laws."[8]

No abolitionist did more to air Ireland's political grievances in the 1840s than James Haughton. Haughton was an active member of the LNRA and unceasing in his efforts to meld Irish nationalism with the transatlantic antislavery movement. To be sure, Haughton always pointed out, as he did in 1852, that the "misgovernment of a people is not to be put on a par with the crime of buying and selling men, like beasts of the field." Such a distinction between political oppression and chattel slavery, however, did not prevent Haughton from voicing his opposition to the former. "We are struggling for our rights and our liberties against power and oppression," Haughton pronounced to readers of the *Nation* in 1847. Haughton's leadership within Irish nationalist organizations, as well as his involvement in several reform movements that aimed to cure the ills of mid-nineteenth-century Irish society, made him the most recognized and respected abolitionist to Irish Catholics in the 1840s. Taking up the causes of Irish tenants, temperance crusaders, disenfranchised voters, and workers, Haughton was the reformer par excellence of his day. His efforts reached across Irish society, including a successful campaign to extend the opening hours at Dublin's zoo so that workers could visit and learn. Importantly, Haughton fused his reform agenda with his antislavery work. In a speech at Dublin's Royal Exchange in 1845, Haughton urged listeners to "give some practical proof of their anxiety to procure liberty for the black man" such as "giving up the use of tobacco, which is a slave-grown produce" and "an expensive luxury, which could be readily dispensed with," thereby leaving more money in workers' pockets. He then urged the crowd to spin and wear home-grown linen and woolen articles to weaken the slave-grown cotton industry and create jobs in Ireland. A reporter from the Dublin *Freeman's Journal* noted the presence of tradesmen in the audience and claimed he had "never seen a more enthusiastic meeting of our fellow citizens."[9]

Some Irish abolitionists went so far as to encourage the redistribution of land in Ireland to solve the island's socioeconomic problems. Richard Allen, for instance, was especially moved by the plight of Irish tenants under callous or absentee landlords. After sporadic episodes of violence in counties Leitrim and Cavan owing to the "oppressively high price of land" in 1845, Allen informed an American correspondent that "the fault lies mainly at the rich man's door." In the same 1847 letter where he lamented "wicked & oppressive laws" in Ireland, Allen described the island's landlords as "absentees, imbarrassed with debt, nominally worth thousands a year but living as splendid beggars." Such absentee landlords left their tenants "committed to the tender mercies of agents whose aim is to collect all the rent they can," giving tenants no incentive to improve their holdings. Even Richard Davis Webb, who rarely expressed sympathy for the Irish masses, griped in 1849 that "English . . . sympathy with the Irish landholders makes it unlikely that any thing effectual will be done to force the land into other & better hands." Without some sort of change in the island's system of landholding, Webb concluded, "there is no hope for Ireland." To be sure, the genteel reformers who convened HASS meetings in Dublin, Limerick, and Cork never put forth proposals for radical social change. But at the very least, Ireland's leading abolitionists were aware of the social and political problems that disproportionately beset their rural, Catholic countrymen and women.[10]

Still, there is ample evidence to suggest that cultural and confessional differences hamstrung abolitionists' efforts to garner sympathy in Ireland for the plight of American slaves. Annie Allen, wife of the HASS's secretary, Richard, believed that abolitionists' lack of success in Ireland resulted from the willful ignorance of Irish people. It was "difficult—seemingly impossible," Allen fumed in an 1844 letter to the American abolitionist Maria Weston Chapman, "to keep alive an interest in the minds and purses of folk who do not read and will not learn the facts and merits of the anti-slavery movement." Isabel Jennings, a member of Cork's most prominent abolitionist family, had difficulty sympathizing with Irish famine victims in 1847, for she had never "known them to care for any intellectual enjoyment." Recalling the years before the famine, Jennings lamented that "all they cared for was—enough of potatoes—education was unknown," concluding that "you could not *feel* they were your brethren." Given the miserable circumstances in County Cork during the famine, Jennings's unwillingness to see those around her as "brethren" because they had shunned "intellectual enjoyment" reveals a critical tone deafness on the part of Irish abolitionists, one that nationalist leaders and Irish Americans alike would later seize upon as part of their criticisms of the antislavery movement. Likewise, HASS members routinely attributed the alleged ignorance of their countrymen and women to the influence of Roman Catholicism. Irish Americans who in the 1850s would ascribe anti-Catholic motives to antislavery reformers need only have pointed to the correspondence of HASS president Richard Davis Webb. Writing to the Boston-based antislavery editor William Lloyd Garrison in preparation for Frederick Douglass's tour of Ireland in 1845, Webb speculated on Douglass's prospects for winning recruits to the cause of the slave. Douglass's Irish audiences, Webb lamented, were steeped in "bigotry & superstition" and "the victims of . . . priestcraft, and religious fanaticism." Four years later, as famine ravaged the Irish countryside, Webb still complained that the "mass of our people are so miserable, degraded, demoralized, & superstitious, so led by the nose by their unscrupulous priests, that it is almost impossible to help them." Echoing the views of American abolitionists like Theodore Parker, who in an 1854 sermon declared that Catholics "love slavery itself; it is an institution thoroughly congenial to them, consistent with the first principles of their Church," Webb found it easy to reconcile antislavery with anti-Catholicism. Webb's brand of anti-Catholicism was especially biting, but his views were symptomatic of HASS members' general distrust of the Irish Catholic peasantry they sought to incorporate into the antislavery movement.[11]

Desirous of involving Irish men and women in the campaign to abolish American slavery but constrained by political, social, and cultural limitations, HASS reformers set about the delicate task of promoting antislavery to an impoverished society. One of their greatest successes came in the form of collecting Irish donations to the Boston Anti-Slavery Bazaar, an annual Christmastime fundraiser organized by Maria Weston Chapman for the American Anti-Slavery Society (AASS). Overseen by leading women in the HASS, the process of soliciting and collecting donations to the Boston bazaar allowed abolitionists to involve Irish workers and peasants in the transatlantic antislavery campaign. Decorative "sea-mosses," made of seaweed that washed up on Irish beaches, were collected from young women in County Cork. Mary Ireland, a Belfast abolitionist, informed Chapman in January 1846 that she was exhorting young women in the area to "use your needle or your pencil for the bazaar" to "evince your sympathy" for American slaves. When the effects of the potato famine manifested in Cork, Jane Jennings worried that Ireland's contributions to the bazaar would be "very far short of what they would have been, in consequence of the distress amongst our working people." An 1848 advertisement for the bazaar emphasized the contributions of rural Irish women, boasting that the "work of our Irish poor has been on former occasions much admired in America, whether knitting, netting, crochet, or embroidery."[12]

Another strategy used by Irish abolitionists was arranging for guest speakers to lecture across the island. In June 1840, members of the HASS attended the World Anti-Slavery Convention in London, where they met and became fast friends with many American abolitionists, especially William Lloyd Garrison and his peers in the American Anti-Slavery Society. Following up on this initial encounter, Garrison and several other AASS members toured the island. An 1841 lecture tour by the African American abolitionist Charles Lenox Remond made a powerful impression. But no sojourning antislavery figure excited more public interest in Ireland in the 1840s than Frederick Douglass. After the publication of his autobiographical *Narrative of the Life of Frederick Douglass, an American Slave* in 1845, Douglass feared that the book's publicity might jeopardize his freedom. As a result, publisher William Lloyd Garrison coordinated with HASS leaders and abolitionists in Scotland and England for Douglass to embark on a two-year lecture tour of the United Kingdom. Douglass's 1845 journey across Ireland, including stops in Dublin, Cork, Limerick, and Belfast, gave abolitionists a chance to convey to a curious Irish audience the horrors of American slavery.[13]

Douglass emphasized the brutality and inhumanity of enslavers in his efforts to convince Irish listeners of the need to act against slavery in America. Newspaper coverage of Douglass's speeches indicate that his audiences were shocked by the brutal punishments inflicted on enslaved people. "I was subject to all the evils and horrors of slavery," he informed listeners at Lloyd's Hotel in Cork, "—to the lash, the chain, the thumb-screw; and even as I stand before you I bear on my back the marks of the lash." The mere mention of devices designed to torture enslaved men like Douglass caused a "sensation" in the crowd at Lloyd's. A report on the lecture in the *Cork Examiner*, a repeal newspaper that also supported abolition and was owned by local Catholic politician John Francis, indicates that Douglass's descriptions were effective. The fact that "such a man should ever have been held as the property of another, his noble frame tasked, flogged, and fettered, and his active, intelligent, and expressive mind cramped and darkened, causes a loathing of the slave system which should be sufficient to enlist all our sympathies," an *Examiner* reporter wrote.[14]

Newspaper reports also indicate that Douglass's audiences in Cork were religiously diverse and, importantly, included Catholics. In a speech at the Wesleyan Chapel, Douglass read "several advertisements of an atrocious character" from American newspapers in which enslavers described fugitives from slavery as "being branded on the cheek or forehead, or bearing lacerations from the lash." During the speech, Douglass was accosted by a Methodist preacher who took offense at the "opprobrium" Douglass had cast on his co-religionists in a previous lecture. The preacher claimed that Catholics had not received their fair share of criticism for being complicit in slavery. While claiming that he meant no offense, Douglass retorted that since "the majority of persons [at the previous lecture] were Roman Catholics, it showed they felt more sympathy with the slave than did the other sects," a comment that was greeted by shouts of "hear, hear" and applause. Douglass continued to lean into the largely Catholic composition of his audience in Cork by denouncing America as "that Protestant country" and celebrating Ireland's leading Catholic politician, Daniel O'Connell, for his labors in the cause of antislavery. While it is impossible to assess Douglass's success with respect to winning over Irish Catholics to the cause of antislavery, one parish priest in Limerick rejoiced that he "saw some of his own creed, all engaged in renouncing slavery" after Douglass left the city.[15]

Additionally, Douglass's affiliation with the Irish temperance campaign and repeal brought his antislavery appeals to the attention of the millions of Irish who took part in either or both movements. Led by Father Theobald Mathew, the so-called Apostle of Temperance, Ireland's temperance campaign saw approximately half of the island's eight million people pledge never to drink alcohol for the rest of their lives. While the movement peaked from 1840 to 1842, temperance still had enough proponents and participants by 1845 to turn Douglass's anti-drink speeches—including a lecture he delivered on Irish soil—into promising recruitment tools for the antislavery cause. Similarly, Douglass's attendance at repeal meetings thrust the issue of American slavery front and center into Irish nationalist politics. During a September 1845 repeal meeting in Dublin, none other than Daniel O'Connell introduced Douglass to the crowd, and Douglass, amid cheers and applause, told listeners of how he had "heard of the Liberator [O'Connell], when he was a slave, in a way that was dear to his heart—he had heard him in the curses of his masters, and thus he was taught to love him[.]" Through his connections to the temperance and repeal campaigns, Douglass momentarily linked the cause of the American slave to the social and political interests of millions of Irish men and women.[16]

For Irish abolitionists, Douglass's tour of Ireland had several important consequences. The first was a surge in Irish contributions to the Boston Anti-Slavery Bazaar. Belfast abolitionist Mary Ireland informed Maria Weston Chapman that Douglass's lectures led to the formation of a female antislavery society in her city. Wishing to take advantage of the "intense interest" created by Douglass's presence, Ireland requested that Chapman send "a few lines . . . mentioning a number of articles suitable for" the Boston Anti-Slavery Bazaar. Cork's contribution to the 1846 bazaar, noted Irish abolitionist Mary Mannix, was still strong despite the "present distressed state of Ireland" thanks to "the extension of the antislavery principles that Mr. Douglass excited during his short stay" in the city. Richard Davis Webb backed Mannix's assessment of the 1846 bazaar contribution, claiming there could be "no doubt that much of the sweep of the Bazaar this year may be attributed to [Douglass]—for from all I can learn the contributions from this side of the Atlantic will be finer than ever." Douglass's tour, according to abolitionists in Ireland, resulted in a banner year for Irish contributions to one of America's most celebrated antislavery fundraisers.[17]

Gauging how wide an audience Douglass actually reached in Ireland is difficult. Ralph Varian, a HASS member who organized Douglass's lecture at St. Patrick's Temperance Hall in Cork, informed readers of the *Liberator* that a local carpenter offered his services free of charge to prepare the hall for Douglass's visit. Varian believed this was proof of "the interest our poorer trades' people take in the anti-slavery cause." The mayor of Cork claimed Douglass's visit had alerted "the mass of the people" that "they too might do something to hasten the emancipation of the American slave from his debasing bondage—simply by forming a portion of the public sentiment of the world." On the one hand, given that the bulk of Ireland's population was rural and that Douglass spoke only in cities, claims that Douglass had reached "the mass of the people" in Ireland should be treated cautiously. On the other hand, antislavery meetings in Irish cities often attracted would-be emigrants desirous of any information they could obtain on circumstances in the United States. In all probability, tens of thousands of prospective emigrants saw Douglass speak or followed his lectures through newspaper reports.[18]

As this last point suggests, Irish newspapers proved to be especially efficient outlets for disseminating antislavery rhetoric. A thriving print culture had taken shape across Ireland by the 1840s, driven in no small part by the repeal movement's association with several of the island's most widely read newspapers and funding of reading rooms where even illiterate peasants could hear reports on repeal meetings read aloud. James Grant, a journalist visiting Ireland in 1844, observed illiterate workers and peasants listening to the contents of Irish newspapers as they were read aloud at regular communal readings in cities and the countryside. Douglass's speech alongside Daniel O'Connell in Dublin, for instance, was either read or heard by the tens of thousands of Irish who followed newspaper coverage of the repeal movement. The *Cork Examiner*, which reprinted many of the speeches Douglass delivered across Ireland, printed 1,200 copies per day in 1845 and was likely read or heard by several times that number. Annual circulation figures for the *Cork Examiner* alone climbed from 140,000 in 1843 to 157,000 in 1844 to 193,000 in the year of Douglass's Irish tour. In light of pre-famine Ireland's robust tradition of communal reading and the repeal movement's adroit use of print culture, Douglass's speeches and O'Connell's antislavery exhortations must have reached hundreds of thousands of Irish in the mid-1840s.[19]

By 1845, Irish abolitionists had reason to be optimistic about the spread of antislavery sentiment in Ireland. Daniel O'Connell, Ireland's most prominent and popular public figure, unflinchingly denounced not only American slavery but also its defenders. Moreover, Irish abolitionists made strides toward finding a common cause with nationalist politicians. By collecting contributions for the Boston Anti-Slavery Bazaar and sponsoring Frederick Douglass's lecture tour, members of the HASS alerted Ireland's predominantly rural, Catholic population to the problem of American slavery. Even while some Irish abolitionists bemoaned the intellectual and religious condition of their fellow citizens, they continued to do their utmost to rally the Irish masses behind the cause of the American slave. These efforts familiarized myriad prospective emigrants with the issue of slavery in the land they would soon call home, producing indifference at worst and perhaps even generating some sympathy for enslaved African Americans. However, between 1843 and 1845, a debate within Irish nationalist circles over the future of Ireland's relationships with the British Empire and the United States produced the first indications of a distinctly Irish anti-abolitionist backlash.

Between Two Empires: Ireland, Britain, and the United States

By 1843, support for repeal had reached a critical mass in Ireland and continued to draw strength from the United States. In October, O'Connell planned to cap an island-wide series of repeal monster meetings that drew tens and even hundreds of thousands of Irish men, women, and children with a massive rally at Clontarf, just north of Dublin. Alarmed by the numbers and rancor of the crowds at previous meetings, British authorities banned the Clontarf meeting on the specious grounds that the phrase "repeal cavalry," suggestive of military forces and violence, appeared in advertisements for the meeting. O'Connell was arrested and briefly imprisoned, but the Clontarf incident demonstrated repeal's popularity; by some accounts, upward of half a million people were on their way to Clontarf before the LNRA canceled the meeting. Following O'Connell's arrest, contributions to the LNRA's repeal rent reached an all-time high.

Ironically, the popularity of "Repeal year" on both sides of the Atlantic in 1843 led to the first controversies over slavery in Irish nationalist politics. American repealers of both Irish and American birth contributed generously to the LNRA in 1843, even as O'Connell continued to decry slavery and its defenders in the United States. As the historian Angela Murphy has shown, American repealers tolerated O'Connell's abolitionism so long as he remained steadfast in his commitment to Irish liberty. In fact, it was in Ireland that O'Connell's antislavery rhetoric first provoked a backlash from Irish nationalists. Repeal's popularity in the United States had translated into substantial financial support for the LNRA. American donations to the organization in July–August 1843 doubled those from all but one county in Ireland, and O'Connell's arrest and imprisonment by British authorities only further cemented his status as Ireland's national hero among both Irish- and native-born Americans. As American funds poured across the Atlantic and into the coffers of the LNRA, O'Connell's continued criticisms of the slaveholding republic rankled some repealers even as abolitionists in America and Ireland fretted that proslavery interests were attempting to silence O'Connell by contributing to repeal.[20]

The transatlantic abolitionist network led by William Lloyd Garrison took the lead in pressing Irish repealers to reject the aid of slaveholders. Announcing, in 1842, his support for the Irish cause, Garrison declared himself "an Irish Repealer and an American Repealer." He supported the repeal of the political union between Great Britain and Ireland just as he favored a separation between the free and slave states. Garrison claimed that Southern donations to Irish repeal were designed "to stop O'Connell's mouth on the subject of slavery, and to prevent any more 'interference' . . . from that side of the Atlantic." This warning about the potential for proslavery interests to corrupt Irish repeal caught the attention of James Haughton, a regular contributor to Garrison's *Liberator*. In April 1843, Haughton wrote to O'Connell to reiterate his objections to "the hollow sympathy, & the blood stained money, of American Slaveholders." Little more than a month later, O'Connell borrowed from Haughton's letter in declaring before a May 9, 1843, LNRA meeting that he did not want "blood-stained money" from America, as shouts of "hear, hear" echoed through Dublin's Corn Exchange building. By May 1843, then, a debate over whether or not Irish nationalists could accept Americans' "blood-stained money"—a phrase never clearly defined but indicating funds tied to proslavery interests—was percolating in Ireland.[21]

The questions of if and how frequently the LNRA actually returned money to America are difficult to answer with certainty. In 1844, O'Connell returned a donation of £178 from repealers in New Orleans, but his rejection of these funds stemmed from an endorsement of violence attached to the donation rather than the money being tainted by its connection to slavery. At a July 29, 1845, LNRA meeting, O'Connell's son, John, stated that "on two or three occasions," the association returned money that came with letters justifying slavery. The elder O'Connell claimed it was "quite true that from many parts of America we refused sympathy, because the evidence of that sympathy was accompanied by principles we could not adopt," an ambiguous statement that raises the possibility of a distinction between "sympathy" and financial aid. In an 1846 letter concerning efforts to convince the Free Church of Scotland to return donations from Southerners, James Haughton claimed that O'Connell "set the Scotch a good example . . . in refusing the contributions of slaveholders to the Repeal funds." There is no direct evidence to support claims that donations were returned. But at minimum, O'Connell always dangled the threat of refusing donations from American enslavers and their defenders.[22]

Regardless of whether or not O'Connell returned money to America, the possibility that his rhetoric might disrupt the repeal campaign's transatlantic fundraising provoked the ire of some repealers. Members of the Young Ireland faction of Irish nationalists used their editorial control over the *Nation* to dissent from O'Connell's criticisms of American slavery. A January 13, 1844, *Nation* editorial signaled the start of a years-long campaign by Young Irelanders to mute discussion of American slavery within Irish nationalist politics. "Repeal must not be put into conflict with *any* party in the States," the *Nation* warned in its opening salvo against O'Connell's abolitionism. "We might as well refuse English contributions because of the horrors of mill-slavery . . . as quarrel with Americans because of their domestic institutions, however we may condemn and once for all protest against them." Authored by one of the *Nation*'s trio of editors—Thomas Davis, Charles Gavin Duffy, and John Mitchel—this piece drew a response from James Haughton. Questioning the *Nation*'s "disposition . . . to accept aid and sympathy in carrying out measures for Ireland's independence from American slaveholders," Haughton urged the newspaper's editors to reconsider their stance. The *Nation*'s editorial board published Haughton's letter, but they refused to come down from their position that American slavery should be of no concern to Irish nationalists.[23]

The *Nation*'s opposition to O'Connell's anti-American rhetoric coincided with deeper fractures within the repeal movement over the ultimate aims and objectives of Irish nationalists, particularly concerning the future of Anglo-Irish relations. Following his release from prison in 1844, O'Connell blunted the edges of his calls to repeal the Union. Speaking to a crowd in Coventry, England, in March, O'Connell insisted that nothing short of "an Irish Parliament will give justice to Ireland" but concluded his remarks by calling for "a strong pull and a long pull for England and Ireland—for Ireland and for England; a strong pull and a long pull, and a pull altogether." At Coventry, O'Connell framed repeal not as a measure that would sever Anglo-Irish relations but as one that could "unite the two countries more closely" through a federated partnership. Over the coming months, he elaborated on the nature of such a federated Anglo-Irish government. A restored Irish Parliament in Dublin would legislate Irish domestic affairs while Irish MPs would remain at Westminster to weigh in on "questions of imperial concern, colonial, military, naval, and of foreign alliance and policy." Never fully fleshed out, federalism proposed to make Ireland a genuine partner in the British Empire, giving what O'Connell described as "a right to Ireland . . . to interfere directly in imperial concerns, in foreign treaties, and in colonial affairs."[24]

While O'Connell's shift toward federalism initially won praise from some Young Ireland nationalists, others were dubious of any plans that kept Ireland part of the British Empire. On the one hand, *Nation* editor Thomas Davis pledged to "welcome Federalism" on the grounds that it conceded "Irish supremacy in Ireland." By the 1840s, tens of thousands of young Irishmen served the British Empire as soldiers and sailors. At the same time, a growing body of middle-class Irish Catholics sought out government patronage positions in England. Given the extent of Irish participation in the British Empire and the potential for federalism to win over otherwise skeptical Irish Protestants and Conservatives at Westminster to the cause of repeal, O'Connell's strategy seemed poised to carry the day. Yet not all Young Irelanders were convinced. Charles Gavin Duffy, another *Nation* editor, saw in federalism a vehicle for English culture to continue stamping out Irish national consciousness. Duffy insisted that only a complete and total repeal of the Union could resurrect Irish nationality, a view that Davis eventually embraced. The federalist debate in 1844 was only a harbinger of further divisions between O'Connell, the pragmatic constitutionalist, and the puritanical Young Irelanders.[25]

O'Connell's flirtation with federalism failed to achieve the goal of repeal, and by the end of 1844 he backed down from the proposal. Yet the question of Ireland's relation to the British Empire resurfaced in 1845 thanks to the looming prospect of war between Great Britain and the United States. In his inaugural address on March 4, President James K. Polk called for an end to British and American joint occupation of the Oregon territory, signaling American intentions to bring Oregon squarely under Congress's control. Moreover, Polk's election on an aggressive expansionist campaign had all but guaranteed American annexation of Texas, a move that was initiated even before Polk delivered his inaugural address. American annexation of Texas threatened to undermine years of careful efforts to cultivate trade ties between Britain and the Lone State Republic and a concomitant campaign on the part of British antislavery reformers to abolish slavery in the former Mexican province. Ever wary of the specter of British abolitionism in North America, proslavery American politicians saw in Texas annexation the chance to shore up the southwestern boundary of slavery while adding to the nation a vast tract of slave-worked soil. As Polk settled into the White House, leading statesmen on both sides of the Atlantic predicted that Texas annexation would lead to the outbreak of a third Anglo-American War. Still dependent on the financial support of proslavery Americans, more and more repealers questioned whether O'Connell's commitment to antislavery and loyalty to the Crown were intertwined. In their eyes, abolitionism seemed contrary to the interests of Irish sovereignty.[26]

At a March 30, 1845, LNRA meeting, O'Connell stepped into the fray of Anglo-American relations in a speech that aimed to leverage British antislavery and foreign policy interests for the return of Irish home rule. Reacting to the news of the American annexation of Texas, O'Connell charged that the government of the United States was "guilty of slavery, the greatest crime that can be committed by humanity against humanity" even as it "boasts of liberty." Such rhetoric was typical of O'Connell's previous condemnations of American hypocrisy. But with the United States on the brink of war with Great Britain, O'Connell went a step further toward arraying Ireland against American slavery by guaranteeing Irish support for British foreign policy, even up to a declaration of war against the slaveholding republic. "The throne of Victoria can be made perfectly secure—the honour of the British empire maintained—and the American eagle in its highest point of flight, be brought down," O'Connell pledged. All that was needed, he continued, was for Britain to grant Ireland its domestic autonomy through the return of "the parliament in College Green, and Oregon shall be theirs [Britain's], and Texas shall be harmless." O'Connell's "American eagle'" speech, according to one of his most loyal supporters, was a "concentrated Denunciation of accursed American 'Land of Liberty' Negro-Slavery," one that aligned Ireland alongside the abolitionist British Empire against American proslavery expansionism.[27]

On both sides of the Atlantic, the fallout from O'Connell's "American eagle" speech was swift and dramatic. The historian Angela Murphy has shown that while Irish American repealers tolerated O'Connell's antislavery rhetoric over the previous half-decade, his suggestion that the Irish would side with Britain in a potential war with the United States forced them to choose between the land of their birth and the land of their adoption. Given that choice amid heightened nativist suspicions of Irish immigrants' loyalties, Irish American repealers overwhelmingly denounced O'Connell's speech, and support for repeal in the United States plummeted.[28] Less understood but just as, if not more, important to the evolution of Irish and Irish American views on slavery and abolitionism is how O'Connell's embrace of the British Empire, rooted as it was in his antislavery convictions, was received by Irish repealers, especially Young Ireland.

O'Connell's "American eagle" speech exacerbated concerns among Young Irelanders that Irish nationalists' denunciations of American slavery jeopardized American support for repeal. The suggestion that the Irish would side with England in a potential conflict with America was especially galling to Irish nationalists who counted America as an ally. Privately, *Nation* editor John Blake Dillon groused that "[e]verybody is indignant at O'Connell meddling in the business. His talk about bringing down the pride of the American Eagle, if England would pay us sufficiently, is not merely foolish, but base and false." The *Nation*'s public reaction to the "American eagle" speech conveyed more clearly why Young Irelanders were loath to criticize the United States. "[N]otwithstanding the slavery of the negro," an April 12 editorial asserted, the United States is "liberty's bulwark and Ireland's dearest ally." Other repeal newspapers, such as the *Dublin Pilot*, *Tipperary Free Press*, and *Waterford Freeman*, likewise stressed the need to privilege repeal above the antislavery cause. As word reached Ireland that O'Connell's speech had precipitated the dissolution of many American repeal associations, the *Nation* tried to correct for O'Connell's alleged error by denying that the United States deserved any criticism for its practice of slavery, "an offence committed by Athens, Rome, Spain, and England." Describing abolitionism as a "Quixotic mission" to redress wrongs in distant lands, the *Nation* averred that Ireland's "suffering and thraldom [sic] require every exertion and every alliance."[29]

O'Connell's promise to help Britain bring down the American eagle if Ireland was granted home rule achieved little for the cause of repeal since the American annexation of Texas went uncontested by British statesmen, rendering O'Connell's pledge of support toothless. Yet the debate over whether repeal should concern itself with American slavery refused to die down. At an August 4, 1845, meeting of the LNRA at Dublin's Conciliation Hall, Dublin barrister and LNRA member Edward Clements spoke in support of O'Connell by denouncing the "horrible and demoralizing system of slavery" that existed in America. As Clements spoke, fellow repealer Richard Scott interrupted. Scott concurred that slavery was indefensible but worried that damning slaveholders at LNRA meetings would alienate American donors. Friends in America, Scott explained, had informed him that after reading antislavery speeches in the published minutes of the LNRA, a repeal association in Cincinnati had voted to retain some £100 in funds that would have otherwise been sent to the organization. He cautioned that repealers "ought to take very good care of how they meddled" in American affairs, as mixed cries of "hear, hear" and "oh, oh" rang through the hall. A lengthy debate ensued between Clements, Scott, John O'Connell, and a nephew of Daniel O'Connell, Captain Broderick, over whether the Association should or should not condemn American slaveholders and proslavery apologists.[30]

Scott was eventually silenced by the LNRA's antislavery faction, although repeated cheers of "hear, hear" for his arguments indicate he was not alone in his opinions. Significantly, a subsequent *Nation* editorial entitled "Ireland and America" endorsed Scott's views. Written by Young Ireland's unofficial leader Thomas Davis, the piece first admonished abolitionists by insisting that slavery's very wickedness made immediate emancipation dangerous, for "the negro has all the vices, ignorance, and wild impulse of a slave." Davis also repeated the threadbare argument that American slavery was "doomed to perish" and should be allowed to die out in its own time. But Davis's central point was that Irish protestations against American slavery harmed the cause of repeal. Irishmen "cannot become blind to the value of such an intimacy" as existed between America and Ireland, Davis insisted before pointing out the importance of American support for Catholic emancipation in Ireland some two decades earlier. Continuing, Davis retraced the steps by which American support for repeal had increased since 1840, calling particular attention to how Americans "swelled the pomp of '43 with their increasing aid." Even as he insisted that Ireland's liberty must be secured "by her own purpose and by her own strength," Davis chastised the O'Connells and others who seemed "ungrateful for the care and zeal of America" through their remonstrance against its peculiar institution. "We are sure, therefore," Davis concluded in reference to the most recent slavery debate within the LNRA, "that the country will not read without some feeling of regret the unhappy discussion of last Monday." The message to the *Nation*'s quarter of a million readers was clear: Irish abolitionism was an impediment to Irish sovereignty.[31]

The *Nation* editorial in Scott's defense revealed that, by 1845, a growing segment of Irish nationalists—especially those belonging to the Young Ireland faction—was fed up with O'Connell's attempts to inject antislavery into Irish political life. Tensions between Enlightenment-influenced thinkers like O'Connell and the more militant and romantic Young Irelanders did not exist in an ideological vacuum. They accompanied disagreements between O'Connell and Young Ireland over the use of violence, O'Connell's flirtation with federalism and Whig MPs, and religion's place in Irish nationalism. In the grand scheme of things, divisions produced by O'Connell's abolitionism and Young Ireland's aversion to it bore only a slight influence on the ultimate fate of the repeal movement. But more important to the present work, the slavery debates in the wake of O'Connell's "American eagle" speech led Young Irelanders to conclude that abolitionism was a divisive, British, anti-American, and therefore unpatriotic cause.[32]

Famine Relief, the Irish Confederation, and Irish Anti-Abolitionism

Before the dust could settle on repealers' debate over the "American eagle" speech, reports began circulating in Ireland about a partial potato crop failure. *Phytophthora infestans*, the fungal infestation responsible for this partial failure of 1845's potato crop, returned in 1846 when the potato harvest dropped some 80 percent from only a few years earlier. Although the blight subsided in 1847, listless and emaciated Irish men and women had been unable to plant anywhere near a sufficient crop for the year, a fate that became all the more tragic in 1848 when the blight reappeared to the utter devastation of farmers whose confidence in the potato had been temporarily restored. As *Phytophthora infestans* returned each year for the next half-decade, potato harvests never exceeded 50 percent of pre-1845 levels. In and of itself, the potato blight would have dealt a severe blow to the millions of Irish smallholders, cottiers, and laborers who depended largely or entirely on the potato for subsistence. But their misery was compounded by a poor relief system funded and overseen by penny-pinching landlords; the belief among some evangelical British politicians, most notably assistant secretary of the treasury Charles Trevelyan, that the potato blight was divinely ordained; and, following the ascension to power of Lord John Russell and the Whig Party in 1846, a dogmatic adherence to *laissez-faire* economics by politicians in London. Under these circumstances, a critical food shortage became the Great Irish Potato Famine, which, from 1845 to 1854, left a trail of starvation, disease, and emigration in its wake.[33]

Even before the inadequacies of Ireland's poor relief system and Westminster's response to the repeated potato crop failures were apparent, humanitarian relief began pouring into Ireland, especially from the United States. American donations to Irish famine relief reignited the now years-long debate over whether or not Irish nationalists should accept rhetorical and especially financial aid from the slaveholding republic across the Atlantic. While this debate unfolded between 1845 and 1847, Irish nationalism was transformed. O'Connell's health rapidly deteriorated, and Young Irelanders became more militant in their demands for Irish sovereignty. In 1847, the debate over Ireland's connections to American slavery reached its zenith, as American and Irish abolitionists' calls for Irish nationalists to reject American aid collided headlong with Young Ireland's determination to do whatever was necessary for what it deemed to be the welfare of the Irish people. From this collision emerged a uniquely Irish critique of abolitionism that proved readily transportable across the Atlantic.

The failure of 1845's potato crop forced Irish nationalists on both sides of the Atlantic to concentrate on alleviating the distress of those whose diets depended on the potato. By December 1845, efforts were underway in Boston to raise funds for the "suffering thousands who will inevitably perish from starvation in case aid is not sent them by their more favored countrymen on this side of the Atlantic." Over the next year, repeal associations in Boston, New York, and Philadelphia shifted their efforts to famine relief, and by January 1847, an Irish-American lawyer in New York City reported that $808,000 had been contributed to famine relief by Irish Americans in New York City alone. In February, the *Nation* reported the news of New York City's contributions and additional aid from Baltimore, Boston, and Philadelphia, which brought the total donations from the four cities to $1.5 million. Between February and June 1847, Boston's Relief Association of Ireland, led by Bishop John Fitzpatrick, collected $150,000.[34] Famine relief efforts quickly reunited the American Irish around the plight of their native land and repaired broken links between Ireland and America caused by O'Connell's denunciation of the "American eagle" in 1845.

Who contributed to famine relief was just as important as how much money finally made the eastward trip across the Atlantic. Irish Americans were among the most eager and, relative to their socioeconomic standing, most generous contributors. United States senators and representatives gave $349 and $972 each, respectively. Choctaw Indians in Arkansas raised $710, while enslaved African Americans on a plantation in Alabama pooled together $50. Millworkers, miners, and railroad workers gave what they could, even as wealthy industrialists like Amos Lawrence made sizable individual donations. Irish famine relief, according to the historian Merle Curti, was "the most impressive, and . . . the first truly national campaign to relieve suffering in another land without respect to political and nationalistic considerations."[35] The diverse backgrounds of famine relief contributors in America gave Irish nationalists additional reason to chide abolitionists who decried American slavery as a stain on Americans' character.

Perhaps no story better illustrates the effects of Americans' famine relief efforts on the relationship between Ireland and America than that of the USS *Jamestown*. Commissioned by Congress to carry provisions from Boston to Ireland, the *Jamestown*, a sloop-of-war that might have otherwise been used in the Mexican-American War, began loading supplies on St. Patrick's Day of 1847. Landing in the port of Cobh in mid-April, the *Jamestown* was greeted by a band, inaugurating more than a week's worth of banquets, celebrations, and speeches to demonstrate the Irish people's gratitude for American generosity. The *Cork Examiner* claimed the *Jamestown*'s arrival had "lifted up our heart a little, and taught us another lesson of the bringing forth of good from evil," and elsewhere lauded "the sort of intercommunion of nations in which we should glory." In Dublin, the *Freeman's Journal* praised "the gallant officers of the Jamestown," while the *Kilkenny Journal* deemed the *Jamestown*'s trip a "glorious mission."³⁶ The *Jamestown*, laden with $100,000 in supplies from Irish Americans and native-born Americans alike, represented all that was great and good in America to the Irish.

Such "laudation of everything American" from Irish pens and mouths in 1847, as James Haughton termed it, concerned abolitionists on both sides of the Atlantic. "The gifts of slaveholders will shut our mouths . . . & close our eyes so that we will not see the wickedness of man stealing," Haughton lamented to the Rev. Samuel May in America. Henry C. Wright warned that slaveholders would "'make capital,' as we say in the United States, out of Irish poverty and distress, in order to win golden opinions of all men . . . which will prove a tower of strength to their cherished '*institution*' of slavery." Richard Davis Webb worried that "the American bounty . . . will confound all distinction in the minds of the recipients, and the bloodiest slaveholder, who sends the price of blood, will be looked on by them as an angel of mercy." Webb certainly knew the perilous conditions afflicting the rural Irish poor; early in 1847, he traveled to some of the worst-affected parts of Ireland in the province of Connaught to investigate potential irregularities in relief works. Despite the horrid conditions in Ireland that American abolitionists read of and Irish abolitionists witnessed firsthand, many fretted over the implication of accepting American aid.³⁷

Editorials in American and Irish newspapers added to abolitionists' fears that aid from America would create a sense of indebtedness among its Irish recipients. An article in the Charleston, South Carolina, *Mercury* is particularly revealing in this regard. "Lavish in their own generosity," the article read, ". . . Irishmen will not fail in a proper appreciation of our exertions on their behalf." The *Mercury* reported on South Carolinians' contributions to Irish famine relief throughout 1847, taking "pride and pleasure" in publicizing the "divine attributes of charity and benevolence" exemplified by contributors. The Charleston daily pointed to proof of Irish gratitude for American aid by reprinting an article in the Dublin *Nation* that predicted "the establishment of 'a cordial understanding' between us [Ireland] and the United States of America" in the aftermath of the famine. As if to confirm abolitionists' fears, the *Mercury* asked Charleston's Irish Americans to "announce . . . to their friends and relations abroad, that they also may come to us, and share with us the blessings it is our lot so bountifully to enjoy."³⁸

Abolitionists' concerns that famine relief from America would blind the Irish to the wickedness of American slavery culminated in a contentious transatlantic debate over accepting donations from Charleston and Baltimore. The funds, £1,300 from the Irish Relief Committee of Charleston and £1,000 from the Irish Relief Committee of Baltimore, were sent to the Central Relief Committee of the Society of Friends, an Irish Quaker body established in 1846 to raise and distribute private relief funds. Although the committee accepted the money at a meeting on March 25, 1847, that decision was preceded by objections from HASS leaders who organized relief efforts. Relief Committee members Richard Allen and Henry Russell argued against acceptance from the outset and publicized their dissent from the committee in the *National Anti-Slavery Standard*. Allen and Wright argued that by accepting aid from people who were certain to have some connection to slavery, Committee members had become "allies of slave-breeders, and slave-traders, and accessories to the robbery, concubinage, and heathenism of Slavery." James Haughton opposed the committee's acceptance of the money and expressed his concern that Irish people would see the Charleston and Baltimore donations as "the spontaneous expressions of benevolent sympathy with us in our late starving condition" rather than the bribes he viewed them to be. For Allen, Wright, and Haughton, enslavers' money came with a moral price that the three were unwilling to let famished Irish men and women pay.[39]

Yet other abolitionists proved more circumspect in their opinions on the Charleston and Baltimore donations. The *National Anti-Slavery Standard*'s editor argued that accepting the money implied no affirmation of slavery and asserted that any "*moral* responsibility" in the matter was owed to the "suffering people." In a letter to Richard Davis Webb, Garrison similarly argued that the aid came "without any sanction of slaveholding being either required, volunteered, or understood." Webb lamented the "bad effect of the American bounty" on Irish minds but acknowledged in the *Standard* that if he were "suffering the pangs of starvation, it is probable my scruples might melt away before the terrible realities of my position."[40] Not wanting to prejudice onlookers against abolitionists and sincerely desiring to assist famine victims, those who advocated acceptance of the Charleston and Baltimore aid demonstrated prudence and compassion.

Ultimately, the arguments of Webb and Garrison persuaded Allen to reassess his position and assent to what was, after all, a foregone conclusion. The committee had decided in March to accept the Charleston and Baltimore donations, yet only in June did Allen reverse tracks and acknowledge in the *Liberator* that it was "justifiable ... to make a rightful application of wealth which may have been wrongfully created." Allen pointed out that if the committee returned enslavers' aid, consistency demanded that it also return aid from bankers and merchants whose income could be traced to slave-grown crops. Whether Allen's change of heart stemmed from a realization that rejecting the money might do more harm than good to the antislavery cause or a genuine concern for famine victims is impossible to determine. It bears emphasis that Quakers' humanitarian credentials during the famine were impeccable.[41]

Viewed as a test of Irish abolitionists' willingness to place the needs of those at home on par with African American slaves, the famine relief debate presumably should not have damaged the antislavery movement's reputation among the Irish. Historians who have addressed the issue emphasize abolitionists' charity and pragmatism during the famine. Abolitionists in America and especially in Ireland, these scholars argue, recognized the dire nature of famine victims' situation and shelved their concerns over "blood-stained money" to administer relief as widely as possible. Thus, as one historian claims, "the abolitionists received enhanced status from their work in famine relief." Irish abolitionists' philanthropy during the famine, in this interpretation, should have put to rest Irish nationalists' argument that labor on behalf of African American slaves came at the expense of political autonomy and social welfare for the Irish.[42]

Yet simultaneous intersecting developments within nationalist politics once again brought the transatlantic antislavery movement into conflict with Irish nationalism. After the untimely death of the *Nation* co-editor Thomas Davis in September 1845, a young Ulster Presbyterian named John Mitchel joined the *Nation* staff, adding to Ireland's most widely read nationalist newspaper an acerbic, uncompromising voice which immediately provoked the ire of Daniel O'Connell. A Young Irelander, Mitchel was one of several romantic nationalists in the LNRA who challenged O'Connell's leadership, a task made easier by the disastrous effects of the "American eagle" speech on American support for repeal and especially by the mounting desperation in the Irish countryside produced by the famine, which made the technicalities of repeal increasingly irrelevant to the Irish masses. By no means should the middle-class, highly educated, and well-coiffured Young Irelanders be mistaken as would-be saviors of the rural Irish poor. But their rhetorical and eventual actual embrace of militancy framed them in stark contrast to the aging constitutionalist O'Connell as Ireland sank deeper and deeper into the throes of famine. By mid-1846, the gulf between O'Connell and Young Ireland had grown too wide to bridge, and the Young Irelanders withdrew from the LNRA; in January 1847, they formed a new repeal organization, the Irish Confederation.[43]

As the split between Young Ireland and O'Connell materialized in 1846 and as Young Irelanders coalesced in the Irish Confederation early in 1847, the thorny question of whether or not Irish nationalists could accept aid from proslavery Americans resurfaced. This was thanks almost entirely to the efforts of James Haughton, who maintained his advocacy of both abolitionism and repeal. Despite being a Garrisonian abolitionist who had counseled O'Connell since 1842 to reject even the sympathies of American enslavers, Haughton sided with Young Ireland in 1846, claiming that O'Connell and his subordinates had stifled free speech within the LNRA. Yet even as Haughton expressed his support for Young Ireland, he cautioned them against receiving any kind of support from the United States. When the *Nation* declared its support for the United States in the Mexican-American War, Haughton penned a letter to the editor calling for the newspaper to recant because the Irish did not deserve independence "if we extend our sympathies to the oppressor in other countries." Americans, Haughton continued, were "striving to conquer Mexico, in order to fill that country again with soul-drivers." Beseeching the *Nation* to "[p]oint the eyes of Irishmen to the glorious temple of freedom," Haughton trusted that the newspaper's editors would fulfill his wishes.[44]

Events soon revealed that Haughton's trust was misplaced. When Young Irelanders gathered in Dublin for the inaugural meeting of the Irish Confederation on January 13, 1847, the venerable Haughton was elected as the new organization's treasurer. Upon taking the floor, Haughton reiterated his plea for Irish nationalists to "indignantly refuse the blood-stained contributions of American slaveholders." Doubtless, many of the Young Irelanders sitting alongside Haughton had heard or read much the same from him before. Just two months earlier, the *Nation* published a letter from Haughton in which he urged the editors to return the subscription payments of Irish immigrants in New Orleans. But this time, Haughton's pleas were met with something more than polite indifference. Father John Kenyon, a Tipperary priest and Young Ireland mouthpiece, responded to Haughton in the *Nation* by declaring that "if, instead of slave-holders, slave-eaters" offered to help Irish nationalists, he would "still accept their aid, and thank them for it, to repeal this abominable Union." Kenyon pushed the argument in an altogether different direction by arguing that the Scriptures did not condemn slavery as a crime. He concluded that all humans were slaves in some sense and dismissed antislavery appeals as "much exaggerated . . . by fanaticism."[45]

Over the coming weeks, a debate between Haughton and Kenyon continued in the *Nation* and hinged on the question of whether accepting aid from enslavers weakened Irish claims to freedom. Accepting an enslaver's assistance, Haughton argued, "coupled as it must be with the implied condition that you are to speak softly of his evil deeds," would morally bankrupt Irish nationalism. With the support of a letter from Dr. R. R. Madden, a Catholic Dublin native involved in the emancipation of slaves in British colonies during the 1830s, Haughton deemed it "an absurdity to talk of the Roman Catholic church not having defined slavery as a crime." But Kenyon was relentless. Demonstrating Irish nationalists' tendency to view the slavery question through an Irish lens, Kenyon asserted that slaveholders' cruelties "shall no more convince the slavery system of evil, than the cruelties of exterminating landlords shall prove that the condition of tenant farming is unchristian." Antislavery, Kenyon declared, was merely "a cheap passport to a character of benevolence and all-embracing charity for persons who, if their hearts were sifted, might be found very bare of either." He was glad, then, to have learned that the Irish Confederation would accept American donations. Refusing to accept defeat, Haughton urged the Confederation to "[l]et the people judge" between Kenyon, "the extenuator, if not the actual advocate of slavery," and himself, "its opponent in all its shapes and forms."[46]

The debate over American aid went unresolved until an April 7 meeting of the Irish Confederation. Dublin's Music Hall was "crowded to its utmost" with a "brilliant array of the beauty and education of the city" as the "middle and operative classes" packed themselves into the building's galleries and onto its floor. Haughton's dispute with Kenyon had not cost him the Confederation's admiration, for he was appointed chairman of the gathering. Upon taking the floor, Haughton raised the question of how the Confederation was to finance itself in the midst of the famine, arguing that "the pecuniary assistance of all classes of Irishmen" was needed. By giving up luxuries like "intoxicating drinks," Haughton suggested, Irish men and women could contribute, but they must not let their "hatred of man-stealing to be buried under the blood-stained dollars of slaveholders."[47] In essence, Haughton was following through on his desire to "let the people judge" the Confederation's policy on slavery.

What followed Haughton's plea was a virtual death knell for American and Irish abolitionists' labors in famine-era Ireland. Before Haughton finished his remarks, a man from the floor shouted, "In an assembly of Irishmen that is not the way America should be spoken of." Another voice from the floor called for "Three cheers for American sympathy," which were heartily given. An exasperated Haughton retorted that he was "taking the best means of advancing the cause of human freedom" as confusion reigned in the hall. Suddenly, a voice cried out, "Repeal! We want no slave lecturing here." After a brief conference with the Confederation's leader, William Smith O'Brien, Haughton made a few parting remarks and took his seat. Adding insult to injury, the organization's secretary, Thomas D'Arcy McGee, soon took to the floor to read an address from the Irish Confederation to the vice president of the United States, George M. Dallas, a leading figure in famine relief efforts. The address disparaged the British Empire for allowing Ireland, which "it calls an integral portion of itself," to "depend on the voluntary contributions of a traduced rival [the United States] for its rescue from famine." The Irish Confederation's scorn for the British Empire stood in sharp contrast to an April 3 *Nation* editorial in which McGee heaped praise upon the United States as "a noble Empire in the West, the spring of enterprise, the seat of commerce, the patron of arts, the refuge of liberty." For all of its devastation, McGee opined, the famine would lead to "the establishment of a 'cordial understanding' between us [Ireland] and the United States of America." With James Haughton no doubt shaking his head in dismay, the address to Vice President Dallas was unanimously adopted by the Irish Confederation's leadership council. Days after the Music Hall meeting, in a final, futile protest against Young Ireland's willingness to accept "blood-stained" American money, Haughton resigned from the Irish Confederation. Reflecting more than a year later on his failed efforts to sever Ireland's connections with American slavery, Haughton could only conclude that the "mind of Ireland needs enlightenment on this question of Freedom."[48]

To grasp the full significance of Haughton's departure from the Irish Confederation, we must recall that his efforts to convince Young Irelanders to reject the sympathy and support of proslavery Americans coincided with the Quaker Central Relief Committee's debate over accepting famine relief donations from Charleston and Baltimore. In fact, Haughton had linked the two debates during his April 7 address to the Irish Confederation. The Central Relief Committee members, he stated, had become "almoners to the women-whippers and cradle plunderers of Baltimore and Charleston" by accepting famine relief from those cities, and only by rejecting slavery-tinged support from the United States could the Irish Confederation avoid a similar fate. Notably, both Irish and Irish-American newspapers reprinted the minutes of the Irish Confederation meeting, conveying to the Irish on both sides of the Atlantic the impression that abolitionists like Haughton would sacrifice both Ireland's political autonomy and the well-being of Irish famine victims on behalf of African American slaves. Thus, the Irish critique of abolitionism expanded beyond strictly nationalistic concerns. Haughton and others who opposed acceptance of the Baltimore and Charleston donations put antislavery at odds with famine relief.[49]

Ultimately, abolitionists' combined objections to the Irish Confederation receiving "blood-stained" money and hesitancy to accept famine relief from the American South bred a uniquely Irish strain of anti-abolitionism in 1847. Such opposition to antislavery was rarely as demonstrative as it was at the Irish Confederation meeting, where James Haughton was jeered off stage to shouts of "[w]e want no slave lecturing here." But in 1847, Irish nationalists flatly rejected the notion that the welfare of Irish men and women should be a concern secondary to or even on par with the fate of African American slaves. A *Nation* editorial that appeared in the midst of Haughton's debate with Father Kenyon summarized Young Ireland's position in maintaining that the Irish had "so very urgent affairs at home—so much abolition of *white* slavery to effect if we can . . . that all our exertions will be needed in Ireland." Moreover, Young Irelanders not only rejected abolitionism but also embraced the slaveholding republic across the Atlantic as Ireland's steadfast ally in their bid for autonomy and as the beneficent guardian of the Irish people in their darkest hour. What the historian Bruce Nelson terms "the convergence of historical circumstances and forces that contributed to [antislavery's] decline and marginalization" in Ireland reached its zenith in 1847.[50]

Yet the fullest effects of abolitionism's nadir in Ireland were to be felt across the Atlantic, where the Irish critique of abolitionism proved readily adaptable to Irish-American circumstances. As Irish immigration to the United States grew by leaps and bounds during the famine years, and as American politics grew rife with dissension over the question of slavery's expansion, Irish Americans would mold Young Ireland's criticism of abolitionism into a powerful critique of antislavery writ large. Ironically, the persistent efforts of Irish abolitionists to convince their compatriots in America to take up the slave's cause would only further inflame Irish-American anti-abolitionism. Most of all, the constant and oftentimes intersecting passages across the Atlantic Ocean made by abolitionists, nationalist exiles, and immigrants, along with the funds and periodicals that all three groups carried with them or shipped to colleagues, friends, or family, continuously colored Irish-American views on slavery, antislavery, and nationhood with a transatlantic tinge.

2

"Over the broad Atlantic": Abolitionist Appeals to Emigrants and Immigrants

In Ballingarry, Tipperary, on July 29, 1848, following more than a year of infighting within the Irish Confederation and heightened vigilance on the part of British authorities in Ireland, Young Irelanders launched a last-ditch and, by that point, symbolic rebellion. The 1848 rebellion lasted a few inglorious hours in the cabbage patch of a widow whose barn was occupied by a few dozen policemen. It might have been little more than a historical footnote if not for the fate of a handful of Young Irelanders who were either captured and subsequently sentenced to transportation by British authorities or made their escape off the island. Over the coming months and years, many of the Young Irelanders involved in the planning or execution of the 1848 rebellion found their way to the United States, joining millions of other Irish immigrants amid the famine migration. There, they became professional exiles, using their folk hero status and an adroit understanding of the power of the popular press to agitate for Irish independence. As polemicists, Young Ireland exiles exercised an outsized influence on how Irish immigrants viewed the famine, migration, and the major political issues being debated in their adopted country, not the least of which were slavery and the fate of the American Union.[1]

Young Irelanders' arrival and influence on the American Irish devastated Irish and American abolitionists' efforts to recruit Irish immigrants into the antislavery movement. Even as HASS members and American abolitionists attempted to cultivate antislavery sentiment in Ireland during the 1840s, they devoted just as much if not more attention to the Irish in America. While their efforts were largely stymied before the famine migration, Young Ireland's growing influence in the United States leading up to and especially after the 1848 rebellion intensified and changed the contours of Irish-American anti-abolitionism. In essence, the Irish critique of abolitionism that emerged from the debates over accepting American aid to repeal and donations to Irish famine relief was transported across the Atlantic by Young Ireland nationalists. It found a receptive audience among Irish Americans. By 1850, Irish-American responses to abolitionist entreaties for them to take up the cause of the slave were nearly identical to editorials in the *Nation* in 1845 or speeches in the Irish Confederation in 1847: The antislavery movement ignored the plight of Irish people and weakened national unity at a time when it was sorely needed.

Thus, the famine migration, including the arrival of Young Ireland exiles between 1848 and 1854, produced important changes in the basis of Irish-American anti-abolitionism. Before the famine, Irish and American abolitionists believed that if a critical mass of Irish immigrants could be brought into the antislavery movement, then they might tip the balance of American politics in favor of mass emancipation. Abolitionists' appeals to the American Irish in newspapers, pamphlets, and addresses argued that Irish people's experience of oppression in Ireland should lead them to oppose the oppression of African American slaves. Ironically, as famine devastated their homeland and newspaper editors—including a growing number of Young Ireland exiles—stoked the flames of resentment, Irish Americans *did* draw from their backgrounds in and connections to Ireland as they responded to abolitionists' entreaties. But rather than blaming enslavers and their enablers for oppressing Black Americans, they blamed abolitionists for turning a blind eye to the political and social troubles of Ireland and for exacerbating political turmoil in the nation that many Irish on both sides of the Atlantic had come to see as Ireland's protector. Under the influence of Young Ireland exiles, Irish Americans also blamed Britain for having caused the famine itself. Many American abolitionists maintained strong ties to British colleagues and expressed admiration for British efforts to combat the slave trade and halt the advancement of slavery in the Western Hemisphere. Under these circumstances, it was not a far leap for Irish Americans to make the case that on both sides of the Atlantic, abolitionism was inimical to Irish interests.

Appealing to the American Irish

Mass emigration to the United States was a fact of Irish society by the 1840s, but the dynamics of Irish emigration and, consequently, the contours of Irish America were undergoing a marked shift as the decade commenced. Between 1815 and 1845, upward of one million Irish people crossed the Atlantic to settle in North America. Within this thirty-year interval, there were important changes in the rate and demographics of Irish migration. While some half a million Irish came to North America during the twenty years after the end of the Napoleonic Wars (1803–1815), roughly the same number made the same voyage in only half the amount of time between 1835 and 1844. Middling farmers and artisans, many of them Ulster Protestants, were a substantial portion of those Irish who arrived in the United States prior to the 1830s, but in the decade and a half prior to the famine, poor, unskilled Catholics came to dominate the ranks of Irish emigrants. Many of these travelers had at least one family member already settled in America and had likely corresponded with them about conditions in their destination, while up to half of those who left Ireland between 1830 and 1845 had part or all of their passage paid for through remittances from family members in the United States.[2] As the pace of Irish immigration to the United States accelerated, and as the ties between prospective emigrants in Ireland and the American Irish thickened, Irish and American abolitionists made targeted appeals to prospective emigrants and recently arrived Irish in the United States.

Letters from abolitionists in Ireland to their American colleagues give evidence of the Hibernian reformers' belief that Irish emigrants, if properly educated, could aid the antislavery cause upon arrival in America. As early as 1840, HASS co-founder Richard Allen informed William Lloyd Garrison that Irish abolitionists would do their utmost to "send out our emigrant countrymen sound on the great principle of man's universal charter to liberty." In 1846, as emigration increased during the famine, the Belfast Ladies Anti-Slavery Society claimed that "if the sons and daughters of Erin ere they leave their own sea-girt isle were intellectually prepared to sympathise with the enslaved and the injured colored inhabitants" of America, "what a difference might the emigrants who are continually leaving our shores carry with them." As late as 1853, Allen told Garrison that "a good deal will be done . . . amongst our emigrant class, both previous to and on their embarkation" to "enlighten them on the sin, the iniquity, the anti-Christianity of holding their fellow-men in bondage."[3] Such talk of intellectual preparedness and enlightenment indicated Allen's detachment from the more prosaic concerns of the great majority of Irish people in the mid-1800s. Still, Allen and other HASS members were persistent in their efforts to capitalize on mass Irish immigration to the United States by arousing prospective emigrants' sympathies for African American slaves before they left Ireland.

An important strategy used by Irish abolitionists to recruit potential emigrants into the antislavery movement was editorializing. The indefatigable Dublin abolitionist James Haughton was especially prolific in his efforts to spread antislavery principles through widely read publications like the Dublin *Nation*. In a revealing 1846 letter to the *Nation*, Haughton declared that the newspaper was, "if not the great educator, at least one of the great educators of the Irish people." It was up to the *Nation*'s editors, according to Haughton, to convey "an utter abhorrence of every degraded Irishman in America who lends himself to the support of slavery." There can be little doubt that the effects of the famine rendered readership of the *Nation* significantly lower in 1846 than its peak in 1845, when the newspaper reached some quarter of a million people in Ireland and tens of thousands more in the United States. Still, Haughton persisted in his efforts to use the popular press in Ireland as a means of incorporating prospective emigrants into the antislavery movement. In 1853, Haughton still demanded that "every newspaper wring with honest denunciation of a system which holds in slavery three and a half millions of men and women." Haughton intended these denunciations to cast shame upon Irish-American proslavery apologists and to develop antislavery principles among those who would soon depart for America.[4] His editorials in Irish newspapers attempted to instill the sort of "intellectual preparation" prescribed by the Belfast Ladies Anti-Slavery Society.

Irish abolitionists also directly appealed to Irish men and women preparing to depart for America. A pamphlet written in 1851 by the Dublin Anti-Slavery Society and printed by Richard Davis Webb is noteworthy in this regard. Entitled *To Irish Emigrants who are going to the United States of America*, it was distributed at points of departure and shipping agents' offices in the south of Ireland. During the famine, cities like Cork and Limerick became important as embarkation ports for emigrants, making the pamphlet's availability in those cities valuable to Irish abolitionists. A letter from Maria Webb, a Dublin HASS chapter member, to Frederick Douglass in September 1851 reveals that the pamphlet was also available in Dublin.[5] Given that most emigrants first went to Dublin and then on to Liverpool before sailing to America, Irish abolitionists seem to have distributed the pamphlet strategically at the most bustling ports of embarkation.

To Irish Emigrants reveals what Irish abolitionists wanted Irish emigrants to know before they left home and, to a lesser extent, what emigrants might have known about slavery before they arrived in America. In four crisp pages, the pamphlet spelled out the moral and economic evils of slavery, emphasizing its unchristian nature and its damaging effects on wages and employment for white workers. Moreover, *To Irish Emigrants* informed emigrants bound for Northern cities (where the overwhelming majority was going) that they would not be outside slavery's reach because the Fugitive Slave Law essentially required all Americans to return alleged escaped slaves to those who claimed them as property. The authors noted that God had "seen fit to colour the African *black*, the European *white*, and on the American Indian he has stamped a copper colour" before asking why whites should receive any greater privileges than non-whites if all humans were made by God. Unlike some modern historians, Irish abolitionists had no doubt where Irish immigrants would fall in America's racial hierarchy. Finally, the authors identified themselves as Quakers who had raised significant amounts of relief for famine victims and asked if the emigrant readers "ever felt grateful for that assistance." If so, they should show their appreciation by working to end American slavery.[6]

It is difficult to arrive at even a rough conclusion on how many emigrants took notice of antislavery rhetoric, editorials, and pamphlets before their departures. The *Nation*, along with several other less widely read repeal newspapers like the Dublin *Freeman's Journal*, the *Galway Vindicator*, and the *Cork Examiner*, routinely published the minutes of repeal meetings at which Daniel O'Connell and his surrogates denounced American slavery and its supporters. James Haughton's letters to the editors of the *Nation* in protest of Irish nationalists or philanthropists accepting "blood-stained money," several of which predated the famine and were therefore more likely to reach the newspaper's readership at its peak, typically inveighed against Irish-American defenders of slavery. Surely, that message did not escape the notice of those prospective emigrants who read or listened to readings of Haughton's scathing words. Additionally, the title of the Dublin Anti-Slavery Society's pamphlet (*To Irish Emigrants who are going to the United States of America*) was likely to catch the eye of emigrants who wanted as much information as possible about their destination, and its availability at main ports of departure suggests at least the potential for a wide readership. However, it is impossible to gauge with any precision how many prospective Irish emigrants seriously considered the antislavery appeals of O'Connell or Irish abolitionists like Haughton. As one historian has observed about the pamphlet, in particular, its "relevance to the needs and occupations of emigrating Irish families was questionable at best."[7] Many of those who read the pamphlet no doubt felt some resentment at the notion that as they awaited the ship that would take them from friends, family, and their homeland, they were being asked to rescue strangers in a foreign land.

In all likelihood, Irish abolitionists knew full well that their appeals were unlikely to make a significant impact on most emigrants before they left Ireland. As a result, they also made direct appeals to Irish immigrants (those who had arrived in America) throughout the 1840s. None of these appeals received more notoriety than the *Address from the People of Ireland to Their Countrymen and Countrywomen in America* (1841). The genesis for the so-called Irish Address was the World Anti-Slavery Convention of 1840, where Garrisonian abolitionists and HASS members became fast friends and strategized over how to bring the American Irish into the antislavery movement. Cognizant of the transatlantic fame of Daniel O'Connell, who was also in attendance at the convention, the American and Irish abolitionists concocted a plan for O'Connell to send one of his "powerful appeals," in James Haughton's words, to the Irish in America in the hopes of setting them straight on the matter of American slavery. With O'Connell's leadership of the repeal movement preoccupying him, HASS members composed the Irish Address in 1841. It began by celebrating the intertwined relationship between Ireland and the United States before warning Irish immigrants that America would never "be the glorious country that her free Constitution designed her to be, so long as her soil is polluted" by slavery. "By all your memories of Ireland," the appeal concluded, "continue to love liberty—hate slavery—CLING BY THE ABOLITIONISTS—and in America you will do honor to the name of Ireland." With the appeal completed, it was left to the African American abolitionist Charles Lenox Remond to gather enough signatures from Irish men and women so that the Irish Address would pack a powerful punch once transported across the Atlantic. During a lecture tour that took him through Dublin, Waterford, Wexford, Cork, Limerick, and Belfast, Remond and other HASS members convinced some 60,000 Irish men and women to sign the Irish Address. Most prominent among the signatories were O'Connell and the almost equally revered Father Theobald Mathew, Ireland's temperance crusader. On January 28, 1842, William Lloyd Garrison read out the Irish Address to a crowd of 5,000 (of whom some 1,500 were Irish) in Boston's Faneuil Hall.[8]

Despite abolitionists' high hopes that the Irish Address would engender Irish-American support for antislavery, it can only be described as an abysmal failure. The *Freeman's Journal*, a newspaper popular with the Irish in New York City, questioned the authenticity of O'Connell's signature, while the more widely read Boston *Pilot* lamely argued that O'Connell's mere signature did not mean his total agreement with the Address's sentiments. Virtually all Irish-American journalists agreed that even if O'Connell's signature was genuine, and even if they disliked the idea of one person owning another, Irish concerns took precedence over those of Black slaves. The *Pilot*'s reaction to the Irish Address was revealing of how the Irish critique of abolitionism was gaining traction among Irish Americans. "We abhor slavery," editor Patrick Donahoe declared, "but we are weak enough to love our own kindred and native land with an intenser [sic] love than the people or land of Russia or Africa." Ultimately, the success of Irish repeal networks in America hinged on Irish Americans' abilities to assert their fidelity to America and disprove nativists' charges of disloyalty. Thus, as Angela Murphy argues, Irish Americans' indignant response to the Irish Address in 1842 was born out of a desire to assert their patriotism by rejecting the foreign influence of Irish abolitionists, even one as revered as O'Connell.[9]

Yet abolitionists persisted in their efforts to recruit Irish immigrants into the antislavery movement by continuing to nudge O'Connell to appeal to his compatriots in the United States. In the spring of 1843, the American abolitionist Henry C. Wright arrived in Ireland with an address from the Pennsylvania Anti-Slavery Society to the LNRA. Wright delivered the document to Haughton, who, in turn, gave it to O'Connell. Impressed by the Pennsylvania abolitionists' defense of abolitionism and frank description of slaves' suffering, O'Connell read the address before the LNRA on May 9 and replied to it with a direct appeal to Irish immigrants. "Over the broad Atlantic," O'Connell thundered, "I pour forth my voice saying 'Come out of such a land, you Irishmen; or if you remain, and dare countenance the system of slavery that is supported there, we will recognize you as Irishmen no longer.'" After this address elicited a negative reaction from several American repeal organizations, particularly the Cincinnati club, O'Connell again used the platform of the LNRA to appeal directly to Irish immigrants in the United States. At an October 1843 LNRA meeting, O'Connell responded to the stridently proslavery stance adopted by the Cincinnati repealers. "It was not in Ireland you learned this cruelty," he fumed before reiterating his call for Irish immigrants to dissociate themselves from proslavery interests. Taking the Cincinnati repealers as representative of most Irish Americans, O'Connell expressed "utter astonishment" that Irishmen could "speak of man being the property of man . . . as if you were speaking of the beasts of the field. . . . It is this," he declared, "that makes us disclaim you as countrymen."[10]

O'Connell's repeated pleas for the Irish in America to unite with abolitionists in opposition to slavery and in favor of racial equality drew overwhelmingly negative responses. Only one American repeal association with a substantial body of its membership made up of Irish Americans supported O'Connell's position on slavery. Otherwise, most Irish-American repealers echoed the anti-abolitionist, proslavery sentiments put forth in the Cincinnati organization's address to the LNRA. Still, O'Connell's antislavery appeals to the Irish in America did not endanger the repeal movement in the United States. Irish Americans rejected and yet tolerated O'Connell's antislavery rhetoric to advance the cause of Irish repeal. Only when O'Connell threatened an alliance between Britain and Ireland against the United States in the "American eagle" speech of 1845 did the repeal movement in America collapse.[11]

The significance of O'Connell's appeals and abolitionists' efforts to recruit prospective emigrants lies not so much in the fruits of their labors as in a pattern established in the relationship between the American Irish and the transatlantic antislavery movement. As the pace of Irish immigration to the United States accelerated in the years before the famine, American and Irish abolitionists invested their hopes in the belief that Irish immigration might tip the scales of the slavery debate. Through editorials, speeches, lecture tours, and pamphlets, they sought to build up Irish sympathy for African American slaves. These efforts no doubt familiarized countless emigrants with the slavery question before they left Ireland. But they also conveyed the impression that abolitionists were so singularly concerned with slavery that they slighted the difficulties faced by Irish migrants themselves. Even as tensions escalated between abolitionists and nationalists within Ireland, the famine and the resultant Irish famine migration to the United States added a new layer of complexity to the fraught relationship between the antislavery movement and the Irish.

The Famine Migration and Irish-American Identity

Beginning in 1845, the Great Irish Potato Famine and resultant famine migration transformed Irish-American identity in ways that would sharpen Irish Americans' criticisms of the antislavery movement. By this time, Irish Americans had a well-deserved reputation as foes of abolitionism. But reports of the miserable conditions in Ireland during the potato famine and the pitiable circumstances of the famine immigrants teeming in American cities gave rise to a new sense of grievance among Irish Americans. In turn, those grievances fanned the flames of bitterness and resentment against those who held up African American slavery as a greater evil than Irish poverty or British misrule. After the botched 1848 Irish rebellion, several influential Young Ireland nationalists found their way to the United States, where they tapped into Irish-American outrage over the famine by charging the British government with deliberately starving the people of Ireland and forcing millions of Irish men and women into exile across the Atlantic. This interpretation of the famine as an act of genocide and the idea that all Irish immigrants were somehow exiles filtered down to Irish Americans through ethnic newspapers and the published writings of popular Young Irelanders. Whether rightly or wrongly, more and more Irish immigrants viewed themselves as exiles and were therefore embittered over efforts to convince them that Black chattel slavery was the most pressing matter of concern for reformers on either side of the Atlantic.

The potato blight first became widespread across Ireland in the fall of 1845, by which time most emigrants for the year had left the island. Still, a then record-high 75,000 Irish departed that year. The blight was even more widespread in 1846, producing chronic food shortages for the millions of Irish who depended on the potato largely or exclusively for their diet. Hunger and malnutrition-induced diseases soon stalked the land, leaving a great many Irish smallholders unable to plant a sufficient crop in 1846 for the following year. Thus, during "Black '47," only 10 percent of the total potato crop yield from 1844 was harvested, touching off a mass departure of people from Ireland, the likes of which were unprecedented and would never again be matched. In 1846, 106,000 Irish departed—a figure that more than doubled in 1847 when 214,000 people left the island. The year 1848 saw a temporary drop in departures—although an impressive 177,000 Irish emigrated in that year—before the pace of emigration quickened in 1849, 1850, and 1851, when an all-time high of 245,000 emigrants set sail. Not until 1855 did annual rates of emigration reach pre-famine levels. All told, out of a pre-famine population of 8.5 million, some 2.1 million people left Ireland during the famine years of 1845–54; 1.5 million of them were destined for the United States. Between 1.1 and 1.5 million Irish perished during the potato famine.[12]

The famine immigrants' backgrounds in Ireland conditioned their prospects in America and how they perceived life in their adopted country. Amplifying trends in the decade before the famine, famine immigrants were overwhelmingly poor, rural, and Catholic. Because the poorest of the poor could not afford the transatlantic fare, cottiers, smallholders, and middling farmers dominated the ranks of the famine migration. Even if these classes were not wholly impoverished in Ireland, they could rarely afford anything other than small, sparse living quarters in the United States, where the Irish quickly became the most urbanized people in the nation at a time when three-quarters of Americans lived in rural areas. Upward of nine out of every ten emigrants in the famine years were classified as either laborers or servants. Whether in major cities like New York, Philadelphia, or Chicago or in smaller industrial settings like the mining town of Pottsville, Pennsylvania, or the mill town of Lowell, Massachusetts, the famine immigrants took whatever low-paying, dangerous, and unstable work was available to them as unskilled, urban workers in an industrializing economy. Clustered in urban and industrial centers—by 1860, for instance, one out of every four New Yorkers and Bostonians had been born in Ireland—the famine immigrants were more visible than any other immigrant group, a circumstance reinforced by their culture. All but 10 percent of the famine immigrants were Catholic, and many came from the heavily Gaelic provinces of Munster and Connaught, where half the population still spoke the Irish language. Between 1845 and 1855, hundreds of thousands of these men, women, and children took up residence in some of the most bustling metropolises in the Western Hemisphere, with New York City, the commercial capital of North America, chief among them. In short, Irish immigrants during the famine years were the poorest, least skilled, and most foreign group of people to inhabit the United States.[13]

Even as the famine's toll manifested in the form of disheveled Irish immigrants alighting along the eastern seaboard, Irish-American newspapers provided extensive and inevitably heart-wrenching coverage of affairs in Ireland to a growing subscribership. During the famine, established Irish-American Catholic weeklies like the Boston *Pilot* and New York *Freeman's Journal*, named after Dublin newspapers, were joined by newcomers like the New York *Nation* and New York *Irish-American*, owned and edited by Young Ireland exiles. Irish newspapers reached American audiences by reprinting parts or the entirety of articles from other publications. Whether in the ethnic press or partisan Democratic newspapers, Irish Americans kept abreast of the wretched conditions in Ireland during the famine. A February 8, 1847, article in the Democratic Charleston *Mercury*, for instance, bemoaned that the "distress" in Ireland had reached "a degree of destitution and suffering, that is absolutely fearful to contemplate." Two months later, the Cincinnati *Catholic Telegraph* reprinted a piece from the *Pittsburgh Catholic* lamenting the "heartrending scenes" that afflicted Ireland, "this suffering country." More explicitly, Irish-American newspapers set aside columns dedicated to "The Latest Irish News," as New York's *Irish-American* labeled its Irish news column, featuring stories of evicted tenants, starving families, and heartless landlords. The emaciating effects of dysentery, typhus, and scurvy—some of the most common famine-related diseases—were regularly reported on in the United States. Just as important, American newspapers extensively covered stories on the British government's callous response to the rapidly deteriorating situation in Ireland. In 1846, the Tory government handed over power to Lord John Russell's Whig Party, whose *laissez-faire* ideology, coupled with a widely shared belief in Irish degeneracy, led British administrators in Ireland to enact more stringent conditions for poor relief that left Irish tenants with the choice of starvation or eviction.[14]

In and of themselves, the pitiful circumstances of the famine immigrants, coupled with reports of dire conditions in Ireland and the British government's inept response, were enough to produce a sense of embittered forlornness among Irish Americans. But the arrival and subsequent influence of Young Ireland exiles in the late 1840s and early 1850s added a new element of aggrieved indignation to Irish-American views on the famine, the famine migration, and what it meant to be an Irish immigrant in America. Following the botched 1848 rebellion, several Young Irelanders were convicted of treason-felony and sentenced to transportation to the British penal colony of Van Diemen's Land, from which a handful eventually escaped to the United States. Others who had evaded capture in 1848 fled directly across the Atlantic. In the late 1840s and early 1850s, these Young Ireland exiles established themselves as key players in the Irish-American press. Thomas D'Arcy McGee established the New York *Nation* in 1848 and later operated the *American Celt* out of Boston. John Mitchel arrived in the United States in 1853 and soon attained both notoriety and infamy as editor of the New York *Citizen* and the Richmond *Southern Citizen*. Like Mitchel, Thomas Francis Meagher escaped from Van Diemen's Land to settle in New York City. His entrance into the Irish-American press was delayed until 1856, when he began operating the New York *Irish News*, employing fellow Young Ireland exiles P. J. Smyth, John Savage, and Richard J. Lalor as subeditors. In these publications and other Irish-American journals that provided extensive coverage of the whereabouts and speeches of Young Ireland exiles, Irish immigrants found a voice that spoke on their behalf. Although the Young Ireland journalists found much to disagree over in their exile, they shared a common sense of outrage over Britain's alleged culpability for the potato famine and its tragic consequences in the form of evictions, departures, and deaths.[15]

No Young Ireland exile did more to influence Irish-American views on the famine, the famine migration, and the condition of Ireland than John Mitchel. Mitchel was arrested, tried, and convicted of treason-felony for publishing incendiary articles in his newspaper *United Irishman* well before the 1848 rising, by which time he was *en route* to the penal colony of Van Diemen's Land. Escaping to the United States in 1853, Mitchel arrived with great fanfare in New York City, where he soon revived his career in journalism as editor of a new weekly newspaper, the *Citizen*. As we shall see, Mitchel quickly became a lightning rod of controversy for his enthusiastic endorsement of Black slavery in the *Citizen*. But for countless Irish-American readers, it was the serial publication in the *Citizen* of what was later published in book form as Mitchel's *Jail Journal* that made him the founding father of a new brand of Irish-American nationalism. In *Jail Journal*, Mitchel charged British politicians with deliberately turning the potato crop failure into a famine. According to Mitchel, the British government's intentions were to free up Irish land for English landlords, to stamp out once and for all Irish resistance to British rule, and to complete the Anglicization of Ireland through the erasure of native Irish culture. For these reasons, Mitchel alleged in a subsequent work entitled *The Last Conquest of Ireland (Perhaps)*, "A million and a half of men, women, and children were carefully, prudently, and peacefully slain by the English government." Readers of both the *Jail Journal* and *The Last Conquest of Ireland (Perhaps)* were instructed that whether by facilitating the exportation of other Irish-grown crops, denying relief to the poor, or essentially forcing millions of Irish to emigrate, British administrators in Ireland had attempted to depopulate the island. Thus, in lines that would reverberate through generations of Irish-American nationalists, Mitchel summed up the famine as follows: "The Almighty, indeed, sent the potato blight, but the English created the Famine." Convinced by the British government's response to the potato crop failure that only an independent Irish republic could save the Irish people, Mitchel doubled down on his advocacy of violent revolution against Britain.[16]

Before taking stock of the significance of Mitchel's views, several qualifiers must be inserted. Modern historians have thoroughly debunked Mitchel's interpretation of the Great Irish Potato Famine as an act of genocide by British politicians. Additionally, Mitchel's support for violent revolution in Ireland put him at odds with several prominent former Young Irelanders there who channeled their energies into the political arena in the wake of the failed 1848 uprising. Finally, Mitchel's eventual labors as a propagandist for the Confederate government during the Civil War clouded his legacy among a substantial number of Irish Americans who remained thoroughly loyal to the Union. But in terms of how Irish Americans made sense of the calamity that caused the deaths of more than a million people in Ireland and led more than two million others to leave the island, Mitchel's views became canon. Generations of Irish-American nationalists, including Mitchel's fellow Young Ireland exiles in antebellum America, took inspiration from the inflammatory rhetoric found in *Jail Journal* and *The Last Conquest of Ireland (Perhaps)*. Thomas D'Arcy McGee, for one, claimed that the Irish were being "exterminated as a people" through the British government's response to the famine. For untold numbers of immigrants, many of whom came from a culture that viewed emigration not as a rational choice but rather as banishment, Mitchel's interpretation had a certain logic to it. No longer were they panicked peasants who had been forced to flee their homeland; in the pages of *Jail Journal*, they became hardened exiles whose vengeance might one day come through Ireland's redemption from British tyranny. Not only did this interpretation of the famine migration imbue antebellum Irish-American identity with a vicious strain of Anglophobia, but also it gave rise to the idea that all Irish immigrants, regardless of whether or not they came during the famine years, shared a common background of oppression and tyranny.[17]

Such bitterness over Ireland's condition coursed through the writings of famine-era Irish Americans. "Perhaps 'tis only the *sense of remoteness*," wrote an Irish immigrant living in Boston to the *Cork Examiner* in 1849, "but I often find myself looking at nothing through tears . . . when I think of the misery—the patient misery that afflicts her [Ireland's] people." Timothy McCarthy, who settled in upstate New York during the famine by way of Montreal and Cork, lamented the "stress and starvation that the people of Ireland endure" in an 1849 letter to his mother. He took solace, however, in the relatively comfortable life he found in America, where, unlike his native Ireland, there was *"no haughty lord to command your obeisance, no despot to grind the faces of the poor,* and to take from them their hard-earned subsistence." Patrick Hanlon, who left Ireland for Allegheny City, Pennsylvania, wrote to his family in Ballymote, County Down, in 1851, telling them how a friend had given "a rather gloomy picture of the present state of Ireland which I believe is not at all exaggerated." That "gloomy picture" was captured lyrically in "A New Song on Skibbereen," an early 1850s ballad popular among Irish Americans in which a father explained to his son why he had left his home in Skibbereen, County Cork, where burial pits lay claim to thousands of famine victims. One version of the song closed with the lines, "we may some day remember, / If we're wanted by the Queen, / That hundreds patiently lay down / And starved in Skibbereen."[18]

To be sure, Irish-American identity in antebellum America encompassed much more than Anglophobia and lamentations for the plight of their native land. The Catholic Church, the Democratic Party, and, for some at least, a budding spirit of working-class comradery exerted strong influences on Irish Americans' perspectives on their adopted country and their place in it. But the raw sense of grievance found in Mitchel's writings, in Irish-American newspapers' reports on the famine, and in the letters of Irish immigrants themselves loomed large in how the Irish in America perceived and responded to the entreaties of reformers seeking their support for another oppressed people. As nationalist exiles and ethnic journalists constructed the ramparts of Irish-American identity in the late 1840s and early 1850s, American abolitionists soon discovered that they were surprisingly strong redoubts against their continued efforts to bring the American Irish into the antislavery movement.

"Hibernianism" or "Americanism"? Irish-American Anti-Abolitionism during the Famine

Most American abolitionists, especially the Garrisonians, grasped the political and social ills that beset the Irish people. In 1842, Garrison declared his enthusiastic support for O'Connell's repeal campaign, and American abolitionists of all persuasions drummed up support for Irish famine relief. Some Garrisonians traveled extensively in Ireland and saw firsthand the miserable circumstances of the peasantry, while others read accounts by Garrisonians who toured or, in the case of HASS members, lived on the island. Their reactions to seeing or reading of poverty in Ireland suggest that few antislavery reformers disputed the notions that Ireland was badly misgoverned and that the condition of the rural poor, in particular, was desperate. In 1845, an anonymous author in the *Liberator* went so far as to express his concern that Irish immigrants would "find on their arrival that those slaves, about whom they heard so many pathetic appeals, are a far sight better fed, better clothed, better housed, and less worked than *they* used to be while in Ireland." In March 1847, Richard Davis Webb made the case to readers of the *National Anti-Slavery Standard* that "at the present time, there can be no doubt, that so far as respects the mere supply of food, the ill-fed slave is better off than the starving Irishman." Two years later, Webb characterized the "bleakness of the country, the poverty of the soil, the loathsome huts, the filth and rags of the people in those poor districts" as "truly disheartening."[19]

Such comparisons between the Irish poor and enslaved African Americans, especially when coming from Garrisonian abolitionists, are arresting. At an abstract level, enslaved African Americans and Irish peasant farmers were both landless, exploited classes within a global capitalist system that denied them the fruits of their labor. But contemporary comparisons between the condition of African American slavery and Irish poverty typically came from slavery's proponents, as Frederick Douglass pinpointed in an 1850 speech. "It is often said, by the opponents of the anti-slavery cause," Douglass observed in December 1850, "that the condition of the people of Ireland is more deplorable than that of the American slaves." Douglass would have been the last abolitionist to discount Irish poverty, but he would not equate it to slavery. "The Irishman is poor," he conceded, "but he is not a slave." "The Irishman has not only the liberty to emigrate from his country," Douglass continued, "but he has liberty at home. He can write, speak, and cooperate for the attainment of his rights and the redress of his wrongs." Like other Black abolitionists who lectured in Ireland in the 1840s and 1850s, Douglass understood that proslavery apologists would weigh his characterization of Irish poverty against his efforts to persuade a transatlantic audience of the singular injustice of Black slavery. American abolitionists less knowledgeable than Douglass of the social and political landscape of Ireland looked upon the symptoms of Irish poverty more as habits to be reformed than products of inequity and dismissed comparisons of the Irish poor with Black slaves as little more than proslavery sophistry. For his part, Webb concluded his comparison of famine-starved Irish peasants and enslaved African Americans by claiming that "there is not a peasant in Ireland, dying with hunger, on his naked cabin floor, who would consent to purchase food and competence for his perishing family, on the condition that, when restored to health and plenty, they should become the property of any man."[20]

Yet even as he denied an equivalency between Black slavery and Irish poverty, no American abolitionist evinced as deep a sympathy for the Irish poor as Douglass. As Douglass traversed Ireland in the autumn of 1845, he reveled in the absence of "prejudice against me, on account of the color of my skin," as he wrote in a January 1, 1846, letter to Garrison. Relatively secure in his freedom for the first time since his escape, Douglass felt liberated by the Emerald Isle. At the same time, he could not ignore the scenes of distress that surrounded him. Writing to the *Liberator* from Scotland in 1846, Douglass recalled how he had once believed that stories of Irish poverty were designed to impeach "the characters of British philanthropists" and thus to cover up "the dark and infernal character of American slavery." While he maintained that many Irish and American authors who lamented the condition of the Irish poor cared less about "the wrongs of Irishmen, than they care about the whipped, gagged, and thumb-screwed slave," Douglass was genuinely shocked by Irish poverty. As he wandered the streets of Dublin and toured the surrounding countryside, he was aghast at what he found, observing that "of all places to witness human misery, ignorance, degradation, filth, and wretchedness, the Irish hut is pre-eminent." Foreshadowing Webb's comparison of Irish peasants with African American slaves, Douglass observed that "men and women, married and single, old and young, lie down together, in much the same degradation as the American slaves." After seeing how the Irish poor lived, Douglass concluded that there was "much here to remind me of my former condition." He confessed that he would "be ashamed to lift up my voice against American slavery, but that I know the cause of humanity is one the world over. He who really and truly feels for the American slave, cannot steel his heart to the woes of others."[21]

Ironically, it was this very intimate knowledge of Irish impoverishment during the famine that led many abolitionists to assume that Irish immigrants would be their natural allies. Douglass's dictum, "He who really and truly feels for the American slave, cannot steel his heart to the woes of others," might just as well be reversed. How, reasoned both American and Irish reformers, could any people who had lived under such tyranny and amid such squalor as the Irish not join in their efforts to liberate and uplift another oppressed people? Firmly convinced that the Irish had a singular understanding of what injustice was and would seize the opportunity to attack it in their adopted country, abolitionists were correspondingly perplexed by Irish immigrants' hostility to their cause. The American

Anti-Slavery Society's official newspaper, the *National Anti-Slavery Standard*, noted in 1849 that the Irish had escaped from "a wretched bondage at home," leaving the editor confounded as to why Irish immigrants "have . . . produced some most repulsive specimens of pro-slavery advocacy." In 1851, the Garrisonian abolitionist Henry C. Wright inquired of James Haughton as to why "emigrants from . . . your own dear Green Isle, escaping from the despotism of the old world, at once join the ranks of the slave-breeders and slave-holders." Later that year, "W. J. W.," a correspondent to Garrison's *Liberator*, recollected that for years he had been congratulating himself "on the strength the English and Irish emigrants would give to the cause of abolition," never thinking that "a voyage across the Atlantic could . . . transform born freemen" into defenders of slavery. Such statements typified abolitionists' shared belief that, given their backgrounds in Ireland, Irish Americans should have been natural foes of American slavery.[22]

Black abolitionists were especially vexed that immigrants who had borne the brunt of injustice in Ireland opposed abolitionism in the United States. Speaking at an 1847 African American convention in Troy, New York, Amos G. Beman observed that "nine-tenths of the Irish residents in Connecticut [his home state], voted against the colored man" in a recent statewide ballot on Black suffrage. Continuing, Beman emphasized that he "loved Ireland, revered her great men, [and] sympathized with her present and past afflictions" but could not overlook Irish "recreancy" when it came to a question of "human right." Elaborating on Beman's remarks in a report on the convention, the Black abolitionist William C. Nell posited that Irish-American anti-abolitionism had to be the result of American influences. The "opposition of Irishmen in America to colored men," Nell averred, "is not so much an Hibernianism as an Americanism." Similar sentiments were expressed six years later by a speaker at a Chicago convention on Black emigration, who alluded to the American Irish while arguing that African Americans should remain in the United States. The Irish had "recently fled from the struggles in their native land between justice and oppression." Heedless of their backgrounds, they had "enlisted here on the side of the oppressor and proved themselves the most inveterate enemies of freedom." If African Americans followed the Irish model of emigration to escape oppression, the speaker reasoned, they too might become oppressors in their new homelands.[23]

Yet abolitionists who believed Irish immigrants' opposition to the antislavery movement was the product of American influences were wrong. In the late 1840s, Irish-American anti-abolitionism became just as much a "Hibernianism as an Americanism," to borrow William C. Nell's phrasing. During the transatlantic repeal campaign, Irish Americans had watched in dismay as abolitionists' lobbying led the repeal leadership to denounce their adopted country. At the same time, debate within the repeal movement over Irish nationalists' connections to American slavery contributed to the fracturing of the Loyal National Repeal Association itself. Young Irelanders' praise for the United States and criticisms of those repealers who spurned "blood-stained" American donations were broadcast to prospective emigrants in Ireland and to Irish Americans through the repeal press. Many of those same Young Irelanders who denounced abolitionism in Ireland made their way to the United States during the famine, where they enjoyed a cult-like status and exercised a powerful influence on Irish-American views. Thus, as abolitionists continued to beseech the Irish in America to unite with them, Irish Americans grew more and more likely to explain their opposition to the antislavery movement with reference to their backgrounds in or connections to Ireland.

By 1847, the influence of Young Irelanders' rhetoric on the style and substance of Irish-American anti-abolitionism was unmistakable. Recall, for instance, the debate in January 1847 between the Young Ireland priest Father John Kenyon and the Irish abolitionist James Haughton over whether or not the newly formed Irish Confederation would accept contributions from slaveholding and proslavery Americans. As part of his argument for why the Irish Confederation could justifiably accept slaveholders' support, Father Kenyon claimed in a letter to the *Nation* that Southern masters "maltreat their negroes half as much as our poor Irish slaves are maltreated by their English masters." A few weeks after these lines appeared in the *Nation*, Quaker famine relief overseers in Dublin received a letter from an Irish immigrant in New York City in accompaniment of his donation; included in the letter was the author's opinion that "the condition of our [Ireland's] starving poor is infinitely worse than that of the Southern slave." An even more transparent cribbing of Father Kenyon's argument appeared in the May 1, 1847, edition of the Boston *Pilot*, one of the most widely read Irish-American newspapers. Editor Patrick Donahoe criticized abolitionists like Haughton who wished to return slaveholders' famine relief donations, claiming that such reformers neglected the plight of the "*white slaves* of England" in favor of the "well fed and well clothed blacks of this country."[24]

Rooted in the Irish debate over accepting "blood-stained" American donations, the argument that Irish poverty was a graver evil than African American slavery became a staple of Irish-American anti-abolitionism during the famine years. Two factors animated this particular claim of grievance. First, Irish-American leaders called upon it to deflect Irish and American abolitionists' persistent efforts to recruit Irish immigrants into the antislavery movement. Second, prominent Young Ireland exiles invoked it as part of a broader Anglophobic agenda in the United

States. In 1849, for example, Thomas D'Arcy McGee, a Young Ireland exile who now edited the New York *Nation*, responded to a published letter by the Dublin abolitionist Richard Davis Webb. Indignant that Webb had chided exiles like himself for failing to unite with American abolitionists, McGee asserted that Young Irelanders' mission was to "liberate their slaves, not to travel across the Atlantic for foreign objects of sympathy." Boston *Pilot* editor Patrick Donahoe perceived a parallel between British and American abolitionists who, Donahoe alleged, ignored suffering in their own backyard. "[Abolitionists'] philanthropy," Donahoe averred in an 1851 editorial, "is a love of men in general, and a hatred of every body in particular. In England, they have tears for unborn negroes, and stripes for Irish peasants, English miners and other operatives. In this country, they act in the same fashion," Donahoe complained. One Irish American from New York City aired his grievances with antislavery reformers in the pages of the *National Era*, a Washington, D.C., abolitionist weekly. "Manhattan," as he signed his letter, argued that Irish exiles in America should not be expected to speak out against American slavery given that "Anti-Slavery agents, when in England, on Anti-Slavery visits, do not feel called upon to declaim against the oppression of the Irish, or the sufferings of the operatives at Manchester."[25] Thinking of themselves as exiles forced from their native land by the cruel tyranny of British rule, these Irish-American commentators chided abolitionists for expecting them to agitate against chattel slavery while famine and tyranny stalked Ireland.

As Irish Americans imbibed the Anglophobic rhetoric of McGee, John Mitchel, and other Young Ireland exiles, they found that it blended neatly with American politics and foreign policy. By the 1840s, Anglo-American relations were at their worst since the War of 1812, with slavery acting as a wedge to drive the two nations apart. By abolishing the slave trade in 1808, freeing slaves in Britain's West Indian colonies in 1833, and directing the Royal Navy to disrupt the illicit Atlantic slave trade, British policymakers had signaled that the Empire would flex its considerable might against slavery in the Atlantic World. While a mixture of economic and cultural imperatives led many Americans to oppose the expansion of the British Empire generally, Southern enslavers were particularly concerned that British statesmen's design to expand the Empire's influence in the Western Hemisphere was a thinly veiled plot to foment slave insurrection and to hasten the demise of American slavery. Throughout the 1840s and 1850s, influential Southern Democrats concentrated American foreign policy objectives on countering what one historian describes as "the imperial abolitionism of Great Britain." The Anglophobic rhetoric that peppered their speeches would have been right at home in the pages of the Dublin *Nation* in 1845 or the Boston

Pilot in 1850. No less a figure than then Senator John C. Calhoun asked his fellow senators in a March 1840 speech how antislavery British policymakers could hold that it was "contrary to the laws of nature or of nations for man to hold man in subjection" in light of how the Irish fared under British rule. Democratic politicians' connecting of the dots between Ireland's plight under the Act of Union and the purported hypocrisy of British abolitionism gave Irish Americans the chance to assert their credentials as American patriots while simultaneously airing Irish nationalist grievances. As rumors swirled in 1845 that British agents in Texas were deepening Britain's influence there to undermine American annexation of the Lone Star Republic, a Boston-based correspondent to the Dublin *Nation* noted wryly that "Texas, with all her slavery laws, is to be supported by England now—though she cried like a crocodile, over the sins of [President] Tyler, who promoted by annexation the extension of slavery. Such is England ever." Such allegations of hypocrisy against British abolitionists and their American colleagues grew all the more convincing in the years to come, as the tragic consequences of British misrule in Ireland manifested in ghastly ways during the famine.[26]

Given the virulent Anglophobia that by the late 1840s was a pillar of Irish-American identity, it comes as a surprise to find American abolitionists ignorant of how their connections to English reformers might taint the antislavery cause in the eyes of Irish immigrants. At no point in Irish and American Garrisonians' extensive correspondence over how to bring the American Irish into the antislavery fold was abolitionism's association with the British Empire raised. In fact, some American Garrisonians were unabashed Anglophiles who celebrated the victories of their English colleagues and venerated their English ancestors as the heirs of a centuries-old tradition of English liberty. By the late 1840s, Garrison himself had traveled to England three times since his first trip in 1833, when the passage of the British West Indian emancipation bill inspired him and other American reformers to establish the American Anti-Slavery Society. To be sure, Garrison and a number of his supporters trumpeted the cause of Irish repeal; in 1842, O'Connell's movement to break the Act of Union of 1801 even inspired Garrison to call for the dissolution of the American Union in hopes that the mere threat of disunion might frighten Americans into abolishing slavery. Ultimately, however, American abolitionists, generally, and Garrisonian reformers, particularly, were conspicuous Anglophiles.[27]

As Irish-American Anglophobia ratcheted up and antislavery reformers struggled to make inroads with the American Irish, the English abolitionist and MP George Thompson embarked on a lecture tour of the United States in 1850. An intimate acquaintance of Garrison, Thompson had been forced to beat a hasty retreat from his first American tour in 1835 when mobs in Massachusetts, New Hampshire, and New York threatened his life amid a nationwide spasm of anti-abolitionist violence. Thompson's 1850–51 tour was tame by comparison. However, American abolitionists' hopes of currying favor with Irish Americans were dashed by Thompson's stops in Boston, New York, and Philadelphia, where Irish-American newspaper editors whipped up mobs to protest the visiting English reformer's presence. The New York *Irish-American* typified its readers' views on Thompson as it railed against abolitionists who "neglect the monstrous social evils, which meet them at every turn in their native land, and hunt across the ocean after reforms which are impracticable, if not impossible." Before Thompson even reached Philadelphia, an Irish immigrant named John Campbell advertised that he would protest his lecture by exposing "the cant and hypocrisy of sham philanthropists, who come over to play the negro, while they are blind to the white man's slavery in the British Isles." On June 21, 1851, according to one observer, a mob of "*Irish-American* Democrats" assembled to hear speeches by Campbell and other Irish Americans. Campbell proclaimed that "the masses in Britain and Ireland were infinitely worse off than chattel slavery; [and] that no white man had a right to speak against negro chattel slavery till he had freed white laborers from wages slavery." Thompson, Campbell raved before the mostly Irish-American mob, was "a foreigner, a member of Parliament, a part of the British Government, the most bloody tyranny on the globe." Taking his antiabolitionist invective to its proslavery conclusion, Campbell insisted that "God designed the blacks to be the slaves to the whites" and implored Irish immigrants to "join the slaveholders against the slaves in this country." Listening in horror to Campbell's tirade was the Garrisonian abolitionist Henry C. Wright, a frequent correspondent with the HASS leadership who had visited Ireland in 1843. Wright wrote at once to James Haughton to apprise him of Campbell's screed, adding that some half a dozen other Irish-born speakers at the anti-Thompson rally delivered similar remarks. "Can you conceive it possible," Wright asked Haughton at the close of his letter, "that Irishmen . . . fleeing from British oppressors, should come here and utter such sentiments?"[28]

Haughton's reply to Wright merits extended discussion, for it reveals how abolitionists' assumptions about Irish immigrants' views clashed against a hardened, embittered Irish-American identity during the famine. "If my feeble voice could reach the hearts of Irishmen in your land," Haughton began an open letter published in the *Liberator*, "I would pour upon them my soul's anathema for their traitorous conduct to liberty, to humanity, for the deep disgrace they are heaping upon that country in which I dwell." Continuing, Haughton agreed that the conduct of Irish Americans like those at the anti-Thompson rally in Philadelphia was humiliating, but he disagreed with Wright's characterization of the Irish in America. "Our people," Haughton wrote of Irish emigrants, "do not quit the home of their fathers so much for the purpose of 'escaping despotism in the old world,' as for improving their fortunes in the new." In other words, Irish immigrants were not exiles; they made a rational choice to seek a better life in the United States. This being the case, Haughton explained that it was only natural for Irish immigrants to "go into the ranks of the pro-slavery party," for "to gain a living in your land, they must unite with the prevalent feeling of the community by whom they are surrounded." Given his bitter disappointment with the conduct of Young Irelanders, Haughton was not surprised that an Irish immigrant less educated than the likes of Thomas D'Arcy McGee or John Mitchel would "take the vilanous [sic] course towards prosperity too often pointed out to him in America" by proslavery interests. In these lucid terms, Haughton dissected the socio-economic basis of Irish immigrants' hostility to the antislavery movement.[29]

Yet, as for what could be done about the fact that Irish immigration was strengthening enslavers' grip on the nation, Haughton floated a solution that could only have further inflamed Irish-American animosity toward antislavery reform. "I would, if it were in my power," Haughton suggested, "prevail on my countrymen to remain at home, rather than to proceed to a land in which, whatever advantages of a temporal nature may be found, the moral atmosphere is too polluted to allow them any reasonable chance of escaping from a most damning pollution." In other words, Haughton proposed an end to Irish emigration to avoid strengthening the hand of proslavery interests. Of course, Haughton knew such power was not at his or any abolitionist's disposal. The point is not what he proposed, which he knew to be impossible, but rather the perspective on Irish emigration that informed these lines. Historical scholarship backs up Haughton's assertion that even during the famine years, emigration was driven by opportunities for socioeconomic betterment. But his casual dismissal of the immigration-as-exile motif bespoke a critical misreading of Irish-American identity during the famine. Molded by an Irish peasant cultural view of emigration as a form of banishment, by reports of mass starvation, deadly diseases, and heartless evictions in the Irish countryside, and by a broken nationalist movement whose exiled leaders in America fumed over British tyranny to a receptive audience, Irish-American identity had come to embrace exile as its *sine qua non* by the early 1850s. Whether real or imagined, an exile's bitterness lay behind the vehemence with which Irish Americans rejected abolitionists' calls for them to join the antislavery crusade.[30]

Throughout the 1840s, abolitionists in Ireland and the United States had appealed to both prospective emigrants in Ireland and Irish immigrants in the United States to join them in their efforts to abolish American slavery. By circulating their appeals in widely read Irish nationalist newspapers and at the ports where emigrants embarked on their journey to the United States, as well as recruiting the Irish nationalist leader Daniel O'Connell to speak directly to the American Irish on the subject of slavery, abolitionists hoped to bring a critical mass of Irish Americans into the antislavery movement. Their chances of success diminished as the famine exodus transformed Irish-American identity in the late 1840s and early 1850s, imbuing it with a sense of grievance that stemmed from the belief that *all* Irish immigrants were, in some basic sense, exiles from an oppressive British regime. Promoted by Young Ireland exiles in America, this sentiment percolated among Irish Americans during the famine years. As it did, the Irish critique of abolitionism born in the debates over accepting American support for repeal and famine relief was adopted and adapted by Irish Americans. Much like the members of the Irish Confederation who argued that abolitionism slighted Irish suffering and weakened their efforts to save the Irish people, Irish Americans responded to abolitionists' entreaties by denouncing their supposedly singular focus on African American slaves and condemning their ties to Ireland's oppressor, Great Britain.

For all of their frustration over Irish Americans' refusal to embrace the cause of antislavery, abolitionists would continue to seek their support in the early 1850s. Irish-American commentators continued to reject such efforts by rehashing arguments similar to those heard at the Irish Confederation's meetings in 1847 or printed in Irish-American weeklies during the early years of the famine: Irish poverty and Ireland's oppression under British rule were just as evil, if not more, in comparison to African American slavery. However, as the slavery debate in America intensified in the early 1850s, Irish-American anti-abolitionism took on another layer, one that looked not only backward at the alleged wrongs inflicted on Ireland but also forward to a redemptive future for the Irish on both sides of the Atlantic. From across the United States, the chorus of "Repeal!" had rung out in support of O'Connell, not to mention the vast sums of money that flowed eastward across the Atlantic into the coffers of the Loyal National Repeal Association and, after 1845, into the treasuries of famine relief organizations. Millions of Irish now resided in the United States, where, despite the grueling work they performed, the pitiful living quarters so many called home, and a groundswell of nativist angst about their presence, many of them were on the make, and all enjoyed the right to become citizens if they wished. Young Ireland exiles who had been banished to the other side of the world by British authorities, along with less seasoned Irish-American nationalists, congregated in New York City to plot the violent overthrow of British rule in Ireland from cluttered newspaper editors' offices or the well-appointed parlors of the more fortunate among them. The American Union had provided refuge to Irish immigrants in their most desperate hour, and Irish nationalists on both sides of the Atlantic now considered the United States as their most important ally in the cause of independence. Thus, when debate over the future of slavery threatened to tear asunder the American Union and thereby imperil the welfare of the Irish in Ireland and the United States, Irish-American anti-abolitionism became a nationalistic fervor.

3

Irish-American Unionism and Slavery

On the surface, it seems ironic that the American Irish in the 1840s lent fervent support to Daniel O'Connell's campaign to repeal the Act of Union while, in the debate over slavery's expansion in the 1850s, they proclaimed that the American Union must be preserved at all costs. Yet, by 1850, there was much in the recent past to suggest to Irish Americans that a robust American Republic played a vital role in the futures of Irish people on both sides of the Atlantic. Vast sums of money sent from the United States to the repeal campaign and famine relief overseers in Dublin reinforced Ireland's economic ties to the United States, while remittances from Irish immigrants to their families financed many of the famine migrants' voyages. Several years of American support for Irish repeal taught many Irish nationalists the value of friendly relations between Ireland and the United States. By 1850, with a growing population of exiled Irish nationalists plotting their next moves from Boston and New York, the United States seemed destined to play an essential part in the fate of Irish nationhood. Finally, there were the awesome and inescapable facts of Irish immigration to the United States during the famine. In less than a decade, 1.5 million of a total pre-famine population of 8 million Irish crossed the Atlantic to settle in the United States. By the mid-1850s, a full quarter of the populations of New York City and Boston had been born in Ireland. Given the sheer scale of this migration and the circumstances behind it, many Irish-American commentators came to see the United States as a refuge or a haven for Irish people.

The upshot of this was that many Irish Americans developed a virulent attachment to the American Union precisely as the Union itself was imperiled by a debate over the future of slavery. Irish-American Unionism, as it will be referred to here, emerged from the convergences in Irish and American history during the mid-1800s and was rooted in a set of expectations for the future. One such expectation was that the United States' constitutional democracy would allow Irish immigrants denied sovereignty and political freedoms in their native land to participate in its representative self-government. Second, American prosperity would allow the United States not only to serve as a refuge for future Irish immigrants fleeing impoverishment and oppression but also to sustain the people of Ireland. Third, the cause of Irish nationhood could only be advanced with significant assistance from the United States. For all of these reasons, Irish Americans argued, the United States had to remain robust in its economic prosperity and unified in its politics. An elastic principle that could be selectively interpreted and applied, Irish-American Unionism became a potent force in how editors, exiled nationalists, and politically engaged immigrants gauged the political landscape of the 1850s.

This emphasis on the need to preserve and strengthen the Union was indicative of the tide of disunionist sentiment and rhetoric that swept across parts of the United States in the early 1850s. While fears of disunion were as old as the nation itself, they took on added immediacy just as the famine migration peaked. In 1842, Garrisonian abolitionists began to call for the dissolution of the American Union, and debates later in the decade over whether or not slavery would be sanctioned in the formerly Mexican lands conquered by the United States demonstrated that the question of slavery's expansion was a potentially explosive one. The so-called Compromise of 1850—an attempt to carve out a middle ground between proslavery expansionists and those who wished to halt slavery's westward march—raised more questions than it settled. One of those questions pertained to the status of escaped slaves residing in free states and ensnared Irish Americans in one of the great flashpoints of the antebellum slavery debate.

It was in this context of escalating sectional tensions over slavery that Irish-American Unionism took shape and was conjoined to the Irish critique of abolitionism that arose during the famine. As Irish Americans invested their hopes in preserving a robust, prosperous American Union, they framed their opposition to abolitionism as an impassioned defense of their adopted country. Like most other Americans, Irish immigrants viewed abolitionists as fanatics. But the vehemence they directed against antislavery reform was grounded in a uniquely Irish-American brand of Unionism that venerated the United States as a refuge and land of opportunity for immigrants and as both an inspiration and incubator for an independent Irish republic. Thus, as they had since the mid-1840s, Irish-American views on the slavery question remained grounded in transatlantic concerns, even as those concerns expanded beyond abolitionists' alleged neglect of poverty and political oppression in Ireland. During the early 1850s, then, the recent history of and future hopes for the transatlantic relationship between Ireland and the United States animated Irish-American involvement in debates over slavery. Importantly, actual transatlantic crossings by Irish people—including, most notably, the Irish temperance crusader Father Theobald Mathew—along with abolitionist-authored missives continued to sway Irish Americans' positions in the antebellum slavery debate. On the one hand, Irish-American Unionism and Irish-American anti-abolitionism reflected uniquely Irish experiences and concerns.

On the other hand, events specific to the domestic politics of the United States, especially the acrimonious debate over slavery's expansion, inevitably weighed upon Irish immigrants' views. Virtually all white Americans agreed that expansion across the North American continent was the Manifest Destiny of the United States, but once they acquired the lands of the West through conquest, the questions of if and how slavery would be sanctioned there reoriented the nation's politics along sectional lines. While the Compromise of 1850 attempted to restore sectional balance to the two-party system, more and more Americans in the free states protested their compulsory complicity in the slave system, especially through a revamped Fugitive Slave Law that turned all white Americans, regardless of where they lived, into potential slave catchers. For their part, white Southerners cried foul over Northern resistance to the capture and return of runaway slaves while insisting that slavery itself was a positive good that ought to be federally sanctioned in the West. Believing that the preservation of the Union was of the utmost necessity, Irish Americans acceded to proslavery Southerners' demands, especially when it came to the return of escaped slaves. But even as Irish immigrants supported enslavers' efforts to recapture runaways, they did not embrace white Southerners' views of Black chattel slavery as a positive good. In 1854, a transatlantic dispute between the exiled nationalist John Mitchel and the Irish abolitionist James Haughton brought to light nuance and complexity in Irish-American views on slavery itself.

Irish-American Unionism and the Father Mathew Controversy

By 1850, many Irish in America were convinced that the United States had played and would continue to perform a singular role in improving the lives of Irish men and women on both sides of the Atlantic. This sentiment meshed neatly with a popular belief among antebellum Americans that it was the destiny of the United States to nurture the growth of representative government worldwide. In 1848, a tide of revolution swept across Europe as nationalists and liberal reformers besieged and, in some parts of the continent, momentarily triumphed over monarchs and aristocrats. Although most of these revolutions quickly fizzled—none more ingloriously than Ireland's—they affirmed decades-old expectations that the example of the American Republic would inspire republican revolutionaries the world over. Irish-American Unionism emerged within this broader context and through the distinctive transatlantic relationship between the United States and Ireland. The parallel growth of mass participatory politics in Ireland and the United States, American aid to Ireland during the famine, and American support for Irish nationalism all contributed to Irish Americans' belief that they had a singular obligation to maintain a robust American nation-state.[1]

As Americans gazed approvingly at the nationalistic and frequently republican thrust of European political unrest in the late 1840s, Irish immigrants marveled at the liberties afforded by their adopted country's constitutional democracy. Indeed, part of the reason why Irish-American Unionism put a premium on maintaining the status quo in American political life was that it seemed to provide the freedoms that decades of political agitation in Ireland had failed to win. Mass participatory politics were nothing new to Irish immigrants by 1850; three decades earlier, Daniel O'Connell's campaign for Catholic emancipation in Ireland had "developed a mass membership, had staged monster meetings and popular demonstrations, and had made use of the arts of propaganda in swaying public opinion," in the words of one historian. The same was true of O'Connell's campaign to repeal the Act of Union, which between 1840 and 1845 enjoyed the support of millions of Irish who attended massive rallies, contributed money to the repeal cause, and tracked the movement's progress in the repeal press. At the same time, American democracy was evolving, as the abolition of property requirements for voting, the introduction of popular conventions to elect candidates, and the courting of the "common man" by politicians made the nation a more egalitarian republic for white men. Familiarized with the tactics of mass participatory politics by O'Connell but stymied in their efforts to bring about systemic political change in Ireland, Irish immigrants reveled in their ability to shape American politics.[2]

Augmenting Irish Americans' aptitude for the rough and tumble world of antebellum American politics was the eagerness with which the Democratic Party embraced them. Beginning in the 1820s, Democrats courted the immigrant vote and sometimes rewarded Irish-American party loyalty by nominating Irish Catholic politicians for office. Such a strategy was anathema to most members of the Whig Party, which, in the eyes of Irish immigrants, had inherited the Federalist Party's legacy of anti-immigrant, anti-Catholic bigotry. As sectional tensions worsened in the 1840s, Irish Americans' affiliation with the Democratic Party also became a means for them to assert their patriotism amid a nativist backlash against the famine immigrants. The historian Jean Baker points out that the party's deep connections to the South allowed Democrats to depict their party as "a Unionist institution that included Southerners long after other institutions had divided on regional issues." For their part, Democratic politicians' rhetoric played upon Irish-American grievances against British imperialism during the famine years. "[How] had Ireland been brought to this condition?" queried Democratic Senator Andrew Butler during a debate over appropriations for Irish famine relief. "Was it not," Butler proposed, "by the blighting hand of oppression?" In January 1846, Representative Felix McConnell, an Alabama Democrat, went so far as to introduce resolutions to the effect that the House of Representatives would welcome any communication from the "high-minded and liberty-loving" people of Ireland seeking admission to the American Union. "The Irish people, as a nation," McConnell's resolution read in part, "have long been ground down by the tyranny of *British misrule and misgovernment*; and while her people have for centuries groaned under a foreign monarchical yoke, they have always cherished the democratic principle of republican government." Coming as it did amid a more serious debate over the Polk administration's aggression concerning British claims in the Pacific Northwest, McConnell's resolution seems to have been a political farce intended to rib British policymakers while buttering up Irish-American Democratic voters. But that is precisely the point. By 1850, Irish Americans were loath to destabilize a political system and especially a political party that, respectively, counted and assiduously courted their votes.[3]

Irish-American expressions of admiration for American democracy frequently took the form of a contrast against the absence of liberty in Ireland. "Outis," a County Cork–born Bostonian whose letters appeared regularly in the *Cork Examiner*, observed in one 1849 letter, "When I look around me on this republic Ireland looks deplorable, by contrast." Even though he felt out of place at times, Outis continued, he had taken a liking to what he described as the American spirit: "All the democracy of my heart warms to them when I see them enjoying their noble equality—proud of their free republic, and owing no lord under the Lord God himself." From Allegheny City, Pennsylvania, County Down native Patrick O'Hanlon wrote to his father in 1851 about the contrast between America and Ireland. "Suffice it to say," Hanlon observed, "America seems to be the last refuge of the oppressed of every clime where they can obtain however poor and unprotected, equal rights and privileges. If the Tree of liberty cannot flourish here it has little to hope for any where else besides." One of several new Irish-American newspapers to emerge during the years of the famine migration, the New York *Irish-American* in 1850 acknowledged that many of its immigrant readers came to the United States with preconceived political views based on their backgrounds in Ireland. But, the *Irish-American* advised, "the influence of Irish prejudice, Irish politics, Irish impulse should be swallowed up in one wholesouled desire and anxiety to prove worthy of the institutions, the franchises, the freedom, the advance, the glory, [and] the power of this land of adoption." Greeted with open arms by the Democratic Party and awestruck by the leveling powers of American democracy, many Irish Americans by 1850 were vested in maintaining the political status quo, which, in the words of one Irish immigrant, represented nothing less than "the most unanswerable evidence of man's capacity for self government."[4]

Famine relief contributions from the United States also helped to convince Irish Americans of their adopted country's singular role in uplifting the people of Ireland. For both Irish immigrants and their families and friends in Ireland, American donations to Irish famine relief affirmed the idea that the United States was a refuge, an idea that provided the second element to Irish-American Unionism. Irish newspapers like the *Galway Vindicator and Connaught Advertiser* were effusive in their thanks, with one 1847 editorial proclaiming that it was "impossible to exaggerate the noble spirit of christian philanthropy which the American people, in every state of the union, have displayed." The Young Irelanders who edited the Dublin *Nation* concurred, declaring that they would not "look upon this aid as alms, but as a loan." "In the day of your trial, in the night of your calamity," the *Nation* addressed Americans, "Ireland will be nearer to you than you may deem, watching for the hour of requital." As the historian Merle Curti has argued, American famine relief "encouraged immigrants and would-be emigrants to think of America as a place of refuge, as offering a chance to share in an abundant society." These ideas were reinforced over the first few months of 1847 as President James Polk and Vice President George Dallas, along with prominent Whig senators Daniel Webster, Henry Clay, and John J. Crittenden, worked in conjunction with the Committee for the Relief of the Suffering Poor of Ireland to mobilize public support for a humanitarian mission to Ireland. Their efforts succeeded when, on March 3, Congress passed a joint resolution authorizing the US Navy to lend two vessels, the *Macedonian* and the *Jamestown*, to Captain George C. DeKay and Captain Robert Bennet Forbes, respectively, "for the purpose of transporting to the famished poor of Ireland and Scotland such contributions as may be made for their relief."[5]

While the *Macedonian* mission was delayed by several months, the *Jamestown* was soon provisioned thanks to a nationwide charitable campaign that brought native- and Irish-born Americans together on behalf of the Irish poor. Because of the relatively high cost of food in Britain, Americans' sizable monetary contribution to famine relief was less effective than shipping actual foodstuffs. Even as it lobbied Congress to loan two ships of war, the Committee for the Relief of the Suffering Poor of Ireland had also recruited the mayors of the nation's busiest ports—New York, New Orleans, Baltimore, Philadelphia, and Boston—to raise funds and accept donations of food for Irish relief. Soon, famine relief committees sprung up in smaller cities, towns, and hamlets across the country. Docked in Massachusetts' Charlestown Navy Yard, the *Jamestown* was laden with some eight thousand barrels of food, including "meal, corn, bread, beans, beef, pork, peas, hams, oatmeal, dried apples, flour, potatoes, rice, rye, wheat [and] fish" gathered from farms throughout New England and shipped free of charge on railroads whose owners joined in the charitable campaign. In Boston, Irish immigrants brought sacks of potatoes or flour to the *Jamestown*, while others gave what they could from their meager earnings. Galway-born George Crosby wrote to his mother back in Ireland to inform her that "two men of war ships laden with provisions" would soon deliver famine relief donations to Cork. Crosby proudly noted that he had given "2 pounds towards it myself." The men who loaded the vessel belonged to the Boston Laborers' Aid Society, a predominantly Irish-American organization, and commenced work on St. Patrick's Day. Within two weeks, the *Jamestown* was sailing east across the Atlantic.[6]

Given that the United States was at war with Mexico, Irish immigrants like Crosby no doubt viewed the decision to spare two naval vessels for Irish famine relief as a sign of their new nation's magnanimity. Many of the congressmen, Whig or Democrat, who voted for the joint resolution to authorize the *Macedonian* and *Jamestown* missions eyed an opportunity to make inroads with Irish-American voters. Whig politicians, especially, hoped to shed their party's nativist legacy by aligning it with the cause of Irish famine relief; many Whig congressmen, like Abraham Lincoln of Illinois, donated the not insubstantial sum of ten dollars to famine relief. But explaining American famine relief as a purely partisan endeavor misses the bigger picture. The *Jamestown* mission was only the most prominent of the hundreds of Irish famine relief campaigns that arose in response to the increasingly dire news from Ireland. A little more than a year after the *Jamestown*'s voyage, Americans shipped 9,900 tons of food and 650 crates of clothing to Ireland, with American vessels docking in Belfast, Cork, Donegal, Dublin, Limerick, Derry, Sligo, and Waterford. Historian Stephen Puleo observes that a consistent refrain in the speeches, pamphlets, and newspaper articles calling for these donations was that "the United States had been blessed by God with rich, productive land and teeming oceans that provided its residents with seemingly endless abundance." In these circumstances, lawmakers' motivations for authorizing the *Jamestown* and *Macedonian* missions likely mattered little to a recently arrived immigrant who found their new home engaged in a massive charitable endeavor to aid their suffering countrymen and women. What better proof was there that the United States was a refuge for the Irish people than its two political parties competing to ameliorate Irish hardship?[7]

A third critical development behind the emergence of Irish-American Unionism in the late 1840s and early 1850s was the rejuvenation of Irish-American nationalism following the collapse of American repeal organizations in 1845. As we have seen, in 1848, Young Irelanders, frustrated by the British government's inadequate response to the famine and seeing their opportunity for action slipping away as British authorities suppressed political dissent in Dublin, launched a hastily organized and ultimately failed rebellion. But before British authorities detected the plot and brought Ireland's 1848 moment to an ignoble end, Irish nationalists in America were invigorated by signs of rebellion in Ireland and ongoing revolutions across Europe. In New York City, they formed a new organization, the Irish Republican Union (IRU), and pledged to deliver "a few thousand Americanized Irishmen" to Ireland to correct "a want of Republican spirit, and a want of military science" among nationalists there. The IRU included a curious mixture of Democratic operatives hunting for votes and, according to a Boston *Pilot* reporter who attended one of its meetings, "honest mechanics and labourers, and men fully determined to go to Ireland, to 'conquer or die.'" By August 1848, Irish-American nationalists and their American supporters in Boston and New York City had formed committees to raise funds exclusively for the armed liberation of Ireland.[8]

Ultimately, these efforts fell apart almost as suddenly as they came together once news of Young Ireland's failed rising reached the United States. But the embers of Irish-American nationalism had been stoked. In the aftermath of 1848, Irish-American nationalists were primed to plan, fundraise, and launch an armed invasion of Ireland in the hopes of liberating the island from British rule. As sundry Young Ireland exiles made their way to the United States over the coming years, they provided the intellectual grist for transforming Irish-American nationalism from a peaceful pursuit of domestic sovereignty into a physical force movement whose aim was an independent Irish republic. Crucially, Irish-American nationalists in 1848 and beyond held up the United States both as a model and as a principal ally for their would-be Irish republic. Defending itself against charges that meddling in another nation's governance from the United States violated the Constitution, the IRU resolved in 1848 that its aim was to bestow upon the Irish people "that republican freedom, which all happily enjoy in the United States." Another supporter of the IRU described the armed invasion of Ireland by Irish-American nationalists as a means to "plant the Republican Tree of America on the Hill of Tara," a reference to an ancient

Irish seat of power. While these sentiments championed the United States as a beacon for republican liberty, even Irish-American nationalists less enamored with their adopted country realized its potential as a training ground for Ireland's future liberators. Dublin native Thomas Reilly was embittered by life in his adopted country. While he admitted in a June 1848 letter to a friend back in Dublin that he would "encourage the Irish peasantry to come to America," Reilly believed that America's uncongenial climate and the hard toil demanded of immigrant laborers would cause many immigrants to die young. Still, his letters in 1848 were peppered with excited descriptions of IRU efforts to recruit and train Ireland's would-be liberators. "The fife and drum went thro' the streets of New York beating up for recruits to proceed to Ireland," Reilly wrote amid the summer excitement of 1848. "There is great enthusiasm in this land among the irish. There are good irish patriots here anxious for the moment to help rescue their native land from bondage." Disappointed that the Young Ireland rebellion collapsed before he and his aspiring revolutionaries could sail back to Ireland, Reilly and many other Irish-American nationalists realized the importance of the United States as a recruiting and training ground for their cause. In the years to come, Irish-American military companies in New York City, along with private clubs founded by Irish-American nationalists across the Northern states, plotted Ireland's liberation.[9]

By 1850, the core tenets of Irish-American Unionism had emerged from a confluence of developments in Ireland and America. Collectively, these events led many Irish Americans to conclude that the United States was singularly capable of improving the lives of the Irish on both sides of the Atlantic. Thus, Irish Americans reacted with particular scorn to anything that portended to weaken or divide their adopted country, and in 1850, they directed that fervor at the Boston-based abolitionist William Lloyd Garrison. Since 1842, Garrison and his circle of antislavery reformers had called for the dissolution of the American Union. As the historian Caleb McDaniel has shown, Garrison's advocacy of disunion was itself inspired by Irish nationalists' campaign to repeal the Act of Union between Great Britain and Ireland. Indeed, Garrison was an avid supporter of the Irish repeal cause, and he saw his own campaign for "the repeal of the union between the North and South" in a similar vein. In both cases, Garrisonians believed, reformers' task was to mobilize the masses to bring about systemic change from outside the political system. O'Connell had repeatedly hinted that repeal was more of a lever to win concessions from Parliament than a blunt instrument designed to smash the Anglo-Irish partnership. Similarly, Garrison viewed his rallying cry "No Union with Slaveholders" more as a means to convince Americans, especially Southerners, of the need to abolish slavery lest the nation itself be destroyed first than as an actual program for the secession of the free states. But these subtleties were lost on most Americans, who saw in Garrisonian disunionism—which many defenders of slavery associated with all varieties of antislavery—nothing less than treason. Viewed through the prism of Irish-American Unionism, Garrison's calls to dissolve the American Union not only threatened immigrants' political and socioeconomic prospects but also imperiled the chances that the American republic would aid in the liberation of Ireland.[10]

While Garrison had a vexed relationship with the American Irish in the 1840s, to say the least, the forces of Irish-American Unionism and Garrisonian disunionism clashed head-on in 1849–50 as a result of Garrison's encounter with the Irish temperance crusader Father Theobald Mathew. A Capuchin priest from Cork, Father Mathew was the most famous and influential reformer in Ireland and one of the most recognizable Irishmen abroad. His notoriety stemmed from his leadership of the Cork Total Abstinence Society (CTAS) and the crusade he led across Ireland and throughout the United Kingdom to eliminate the consumption of alcohol. By 1843, perhaps one-half of all Irish adults had pledged never again to imbibe, earning Father Mathew the nickname "Apostle of Temperance." But by 1849, the famine had ground the temperance campaign to a halt, and Mathew was in ill health. In need of healthful respite and realizing that emigration had transplanted hundreds of thousands of pledge-takers to America, Mathew left Ireland in 1849 to carry on his work among the American Irish. From 1849 to 1851, Mathew administered the temperance pledge to tens of thousands of Americans, with the American Irish foremost among those who lined up to meet him in dozens of cities and scores of small towns and hamlets across the country. However, a confrontation between Father Mathew and William Lloyd Garrison in July 1849 dogged Mathew throughout his travels and added fuel to the fire of Irish-American anti-abolitionism.[11]

Before delving into the particulars of the Garrison-Mathew encounter and the ensuing controversy, it is critical to grasp the high expectations held by Irish- and native-born Americans alike for Mathew's American tour. Members of the largely Irish-American Roman Catholic Total Abstinence Beneficial Society of New York greeted Mathew's arrival there by declaring their "inexpressible delight at the arrival of so illustrious an Irishman on the shores of this our beloved and adopted country" and welcomed him "in the name of our exiled brethren, so numerously scattered over this vast and mighty Republic." The Boston *Pilot* predicted that the story of Mathew's visit would "read like a history of some of the primitive ages, when the St. Patricks and the St. Galls and a host of others used to cross oceans and do wondrous things in foreign lands." Many native-born Protestant Americans, meanwhile, believed that disproportionately high rates of crime and poverty among Irish immigrants stemmed from alcohol abuse and expected Mathew's temperance campaign to uplift such miscreants. In New York, W. E. Dodge, a representative of the city's temperance societies, proclaimed Mathew's temperance pledge to be "the passport to employment and prosperity" for Irish immigrants. Noting that he had always welcomed the Irish, Dodge added that "there is room enough for all and to spare; but let them come with the pledge" from Mathew. The *Boston Evening Transcript* observed that Father Mathew could "do that for temperance, among the Catholic Irish, which a whole army of teetotal protestant advocates could never do." Similarly, a reporter for the antislavery *National Era* who attended a Washington, D.C., temperance event noted with evident satisfaction that Mathew's "influence over the Irish is immense." "Outis," the Cork-born, Boston-based correspondent to the *Cork Examiner*, took note of these predictions. "The Americans are delighted with" Mathew's labors, Outis explained, for Father Mathew would strengthen the American Republic by uplifting Irish immigrants. "There are three millions of Irish here," Outis observed, ". . . and the great change Father MATHEW will effect in their habits, ideas, &c., will be as much a benefit to the United States of America as to the Celts themselves." With the approval of Protestant elites, Mathew's work afforded Irish Americans the opportunity to revel in their Irish backgrounds while demonstrating their abilities to lead sober, moral lives in America.[12]

From the outset, however, Mathew's temperance campaign in America was surrounded by controversy over his views on slavery—a controversy brought on by an encounter between Mathew and William Lloyd Garrison on July 27, 1849, in Boston. Garrison knew full well Mathew's influence with Irish immigrants and recalled that his name was second only to O'Connell's among the sixty thousand signatories to the antislavery Irish Address in 1841. Hoping to procure a renewed affirmation of abolitionism from the Apostle of Temperance and thereby enlist some of Mathew's Irish-American pledge-takers in the antislavery movement, Garrison visited Mathew and invited him to the American Anti-Slavery Society's annual August 1 celebration of emancipation in the British West Indies. Mathew demurred, claiming his mission to "save men from the slavery of intemperance" prevented him from "attempting the overthrow of any other kind of slavery[.]" Garrison countered that he did not intend to weaken the temperance campaign but felt that Mathew must "bear a clear and unequivocal testimony . . . against the enslavement of any portion of the human family," especially since Irish

Americans had "given little or no heed" to the Irish Address. Informing Garrison that his endorsement of the Irish Address had subjected him to "a good deal of odium," Mathew reiterated his refusal to attend the West Indies emancipation celebration and ended the conversation. Stung, Garrison published in the *Liberator* his recollection of the encounter with Mathew accompanied by a copy of the Irish Address signed by Mathew in 1841.[13]

As news of Garrison's confrontation with Mathew spread, it reignited the on-again, off-again war of words between Irish Americans and Garrisonian abolitionists in both the United States and Ireland. The Garrisonians' frustrations with Father Mathew stemmed from their continued belief that if a sufficient number of Irish immigrants were converted to the antislavery cause, they would tip the balance of the slavery debate in favor of abolition. Garrison himself insisted during his call upon Mathew that Irish Americans held "the key of the slave's dungeon, as the balance of political power is in their hands." Writing to the Irish abolitionist James Haughton, Wendell Phillips dismissed Mathew's concern that speaking in favor of abolitionism would damage his labors among the American Irish. "Would a frank expression of his opinion on this subject, 'occasionally,' (all we asked) have injured him with the Irish?" a vexed Phillips asked. One Garrisonian went so far as to disavow the temperance pledge he took from Mathew, writing in the *National Anti-Slavery Standard* that, "in the name of Daniel O'Connell, seventy thousand Irishmen, and the American slaves, I protest against the compromise you have made with woman-whippers and baby stealers." Throughout Mathew's American tour, abolitionists excoriated the Apostle of Temperance, no doubt seeing in Garrison's failed overture to Mathew a microcosm of their collective inability to win the support of the Irish in America.[14]

Irish-American commentators responded to abolitionists' criticisms of Father Mathew in kind. Importantly, they did so by reiterating the Irish critique of abolitionism born out of the debates over American repeal aid and famine relief and by harkening to the tenets of Irish-American Unionism. The New York *Irish-American* led the charge by reminding its readers that abolitionist meddling in Irish nationalist politics had sown seeds of discord in Ireland. Referring to the Irish Address, the *Irish-American* thundered that "it and subsequent observations made on the question of American slavery . . . WERE THE FIRST—THE VERY FIRST—CAUSES OF THE DIVISIONS" in the repeal movement. In language reminiscent of the Dublin *Nation*'s 1847 anti-abolitionist editorials, the Boston Irishman "Outis" argued that Mathew would "*destroy his own influence, and leave himself nearly powerless to rescue his white slaves*" if he endorsed abolitionism. Such criticism of Garrison's attempt to recruit Father Mathew into the antilavery movement played upon the idea that abolitionism slighted the suffering of Irish people and weakened the efforts of Irish nationalists. At the same time, both Irish-American and native-born partisan commentators claimed that Garrison's lobbying detracted from Mathew's efforts to uplift the Irish in America and thus strengthen the social and moral integrity of the nation itself. Irish-American correspondents to the Dublin *Nation* averred that Mathew was "absorbed in the one idea of their [Irish immigrants'] social and moral regeneration," a sentiment that was echoed by Thomas D'Arcy McGee's New York *Nation*. "Who has dried so many tears as Father Mathew? Who has saved so many lives as Father Mathew?" McGee queried rhetorically in the wake of the Garrison-Mathew encounter. Now, these Irish-American journalists fretted, Garrison's meddling jeopardized Mathew's efforts to uplift the Irish in America. Similarly, the Democratic *New York Herald* lamented that "the moralising influence which [Mathew] was calculated to have on this country" would be negated by his association with Garrison. As Mathew proceeded down the Atlantic seaboard on his American tour, Irish Americans seethed with anger over what they perceived as abolitionists' continued indifference to Irish woes and hoped to salvage whatever "moralising influence" Mathew might have on their compatriots and their adopted country itself.[15]

An important element of the Garrison-Mathew controversy was that it prompted Irish Americans to reflect on what they thought about Black chattel slavery. In Boston, the *Pilot*'s influential editor, Patrick Donahoe, and the *Cork Examiner*'s Irish-born correspondent, "Outis," couched their criticisms of Garrison by expressing a desire to see the demise of American slavery. "Outis" claimed that he would "gladly see [abolitionists'] object attained to-morrow, and slavery prostrate in the dust," while Donahoe insisted that antislavery was, in the abstract, a "good cause." Both authors argued that antislavery was made repugnant by the alleged fanaticism with which abolitionists pursued their ends; Garrison, in Donahoe's words, made "the cause of the poor negro disgusting to those who would otherwise favor it." Patrick Lynch, the New York *Irish-American* editor, similarly condemned chattel slavery even as he upbraided abolitionists. Lynch's commentary came in response to a letter to the editor written by a self-described Black Catholic author who chided Lynch for his "cruel, wanton, and brutal attack on the measures advocated by messrs. Garrison and Douglass, (which are identical with those you struggle for in the case of Ireland)." Lynch published his reply beneath the reader's letter, starting with an unequivocal statement on slavery itself. "Slavery—that is the purchase and use, as property, by one human being, of another—is an evil which should be abolished," Lynch wrote. "No man that ever handled a pen, or wagged a tongue," he put forth, "would sooner see Slavery rooted out of the world than the writer of these observations." Like Donahoe and "Outis," however, Lynch ultimately opposed abolitionism, branding Garrison a "traitor" and his followers proponents of "Slave insurrection." Slavery, in the opinions of these Irish-American commentators, was wrong. But the greater wrong, in their eyes, would be to break apart the nation whose existence they understood to be vital to the welfare of Irish people on both sides of the Atlantic Ocean.[16]

The Debates of 1849–50

If Irish Americans hoped that Father Mathew's refusal to endorse abolitionism would shift public attention squarely onto his efforts to combat drink, then they would soon be disappointed. After fruitful stops in New York City, Boston, and other Northern cities, Mathew made his way south early in the winter of 1849. Before Mathew arrived in Washington, D.C., Georgia temperance advocate Judge Joseph Lumpkin sent him a letter questioning whether he still adhered to the antislavery principles he endorsed in 1841 via his signature to the Irish Address. Although Mathew later eased Lumpkin's concerns over his signature to the Address, Lumpkin's letter was published nationally. The net effect of Lumpkin's letter was to tip off white Southerners that a foreigner who had once signed an antislavery appeal to Irish immigrants was on his way to the slave states. When Mathew arrived in D.C., the House of Representatives welcomed him unanimously, no minor feat in light of the rancorous and as yet inconclusive debate over the speakership that coincided with Mathew's arrival. But with Judge Lumpkin's letter having made the rounds, proslavery Southern senators objected to Mathew's presence on the Senate floor. A warm debate ensued as Mathew watched from the Senate gallery.[17]

The Senate debate over welcoming Father Mathew foreshadowed the nine months of bickering and recriminations that culminated with the Compromise of 1850. Proslavery senators opposed Mathew's admission to the Senate floor based upon his signature to the Irish Address in 1841, which Judge Lumpkin's letter brought to light. Jeremiah Clemens of Alabama argued that since Mathew had on a former occasion "denounced one portion of the people of this Confederacy as little better than a band of lawless pirates," he was unwelcome in the Senate. Mississippi's Jefferson Davis concurred, noting that while he lauded Mathew's temperance work, Mathew was "the ally of Daniel O'Connell in his attempt to incite the Irishmen . . . to unite as a body with the abolitionists in their nefarious designs against the peace, the property, and the constitutional rights of the southern States." Virginia's James Mason also expressed admiration for Mathew's temperance work before questioning how the Senate could know that he would not "connect his mission in some manner with the destruction of slavery in the southern States[.]" Such objections from slave state senators reflected their belief that signing the Irish Address made Mathew an enemy to half of the nation.[18]

Mathew's support in the Senate came mainly from those who hoped to dampen sectional animosity as the Senate prepared to debate slavery's presence in new states and Territories. Mathew's visit to Washington came on the eve of Kentucky senator Henry Clay's attempts to forge a compromise between North and South over where slavery would be permitted to spread in land acquired after the Mexican-American War. Clay feared that the Mathew controversy might rally proslavery Southerners against his compromise and, in the hopes of pacifying Mathew's opponents, lamented "this pushing the subject of slavery in its collateral and remote branches upon all possible occasions" in the Senate. Isaac Walker of Wisconsin, who had proposed to welcome Father Mathew on the Senate floor in the first place, along with Stephen Douglas of Illinois, joined Clay in voting for Mathew's admission, hoping to foster collegiality ahead of what promised to be a divisive debate. Only Senator William Henry Seward, one of the chamber's staunchest opponents of slavery, argued that the Senate should recognize equally Mathew's dedication to the causes of antislavery and temperance. Mathew's supporters carried the day by a tally of 33 to 18, and Father Theobald Mathew became the first noncitizen since Lafayette to be invited onto the Senate floor; unfortunately, he had already departed from the Capitol by the time the vote concluded.[19]

Reactions to the Senate's debate over Father Mathew from two leading Irish-American newspapers focused primarily on the ominous signs of disunion that festered beneath the surface. While Mathew had been "exorcising one sort of evil spirit in Ireland," the *Pilot* observed, he had met with "another evil spirit, which may be fairly considered as vile and as injurious as the former" in America. This was the spirit that pitted "the North and South of this continent, one against the other, to threaten, throttle, and worry each other, like two dogs." Within this metaphor was a warning that the *Pilot* clarified in a later article: the "violent abolitionism of the North" threatened to "injure our union, by provoking civil war." When the Senate took up Clay's proposed legislation in late January of 1850, the *Irish-American* implored legislators not to recreate the bitter divisions that arose during Mathew's visit a month earlier. It was the Senate's duty to thwart those who would "pull down to earth the temple of power which the popular American heart has built and dedicated to Republican Liberty." The Senate debate over Mathew's views on slavery foreshadowed months of debate over the future of slavery in the expanding nation. As a result, these Irish-American editors concluded that abolitionism threatened their adopted country's harmony and growth.[20]

Irish Americans had anticipated that Father Mathew's tour would act as a much-needed balm for their famine-scarred countrymen and women. Thus, when abolitionists' overtures to and criticisms of Mathew threatened to detract from his mission, Irish-American editors accused those reformers of indifference to the well-being of Irish men and women. That accusation mirrored one leveled at Irish abolitionists in 1847 who had objected to receiving "blood-stained" famine relief donations from the United States. The senatorial debate over Mathew not only confirmed to Irish Americans that his earlier opposition to slavery had damaged his reputation in America but also suggested that the sectional division over slavery brought on by radical abolitionists, from their point of view, threatened the political unity of their adopted nation. In these respects, the Father Mathew controversy served as a blueprint for how the interconnected Irish and Irish-American critiques of abolitionism would influence Irish immigrants' position in national debates over slavery throughout the 1850s.

Having settled the Father Mathew controversy in December 1849, senators turned to more pressing business in January 1850. Festering for years in the halls of Congress and editorial columns across America was the question of whether slavery would be permitted to exist in the vast swath of territory—stretching from the southernmost tip of Texas to the northern border of California—acquired as a result of the Mexican-American War. In 1846, with that debate still in its infancy, Pennsylvania congressman David Wilmot had proposed to ban slavery in any territory purchased from Mexico during postwar treaty negotiations. Importantly, in the debate that ensued from this proposal, the two sides broke a traditional Whig-Democrat divide and aligned along sectional lines, with antislavery Democrats and so-called conscience Whigs joining forces in support of Wilmot's proviso. While the Wilmot proviso was ultimately voted down in the Senate, the bitter divisions it engendered were readily apparent during the first session of the 29th Congress, which began with a three-week debate over the speakership of the House of Representatives that was settled only after sixty-three ballots and a handful of fistfights between Northern and Southern congressmen. At stake was not only the question of free or slave labor in new American territories, but also the balance of power in the Senate between the free and slave states. The threat of discord and even disunion was palpable.[21]

Even before Congress began to debate the legislation that eventually formed the basis of a compromise, Irish-American editors and journalists counseled moderation to both proslavery and antislavery lawmakers. The Boston *Pilot* predicted the bitter senatorial debate that unfolded in 1850 in its condemnation of Southern senators who voted against Mathew's admission to the Senate. The Father Mathew debate "prefigure[s] but too truly the dreadful storm which must arise when that great question of Slavery, isolated and alone, is before the consideration of Congress," the *Pilot* asserted on January 5. Editor Patrick Donahoe condemned Southern senators' "fanaticism," which outdid that of "the most hotheaded abolitionist of the North." A week later, the *Pilot* took aim at antislavery Northerners when it warned Irish-American readers of the "insane attempts of those who, for the sake of a small minority of the inhabitants . . . would peril the integrity of this glorious confederation." The United States, Donahoe wrote in a full-throated trumpeting of Irish-American Unionism, was destined to "abolish a wider and more woful [sic] slavery" than that which existed in the South, meaning the oppression of people in would-be nations like Ireland. Those who imperiled this mission through antislavery agitation were "more effective advocates of human degradation than the worst planters with the bloodiest whips." In New York, an Irish immigrant correspondent for the Dublin *Freeman's Journal* described the situation in Congress bluntly as "disunion rampant" and predicted that proslavery Southern politicians would convene to "dissolve the union" if Congress prohibited slavery in the territories. Irish-American commentators urged partisans on both sides of the slavery question to move toward the middle for the sake of national unity.[22]

After Senator Clay initiated a debate in the Senate on January 29 with eight resolutions on the question over slavery in the Territories, Irish-American journalists doubled down on their calls for national unity. The *Irish-American* lauded a speech Clay delivered in support of his resolutions, with editor Patrick Lynch condemning sectionalist politicians who threatened to turn the nation against itself. In early March, the same newspaper proudly reported on a public gathering at New York's Castle Garden where attendees from all parties had united against "the demon of dissension and destruction." Predicting that similar gatherings would follow New York's model, the *Irish-American* concluded that the "distructionists' [sic] and disturbers' tongues shall be paralyzed and silenced forever, and their evil deeds, their fanaticism, and treason held up to the malediction of millions." A few weeks later, both the *Irish-American* and the *Pilot* lauded the infamous New York City politician Isaiah Rynders for leading a mob that broke up an abolitionist convention in Manhattan. "Clay, Webster, Cass, Taylor and the rest, will extinguish abolitionism," the *Pilot* predicted about leading figures in the ongoing congressional debates.²³ Believing that compromise in 1850 hinged on silencing antislavery voices, Irish-American editors attempted to drown out those who they alleged would subvert national integrity to end slavery.

The tenets of Irish-American Unionism continued to shade Irish-American journalists' perspective on Congressional debates over the future of slavery as they continued in the spring of 1850. "An Exile," writing to the Dublin *Nation* from Washington, D.C., lamented that "some few fanatics north and south have endeavoured to raise a cry of disunion." The "fanatics in the north," he postulated, were led by William Lloyd Garrison, who had condemned the Constitution as "'an agreement with Death and a covenant with Hell.'" Meanwhile, proslavery "Southern *Hotspurs*" were gathering in Nashville, Tennessee, to "consider the feasibility of a Southern Republic!" Indeed, while the Nashville Convention had been planned since the fall of 1849, proslavery extremists there now conspired to threaten secession if their demand for a federal guarantee of slavery in the Territories was not met. Such a blatantly treasonous position won little support outside a handful of Deep South states, and moderation eventually prevailed at the Nashville Convention in the form of a platform that called for an extension of the Missouri Compromise line across the continent. As the *Nation* correspondent relayed news of these developments across the Atlantic, his expression of confidence that the Union would be preserved revealed precisely why Irish Americans were so willing to accede to the demands of proslavery Southerners. "[L]et not our step-dame, Britain, rejoice too soon" at the prospects of disunion, he warned, illustrating Irish Americans' conception of the American Republic as a foil to Ireland's oppressor. "Let not those who look to the New World for improvements on the polity of the old be cast down, for the great experiment of Federal Republicanism is in no danger of any more serious interruption than the hisses that may greet an indiscreet ovation," he concluded. Like many other exiled Irish nationalists in America and liberals across the European continent, this writer conceived of the American Union as a "great experiment" in self-governance whose very existence mocked the pretensions of Old World monarchs and aristocrats. He and other Irish-American journalists, therefore, feted advocates of compromise in Congress whose labors would, they hoped, sustain the Union.²⁴

It took seven months of deliberation, lofty rhetoric, and failed votes to arrive at what historians refer to as the Compromise of 1850. California was admitted as a free state; the slave trade was banned in Washington, D.C.; a border dispute between Texas and New Mexico was settled; Utah and New Mexico were organized as Territories without restrictions on slavery; and a stronger fugitive slave law was enacted. Because the "compromise" was not one omnibus bill that Northern and Southern congressmen had agreed to but rather a series of measures passed along mostly sectional lines, it was more of a stay of execution than anything else. But as the historian James McPherson observed, it "seemed to have broken the deadlock that had paralyzed the government and threatened the republic since 1846." After four years of rancor, the future of American nationhood seemed secure. Irish Americans shared with most Northerners a sense of relief over a crisis having been averted, but the debate leading to the compromise had hardened their uniquely transatlantic perspective on the necessity of preserving the Union.[25]

"The Wages of Infamy": Irish Americans and Fugitives from Slavery

As we have seen, Irish-American editors like Patrick Donahoe and Patrick Lynch attempted to disassociate their disdain for abolitionism from their views on African American slavery itself. Throughout the 1840s and during the debate that preceded the Compromise of 1850, Irish-American commentators claimed to oppose all forms of oppression—including Black slavery—even as they lashed out against antislavery reformers. After all, a sense of grievance over the injustice of British rule in Ireland was one of the planks of Irish-American identity during the famine years, and O'Connell's appeals for Irish immigrants to oppose all types of oppression had forced even the most strident Irish and Irish-American foes of antislavery to concede that African American slavery was one such type. And while the American Catholic hierarchy conspicuously refused to stake out a position in the slavery debate or even to condemn slavery as a moral wrong, its leaders also pointed to the Church's record of protesting against particular abuses in the master-slave relationship and, in centuries past, bringing about the gradual emancipation of slaves in Europe. No less a figure than John Hughes, the influential Irish-born Archbishop of New York, had proclaimed in 1842, "I am no friend of slavery, but I am still less friendly to any attempt of foreign origin to abolish it." Hughes's logic—that slavery was bad but abolitionism, especially of foreign origins, was worse—held sway among lay Irish Americans like Donahoe, who argued in an 1850 editorial that Catholics desired the "gradual, legal, and peaceful abolition of slavery," an end that "wild fanaticism" on the part of abolitionists had postponed by "a hundred years, perhaps longer." Such arguments were specious at best but nonetheless persuasive among Irish Americans who held no particular affinity for Black slavery and sought, above all else, to ensure the viability of the American Union.[26]

Events between 1850 and 1854 forced prominent Irish-American journalists, clerics, and exiled nationalists to address more forthrightly where they stood with respect to the morality and practice of slavery itself. The first was the passage of the Fugitive Slave Act as part of the Compromise of 1850. In the preceding decade, Northern states enacted personal liberty laws that barred the use of state facilities to enslavers and slave catchers attempting to capture and return fugitives from slavery. Incensed by these personal liberty laws, proslavery legislators wrenched out of the negotiations in 1850 a new Fugitive Slave Act. Unlike the Fugitive Slave Act of 1793, the new law allowed federal commissioners and marshals to deputize state officials and residents to assist in capturing runaways. Other parts of the law empowered new federal commissioners to rule on enslavers' claims; awarded larger bonuses to commissioners who ruled in favor of claimants than to those who upheld Blacks' freedom; placed the burden of proof of freedom on captured African Americans (who could not testify on their own behalf); and set harsh criminal penalties for those who aided or harbored fugitives. Perhaps most galling of all, the Fugitive Slave Act of 1850 required only the claim of an enslaver to permit federal commissioners and marshals to apprehend alleged fugitives, effectively rendering the entire free Black population of the North liable to kidnapping.[27]

Over the next few years, Irish Americans defended the Fugitive Slave Act even as they continued to insist that they desired the ultimate extinction of slavery itself. The Boston *Pilot*, in particular, mounted an enthusiastic defense of the legislation that revealed where Irish Americans' opinions conformed to and departed from Northern whites' attitudes on the issue. A word on the *Pilot*'s influence and that of its owner, Patrick Donahoe, is necessary here. Donahoe was born in County Cavan, Ireland, and arrived in the United States as a ten-year-old with his father in 1821. He cut his teeth with Boston's first Catholic newspapers before assuming control over a newspaper that he renamed the *Pilot* in 1838 after the popular Catholic, nationalist weekly published in Dublin. By the 1850s, the *Pilot* had tens of thousands of readers and was the most widely circulated Irish-American newspaper in the country, earning it the nickname of the "Irishman's Bible." Its perspectives on the Fugitive Slave Act and fugitive slave cases in the early 1850s provide revealing glimpses into Irish-American opinion on one of the most controversial issues of the sectional crisis.[28]

Above all else, the *Pilot* insisted that the newly enacted Fugitive Slave Act was constitutionally legitimate and necessary for preserving law and order. Donahoe's first pronouncement on the measure came in response to a pamphlet published in 1850 by the New York abolitionist Lewis Tappan. Encouraging his white readers to resist the "wicked Bill" by defending their Black neighbors from being "kidnapped," Tappan described the Fugitive Slave Act as a "disgrace to the nation" foisted upon residents of the free states by a "Slave Power." In early November, Donahoe published notice of Tappan's pamphlet as part of a lengthy editorial on the law. Writing on behalf of his tens of thousands of Irish-American readers, Donahoe first insisted, "We are an abolitionist, also, for we believe in the Holy Roman Catholic Church." Continuing, Donahoe rehashed the familiar argument that "fanatic" abolitionists like Tappan did more harm than good to the cause of antislavery by placing enslavers on the defensive and alienating law-abiding Americans from the cause of the slave. "Really," Donahoe insisted, "the South asks nothing more, and the new Fugitive Slave Law aims at nothing more" than enforcement of constitutional law. A few weeks later, Donahoe editorialized similarly after the abolitionist Unitarian clergyman Theodore Parker counseled his Boston congregation to resist the Fugitive Slave Law. The *Pilot* responded by telling readers they were "only to abide by the letter and spirit of the Constitution, which says that fugitive slaves must be restored." Shortly after, the *Pilot* reported on a "Great Union Meeting at Faneuil Hall," where attendees passed a resolution declaring "that all the provisions of the Constitution of the United States ... are equally binding upon every citizen." Another resolution proclaimed that "every species and form of resistance to the execution of a regularly enacted law ... tends to anarchy and bloodshed." The resolutions mirrored the *Pilot*'s argument that the nation's political integrity hinged on compliance with the Fugitive Slave Law.[29]

The *Pilot*'s support for the Fugitive Slave Law also reflected a uniquely American Catholic strain of thought regarding antislavery reform and human enslavement itself. In his response to Tappan's pamphlet, Donahoe attacked what he perceived as the godless philosophy undergirding abolitionism and virtually all other types of reform. "Their [abolitionists'] principle," Donahoe huffed, "is the same as that of the Socialists, Women's rights, Female men, Peace men,—it is *Atheism*. It is the assumption that man has no home excepting upon earth, and that the whole duty of man is, to live as long, and as happily as he can." The essence of this anti-reformist logic was that the natural world created by God was not equal, and to try to remedy natural inequalities was to subvert God's order. Archbishop Hughes of New York captured this sentiment in more simplistic terms. It was "a crime for one man to reduce another, both being equally free, into bondage and slavery," Hughes observed. But, he continued, American slaves were born into slavery, and Church teaching held that the master-slave relationship must not be disturbed once established. So long as a master acted as "guardian and protector of his slaves" and the slave was "obedient, faithful, moral and loyal to his master," both were "in the line of obedience to the Supreme Master who created all." Hughes and other Catholics viewed slavery as "a social evil," in the words of one Catholic newspaper, but because the Church held only the enslavement of free men and the abuse of slaves to be moral sins, American Catholic leaders regarded slavery in and of itself as a legitimate institution. Thus did lay Irish-American Catholic leaders like Donahoe and leading clerics like Hughes align their interests in preserving national unity with the teachings of their Church.[30]

Subsequent developments in Boston confirmed for Donahoe the merits of his efforts to justify the Fugitive Slave Law. On February 15, 1851, dozens of Black Bostonians liberated and whisked away to Canada a fugitive from slavery named Frederic Wilkins, otherwise known as Shadrach, who had been captured and was awaiting trial in a Boston courthouse. After the arrest of another fugitive, Thomas Sims, in the city less than two months later, Boston was put on lockdown by a combined local and federal force mobilized to prevent a repeat of the Shadrach rescue. Attempts by abolitionists to stage protests outside the Massachusetts State House and at Faneuil Hall were thwarted by state legislators, and on April 12, 1851, Sims was escorted by hundreds of soldiers and volunteers to a ship that returned him to slavery in Savannah, Georgia. Donahoe proudly observed that Boston's "orderly and peace-loving Irish population" had no involvement in the "Rowdy and disreputable" conduct of abolitionists during the Sims affair, but one of the *Pilot*'s readers took Donahoe to task for his seeming delight at the return of the captive. John Lambert, an Irish-born resident of Factory Point, Vermont, chided Donahoe for supporting Sims's return, a position that Lambert found "unbecoming one who is publicly pleading the cause of the oppressed and abused Irish people, and the persecuted Catholics." Echoing Daniel O'Connell, Lambert averred that as a "native of Ireland, as a Catholic Christian, as one whose heart bleeds for the suffering children of my oppressed country, I can not but feel for the whole human race who are suffering in bondage and oppression." Put on the defensive, Donahoe insisted in an editorial reply to Lambert that the reader was "in error when he says we defend the institution of slavery. We have simply insisted upon our duty to be loyal citizens of the nation." The *Pilot* editor continued, "We, too, desire to see slavery abolished. But, as a Catholic, we cannot countenance any mode of abolishing slavery, which is not approved by the church." In an implausible flourish, Donahoe concluded that the Catholic Church "has emancipated millions of slaves, she emancipated the slaves of Europe, she alone can do it in America, and very possibly, will."[31]

Donahoe's perspective on the Fugitive Slave Law offers important insights into how the *Pilot*'s Irish-American readership understood what many Northerners viewed as the most detestable element of the Compromise of 1850. Those who upheld the law, Donahoe counseled, were both fulfilling their duties as citizens and helping to preserve sectional harmony, arguments not easily lost on readers whose allegiances were uncertain in the eyes of many native-born Americans and who subscribed to the tenets of Irish-American Unionism propagated in the pages of the *Pilot*. Besides, Donahoe and other Irish-American Catholic leaders argued, resistance to the Fugitive Slave Law was not only unlawful but also unchristian, for the practice of slavery was no less legitimate in the eyes of the Church than it was under the Constitution. And yet, Donahoe stood firm in the claim that he and all true Catholics sought an end to African American slavery. Abolitionists who encouraged resistance to the Fugitive Slave Law, be they pamphleteers like Lewis Tappan or the mobs that took to the streets of Boston during the Sims affair, set back the cause of the slave by stiffening the spines of enslavers and exacerbating sectional animosity. No doubt, many *Pilot* readers who took Donahoe's words to heart were convinced that Irish Americans had a particular duty to uphold the law.

They found their chance in 1854. By this time, Northern outrage over enforcement of the Fugitive Slave Act had subsided considerably since 1851, when the Shadrach and Sims cases in Boston and instances of concerted resistance to the capture of fugitive slaves in Christiana, Pennsylvania, and Syracuse, New York, portended a potential nationwide conflict. Over the coming years, thousands of fugitives from slavery fled to Canada. But in March 1854, an enslaved Virginia man named Anthony Burns escaped to Boston, where on May 24, he was seized by a deputy marshal as he walked down Court Street after leaving his job at the Mattapan Iron Works. Two days later, an incensed mob tried to break into the courthouse where Burns was held, intending to whisk him away to freedom. As the crowd tried to gain entry, James Batchelder, a twenty-four-year-old Irish-born truckman employed at the Boston Custom House who had been deputized to guard against an attempted rescue of Burns, held the door shut. Amid the tumult, Batchelder was shot and soon bled to death, leaving behind a widow and two young children.[32]

Batchelder was only the first of hundreds of Irish-born Bostonians to aid in the reenslavement of Anthony Burns. Following the courthouse attack, Mayor Jerome V. C. Smith ordered the Columbian Artillery, an Irish-American militia company captained by one of the city's most respectable Irish Catholic immigrants, Thomas Cass, to guard Court House Square. Additionally, both the Columbian Artillery and the Sarsfield Guards, another militia company comprising almost exclusively Irish Catholic immigrants, aided federal troops on June 2 in securing the route by which armed guards marched Burns to the *John Taylor*, the ship that returned him to slavery in Virginia. While the militiamen acted on official orders, dozens of Irish-born tradesmen and laborers from the Bay State Club voluntarily armed themselves with pistols and swords, guarding against any attempts to liberate Burns as he was marched down State Street to the *John Taylor*. Irish-American militiamen's prominent role in preventing an attempted rescue of Burns provoked a fierce response from abolitionists. A widely distributed handbill asked Bostonians if they would "submit to have our Citizens shot down by a set of Vagabond Irishmen," singling out the Columbian Artillery for allegedly volunteering to "shoot down the citizens of Boston . . . [and] defend Virginia in kidnapping a Citizen of Massachusetts!" To be sure, hundreds of native-born militiamen, federal troops, and thousands of native-born Bostonians turned out to aid in and cheer on the reenslavement of Burns. Thomas Wentworth Higginson, a Unitarian minister and militant abolitionist who was one of the few men to break into the courthouse during the attempted rescue of Burns, claimed that one of the men at his side, Henry Kemp, was an "energetic Irishman." But reports on the Burns case in antislavery newspapers emphasized Irish immigrants' alacrity in serving the interests of Burns's captors. According to the Brooklyn *Independent*, it was "Irish steel and Southern fraud" that re-enslaved Anthony Burns. Ever hopeful that his compatriots in America would take up the slave's cause, James Haughton lamented that Boston's Irish-born community had "earned the wages of infamy" for doing the "business of the oppressor" in the Burns rendition.[33]

One reason why abolitionists singled out Irish immigrants' involvement in the Burns case was Irish-American editors' laudation of their countrymen who took part in his reenslavement. The *American Celt*'s Thomas Sweney disputed an erroneous report that James McClure, one of Burns's attempted rescuers, was Irish (in fact, he was a Scot). Irish immigrants, Sweney declared, "never have, and never will be found to act inconsistently with the proper observance of that solemn obligation" to the "Constitution and Laws of this glorious Union." The *Pilot* criticized the "free soilers" from the surrounding towns and countryside and abolitionists in Boston who attempted to liberate Burns, arguing that "men who combine to hinder the execution of a law of the land should be put down." The Irish revolutionary exile and editor John Mitchel came out just as forcefully in support of Burns's rendition and the Irish-born Bostonians who abetted it. Mitchel's *Citizen* proclaimed that it was "satisfactory, that the Irish, as soldiers and citizens, took the side of justice and the Constitution during the disturbance." Such chest-thumping for enforcement of the law and protection of the Constitution reveals how the tenets of Irish-American Unionism informed Irish immigrants' actions in the thick of the sectional crisis.[34]

As newspapers reported the particulars of the Burns case in the weeks after his reenslavement, they reinforced key elements of the Irish critique of abolitionism and Irish-American Unionism. The Irish-born truckman John Batchelder's murder at the hands of abolitionists who attempted to liberate Burns breathed new life into the Irish critique of abolitionism, especially because it occurred shortly after a brawl in Boston's North End between the neighborhood's Irish residents and nativist supporters of the infamous anti-Catholic street-preacher John Orr (better known as the "Angel Gabriel"). Comparing the two incidents, the *Pilot* found it outrageous that "tumults against the Catholics were, and are winked at by a large class of citizens and the perpetrators have so far escaped punishment" even as the murdered Batchelder and Irish-American militiamen in Boston were castigated by abolitionists for defending the law. The *Pilot* was not alone in its outrage over abolitionists' conduct in the Burns affair; two of the abolitionists who exhorted a crowd at Faneuil Hall to attempt the rescue, Theodore Parker and Wendell Phillips, asked for police protection in the days that followed, "being fearful of the Irish, who . . . threatened to avenge the death of Batchelder." While Phillips had previously demonstrated sympathy for Irish causes in his words and deeds, the same could not be said of Parker. A Unitarian minister who by 1854 was the most popular preacher in Boston, Parker was among the most inveterate anti-Catholics in America. The Irishmen who threatened Parker and Phillips likely saw the antislavery mob that killed Batchelder as little different from the anti-Catholic mob that wreaked havoc in the North End. At a time when nativist sentiment coursed throughout America and especially Boston, Irish Americans interpreted Batchelder's death as yet another indication that abolitionism and anti-Irishness were two sides of the same coin.[35]

Moreover, Irish Americans soon found reason to believe that their service in support of the Fugitive Slave Law would be rewarded. Three days after the courthouse fracas that resulted in Batchelder's death, C. J. Faulkner, a Whig congressman from Virginia, proposed a liberal bounty for Batchelder's widow in light of her deceased husband's "patriotism and courage . . . against the violent assaults of a domestic foe." The matter went to the Committee on Pensions, which by a vote of 3-2 (the nays coming from antislavery senators William Henry Seward and Charles Sumner) asked the Senate to award the widow with "a sum adequate to provision her for her future support," leaving her with $3,000 after the Senate's decision. In its final report, the Senate Committee on Pensions awarded the widow Batchelder a bounty in recognition of her husband's efforts to maintain "the harmony, peace, and perpetuity of the Confederacy." Such language meshed neatly with the tenets of Irish-American Unionism, which saw in "the perpetuity of the Confederacy" the opportunity for the United States to remain a haven for immigrants and an ally to Irish nationalists. The pension committee's decision indicated that enforcement of the Fugitive Slave Law would not only advance that national purpose but also provide immigrants with the thanks of a grateful nation and more tangible economic rewards.[36]

More than any other single incident to this point in time, the Anthony Burns case revealed how the Irish critique of abolitionism and Irish-American Unionism propelled Irish immigrants to act in support of slavery. Donahoe maintained that his readers understood "the feelings of men who dislike the fugitive slave law" and desired nothing more than for such men to seek a "peaceful, legal remedy for their grievance." But these and similar protests could not disguise the fact that the *Pilot* was openly calling for its readers to aid and abet the reenslavement of Black captives like Shadrach, Thomas Sims, and Anthony Burns or the fact that its readers were listening. Whatever space had existed for Irish Americans to walk a tightrope between an abstract opposition to slavery on the one hand and explicitly proslavery deeds on the other had vanished with the passage of the Fugitive Slave Act. It was for this very reason that a great many moderates across the North, to quote one convert's reaction to the Burns case, "went to bed one night old-fashioned, conservative, compromise Union Whigs & woke up stark mad Abolitionists." Irish Americans' abiding distrust of antislavery reformers did not permit such a dramatic turn, nor did their steadfast belief that deference to proslavery interests was necessary for the preservation of the Union. But just how far down the path of proslavery extremism would they travel?[37]

The Mitchel Controversy

Almost simultaneously with the Burns case, another controversy over Irish immigrants' involvement in the slavery debate was brewing in New York City, where the exiled Irish revolutionary John Mitchel had recently taken up residency and launched a new Irish-American newspaper, the *Citizen*. Mitchel, as we have seen, played an instrumental role in remaking Irish-American nationalism into a militant republican movement rooted in an unremitting sense of grievance against British misrule in Ireland. While his lectures and writings as an Irish immigrant in America served as fodder for Irish-American identity from the mid-nineteenth century onward, his enthusiastic endorsement of African American slavery quickly turned him into a lightning rod of controversy nationally, forcing prominent Irish Americans to clarify where they stood concerning the practice of slavery itself.[38]

Mitchel's first pronouncement in support of Black slavery in the pages of the *Citizen* was prompted by one of the many transatlantic appeals to Irish immigrants made by Irish abolitionists in the antebellum period. In November 1853, James Haughton wrote an open letter in the Dublin *Nation* to another exiled Young Irelander (and co-owner of the *Citizen*), Thomas Francis Meagher. Knowing that Meagher read the *Nation* in his American "exile," Haughton asked him to live up to a speech Meagher made in New Jersey in which he professed to "hate slavery with a deep and intense hatred." If Meagher truly believed these words, Haughton counseled, he would apply them to all God's people. Haughton urged Meagher to "sanction not [the] denial of civil and social rights to the colored people by your silence, or you will become a participator in these wrongs." He concluded by noting that while he had distrusted other professed lovers of liberty who left Ireland for America, he believed that Meagher, Mitchel, and other Young Irelanders would remedy the "conduct of the Irishmen in America towards the colored people."[39]

While Meagher replied to Haughton with what amounted to a non-answer, Mitchel published his own reply to Haughton's letter in the second issue of the *Citizen*. Mitchel's response combined a blistering attack against Haughton personally and abolitionism more generally with an open embrace of Black slavery. He began by claiming that "while the doomed white slaves of his own country were in the very crisis of their own agony" during the famine, Haughton "was seized with a paroxysm of violent sympathy with the fat negroes of America." Here, Mitchel referred to Haughton's objections to accepting famine relief funds from Charleston and Baltimore in 1847. Mitchel then accused Haughton, "a deep political economist" and corn merchant, of having "stored up corn, hoarded like gold, always hoping the market would come to the very dearest, until it rotted in his store, and was thrown into the river Liffey." Such callousness combined with Haughton's persistent antislavery exhortations during the famine, Mitchel claimed, led Irishmen to "abhor the very name of negro." That Haughton still asked the Irish people to "take up his wearisome song—which they always refused to sing at home"—revealed how little Haughton cared for "Irish serfs." Denying that it was a "crime, or a wrong, or even a peccadillo" to own, buy, sell, work, or whip slaves, Mitchel concluded by wishing for "a good plantation well-stocked with healthy negroes in Alabama."[40]

Mitchel's letter to Haughton stands out as one of the strongest indicators that Irish-American anti-abolitionism originated in famine-era Ireland. Whether or not Irish Americans knew of Haughton's objections in 1847 to receiving famine relief from the American South—presumably, many of them did not—Mitchel gave new life to the incident in the 1854 letter. As fugitive slave cases and congressional debates over slavery in the Nebraska Territory caused sectional tensions to escalate early in 1854, antislavery had a groundswell of support in the Northern political landscape. By rehashing abolitionists' alleged pitilessness toward Irish suffering during the famine, Mitchel gave new relevance to the Irish critique of abolitionism just as antislavery politics was on the rise in the free states. Then, too, Mitchel had an even simpler argument: Why should immigrants take up the "wearisome song" of antislavery in America when they had already "refused to sing" it in Ireland? Here, Mitchel repackaged a line used by another Young Ireland exile in America, Thomas D'Arcy McGee, who in 1849 had rejected a transatlantic appeal from Haughton by pointing out that "out of fifty Irish Nationalists" in the Irish Confederation, not one had taken up "that black hobby of yours." In the plainest and ugliest terms possible, the "Alabama plantation" letter reveals how the Irish critique of abolitionism was adapted to American circumstances during the antebellum slavery debate.[41]

Mitchel's claim that Haughton purposefully dumped food during the famine demands further scrutiny. In June 1847, Richard Davis Webb informed an American correspondent that Haughton "lined his purse pretty well this hard year" as a corn merchant and was accused of being "a grinder of the faces of the poor, [and] a destroyer of provisions . . . that prices should come down." Webb's 1847 letter shows that Mitchel was not the first to level this accusation against Haughton. The abolitionist Henry C. Wright, who was in Dublin in 1847 and lived with Haughton for a time, responded to Mitchel's claims in 1854 by acknowledging that while Haughton had dumped a large quantity of corn into the Liffey, "it was shipped in America in bad condition, and reached Ireland in a worthless state." This defense of Haughton was seconded by fellow abolitionist Parker Pillsbury in February 1854. Webb also weighed in on the issue, informing the *National Anti-Slavery Standard* that a Dublin whiskey dealer, who saw Haughton's temperance work as a threat, started the corn-dumping rumor around the same time that

Mitchel did, adding that "no honest man" believed Mitchel or the "Dublin publican." Haughton's son did not even feel the need to address the corn-dumping rumors in a memoir of his father's career, and for good reason, for there is no evidence that Haughton purposefully withheld or dumped usable food during the famine.[42]

Baseless as it was, Mitchel's accusation of food dumping conformed to the persistent Irish critique of abolitionism as inimical to the welfare of Irish people. But even more so than his libel against Haughton, Mitchel's wish for "a good plantation well-stocked with healthy negroes in Alabama" provoked outraged responses from antislavery Northerners. It bears emphasis that abolitionists and other commentators who wrote in reaction to Mitchel's "Alabama plantation" letter did so amid the much more politically consequential and divisive debate over the fate of slavery in the Nebraska Territory. At the urging of Southern politicians in January, Illinois senator Stephen Douglas amended his bill to organize the Nebraska Territory by adding a provision that repealed the Missouri Compromise of 1820. Essentially, Douglas's revised Nebraska bill opened up the possibility that through popular sovereignty, voters in the territory could sanction slavery across a vast swath of North America where it was previously banned, or at the very least in the newly carved out Kansas Territory, whose soil and climate seemed more congenial to cash crop agriculture than the more northerly Nebraska Territory. Douglas's revisions to the Nebraska bill sent shockwaves across the free states, where Democrats and Whigs alike spied yet another attempt by the Slave Power to browbeat Northerners into accepting no limits on slavery's expansion. Against the backdrop of the Kansas-Nebraska debate, abolitionists and even more moderate antislavery Northerners saw in Mitchel's positive endorsement of slavery a sign that Irish immigrants throughout the free states would add to the Slave Power's grasp on the reins of government. D. S. Grandin, a correspondent of Garrison, observed that he had yet to encounter an Irishman in America "who did not hate a negro," despite the "love of liberty" they professed, while fellow Garrisonian Henry C. Wright worried that Irish immigrants would "more urgently seek to become slave-drivers and slave-hunters" thanks to the tutelage of Mitchel, the "Irish Benedict Arnold." Horace Greeley's New York *Tribune* claimed that Mitchel would "increase the popularity of his paper among the Irish-Americans" by his proslavery avowals.[43]

As the historian Cian McMahon observes, modern scholars have erroneously followed the lead of abolitionists like Wright and antislavery editors like Greeley in assuming that Mitchel's "Alabama plantation" letter was indicative of broader Irish-American opinion. Responses to Mitchel's infamous letter reveal important nuances in how Irish Americans thought about American slavery. Most immigrants likely agreed with Mitchel's indictment of abolitionists, for, on this subject, he was merely reiterating the critique of abolitionism developed by Irish nationalists during the famine and made popular in America by exiled Young Irelanders. Yet Irish nationalists in America and Ireland denounced Mitchel for arguing that slavery was a positive good, with some even expressing concern that Mitchel's views would set back the Irish national cause. One of the tenets of Irish-American Unionism was that the United States would play a pivotal role in creating an independent Irish nation, and Mitchel's proslavery extremism threatened to dampen American sympathy for Irish nationhood. Some Irish Americans argued that Mitchel's zealous support for Black chattel slavery was simply irreconcilable with their desires for Irish freedom. Thus, both Mitchel's critique of abolitionism and Irish Americans' rejection of his endorsement of Black slavery were rooted in particularly Irish concerns.[44]

Irish nationalists in America and Ireland had good reason to fear that Mitchel's proslavery views alienated potential American supporters of the Irish national cause. Mitchel himself had rejuvenated Irish-American nationalist circles by aiding in the creation of the Irishmen's Civil and Military Republican Union—a group that coordinated its efforts with Irish-American militiamen in New York. As British soldiers departed Ireland for the Crimea in 1853, Mitchel and other plotters opened a backdoor channel to the Russian Czar, hoping that Britain's distraction might provide an opening for a rising in Ireland. However, the controversy created by the "Alabama plantation" letter threatened to sap potential American support for such an endeavor. In an article picked up and reprinted by the *Pilot*, the Boston *Commonwealth* claimed that Mitchel's attempts at revolution in Ireland had merely aimed to convey "mastership of the soil and peasantry of Ireland" to him and a few others. According to this interpretation of Mitchel's views, which the *Commonwealth* ascribed to Young Irelanders across the board, exiled Irish nationalists in America were unworthy of American admiration or support, for Mitchel's words suggested that they would have no qualms about lording over the rural Irish poor. Similar arguments substantiated Irish-American concerns that the cause of Irish nationalism in America would suffer because of Mitchel's advocacy of slavery. Henry Ward Beecher's *Independent* best illustrated what Irish Americans like Donahoe feared would result from Mitchel's proslavery writing: "If this was the thistle that was growing in Ireland," Beecher reflected, ". . . then England has put the world in debt to her for cutting it up by the *root*." A group of Irishmen in New York City observed that British officials would now be able to silence Irish nationalists "by reminding the people of the renowned patriot John Mitchel, who so bitterly condemned the British Government, and then apologized for American Slavery!"[45]

To be sure, not all condemnations of the "Alabama plantation" editorial reflected purely Irish nationalist concerns. Editors of Irish-American Catholic newspapers found religious grounds to oppose Mitchel's denunciation of abolitionists. In his initial response to Haughton, Mitchel had asserted that he was no more an abolitionist than "Moses, or Socrates, or Jesus Christ." Patrick Donahoe's *Pilot* had long since expressed concern over Mitchel's anticlericalism. In his response to the "Alabama plantation" letter, Donahoe chided Mitchel for bringing Moses and Jesus into what should have been a purely secular discussion, labeling such language as "blasphemy" and arguing that Irish Catholics should no longer read the *Citizen*. In an article that was copied into Chicago's *Western Tablet*, the *American Celt* dismissed Mitchel altogether for his "*irreverence and imprudence*" and chastised him for his alleged blasphemy. Mitchel's record of questioning clerical influence and supporting secular nationalist revolutionaries in Europe had won him no favors in the Irish-American Catholic press, and the particular language he used in the "Alabama plantation" letter offered a convenient off-ramp for editors who sought to distance themselves from his extreme proslavery views. His fiercest Catholic critic in America, Archbishop Hughes, went so far as to assert that Mitchel, a Presbyterian, came from an "Orangeman" background and was therefore "accustomed . . . to oppressing people."[46]

Most revealing of all the responses to Mitchel's "Alabama plantation" letter were those from exiled Young Irelanders and Irish-American editors who condemned, first and foremost, its endorsement of African American slavery. Young Irelanders' reactions were significant, for they continued to play an outsized part in shaping Irish-American opinion. In responding to the "Alabama plantation" letter, most Young Irelanders sought to preserve their reputation and the cause attached to it by disassociating Mitchel's extreme proslavery sentiment from Irish nationalism. Rather than coming to the defense of his friend and co-owner of the *Citizen*, fellow New York exile Thomas Francis Meagher remained silent as he sojourned in California, leaving Mitchel to take the heat for his editorial in the *Citizen*. Over the next few years, Meagher studiously avoided unequivocal statements on slavery. On the few occasions he addressed the subject, he emphasized his desire to see slavery abolished but only at such a time when abolition would not endanger the Union. More outspoken and direct than Meagher was Michael Doheny, another exiled Young Irelander in New York City who soon became a crucial player in recruiting and training Irish-American nationalists. Doheny responded to Mitchel's editorial with a lengthy counterargument—one that he would repackage both in open letters to the Irish-American press and public lectures throughout the 1850s. He attacked the white supremacist basis of Mitchel's endorsement of Black chattel slavery, labeling it "fraudulent, barbaric, brutal, and contemptible." For himself, Doheny claimed to "detest and abhor the slavery of an African negro . . . precisely as I detest and abhor the slavery of a white Irishman." Another Young Irelander responded to Mitchel by stating that the "language of Mr. Mitchel expresses sentiments of Mr. Mitchel alone—not mine, nor, as I believe in this instance, the sentiments of the overwhelming majority of his countrymen." Even more blunt was the New York *Irish American*, which stated baldly in the wake of Mitchel's "Alabama plantation" letter that "Irish Americans are not advocates of, and do not stand up for, the institution of Slavery, its wrongs and evils."[47]

Ultimately, Mitchel's proslavery advocacy weakened his clout with the Irish in America. Even those Irish Americans in the South who supported Mitchel's stance on slavery recognized that it lessened his influence among the exponentially larger Irish-American population in the free states. Robert and William McElderry of Lynchburg, Virginia, defended Mitchel in letters to their family in Ireland by offering a Biblical justification for slavery and arguing that "preachers and others who denounce slavery on every occasion in Ireland had better come . . . to the slaveholding state of Virginia and see how slaves are treated here and go home and treat their white servants better." Yet both reported that Mitchel's advocacy of slavery had precipitated a steep decline in subscriptions to the *Citizen*. Mitchel himself claimed at the end of 1854 that the "Alabama plantation" letter had "swept off ten thousand readers at one blow" from his subscription list. Mitchel's biographer notes that the decline in readership was partly the result of Mitchel's disputes with the Catholic clergy, but his extreme proslavery views won him few friends outside of the South, even among Irish Americans who were well-inclined to share in his disdain for abolitionism.[48]

As for Mitchel himself, the blowback from his "Alabama plantation" letter was only one of several disagreeable incidents of his first year as an Irishman in New York City. Frustrated by the incessant infighting that hampered Irish-American nationalist organizing in New York and disgusted by what he viewed as the money-grubbing, individualistic culture of the great metropolis, Mitchel removed his family in 1855 to Tuckaleechee Cove, Tennessee, and thence to Knoxville and Richmond. Though he never owned slaves, Mitchel was a tenacious Southern partisan in the years before the Civil War and expanded on his advocacy of racial slavery by pushing for the reopening of the transatlantic slave trade, which he argued would lower the market value of enslaved people and thus redound to the benefit of poor whites. Historians have explained Mitchel's decision to relocate to the South by emphasizing his rejection of Northern society's liberal conceptions of progress, his frustration with the religious sectarianism that ran rife in the antebellum North, and his exultation of Jeffersonian republican virtues. Looking at his move from a different perspective suggests that Northerners forced Mitchel's hand by resoundingly rejecting his proslavery extremism, and Irish Americans were among his critics.[49]

Coming as it did amid the national political storm that formed over the Kansas-Nebraska Act and on the cusp of the Anthony Burns case, the fallout from John Mitchel's endorsement of Black slavery imparted important lessons to Irish Americans as they navigated the treacherous waters of the antebellum slavery debate. First, the incident not only aggravated the already fraught relationship between abolitionists and the Irish in America but also reinforced the notion that taking up the slavery question only divided Irish nationalists from each other. Second, the controversy swirling around John Mitchel in 1854 served as a reminder that the slavery debate itself remained transatlantic in nature for Irish Americans. After all, not only did Mitchel's critique of abolitionism refer back to events in Ireland during the famine, but also Mitchel's "Alabama plantation" letter was a response to a transatlantic missive by the Irish abolitionist James Haughton. "Words, ideas, and memories from Ireland," Cian McMahon rightly argues, "played a critical role in how Irish Americans thought about [slavery]." Finally, when viewed alongside the Father Mathew controversy, the Mitchel affair suggested that Irish Americans who waded into the slavery debate faced a no-win proposition. Mathew's signature to the antislavery Irish Address had jeopardized his reputation and his ability to travel in the South. Mitchel's enthusiastic endorsement of slavery cost him thousands of readers and made him a pariah among most Northerners. As white Northern public opinion underwent a seismic shift from proslavery or neutrality to antislavery, Irish Americans concluded from these incidents that moderation, compromise, and preservation of the status quo were laudable aims.[50]

The upshot of this was that from 1850 to 1854, Irish Americans in the North occupied a precarious position on the slavery issue. Because most immigrants believed the United States would improve the lives of Irish men and women on both sides of the Atlantic, they adopted an unequivocally Unionist position when it came to sectional debates over slavery. In effect, this strain of Irish-American Unionism led them into the proslavery camp, as the fugitive slave debates and the Anthony Burns case revealed. Yet, at the same time, few Irish Americans admitted to favoring slavery on principle. Reactions to John Mitchel in 1854 indicated that Irish Americans' interests in preserving the Union had not produced a rigid devotion to slavery, even if their opposition to the antislavery movement was uncompromising. It bears emphasis nonetheless that in the context of the sectional crisis, the Irish-American position was effectively proslavery. In January 1850, Patrick Donahoe's *Pilot* called abolitionists "effective advocates of human degradation" because opposition to chattel slavery alienated Southerners and, as a result, imperiled the nation. From the *Pilot*'s point of view, the American nation had the potential to improve the circumstances of people not only in America but also in Ireland and elsewhere around the world. Because enslavers were a vital segment of the nation, their interests demanded protection. By working in the interests of enslavers in the 1850s, Irish immigrants themselves became "effective advocates" of American chattel slavery.[51]

Notably, the domestic crisis over the expansion of slavery gave added weight to the transatlantic influences on Irish Americans' position in that crisis. In other words, events in America and influences from Ireland moved in sync. It mattered to Irish Americans that the bitter debate preceding the Compromise of 1850 came immediately after the Senate nearly refused to welcome the Irish national hero Father Theobald Mathew because he had at one time signed an antislavery declaration. So, too, was it meaningful that John Mitchel's "Alabama plantation" editorial threatened to tarnish the cause of Irish nationalism just as Northern antislavery sentiment escalated during the fugitive slave controversy and especially the Kansas and Nebraska debate in Congress. Irish Americans' reasons for opposing antislavery reform and doing the bidding of enslavers to foster national unity had essential origins in and connections to Ireland. Events in the United States from 1850 to 1854 legitimized those reasons, nurturing a particularly Irish-American commitment to protecting and even expanding slavery that would only deepen as the sectional crisis itself accelerated through the 1850s.

4

"As if I was a common Irishman": The Irish-American Critique of Antislavery

By the time John Mitchel arrived in New York City in 1853, the American Irish had never been and would never again be such a significant presence within the broader American population. In 1854, two out of every five foreign-born Americans were Irish—a ratio all the more impressive when one considers that never before had immigrants constituted a larger percentage of the total national population, nor would they again until the early twentieth century. New York City had more Irish-born residents than any city in Ireland, including Dublin. For every Irish-born American, there were only five people in Ireland. By contrast, for every German-born American (Germans constituting the largest foreign-born population in the United States), thirty-three Germans remained in Europe. Also worth pointing out is the sectional preponderance of Irish-American settlement in northern urban and industrial communities. By 1860, approximately 84,000 Irish lived in the American South, well below the number of Irish-born Philadelphians (about 97,000) and paling in comparison to the number of Irish-born residents of New York City (more than 275,000). In both New York City and Boston, one out of every four residents had been born in Ireland, a proportion exceeded in some smaller cities and industrial regions of the free states. The sheer size of the nation's Irish-born population, clustered as it was within urban-industrial communities, ensured that Irish Americans would play a pivotal role in the political crisis of the 1850s.[1]

While it is impossible to know just how many of the 1.5 million Irish who took up residency in the free states between 1845 and 1854 arrived with a memory of abolitionism in their native land, the key point is that some of them did. Many others learned of the Irish famine relief debates and the divisions within the repeal movement over American slavery through the Irish-American press or the Irish communities in which they resided. As we have seen, an Irish critique of abolitionism crossed the Atlantic with the famine migrants and, just like the migrants themselves, was adapted to American circumstances while retaining its distinctively Irish roots. But developments in the Northern economy, especially across the political landscape from 1854 to 1860, led Irish Americans to bend the Irish critique of abolitionism more to their whim. As the sectional crisis over slavery's expansion into the territories deepened during the second half of the decade, the Irish critique of abolitionism morphed into a broader Irish-American critique of the North's socioeconomic system and its increasingly well-defined politics of antislavery.

Even as Irish Americans championed their adopted country as a haven for the oppressed and a beacon of liberty, they also lamented the exploitative conditions that awaited immigrant laborers in Northern cities, mines, and railroad camps. Poorly paid, frequently unemployed, and unfairly dealt with by unscrupulous employers, Irish immigrant workers routinely described their situation as little better, if not worse, than enslaved African Americans. By flipping on its head the antislavery argument that a society of "free labor" was more virtuous and efficient than a slave society, Irish Americans aimed to procure better treatment and pay from Northern industrialists and employers by forcing antislavery Northerners to confront the flaws of their own exploitative economy. Yet, to many native-born Americans in the 1850s, the problem was not the free labor system but rather immigrants themselves, especially Irish Catholics, who could not improve their condition through diligent labor. Moreover, Irish immigrants' preference for the proslavery Democratic Party suggested an innate tendency to choose oppression over freedom. Such sentiment combined with the collapse of the Whig Party in 1854 to allow the nativist Know-Nothing Party to sweep into power across the North. The Northern Know-Nothings espoused an opposition to the spread of slavery and a desire to curtail immigrants' participation in American politics. Their stunning electoral success from 1854 to 1856 convinced Irish Americans that all opponents of slavery, no matter how moderate, were inherently anti-Irish, adding a new layer to the Irish critique of abolitionism. When, in 1856, the Republican Party supplanted the Know-Nothings as a Northern antislavery alternative to the Democratic Party, Irish Americans insisted that Republicans' opposition to the extension of slavery into the territories masked the party's true nativist agenda.

Thus, between 1854 and 1860, the famine-era Irish critique of abolitionism evolved into a broader Irish-American critique of antislavery. On the one hand, this shift was evident in editorials and letters to the editor in Irish-American newspapers that leveled accusations of anti-Irish prejudice against antislavery Know-Nothing and Republican politicians. On the other hand, the Irish-American critique of antislavery also implicitly—and at times, quite explicitly—constituted a challenge to the free labor society that Northern Know-Nothings and Republicans championed. Irish immigrants' experiences in the Northern labor market suggested that preserving the West as a free labor redoubt was hardly worth exacerbating sectional tensions and risking the integrity of the American Union. As a result, Irish Americans rejected the free-soil argument that the West must remain open to free labor at all costs, even pushing Southern proslavery expansionists to the brink of severing their ties with the United States. As those expansionists acted more aggressively to enact their agenda, especially through their outsized influence within the Democratic Party, Irish Americans often struggled to explain their allegiance to a party that did the bidding of enslavers. Adapted from the Irish critique of abolitionism, the Irish-American critique of antislavery helped Irish-born editors, politicians, and laborers reconcile their self-professed disdain for oppression with their votes for a party committed to the expansion of Black chattel slavery.

Exceedingly well-chronicled by historians, the political crisis that unfolded in the United States between 1854 and 1860 will be familiar to many readers. In key respects, Irish-American perspectives on that crisis, as well as the actions of Irish-born workers, voters, and politicians in it, mesh seamlessly with those of native-born editors, ward bosses, congressmen, and laboring classes who voted the Democratic ticket. Yet, at critical junctures in the nation's descent into civil war over the latter half of the 1850s, Irish Americans interpreted events through a uniquely Irish lens. The transatlantic tenets of Irish-American Unionism that took shape during the famine years remained intact during the culmination of the sectional crisis. Editors, exiled nationalists, and the occasional workingman argued that the Union must be preserved as a haven for oppressed immigrants and as a potential ally for Ireland. Additionally, the Irish-American critique of antislavery at times bore an uncanny resemblance to the Irish critique of abolitionism, especially when Irish-American editors drew parallels between the politics of antislavery in Great Britain and the rise of the antislavery Know-Nothing and Republican parties in the free states. Some Irish-American commentators even went so far as to claim that antislavery Northerners who fanned the flames of sectionalism—most notably John Brown—were conspiring with British colleagues to topple the world's greatest hope for republican government. Irish immigrants' opposition to all forms of antislavery as a means of preserving the Union continued to operate under important transatlantic influences as the sectional crisis inched closer to civil war.

"To us poor men, turn your commiseration":
The Irish-American Critique of Free Labor

Early in 1850, the New York *Irish-American* printed and disputed the contents of a letter from former Young Ireland rebel and newly arrived immigrant Joseph Brenan. Writing to the Dublin *Nation* from his new home in Manhattan, Brenan described his fellow Irish immigrants as mere "'hewers of wood and drawers of water' in a stranger's land." Irish immigrants were no better off in America than they had been in Ireland, Brenan claimed, and for proof, he offered up the purported commentary of an anonymous enslaved man: "'My master is a great tyrant ... he treats me as badly as if I was a *common Irishman*.'" The *Irish-American* declared Brenan's letter to be a libel upon the Irish in America, claiming that Brenan ignored Irish-American workers' accumulation of property and Irish-American women's gainful employment. Only weeks earlier, the newspaper had acknowledged that Irish-American men performed "the labor and drudgery of the nation." But, editor Patrick Lynch argued, it was their privilege to do so, for their labor allowed them to acquire property and avoid starvation, neither of which had been possible in Ireland.[2]

The disjuncture of the *Irish-American*'s rosy picture of Irish immigrant socioeconomic mobility and Joseph Brenan's dour appraisal of Irish-American prospects was emblematic of a more substantive debate over labor in the United States. That debate had significant implications for how the Irish in the North acted in the sectional conflict over slavery. Like Lynch, most Irish-American editors argued that immigrants' labor in America afforded them opportunities for advancement that did not exist in Ireland. Yet, by 1850, most Irish-American workers found that the payoff for performing the "drudgery" of the nation was sporadic employment, inconsistent pay, and deceitful bosses. As a result, even those like Lynch, who championed the progress of Irish-American labor, saw glaring deficiencies in a Northern economy that exploited its most vulnerable workers. The North's economy of "free labor" needed to be reformed, making it not only undesirable but also ill-intentioned to spread such an economy in the West. In arguing that immigrant laborers in the North were treated worse than chattel slaves in the South, Irish-American journalists and workers were not supporting slavery. Instead, they aimed to draw the attention of free labor's proponents to the inequities and exploitative practices that prevailed in the Northern economy.[3]

Between the American Revolution and the 1850s, residents of the free states came to believe in the superiority of a society whose workers earned the fruits of their labor. The emergence and growth of "free labor" thought in the free states during the first half of the nineteenth century coincided with the gradual abolition of slavery in Northern states, the end of indentured servitude and apprenticeship, and a steep rise in wage earners. Proponents of free labor held that workers who benefited from the fruits of their labor, first as wage earners and then as self-employed entrepreneurs, could achieve economic and political independence and therefore become ideal republican citizens. Within that process, their labor would create capital to fuel the nation's economic expansion—a process that appeared to have accelerated by the 1850s. Since workers possessed a common ability to achieve social mobility through honest, diligent labor that would fuel economic growth, there was no conflict between labor and capital—or so free labor's boosters claimed.[4]

In the abstract, Irish Americans admired this idealized free labor society, especially its assumption that workers would improve their circumstances through diligent labor. From upstate New York in 1849, Timothy McCarthy told his mother in Ireland that in America, there was "*no despot to grind the faces of the poor,* and to take from them their hard-earned subsistence," indicating his belief that honest labor would be rewarded. An Irish-born Bostonian lauded the Irishmen in Boston who laid pipes, carved roads into hillsides, and filled the city's estuaries with earth, for he believed they would profit materially and morally from the work. Even the generally embittered Boston *Pilot* ran a series of articles in 1854 on "Practical Lessons for the Working Man," one of which claimed that mill hands would eventually have the opportunity for promotion and could even own the mills where they worked when their employers retired. Several years later, and in the aftermath of a vicious nativist movement, the noted Irish priest and scholar Daniel W. Cahill wrote during a tour of the United States to encourage tenant farmers, laborers, and tradesmen in Ireland to cross the Atlantic. "[N]o man of any trade or class," Cahill advised, "can want employment in the United States of America if he be a good workman and have good conduct."[5]

Such glowing descriptions of what immigrants could obtain from their labor did not match the reality for most Irish-born workers. While pockets of Irish-American economic success and prosperity could be found in every major antebellum Northern city, Irish-born skilled workers and professionals in the United States overwhelmingly came from the relatively thin ranks of artisans and professionals who left Ireland prior to and during the famine. Upward mobility was exceedingly rare for most Irish immigrants who had been small farmers, cottiers, or common laborers in Ireland. While the sheer number and visibility of Irish immigrants who fell into the ranks of the working poor were unprecedented in

American life in the mid-1800s, they were hardly the first Americans whose circumstances raised concerns about the North's emergent wage-based economy. In the 1830s, the pitiful condition of wage earners provoked penetrating questions from artisans and craftsmen displaced by the emergence of industrial capitalism over just how beneficial free labor was to a sizeable portion of its workforce. Whereas these early critics of free labor and "wage slavery" aimed to restore a republican tradition of labor independence, Irish immigrant workers who protested wage slavery in the 1850s could claim no such legacy. But like the native-born artisans and craftsmen of the 1830s who decried so-called wage slavery, Irish immigrant workers in the 1850s drew parallels between their experiences and those of Black slaves to highlight the injustices of free labor.[6]

The fact that many Irish-American comparisons between wage and slave labor were rooted in exaggerations or even fictions did not detract from their contemporary currency. Joseph Brenan, who wrote of an enslaved man complaining that he was treated worse than a "common Irishman," had almost certainly never seen any enslaved African Americans when he included this anecdote in a letter to the Dublin *Nation*. Historians have used Brenan's "common Irishman" quip to claim that Irish immigrants shared common experiences with African Americans, as an example of how Irish immigrant workers anxiously disassociated themselves from African American labor, and as evidence of African Americans' general contempt for Irish immigrants. But no one has considered who Brenan was and in what context he authored the letter to the editor that includes the original "common Irishman" quip. Recall that Brenan was a Young Irelander— one who took part in the failed 1848 rebellion. Like his fellow Young Irelander John Mitchel, Brenan was convinced that British statesmen intentionally turned a food shortage into a famine, and he saw the woefully inadequate famine relief system implemented by Prime Minister John Russell as a calculated ploy to encourage emigration in the hopes of depopulating Ireland. Seen in this light, Brenan's tale of an enslaved man complaining that he was treated as a "common Irishman" was not a credible reporting of the actual condition of Irish-American labor but rather a clever piece of propaganda that aimed to convince Irish men and women not to emigrate. The story itself was surely apocryphal, but it would have had an important meaning to Manhattan's Irish workers, whom Brenan found to be performing the drudgery of the city. For these workers, the story of an enslaved man complaining that he was treated worse than an Irishman served as a damning indictment of the economy into which they had entered.[7]

While Brenan's critique of immigrant working conditions was based on fiction, many Irish-born laborers could relate to its emphasis on the exploitation and abuse of their kind. An 1852 letter in the Chicago *Western Tablet*, an Irish-American Catholic newspaper, told of a young Irishman who went to Illinois on the promise of railroad work. There, according to the letter's author, "Patrick," the young Irishman found that he had been duped into a scheme to glut the labor market to depress wages. "Is it not enough that cruelty is perpetrated on the unfortunate laborers now working on the railroad," Patrick asked, "victims . . . who are worse treated than the slaves at the South?" Several months later, two Irish-American laborers on the Wisconsin and Chicago Railroad complained to the *Western Tablet* that they endured "a taskmaster named Hash, whose brutality and tyranny would eclipse that of any negro driver, and whose general demeanor in ordering the men manifested the peculiar treatment of *'niggerdom.'*" By arguing that wage labor on the railroads was just as exploitative as slavery, these immigrant workers questioned Northerners' belief that their free labor economy was inherently superior to the Southern alternative. Like many of the tens of thousands of Irish who found work on the nation's rapidly expanding railroad network, these men found little agreeable about their situation. "This winter is the worst for labourers and mechaniks they had for the last 20 years," wrote Irish-born Patrick Kennedy of Strasbourg, Virginia, a few years later in 1855. "The labourers on the Rail Roads cannot make their board money," Kennedy apprised his correspondent in Ireland.[8]

Similar lamentations were also found among immigrant workers in factory towns. From Dover, New Hampshire, an Irish-born millhand wrote to the Boston *Pilot* under the initials "A.O.Y." to tell readers of "a number of Irish families, in greater poverty than the Southern slaves" who lived and worked in the town. Employed by the Cocheco manufacturing company, these Irish-American families received measly wages and were forced to pay exorbitant prices for food. A.O.Y. argued that the "principal cause of . . . poverty and slavery of the Irish here in Dover, and every other place like it" was that the company was the only source of employment in town. "You who talk of Southern slavery," A.O.Y. grumbled, "reflect on this; it will certainly excite your sympathy." He ended his letter with a simple but plaintive poem titled "An Operative":

> Sir, how can I live in these hard times,
> When living costs so much.
> For house, garment, food, light and fires,
> And still some opine they may be higher.
> My children have bare hands and feet,
> And scarcely can get enough to eat,

All working for the cotton lord.
Ah then, why not change this cruel system,
To meet butcher, grocer, baker, without trustism.
And to us poor men, turn your commiseration.
And for our hard toil and sweat, give us more compensation.

The author's demand for those who "talk of Southern slavery" to "reflect" on the exploitation of Irish immigrant laborers recalled the Irish critique of abolitionism in famine-era Ireland. It also suggests that Irish-American workers viewed abolitionism as part and parcel with the advancement of industrial capitalism. A.O.Y.'s letter aimed to convince antislavery Northerners that they should reform the factory system before they confronted the slave system.⁹

To this point, we have seen that Irish-American criticisms of the North's free labor economy focused on exploitative working conditions and employment practices on railroad lines and within factories. These were unquestionably Irish-*American* concerns, but conditions in and continued immigration from Ireland sharpened their points. While the gradual end of the potato famine in Ireland over the first few years of the 1850s caused a corresponding decline in Irish emigration, the distinctive qualities of post-famine Ireland's economy and society left many smallholders with no choice but to emigrate. The famine did not so much inaugurate as it did accelerate the consolidation of agricultural land by strong farmers—a fact that was often accomplished by the eviction of smallholders and cottier tenants. This displaced tenantry found no Irish equivalent of New York City, Chicago, or San Francisco to move to; there were precious few factories, mines, or workshops in Ireland where a landless peasant farmer could find readily available employment. As a result, Irish emigration continued at a steady clip throughout the 1850s. Over the second half of the decade, roughly 50,000 Irish per year immigrated to the United States. This impressive, if diminished, flow of unskilled, impoverished rural Irish people to the burgeoning cities and industrial communities of the northeast and Midwest raised pressing questions about whether Irish immigrants were truly better off in the United States and revived transatlantic comparisons between Irish and Irish-American poverty.¹⁰

As some prominent Irish Americans warned potential emigrants of the trying circumstances that awaited them in America, they framed comparisons between enslavers' treatment of enslaved African Americans and industrialists' treatment of Irish-American laborers within a transatlantic context. After the Irish nationalist politician William Smith O'Brien toured the United States in 1859, he offered an enthusiastic appraisal of immigrants' chances for upward social mobility in a lecture delivered in Dublin. William Lalor, an Irish-American farmer and brother of the Irish social radical James Fintan Lalor, disputed O'Brien's portrayal of Irish-American labor and social status in a letter to the *Irish News* of New York. Lalor stated that "nearly all the drudgery and all the work requiring great physical strength is performed by the Irish in America," and immigrants who desired to escape cities and obtain land in the West had to "work harder by far than the Southern slaves." The pitfalls of life and work in America, Lalor concluded, should convince the Irish in Ireland to remain at home. Other Irish-American commentators suggested that the treatment of Irish immigrant workers was indicative of a "Yankee" contempt for the Irish that spanned the Atlantic Ocean. "J.M.E." vented his frustration over the treatment of Irish immigrants by "Yankee" bosses, whom he connected to the anti-immigrant Know-Nothing Party. "We work like slaves for the mouthful we eat," J.M.E. griped in the *Irish-American*, "and it would be a pleasure to work thuswise were we respected; *but there is not respect shown us*—no more than if we were so many Southern slaves." J.M.E. claimed that "a Southern slave-owner respects his slaves," whereas Northern employers hated Irishmen "as bitter as John Bull did or does." The *American Celt*, edited by former Young Ireland rebel Thomas D'Arcy McGee, similarly claimed that there was "often a more intimate sympathy between the Alabama planter and his African *slave* than between a Yankee employer and his Irish *help*." In both of these analyses, employers' mistreatment of their Irish workers resulted from anti-Irish prejudice, a sentiment that J.M.E. and McGee believed was inherent among capitalists on both sides of the Atlantic.[11]

Irish-American reactions to a catastrophic industrial accident in 1860 reveal how closely their criticisms of industrial capitalists resembled famine-era Irish criticisms of abolitionism. Just before dawn on January 10, 1860, the Pemberton Mill in Lawrence, Massachusetts, buckled and collapsed, killing dozens instantly and leaving dozens more trapped for several hours, only to endure a more tortuous end when a fire swept through the ruins that night. Many of the victims were Irish women. After an investigation revealed that cheaply manufactured iron pillars and an excessive amount of machinery on the shop floor caused the collapse, an Irish-American correspondent to the Dublin *Irishman* asserted that the immigrant victims were "sacrificed by a murderous negligence to the spirit of mammon, or economy, if you will." The *Irish-American* was disgusted to see that, as Northerners railed against the spread of slavery, they did nothing to stop tragedies like the Pemberton Mill collapse. "Shall the black slave of the south monopolize all the sympathies of Massachusetts," the *Irish-American* asked, "while her own white slaves perish in hundreds without a remonstrance in order that cotton may be manufactured at a shade less of cost?" Just as Irish nationalists during the famine castigated abolitionists for privileging the cause of enslaved African Americans over the plight of the Irish poor, these Irish-American journalists wagged their fingers at antislavery Northerners for negating the exploitation and suffering of Irish-American workers in their midst.[12]

While the Irish-American critique of antislavery was often deployed in response to localized instances of labor exploitation, it was given voice at critical moments in the sectional crisis by the few Irish-American politicians who had managed to climb the ranks of the Democratic Party. The congressional debate that culminated with the Kansas-Nebraska Act of 1854 was one such instance. Sponsored by Democratic senator Stephen Douglas of Illinois, the "Nebraska bill" originated as an attempt to organize the remaining portions of the Louisiana Purchase lands, all of which were north of the Missouri Compromise line. Douglas's initial bill passed the House but received lukewarm support from Southern senators, for under the terms of the Missouri Compromise, slavery was barred from any states carved out of the proposed Nebraska Territory. After consulting with a cadre of proslavery senators, Douglas amended the bill so that it not only allowed voters in two proposed territories—Kansas and Nebraska—to give an up or down vote on the legality of slavery but also repealed the Missouri Compromise altogether. Douglas's proposal to let popular sovereignty decide the fate of slavery in a vast swath of the trans-Mississippi West—land that for more than three decades was reliably free soil—quickly became the all-consuming matter of congressional politics over the first few months of 1854. Free-Soil representatives and senators howled, claiming Douglas's turnabout was yet another sign that a corrupt "Slave Power" controlled the Democratic Party. Meanwhile, Northern Whigs and more than a few Northern Democrats contemplated bolting their parties to form a sectional antislavery coalition as the Nebraska bill trudged its way through Congress on the support of an almost uniformly Southern bloc.[13]

Amid the debate over Douglas's bill, the Irish-born New York Democratic congressman Mike Walsh loudly criticized Northern politicians who cried foul over the potential for slavery to advance into the territories. Like most of the few Irish immigrants who broke through antebellum ward-level politics, Walsh came to the United States before the famine. Through an appropriately named newspaper, *The Subterranean*, which he established in the 1840s, Walsh garnered enough support in the tumultuous world of New York City politics to win Tammany Hall's endorsement for a seat in the state assembly, and in 1852, he was elected to Congress. Walsh's politics were of the radical Jacksonian variety; he came from Manhattan's Sixth Ward, the "Bloody Ould Sixth," a working-class neighborhood that his district encompassed and where Irish immigrants both competed for jobs with and lived alongside a sizable if shrinking Black community. Having built his political career not just as a champion of the white working man but more specifically as an advocate for the immigrant laborer, Walsh joined the fray of the Nebraska bill debate to mock Northern handwringing over the potential extension of slavery in the West. "The only difference between the negro slave of the South and the white wage slave of the North," Walsh waxed on the House floor, "is that the one has a master without asking for him, and the other has to beg for the privilege of becoming a slave. . . . The one is the slave of an individual; the other is the slave of an inexorable class." Responding to the arguments of a representative from Massachusetts who was "overflowing with sympathy for southern slaves," Walsh recounted the story of a mother from Southbridge, Massachusetts, who had been employed by the town to clean its public buildings. After becoming ill, the woman was deemed to be "an incumbrance on Massachusetts" and banished to her native New York. In the last year alone, Walsh continued, some 1,300 indigent New Yorkers were "deprived of their liberty without any show or color of an offense, but because they were poor, and too honest to commit a crime." Juxtaposing these stories of liberty-deprived, impoverished Northern workers against the heated opposition to the expansion of slavery that emanated from his Free-Soil and Northern Whig colleagues, Walsh did not so much build a case for slavery as he did expose the contradictions within free labor thought. Wages and contracts, Walsh believed, were mechanisms by which capitalists bound their workers in a state of dependency, one that left them just as vulnerable to various forms of exploitation and abuse as human chattel. "You are slaves," Walsh had once told his electorate, "and none are better aware of the fact than the heathenish dogs who call you freemen."[14]

Walsh's vote was one of 44 "yeas" from Northern Democrats that secured passage of the Kansas-Nebraska Act and thereby added immensely to the potential slave territory of the United States. There can be little doubt that the effect of Walsh's speech on the House floor and its echoes in Democratic newspapers and ward halls throughout Northern cities was to reinforce proslavery polemicists' efforts to defend African American slavery as a benign institution, a "positive good" that afforded its laboring classes a level of material comfort unavailable to the victims of Northern "wage slavery." But there was more to Walsh's pro-Nebraska speech and vote than partisan pandering or kowtowing to proslavery interests. While Walsh and the other Northern Democrats in the House who voted for the Kansas-Nebraska Act might have thought they were shoring up their party unity across sectional lines, their hopes were dashed by congressional elections in 1854 and 1855 that saw the number of Democratic representatives from the free states plummet from a high of 91 in 1854 to just 25 by 1855. Of the 44 Northern Democrats who voted for the measure, only seven won reelection. As for the contemporaneous claim—repeated by some latter-day historians—that Walsh and his pro-Nebraska Democratic colleagues were the proverbial dogs being wagged by the tails of proslavery ideologues, Walsh himself anticipated and raised considerable objections to such a characterization. "I . . . cannot be justly accused of pandering to the slave power," Walsh stated to his colleagues. "I am in the position of a man who never had a dollar from the earnings of any human being but myself. . . . I have always been the employee and never the employer. Sir, I am no lover of oppression." Having experienced or seen firsthand the dark underside of the Northern free labor economy, Irish immigrants like Walsh found little in that system worth antagonizing sectional strife. Instead, they argued that until Northern employers paid a living wage, treated workers with dignity, and guaranteed the availability of work for those who needed it, the free labor vision would remain hollow. A society of free laborers was not necessarily superior to a slave society and was certainly not worth fighting for if doing so meant alienating one section of the country from the other. In the political climate of 1854, then, the interests of Irish immigrant workers blended neatly with those of proslavery Southerners. This arrangement was to have momentous consequences for how Irish Americans reacted to the growing strength of Northern antislavery political parties.[15]

"A raw head and bloody bones": The Rise and Fall of the Know-Nothings

The fallout from the Kansas-Nebraska Act was swift and sweeping. As we have seen, Northern voters demonstrated their displeasure with pro-Nebraska Democrats like Walsh during the midterm elections of 1854. While Democrat James Buchanan went on to capture the presidency in 1856, by that point in time the Pennsylvanian president found himself at the head of what was, for all intents and purposes, a Southern proslavery party. For the rest of the decade, Southerners made up a decisive majority of Democratic congressmen and senators, using their newfound dominance to push the party toward a more unabashed and militant embrace of proslavery expansionism. Meanwhile, a Whig Party whose Northern wing was already weakened by the much-despised Compromise of 1850 saw its last strings of cross-sectional unity snap in the wake of the Kansas-Nebraska Act. Most of the remaining antislavery Whigs bolted from the party in search of an organization that could loosen the Slave Power's grasp on national politics. While some established new antislavery state party structures under the Republican moniker, others did so as Fusionists or anti-Nebraskaites; in the frantic realignments that played out in 1854, it was by no means a certainty that the Republican Party would soon emerge as the North's preeminent antislavery coalition. Conservative Northern Whigs—those whose primary concern was not the expansion of slavery but rather the preservation of the Union and "traditional" American values amid a rising tide of immigration—also saw the writing on the wall and cast out in search of a new party. As antislavery Whigs debated how to transform their Northern wing into an incontrovertibly antislavery party, conservative Whigs coalesced around a platform of anti-immigrant, anti-Catholic nativism.[16]

The dynamics of the collapse of the two-party system left a lasting imprint on how Irish Americans viewed antislavery politics. Already, Irish-American newspapermen and their working-class readership were critical of antislavery politicians who extolled the merits of a free labor economy while glossing over that economy's exploitation of immigrant labor. In that sense, the Irish-American critique of antislavery built on the established Irish critique of abolitionism, which took antislavery reformers to task for allegedly slighting Irish poverty and political oppression. But as antislavery Free-Soilers, ex-Democrats, and especially ex-Whigs searched for a path to power, they inadvertently added to the Irish-American critique of antislavery by linking hands with nativists who shared their opposition to slavery's expansion. Animated by a core disdain for all things perceived to be foreign, nativists in the early to mid-1850s not only sought to limit immigrants' political and cultural influence but also hoped to curb what they viewed as corruptive, un-American practices, such as parochial schooling, excessive consumption of alcohol, and political corruption. Even if they did not necessarily attribute these problems to immigrants directly, many antislavery Northerners agreed with nativists nonetheless that public schools, temperance, and an end to corruption would promote a more virtuous republican society. In 1854, the Know-Nothing Party emerged from this mélange of antislavery politics and nativism in the free states. As it did, and as the party experienced stunning, if ultimately fleeing, electoral successes in Northern states, Irish Americans found yet another reason to hold in contempt antislavery politics.[17]

The particulars of the Know-Nothing Party's origins merit attention. By 1854, many Northerners were concerned about the volume and qualities of immigrants who had come to the United States over the previous decade. Immigrants now made up over 14 percent of the population, a proportion not eclipsed until the first decade of the twentieth century. In three of the four years between 1851 and

1854, total immigration exceeded 400,000; before 1847, it had never peaked above 200,000. It was not just the number but also the type of people who came and what became of them in their adopted country that raised nativists' ire. While significant numbers of English, Scottish, and Scots-Irish—all of them English-speaking Protestants, many of them at least semi-skilled workers—were among the new arrivals, the vast majority were from Ireland or German-speaking parts of Europe. Nine of every ten Irish immigrants in this period were Catholic, and at least eight of every ten were unskilled workers. Whereas three-quarters of all Americans lived in rural areas, the same ratio of the roughly 1.5 million famine Irish immigrants settled in urban-industrial areas. There, they labored in the meanest of circumstances in the antebellum Northern economy before returning home to neighborhoods where rates of criminality and disease far exceeded those inhabited by other immigrant groups, let alone native-born Americans. While German-speaking immigrants' settlement was more dispersed, in key respects, patterns in German immigration mirrored those of the Irish. Catholic Germans strongly outnumbered Protestants by the mid-1850s, while fewer and fewer skilled Germans made the transatlantic crossing. As early as the late 1840s, nativist organizations like the Order of United Americans (OUA) had decried what they saw as a looming threat to the nation's vitality in the form of increased Irish and German immigration. In the early 1850s, a more secretive nativist organization, the Order of the Star-Spangled Banner (OSSB), welcomed OUA members to its ranks. By October 1854, the organization was commonly known as the "Know-Nothings," with party lodges in place across the country and more than a million members.[18]

Even before the Know-Nothings arrived on the Northern political landscape, Irish Americans were convinced that nativism and antislavery politics marched hand in hand. In 1851, the Boston *Pilot* explained why Irish Catholics should oppose the Free-Soil Party, which aimed only to prevent slavery from spreading and not to abolish slavery in states where it already existed. "As a general thing," the *Pilot* claimed, "whenever you find a free-soiler, you find an anti-hanging man, woman's rights man, an infidel frequently, bigoted Protestant always, a socialist, red republican, a *fanatical* teetotaler, a believer in mesmerism, Rochester rappings, and in every devil but the one who will catch him." Free-soilism, as depicted by the *Pilot*, was shorthand for a collection of radical reforms and beliefs. Notably, the *Pilot*'s reference to "bigoted Protestant[s]" in its description of free-soilers indicated Irish Americans' belief that radical reformers were anti-Catholics. Put more succinctly, as the *Pilot* did in another article, Irish Americans viewed free-soilism as "a recrudescence of Puritanism in its most extreme form." In the columns of the most popular Irish-American newspaper in antebellum America, moderate free-soil opponents of slavery became fanatical religious bigots.[19]

This association between nativism and antislavery politics seemed to be confirmed to Irish Americans when, in 1854, the OSSB suddenly transformed from a secretive nativist fraternal order into a national political party whose Northern wing prioritized stopping slavery's expansion. Stung by their Southern colleagues' support for the Nebraska bill, many disaffected Northern Democrats and Whigs flocked to the Know-Nothing Party (formally, the American Party), seeing in it a vehicle for the type of bold antislavery politics that they believed was necessary to stand up to the Slave Power. Many shared at least some of the anti-immigrant, anti-Catholic prejudices held by nativist members of the OSSB. But if anything held the party together in the North, it was a belief in the limitless potential of a society of free laborers, one that Irish immigration threatened to hold back. In a system that rewarded honest and industrious labor with the opportunity for upward mobility, Irish immigrants were mired in poverty. Those who believed in the inherent supremacy of free labor rejected criticisms of how workers were paid or treated, for such criticism could only serve to validate defenders of chattel slavery. Instead, free labor's proponents claimed that if some workers remained socioeconomically stagnant in an otherwise dynamic society, the fault lay with them rather than the society's system of labor itself, which could only suffer from those who lagged behind. The unmistakable fact that the Northern workers who were least successful in benefiting from the fruits of their labor were predominantly Irish and Catholic led many to conclude that foreignness and Catholicism were threats to the vitality of their free society. At its core, the Know-Nothings' appeal stemmed from a widely held belief throughout the North that American freedom was besieged. In this sense, their opposition to the expansion of slavery, their contempt for immigrants whose poverty raised troubling questions about the free labor system, and their concerns about an influx of Catholics who held a supposedly slavish devotion to Rome all meshed neatly together.[20]

The Know-Nothing Party's origins in local fraternal organizations dedicated to anti-Catholicism thus went hand in hand with its origins as an antislavery party in the North. Many antislavery ex-Whigs and ex-Democrats who joined the Know-Nothings found the movement's strident anti-Catholicism to be part and parcel with their opposition to slavery. A Know-Nothing lodge in Massachusetts, for instance, described Catholicism as slavery's "natural co-worker in opposition to freedom and republican institutions." The fact that Irish Catholic immigrants voted en masse for the proslavery Democratic Party confirmed to antislavery politicians that Catholicism and slavery were twin evils, both of which degraded a society in which freedom of conscience and economic independence were twin pillars. The Irish abolitionist James Haughton observed from Ireland in 1856 that the Know-Nothings' rise was attributable to Irish Americans having sided with enslavers. Irish Americans were "ever to be found doing the dirty work of the oppressor," Haughton explained, which was "the real and all-sufficient cause of the present unpopularity of the Irishmen in the United States." Know-Nothing newspapers and politicians alike demonstrated their hostility to Irish Catholic immigrants as part of a broader condemnation of Northern complicity in furthering enslavers' interests.[21]

Irish Americans who followed politics in the mid-1850s could not have missed indications that nativism and antislavery politics were entwined by Know-Nothingism. George McWhirk, a Protestant Irish immigrant who opposed slavery's expansion, wrote to the antislavery *National Era* in January 1855 to caution antislavery politicians against supporting the Know-Nothings' proposed twenty-one-year wait period before immigrants could become naturalized citizens. McWhirk argued that nativists' preoccupation with Catholicism distracted from the truly important issue of the day. "But what is all this to do . . . about Roman Catholicism?" McWhirk asked. "It is a mere assumption, a raw-head and bloody-bones, to distract and divide the people from the issue of Slavery." Even as he urged antislavery Northerners to leave aside nativist issues, McWhirk's plea itself revealed that antislavery politics and nativism had become powerful allies in the free states. That alliance was also evident in coverage of a Know-Nothing rally held in Worcester, Massachusetts, to celebrate the party's stunning success in a recent state election. When the jubilant crowd burst into song, a Black correspondent for *Frederick Douglass' Newspaper* asked if African Americans could "dance to this Know-Nothing music?" The chairman of the meeting replied that the party knew "no man by the color of his skin," stating that Know-Nothings would "take our colored citizens by the hand as brethren, and . . . do all in our power for their elevation." This provoked the ire of an Irish immigrant who, for some unknown reason, attended the celebration. "Mr. President, do you give the colored population more privileges than you do the Irish, who are white people? Who builds your railroads and your telegraphic wires?" the Irishman asked. The Black newspaper correspondent shot back that "those who build our railroads, and those who fill our alms-houses, are intimately related." The exchange at Worcester's city hall indicated Irish Americans' growing belief that political antislavery and nativist hostility to foreigners were mutually inclusive.[22]

Of the handful of new antislavery parties that fielded candidates in state and federal elections across the free states in 1854 and 1855, the Know-Nothings had the greatest electoral success. In Congress, more than 120 representatives elected in 1854 took their seats in the House with the support of the Know-Nothing Party, and while they lacked the votes to enact a purely nativist agenda at the federal level, Know-Nothings in several states did not. Massachusetts voters in 1854 elected a Know-Nothing governor, a slate of Know-Nothing congressmen, and a nearly unanimous Know-Nothing state legislature save for two representatives. The state legislature, in turn, elected Henry Wilson as United States Senator after Wilson struck a deal with the Know-Nothings whereby he declined the Free-Soil nomination for governor to ensure a Know-Nothing victory in the gubernatorial race. Pennsylvania and Indiana also saw the Know-Nothings sweep into power in 1854, while in 1855, the party scored victories in New Hampshire, Connecticut, Rhode Island, New York, and California. To varying degrees in each of these states, Know-Nothing legislators passed laws intended to limit immigrants' and Catholics' (typically viewed as one and the same) political power and influence. Laws lengthening or making more arduous the process by which immigrants became naturalized citizens effectively aimed to reduce the ranks of foreign-born voters, as did measures that enacted literacy tests for prospective voters. Hoping to reduce what nativists believed was a corruptive concentration of property and wealth in the hands of the American Catholic hierarchy, Know-Nothings passed laws requiring clergymen to cede titles for church properties to lay boards of trustees. In Massachusetts, the party sought to block any potential avenue for the state's sizable Irish Catholic population to assert itself in the public sphere. In an apparent reaction to Irish-American militia units' participation in the rendition of Anthony Burns, Governor Henry J. Gardner disbanded seven Irish-American state militia companies. Massachusetts Know-Nothings also mandated that the Protestant King James Bible be used exclusively in public schools. The most severe Know-Nothing legislative act in Massachusetts was a state "nunnery committee" that belligerently investigated unfounded allegations of licentiousness behind convent walls. In short, through a combination of successful and failed attempts at legislative reform, Know-Nothings across the North demonstrated that their rise in power would coincide with the political and social weakening of immigrants' status.[23]

In this context, Democratic hucksters found it expedient to mobilize Irish-American voters against antislavery candidates by tarring them with the stain of Know-Nothingism. In Ohio, for instance, the Democratic *Cincinnati Enquirer* argued that gubernatorial candidate Salmon P. Chase, running as a member of the Buckeye State's newly formed Republican Party, would mimic the "Abolition Know-Nothing Legislature" of Massachusetts by barring immigrants from office and passing a twenty-one-year law if elected. Chase did court Ohio's Know-Nothings, arguing that Catholics and foreigners had done something "justly censurable & calculated to provoke the hostility which has embodied itself in the Know-Nothing organization." Chase's comments prompted the Democratic *Enquirer* to argue not only that a Chase victory would lead to Blacks being "elevated in the scale of society" above Irish and Germans, but also that it would "disfranchise the foreign population." Antislavery and nativism, in other words, were two sides of the same coin. The *Enquirer*'s demagoguery was all for naught, as Chase claimed victory largely thanks to the support of antislavery Know-Nothings in 1855. In Chicago, Democrats were more successful with rallying immigrants against an antislavery candidate by painting him as a Know-Nothing in disguise. An irate Chicagoan complained in March 1856 that the anti-Nebraska Democratic candidate for mayor, Francis Sherman, had been defeated by the pro-Nebraska Democrat Thomas Dyer through massive fraudulent voting by Irish immigrants. Writing to the *National Era*, the author claimed that in the heavily Irish seventh ward, where the pro-Nebraska Dyer won by 670 votes, 1,218 votes had been cast, more than double the 593 votes cast in that ward the previous year. Irish and German voters, according to the author, "rushed to the polls with a unity and *espirit de corps* never before known" after pro-Nebraska "demagogues" told them that a victory for the anti-Nebraska candidate would lead to a repeat of vicious anti-immigrant riots that struck Louisville and Cincinnati in 1855, a claim that was backed by a second letter to the *National Era* the following month.[24]

As these examples from Massachusetts, Ohio, and Illinois suggest, Irish-American voters in 1854 and 1855 found it difficult to untangle the various strands of antislavery and nativism that were wrapped around Northern politics. The dividing lines between Know-Nothingism and Anti-Nebraskanism mattered little to Irish-American voters who saw in each of these antislavery factions a core nativist element. As a consequence, Irish-American voters strengthened their allegiances to the Democratic Party. It bears emphasis just how potent a force nativism was at this crucial juncture of the sectional crisis. Not only did strictly antislavery candidates like Chase openly court the support of nakedly bigoted voters, but also few pure free soilers spoke out against the nativist tide. Responding to a query of where he stood in the confused post-Nebraska political landscape, Abraham Lincoln wrote privately in 1855 that he was "not a Know-Nothing. That is certain." Observing that Black Americans had been excluded from the nation's founding creed that "all men are created equal," Lincoln mused on how the Declaration of Independence would be construed by a Know-Nothing government. "When the Know-Nothings get control," he cautioned, "it will read, 'all men are created equal, except negroes, and *foreigners, and Catholics.*'" And yet even Lincoln, whose lifelong sympathy for foreign-born Americans has been ably documented by the historian Jason Silverman, did not publicly disavow the Know-Nothing Party until his bid for senate in 1858, by which time the party itself had all but vanished. "If nativism did not crowd antislavery off the track altogether," the historian David Potter has written of the crucial juncture of 1854–55, "the antislavery party, it appeared, would at least have to accept nativist planks in its platforms and nativist candidates on its tickets." One of the Know-Nothings' lasting accomplishments, then, was to push immigrants further into the open embrace of the proslavery Democratic Party.[25]

The Leopard's Spots: Nativism, Disunionism, and the Republican Party

Just as it appeared that the American Party might supplant the Whigs by synthesizing nativism and antislavery, events in Kansas and the nation's capital rapidly reordered the politics of antislavery across the free states. After the Kansas-Nebraska Act left the fate of slavery in those territories in the hands of their voters, antislavery and proslavery partisans descended on Kansas to stage a political and physical battle for control of the territory. With an official proslavery territorial government at Lecompton and an unofficial (though more genuinely representative) antislavery government in Topeka, Kansas became a powder keg. In May 1856, the keg exploded when proslavery ruffians destroyed the antislavery town of Lawrence. The sack of Lawrence prompted Massachusetts senator Charles Sumner to deliver a blistering speech on "The Crime against Kansas" on the Senate floor in which the abolitionist senator excoriated proslavery Kansans and their supporters in Congress, including Senator Andrew Butler of South Carolina. Two days later, Representative Preston Brooks of South Carolina— Butler's nephew—wielded a gold-tipped cane as he beat Sumner within inches of his life on the Senate floor, an act lauded by Southern newspapers. The proslavery assault on Lawrence and the caning of Sumner prompted a particularly zealous antislavery settler in Kansas, John Brown, to exact murderous vengeance on five proslavery settlers near Pottawatomie Creek. Between proslavery violence in Kansas and the brutal assault of an antislavery senator in the Senate chambers, it seemed to many Northerners that there was no limit to what an aggressive Slave Power would do to expand the limits of slavery. Under these circumstances, operatives within the more stridently antislavery faction of Northern politics set in motion a plan to bring nativist voters into the fledgling Republican Party, a process that would bear fruit in the summer of 1856.[26]

As news of conflict between antislavery and proslavery settlers in Kansas reached the East Coast, the two leading Irish-American newspapers blamed both antislavery settlers and their supporters back east for aggravating sectional animosities. "Dido," an Irish-born resident of Detroit, Michigan, wrote to the *Pilot* in the spring of 1856 to express concern about the "large contributions in money and war-like armaments" that flowed into Kansas. "Dido" believed that newspaper reports on "the suffering of the people of Kansas" were "well calculated to keep up the excitements among the *intelligent* and *liberty-loving* people of the North, until after the Presidential election." The author's purposeful use of italics suggests a mocking tone intended to convey the notion that reports on attacks against Free State settlements were embellished to drive Northern voters away from the Democratic Party. After the sack of Lawrence proved that Free State settlers were, in fact, besieged by proslavery ruffians, the *Pilot* gave a more measured, if still deeply partisan, assessment of affairs in Kansas. In a June 1856 article, editor Patrick Donahoe argued that while Free Staters acted from laudable sentiments, they were legally in the wrong. Stripped of its "anti-slavery covering," the *Pilot* argued, the situation in Kansas boiled down to "the question of legal right." If the Lecompton territorial legislature campaigned for temperance rather than slavery, Donahoe claimed, Northerners would have recognized it as a legitimate governing body. The temperance analogy was not coincidental, for many Irish Americans thought that nativist temperance advocates shared a penchant for lawlessness and nativist sentiment with antislavery Northerners. New York's *Irish-American*, meanwhile, argued that Northern newspapers' support for the unrecognized Free State Topeka legislature revealed how ostensibly moderate antislavery politics was being subsumed by radical abolitionism. *Irish-American* editor Patrick Lynch aired his perspective on affairs in Kansas in response to a March 1856 editorial in the *New York Daily Tribune* written by the Boston abolitionist Theodore Parker, whose contempt for Irish immigrants was well known. In his letter to the *Tribune*, Parker chided the Irish for voting Democratic and claimed that Irish Americans had a predilection for spousal abuse and unprovoked attacks against African Americans. The *Irish-American* responded to Parker by arguing that "if Irish emigrants join the Democratic party and take sides against abolitionists," they did so not from an affinity for persecuting Blacks but from a desire to foster unity among the states "for national prosperity and the general good." Notably, the *Irish-American* included *Tribune* editor Horace Greeley in rebuking abolitionists. Greeley's opposition to slavery was rooted in his concern for the fate of workingmen rather than the religious militancy that fueled Parker. By 1856, the *Tribune* generally espoused Republican ideas rather than the calls for immediate and unconditional emancipation made by abolitionists like Parker. But to the *Irish-American*, the radical Parker and the moderate Greeley were equally dangerous, for both men's open support to Free Staters in Kansas would provoke the ire of Southern politicians and further polarize the nation.[27]

As the fall elections approached, Irish-American editors maintained that antislavery partisans were exaggerating violence in Kansas to whip up Northern voters' furor. On September 27, the *Pilot* reported that a correspondent for the *New York Daily Tribune* told a Detroit editor of Free Staters' determination "that war [in Kansas] shall last until November, at whatever cost" to ensure victory for Republican John C. Frémont. The *Irish-American* reprinted the *Pilot* article, adding that if the report was true, "it shows a depth of perfidy on the part of those who employ such tools as we do not think can be equalled [sic] in modern times." The *Irish-American* elaborated on the *Pilot* article by noting that antislavery ministers like Henry Ward Beecher continued to preach "strife and violence instead of peace and good will[.]" As far as the *Pilot* and *Irish-American* were concerned, antislavery politicians were aiding and abetting an illegal insurrection for partisan gains in the 1856 elections.[28]

Historians have long known that what occurred in Kansas in 1856 was less important than what Americans thought was taking place. Hopeful that the plight of Free Staters might buoy the nascent party's electoral prospects, Republican editors dispatched correspondents to Kansas for explicitly partisan purposes. Complaints from the *Pilot* and *Irish-American* that reporters from the *Tribune* embellished or ignored specific facts to the favor of Free Staters did not emanate from a preoccupation with defending proslavery violence or the proslavery cause in Kansas. Instead, they demonstrated a consistency in how Irish Americans evaluated the conflict between opponents and proponents of slavery's expansion throughout the 1850s. Convinced that legal guarantees of the right to own slaves could prevent a rupturing of the Union over slavery, Irish-American editors towed the Democratic Party line when it came to legalizing slavery in the territories, even as they continued to articulate an abstract opposition to slavery in and of itself.[29]

Tellingly, the *Pilot* was consistent in its veneration of national unity when covering Preston Brooks's attack on Senator Charles Sumner. Describing Brooks as "a fierce and hot-headed fool," the *Pilot* noted that although Sumner's speech was in poor taste, Brooks had no right to assault Sumner, and his $500 bail was a "burlesque upon the law, considering the character of the outrage." When Brooks was ordered to pay only a $300 fine for having nearly killed a United States senator, the *Pilot* unleashed its patriotic outrage. "The idea that in the social state, existing under a government of laws, the citizen has no right to take the law into his own hands" never occurred to Brooks, the *Pilot* railed. For Brooks to justify his actions by alleging that Sumner assailed his native state, South Carolina, was equally damning in the *Pilot*'s opinion, for a congressman owed his allegiances to the "supreme law of the land." The reasoning behind the *Pilot*'s denunciation, along with the simple fact that the anti-abolitionist *Pilot* aligned itself on the side of an abolitionist Republican senator, reveals how strongly the newspaper adhered to the principle of law and order under a federal compact.[30]

The *Pilot*'s criticisms of Congressman Brooks might also have reflected Irish Americans' outrage over a lesser-known act of wanton violence perpetrated by a Southern-born congressman. Two weeks before the assault on Sumner, Philemon Herbert, an Alabama-born Democratic representative from California, stepped into the dining room of Willard's Hotel just as the waitstaff began serving lunch at 11:00 a.m. When his Irish-born waiter, Thomas Keating, refused to serve him a full breakfast, Herbert attacked Keating. Using dishes and whatever they could get their hands on, the two grappled until Herbert gained the upper hand. He pulled out a revolver, called Keating a "damned Irish son of a bitch," and shot him dead on the floor of Willard's dining room. Two weeks later, by a vote of 79-70, the House of Representatives decided not to inquire as to whether Herbert should face congressional sanction. All but 6 of the 79 who voted in Herbert's favor were Democrats, while every Republican representative voted for an inquiry.[31]

Irish-American editors were apoplectic that the murderer of an Irish immigrant could not only be acquitted at trial but also exonerated of any wrongdoing by Democrats in Congress. The *Pilot* first claimed that Herbert was a Know-Nothing, but when provided with evidence to the contrary, it condemned Democrats who chose partisanship over justice. New York's *American Celt* went even further than the *Pilot* in stoking its Irish-American readers' outrage after the House refused to investigate Herbert. Proclaiming that "the blood of Thomas Keating was on the hands" of Democrats, the *American Celt* declared that those who supported the Democracy would be "accursed ... until that blood is lawfully purged away." Meanwhile, Southern editors dismissed Irish Americans' outrage over Keating's murder, with the Charleston *Standard* stating blithely, "If white men accept the offices of menials, it should be expected that they will do so with an apprehension of their relation to society." Keating's murder at the hands of a proslavery, Southern-born congressman and Democrats' protection of Herbert showed Irish Americans that flagrant abuses of the law knew no sectional or partisan boundaries.[32]

By the spring of 1856, Irish-American editors had good reason to think that the Democratic Party not only shared some of the blame for allowing the slavery question to exacerbate sectional tensions but also abandoned its Irish-born base. The caning of Senator Charles Sumner by a proslavery Southern Democrat and Southerners' approval of an assault against a United States senator both suggested that antislavery Northerners had no monopoly on divisiveness or aggressiveness in the slavery debate. By refusing to investigate a Democratic congressman who murdered an Irish-born waiter, Democrats also revealed that Irish Americans' loyalties to the party in the sectional conflict might go unrewarded. If coverage in the *Pilot* and *Irish-American* gives any indication, most Irish Americans regarded antislavery Northerners as the aggressors in Kansas. But to the extent that editors Patrick Donahoe and Patrick Lynch cast blame for the open violence that plagued the territory, it was not born out of proslavery expansionism but rather out of concern that the Kansas conflict would irreparably divide the nation.

The 1856 presidential race was therefore a pivotal juncture for how Irish Americans viewed antislavery politics. Elections in Ohio, Pennsylvania, New York, and Massachusetts the previous year had indicated that for the American Party—the official party designation of the Know-Nothings—to fend off a rising Republican challenge in the free states, they would have to position themselves as the better of two antislavery parties. But just as it had done to the Whigs, the question of slavery's expansion into the territories split the American Party, with those who refused to endorse the Kansas-Nebraska Act adopting the moniker North Americans and those who supported the law calling themselves South Americans. Over the protests of most of the party's antislavery delegates, the American Party in February 1856 nominated for president Millard Fillmore, whose actual affiliation with Know-Nothingism was dubious at best but who was sufficiently compliant on slavery's extension into the territories. By the time the North Americans reassembled in June, Northern voters' outrage over proslavery violence in Kansas and the assault against Sumner made it all the more imperative that the party nominate a strong antislavery candidate for president. This was not lost on attendees at the inaugural Republican Party convention, held in Philadelphia simultaneously with the North American Party convention. Realizing that the events of the last few months and fears that a divided antislavery vote would allow Democrats to retain the presidency gave them the upper hand, Republicans nominated John C. Frémont, a political neophyte whose antislavery credentials stemmed from his promotion of a free California while serving in the Army in the late 1840s. At Frémont's nominating convention, Republicans put forth a platform that said nothing about immigrants or Catholics and that called for a ban on slavery, described as a "relic of barbarism," in all federal Territories. Seeing the writing on the wall, the North Americans added their endorsement to Frémont's candidacy. For their part, Democrats nominated James Buchanan, a Pennsylvanian with a long career in public office whose primary attribute in 1856 was that he had been absent from the country amid the heated controversy over the Kansas-Nebraska Act while serving as America's minister to Great Britain.[33]

Even though Fillmore technically ran as the American Party's candidate, Irish-American editors set their sights on Frémont and the Republican Party, insisting that Republicanism and Know-Nothingism were synonymous. Reviving the claim that antislavery partisans were the real culprits behind the violence in Kansas, the *Pilot* reprinted a made-up conversation between an Irishman and a "Beecher-Parker, revolving-Bible-rifle disciple" named Sam who planned to vote for Frémont. After Sam told the Irishman that his five years in America was long enough to permit him to vote, the Irishman retorted that five years was "long enough for a Buchanan voter, but you know it takes *twenty-one-years* to make a Frémont voter." The digs here were subtle but neatly aligned with well-established Irish-American views. Sam, a Republican voter, was described as a militant abolitionist unduly influenced by evangelical Protestant preachers. The Irishman's response, meanwhile, insinuated that Frémont endorsed the Know-Nothings' proposal for a twenty-one-year wait period before immigrants could vote. The *Irish-American* similarly linked Republicans (and their Whig predecessors) with anti-Irishness, claiming that both parties inherited the aristocratic tendencies of England. In an October editorial, the *Irish-American* argued that the Whig and Republican parties had "native American or Know-Nothing sentiments and proclivities" and were full of "bigoted [sic] and denominational parsons" who attacked Irish Catholics. Both articles aimed to convince readers that their votes for the Democratic Party would preserve the Union and beat back a Republican tide of nativism.[34]

A preelection editorial in the *Pilot* encapsulated Irish-American views on the relationship between the politics of antislavery and nativism. After hearing that some Germans in Boston had attended a Frémont rally in June, the *Pilot* explained why it would be a mistake for immigrants to vote the Republican ticket. Frémont supporters were Free-Soilers and, the *Pilot* argued, "free-soilers have been the heart and backbone of the know-nothing movement in this state." Republican opposition to the expansion of slavery was a red herring, the *Pilot* claimed, for the party was led in Massachusetts and across the free states by the same former Know-Nothings who had attempted to prolong immigrants' naturalization process and to implement a religious test for candidates seeking public office. Did these Germans really suppose, editor Patrick Donahoe asked, that once in power, Republicans would "from a sense of gratitude and justice abstain from carrying into effect their know-nothing principles?" And even if embracing Republicans' free soil cause in Kansas did not mean embracing nativism, it would force immigrants to "sustain and ratify an insurrection in their adopted country, for that is what the Kansas affair actually amounts to." Such a course of action was unthinkable, for when naturalized citizens took the oath of allegiance, they swore to "support the Constitution—not the Northern or Southern construction of that instrument." The *Pilot* maintained that Republican nativists were using the German immigrant supporters as pawns in an unconstitutional rebellion that would tear the nation apart. "Thus we see," the *Pilot* concluded, "the Leopard has not changed its spots."[35]

The *Pilot*'s criticism of the Republican "Leopard" in 1856 epitomized the fusion of the Irish-American critique of antislavery and Irish-American Unionism. On the surface, the *Pilot*'s and *Irish-American*'s criticisms should have been reserved for the American Party candidate Fillmore. But Fillmore's campaign focused far less on nativist issues than it did on Republicans' tendencies to polarize the nation on the question of slavery. Conversely, Frémont gained the support of many Northern Know-Nothings who misguidedly believed that he would first resolve the slavery issue and then enact their nativist agenda. While Buchanan handily won the electoral college contest, Frémont and the Republican Party's outperformance of Fillmore and the North Americans signaled the demise of nativism as a potent force in national politics. To many Northern Know-Nothings, the Republican Party now provided the mainstream antislavery political party that they had sought to establish in the first place through Know-Nothingism. Yet, to Irish-American observers, Frémont's candidacy demonstrated a disturbing continuity in antislavery politics. The Republicans' platform was unequivocally one of a sectional antislavery party, one that would only further alienate proslavery expansionists in the South and thereby threaten the unity of the nation that Irish immigrants believed was destined to aid the Irish on both sides of the Atlantic. The party also harbored many ex-Know-Nothings and appeared to have adopted nativist elements, even if it officially shunned nativist policies. Irish Americans saw the Republican Party as merely a new manifestation of a familiar foe whose opposition to slavery, purported disregard for national unity, and alleged anti-Irish proclivities could be traced to famine-era Ireland.[36]

Fanatics North and South: The Final Crisis of the Union

Indeed, the Democratic Party in 1856 could boast a longer and more genuine track record with respect to courting and, to a limited degree, rewarding Irish Americans' votes than any other party in the maelstrom that was American politics in the mid-1850s. Since the party's founding, Democratic candidates in the free states had presented themselves as representatives of the working man regardless of his ethnicity or religion. As we have seen, a select few Irish-American ward politicians like Mike Walsh climbed the ranks of the party to the national stage, while myriad other Irish-born Democratic voters enjoyed the smaller but no less tangible fruits of patronage. Then, too, the fact that the Democratic candidate for president and other party leaders were Northerners lent some credence to Irish-American claims that their Democratic ballots were not so much endorsements of slavery's extension into the territories as they were rivets holding the nation together. Indeed, Democratic editors and politicians in both the free states and slave states in 1856 charged that Republicans were disunionists whose opposition to the Kansas-Nebraska Act and slavery's expansion into the territories not only flew in the face of established law but also revealed their true intentions to elevate Black Americans to a position of equality in American society. In these respects, Irish-American support for the Democratic Party in 1856 fit within both long-established patterns of Irish-American politics and a concerted effort by the party to cover itself under the mantle of Unionism as sectional divisions deepened.[37]

However, after the election of 1856, it became increasingly difficult for Irish Americans to disentangle their support for the Democratic Party from the unfettered expansion of slavery. As the power brokers of a party that now controlled the White House, Congress, and the Supreme Court, Southern Democrats accelerated their drive to expand the limits of slavery both on American soil and abroad. Their first victory was less an immediate consequence of Buchanan's election than the result of a years-long campaign to tilt the balance of the judicial system in favor of enslavers. On March 6, 1857, Chief Justice Roger Taney issued the Supreme Court's decision in *Dred Scott v. Sandford*. Taney wrote on behalf of six other justices in the majority, each appointed by a proslavery Southern president. In *Scott*, the court ruled not only that African Americans were barred from citizenship by the Constitution but also that Congress had no constitutional authority to ban slavery in United States territories. Elated, proslavery Southerners in Congress next attempted to push through a bill that would have admitted Kansas to the Union as a slave state based on a fraudulently conceived state constitution drafted by the unrepresentative territorial legislature in Lecompton and ostensibly approved by a whopping majority of Kansans in a vote that was marred by massive corruption on the part of proslavery partisans. Stymied by a unified bloc of Republican opposition and just enough "nay" votes from Northern Democrats in the House, Southern congressmen now clamored for a federal slave code in the territories, effectively calling for Congress to apply the logic of the *Scott* decision through legislation. Meanwhile, Buchanan's Virginian secretary of war, John Floyd, worked in tandem with Jefferson Davis, Mississippi senator and chairman of the Committee on Military Affairs, to expand the armed forces. As the historian Matt Karp has shown, such maneuvers to enlarge and empower the army and navy in 1857–58 were part of a longer campaign on the part of proslavery Southerners to marshal the nation's armed forces and diplomatic corps in support of a "foreign policy of slavery."[38]

Amid such clear evidence that the Democratic Party was now controlled by proslavery extremists, Irish-American editors struggled to reconcile their readers' Unionist aims with their Democratic votes. In two editorial responses to news of the *Scott* decision, the *Pilot* chose to defend the reputation of the Supreme Court against antislavery Northern critics rather than wade into the particulars of the case itself. "If the decision had been in favor of the [Missouri] compromise," the *Pilot* declared, "we should not have seen any cause for denouncing the court." This convenient hypothetical elided the near certainty that a decision in the *Scott* case upholding Congress's right to limit slavery's expansion in the territories would have ignited a firestorm from Southern Democrats. Instead of calling attention to the true implications of the Court's decision in *Scott*, the *Pilot* beat the drum of Unionism, lamenting the "anarchical spirit which breathes through the presses which assail the decision." Yet subsequent developments in 1857 made it harder still for Irish Americans to defend their Southern allies in the Democratic Party. Through the summer months, the *New York Tablet*, a newly established Irish-American Catholic newspaper edited by Bernard Doran Killian, ran a series of articles that chronicled the return of the filibusterer William Walker to the United States. Two years earlier, Walker led a band of brigands in an invasion of Nicaragua, where he inserted himself into that country's ongoing civil war to carve out a new government and declare himself president. By early 1857, Walker had overplayed his hand and was forced to beat a hasty retreat to American shores, but not before he launched a final desperate power grab that included an attempt to reinstate slavery in Nicaragua. Many Southern Democrats lauded Walker as a hero to the cause of slave expansionism. As it kept readers abreast of Walker's repatriation, Killian's *Tablet* strongly condemned his quixotic campaign in Nicaragua and all other filibustering missions. "If the readers of Irish American journals are . . . zealous supporters of the Democracy," Killian commented, "they are also . . . zealous opponents of filibusterism, whether attempted in Cuba, prosecuted in Central America, or killed in the inception in Sonora." Importantly, the *Tablet*'s weeks-long campaign against the hero's welcome that Southerners afforded to Walker included specific criticisms of his reinstatement of slavery in Nicaragua. Should the Democratic Party not repudiate the type of "brigandage and brigands" represented by Walker, the *Tablet* warned, Irish-American voters would have no choice but to repudiate the party itself. While the *Tablet*'s threat of political mutiny was exaggerated, it indicated a deeper tension within Irish Americans' relationship with the Democratic Party.[39]

Just as it seemed Southern Democrats' proslavery expansionism might force Irish immigrants to choose between their party and their Unionist principles, the abolitionist John Brown's raid on Harpers Ferry, Virginia, in October 1859 shored up the connection between the Irish-American critique of antislavery and Irish-American Unionism. Harpers Ferry was home to a federal arsenal where Brown and his men intended to seize weapons, liberate enslaved men and women in the vicinity, and retreat to the Appalachians to wage a guerilla war against slavery. The raid itself was an abysmal failure, leading to the deaths of most of the raiding party, several residents, and one of the marines dispatched to retake the arsenal. Brown and a handful of survivors were captured, and by year's end, Brown had met his end on a gallows in Virginia. But his serenity and eloquence in court, a public relations campaign undertaken by admiring Transcendentalists, and years of Northern disdain for the haughty "Slave Power" combined to make those gallows "as glorious as the cross," in the words of Ralph Waldo Emerson. And while Republicans repudiated Brown's actions, their statements indicated that only Brown's violent deeds—not his antislavery principles—were objectionable.[40]

Sensing an opportunity to transcend intraparty sectionalism and to gain voters in the 1860 presidential election, Northern Democrats joined Southerners in blaming Republicans for Brown's violent abolitionism. In some ways, Irish Americans' commentaries on the raid reflected these broader Democratic attempts to convince Southerners and conservative Northerners that the Democracy was the party of national unity. The *Pilot* claimed that Brown acted logically from the belief that his free-soil "aiders and abettors in 1856, '57, and '58" would support a more direct assault on slavery. Brown's raid was "merely an amplification of the ideas of the free-soilers," a charge that was seconded in a letter to the editor of the *Pilot* accusing the governors of Massachusetts, New York, and Ohio of complicity in the plot. Similarly, the *Irish-American* saw the "true culprits" of Brown's crime as "safely intrenched [sic] behind their editorial desks, their pulpits and Senatorial chairs," positions that Irish-American readers in New York no doubt associated with Greeley of the *Tribune*, the Reverend Henry Ward Beecher, and Senator William Henry Seward, all firm antislavery Republicans. By associating the whole of the Republican Party with its relatively few radical opponents of slavery in the aftermath of Harpers Ferry, both newspapers positioned the Democratic Party as the party of national unity.[41]

Yet Irish Americans' reactions to Harpers Ferry also harkened to a distinct Irish-American critique of antislavery that had developed over the past decade. Upon learning that Brown was to be hanged, the *Irish-American* alleged that the industrialist Amos Lawrence should share Brown's fate, for Lawrence not only allegedly gave Brown $7,000 for his scheme but also was responsible for the mistreatment of Irish immigrant workers in the textile mills that gave him his fortune. The *Pilot* mocked Brown's supporters as nativist extremists, claiming it had warned Republicans in 1856 against financing men like Brown in Kansas but was told that "as Papists we were wedded to slavery." After Brown stated in court that his actions were guided by a belief in the Bible's teaching of the Golden Rule, the *Pilot* sneered that Protestants' unmediated reading of the Bible was to blame for this new brand of violent abolitionism. In these accounts, editors Patrick Donahoe and Patrick Meehan (who succeeded Patrick Lynch as the *Irish-American*'s editor in 1857) argued that Brown's antislavery fervor was part and parcel with his and his backers' alleged anti-Irish, anti-Catholic tendencies. Yet again, antislavery and nativism loomed as twin foes in the editorial columns of Irish-American newspapers.[42]

The most revealing Irish-American analysis of Harpers Ferry came after Brown's execution. On December 3, the *Pilot* argued that antislavery preachers like Henry Ward Beecher and radical abolitionists like Brown partook in an English plot to divide and conquer America, a plot that had "done its work of blood and desolation so effectually in Ireland and whose evil effects have pursued the Irish working-classes" to America. Just as English "philanthropists" blamed Catholicism for Ireland's pitiful condition, so too did their "know-nothing allies in America" view slavery as a cancer to the United States. A week later, the *Pilot* offered proof that "Old and New England" had conspired to foment Brown's raid, pointing out that two Irishmen, a Harpers Ferry resident named "Burley" (actually Thomas Boerly) and a Marine named Quinn, were among those killed by Brown's men. A grocer by trade, Boerly came from County Roscommon and was a respected brawler in the town with a wife and three children; he was killed by one of Brown's men as he walked from his home to his store. Quinn came to

America from Ireland as a child in 1844 and joined the Marines in 1855. He was killed when commanded by Colonel Robert E. Lee to attack the engine house in which Brown and the surviving raiders had barricaded themselves. In light of this information, Donahoe thundered that the raid's planners were "the natural, the unrelenting, the implacable enemies of the Irish race." Brown and his men, the *Pilot* conjectured, were no different from the nativists who penned the Alien and Sedition Acts in 1798, burned a Charlestown, Massachusetts, convent in 1834, and "labor[ed] in the interest of a foreign government, England," to dismember the United States. Brown's raid pushed the *Pilot* to its most feverish conjuring of the supposed conspiracy that linked abolitionism, nativism, and disunionism.[43]

It is tempting to dismiss out of hand the *Pilot*'s fantastical explanation of the Harpers Ferry raid as a transatlantic British plot that would simultaneously destroy the American Republic and wreak havoc on its Irish-American Catholic population. But doing so would obscure the transatlantic lens through which Irish Americans viewed the relationship between the American Union and their native land. Between 1854 and 1859, Irish nationalists in America continued to plan Ireland's liberation, always keeping a watchful eye for British foreign entanglements that might provide an opening for an invasion, a rising, or some combination thereof. With British forces committed to the Crimea in 1855–56, the Boston-based Irish Emigrant Aid Society—its name a mocking play on the free-soil Emigrant Aid Society—had tried to recruit Irish immigrants to sail east across the Atlantic and liberate their native land. This far-fetched design was disrupted by the arrest of twenty members of an Emigrant Aid Society branch in Cincinnati on charges of violating the Neutrality Act of 1818. But in 1857, an opportunity appeared to knock again when sepoys employed by the British East India Company launched what soon became a massive uprising across northern and central India. Not only did Irish-American editors cheer on the "Indian mutiny," but also exiled Young Ireland rebels John O'Mahony and Michael Doheny sent word from New York to a fellow former Young Irelander named James Stephens that the moment was ripe for revolution. O'Mahony and Doheny's proposal, agreed to by Stephens in Dublin, was for Irish Americans to raise funds and arms for a secret revolutionary organization that Stephens would organize in Ireland. Stephens convened the first meeting of the Irish Republican Brotherhood in Dublin on St. Patrick's Day of 1858, and less than a year later, O'Mahony and Doheny convened an organization that O'Mahony dubbed the Fenian Brotherhood after the mythical ancient Celtic warriors, the *fianna*. Pledging themselves to the overthrow of British rule in Ireland, members of both the Irish and Irish-American organizations were commonly referred to simply as "Fenians."[44]

By the time of Brown's raid, Irish-American nationalists—of which Donahoe was one, even if his strident Catholicism led him to eschew secret societies like the Fenians—were no strangers to transatlantic plots. If Fenians could plot the overthrow of British rule in Ireland from New York City, then surely abolitionists could orchestrate a slave rebellion from Exeter Hall in London.

For their part, white Southerners also detected in Brown's raid a more far-reaching plot, one that emanated from the press and pulpits of the free states and that had turned virtually all white Northerners into radical abolitionists bent on the violent destruction of American slavery. Even Irish immigrants, who for the past two decades had steadfastly defended enslavers' interests, fell under white Southerners' suspicion. In early December, twenty-three-year-old James Powers, a County Wexford native who had immigrated to Philadelphia and worked as a stone-cutter on the new state house in Columbia, South Carolina, became a victim of this collective paranoia. A co-worker alleged Powers to have stated that Black slavery degraded the labor of white men. When a vigilance committee member caught wind of the allegation and told Columbia's mayor, Powers was jailed for nine days and then marched out of town before a crowd of jeering onlookers. Once they marched Powers beyond the limits of Columbia, the vigilance committee ordered an enslaved man to strip Powers and deliver thirty-nine blood-drawing lashes to his back. After being tarred and feathered, Powers was put on a train to Charleston, South Carolina, tarred and cottoned (for want of feathers) at a subsequent stop, and berated at each station on the trip. Following another week in jail, Charleston authorities put Powers on a steamer to New York City, where word of his ordeal quickly spread in the antislavery press and beyond.[45]

South Carolinians' treatment of the Irish-born Powers galled Irish-American editors in the North, some of whom struggled to square their antiabolitionist views with the mob violence perpetrated against their countrymen by proslavery Southerners. "No class of citizens has been truer to the rights of the South than the Irish," the *Pilot* declared, yet merely for stating that "negroes should not be employed in mechanical pursuits," an Irishman had been viciously abused. The *Pilot*'s story pointed out that Powers had "always voted the democratic ticket, which implies that he was disposed to sustain the constitutional rights of the South," only adding to the outrage committed upon him. The *Pilot* paired its coverage of Powers's ordeal with a story on James Cranagle. Cranagle was "an Irish gentleman" who, upon trying to collect a debt in Georgia, was falsely accused as an abolitionist, robbed of one hundred dollars, and jailed for several days. "We would suggest to the Southern people," the *Pilot* concluded, "that a few more outrages of this character will greatly reduce the number of their firmer friends at the North." Patrick Meehan's *Irish-American* was initially more circumspect in its coverage of the Powers story. While lamenting Powers's treatment, the *Irish-American* also reviled antislavery newspapers like the *Tribune* that dwelt on the Powers case but ignored the murder of Thomas Boerly at Harpers Ferry and the illegal deportation of Hugh Carroll, a naturalized Irish immigrant in Massachusetts. For the *Tribune* to "call upon all Irish-born citizens to regard [Powers's] case as a specimen of how their countrymen are used in the South" was sheer hypocrisy, as it had remained silent when Boerly and Carroll were subjected to Northern abuse. Pointing to Virginia Governor Henry A. Wise's past condemnation of Know-Nothingism, the *Irish-American* insisted that "the Irish encounter the least amount of hostile prejudice in the South."[46]

A remarkable turn of events soon forced even the *Irish-American* to see that the Powers case was but a symptom of white Southerners' proslavery extremism. In a mid-February letter to the *Irish-American*, "A Columbia Irishman" alleged that virtually every detail of the Powers story in Northern newspapers was false, including the basic fact that Powers was Irish. These allegations prompted Powers to defend himself and the antislavery editors of New York that first brought his story to light. Shortly after the *Irish-American* published the letter alleging that Powers' account was fraudulent, Powers himself delivered a hand-written account of his ordeal to the offices of the *Irish-American* and confirmed to its editor that he had told his story in person to the *Tribune*. The *Irish-American* published Powers's account, which stated that while in the South, he had "sen [sic] negroes employed in all branches of business and a white working man can get nothing to do except that which a negro can not do." His account concluded that Southerners favored "the extermination of all men whether native or adopted white or black who do not avow themselves in feavor [sic] of" slavery. Previously, the *Irish-American* had declared that Southerners "owe it to us, who have stood by them unflinchingly" to condemn those responsible for Powers's treatment. By printing Powers's version of the events in Columbia, which reads like it was ripped from a Republican stump speech in the coming elections, the *Irish-American* tacitly acknowledged that even Irish immigrants could not expect fair treatment from Southern extremists.[47]

The Powers incident was a potent indication to Irish Americans in the free states that regardless of their willingness to justify slavery's expansion in the hopes of preserving the Union, the sectional conflict had rendered them unalterably Northern in the eyes of white Southerners. By all indications, the vast majority of Irish Americans across the North spurned proslavery Southern Democrats by voting for Stephen Douglas, the Northern Democratic candidate in the four-way presidential race of 1860. To be sure, Douglas was a virulent racist, a rabid anti-abolitionist, and the architect of the Kansas-Nebraska Act, a crime that no Northern antislavery voter could forgive. But the mere fact of Douglas's candidacy in 1860 revealed the "heads I win, tails you lose" choice that confronted Northern Democrats by this point: Put the party's platform entirely in the hands of Southern proslavery expansionists and lose even more support across the free states, or break from their Southern colleagues and split much of the Democratic vote along sectional lines. Douglas's efforts in 1858 to allay Northern concerns about the *Dred Scott* decision by promising that slavery could still be outlawed in the territories through the will of voters on the ground—the so-called Freeport doctrine—had made him anathema to most Southern Democrats. After anti-Douglas Democrats left the party's second nominating convention in Baltimore to nominate John C. Breckinridge on a platform that called for a federal slave code in the territories, Douglas was nominated by what remained of the now broken Democratic Party. Tellingly, Irish Americans were enthusiastic about Douglas's candidacy, giving virtually no attention to the Southern Democratic nominee Breckenridge and focusing instead on the contrast between Douglas and his Republican rival, Abraham Lincoln. Boston's *Irish Pictorial Weekly* reported that Douglas was mobbed by the Boston Irish at a July campaign stop, and the newspaper later endorsed the "Douglas Axe" as the best means of chopping down the "Republican tree." Much of Irish Americans' support for Douglas came by way of denunciations of Lincoln as the standard-bearer of "John Brown Republicanism," nativism, and disunionism. In a sign of how deeply the Irish-American criticism of antislavery politics was lodged, numerous Irish-American newspapers painted Lincoln and his party with the brush of nativism despite Lincoln's numerous repudiations of nativism and the Republican Party having adopted a platform that pointedly opposed any changes to the country's naturalization laws. In short, Irish-American voters who cast their ballots for Douglas aimed to curb the influence of nativism and extinguish the flames of sectional tension that threatened to divide the nation permanently.[48]

Lincoln's victory in November catalyzed a sequence of events that confirmed Irish Americans' fears about antislavery politicians gaining power. Seeing that a political party committed to halting the spread of slavery would grasp the reigns of the federal government, proslavery Southern legislatures in seven states passed ordinances to secede from the Union between December 1860 and

February 1861. Delegates from those states soon convened in Mobile, Alabama, to establish the Confederate States of America. Lincoln entered office on March 4, believing that secessionism was a momentarily powerful fringe movement. But when his administration's attempt to resupply Fort Sumter in Charleston Harbor was met by a Confederate bombardment of the fort on April 12, a war between the Union and Confederacy became a fait accompli. In the days and weeks after Fort Sumter, Lincoln issued a call for seventy-five thousand volunteer militiamen to suppress an armed rebellion while four more slave states seceded from the Union. As Irish Americans had predicted, an antislavery political party had gained national power, and civil war was the result.[49]

During the political crisis of the 1850s, Irish Americans overwhelmingly supported the proslavery policies of the Democratic Party. The reasons for that support were threefold and coalesced around a forceful Irish-American critique of antislavery. Given how poorly Irish immigrants fared in the Northern labor market during and immediately following the famine migration, Irish-American newspaper editors and workers looked skeptically on free soil politicians' plans to advance the Northern free labor economy in the West. They argued instead that the depressed condition of the laboring classes in Northern cities was a far more pressing concern than the potential spread of slavery in the territories. Additionally, the rise of antislavery politics in the North in the form of the Know-Nothings and Republicans coincided with an era of intense nativism in Northern politics, convincing Irish Americans that antislavery politics was a stalking horse propagated by nativists whose ultimate aim was to weaken the influence of immigrants and Catholics in American politics. Finally, the proslavery Democratic Party stood alone until 1860 as the one true national party in American politics. A vote for an antislavery party, Irish Americans argued, was, in essence, a vote for sectionalism.

As the sectional crisis deepened between 1854 and 1860, Irish Americans grew less likely to explain their position on slavery with reference to Ireland. Yet, at critical junctures on the road to the Civil War, Irish-American commentators raised important antecedents, parallels, or influences from recent Irish history that continued to shape their perspective on the future of American slavery. Some likened Irish immigrants' unenviable position in the Northern free labor economy to Ireland's pitiful status in the political union with Great Britain or, more directly, to the miserable condition of Irish peasants. Others argued that John Brown was part of a transatlantic abolitionist conspiracy to sever America's Union and to persecute the Irish in the process. Immigrants' belief that the United States was a haven for the oppressed of Ireland and a future ally for

Irish nationalists lay just beneath the surface of their contempt for antislavery Northerners who seemed to threaten national unity, especially in the late 1850s as exiled Irish nationalists in America regrouped to plot their native land's liberation. During the Civil War, Irish Americans in the North would continue to find reasons to believe that abolitionists possessed a singular contempt for the Irish. But many would also discover that the core tenets of Irish-American Unionism no longer aligned with the expansion or even preservation of African American slavery.

5   Irish Americans and the Union War

Throughout the secession winter of 1860–61, Irish Americans across the free states gave many indications that their sympathies in the sectional crisis lay with proslavery secessionists. However, the Confederate bombardment of Fort Sumter on April 12, 1861, rallied the Irish in the loyal states in support of a war to compel secessionists back into the Union. From Boston and surrounding towns, the 9th Massachusetts Volunteer Infantry Regiment organized around Colonel Thomas Cass and his fellow former members of the defunct Columbian Artillery, a former militia regiment disbanded by the state's Know-Nothing governor in 1854 after its participation in the reenslavement of Anthony Burns. Less than two weeks after the assault on Fort Sumter, the *James Adger* shoved off of Pier 4 in Manhattan and steered south toward Washington, D.C. On board were the 996 enlistees of the 69th New York State Militia Regiment, an Irish-American unit commanded by the famous Irish-American nationalist Michael Corcoran, who was fresh from his court-martial for having refused to parade the 69th New York before the visiting Prince of Wales. The 9th Massachusetts and 69th New York were followed to the seat of war in the coming weeks and months by additional Irish-American units from Massachusetts, New York, Pennsylvania, Illinois, Ohio, Wisconsin, Connecticut, and Indiana. In the months and years ahead, Irish immigrants enlisted in nonethnic units by the tens of thousands.[1]

Much like the Great Irish Potato Famine and the famine migration had a decade earlier, the first shots of civil war in 1861 prompted Irish Americans to expound upon why Irish people on both sides of the Atlantic had a particular stake in the welfare of the American Union. There were many reasons, far from all ideological, why Irish Americans chose to enlist in the Union Army or threw their support behind the Union war effort by writing editorials, speaking at Union rallies, or attending and contributing to fundraisers for Irish-American units. Yet few contemporaries were blind to their individual or communal concerns being wrapped up in a broader and inseparable struggle over the future of American nationhood and American slavery. The resolution to that struggle, they knew, would have momentous consequences not only for the government, economy, and social fabric of the

United States but also for the fate of prospective Irish immigrants—many of them friends and family—and the future of Irish nationhood. Thus, as loyal Irish Americans mobilized for war in 1861 and followed the course of the conflict from the battlefield and home front through the end of 1862, many explained their support for the Union war effort with reference to the tenets of Irish-American Unionism that took shape over the previous decade. In editorials, speeches at recruitment rallies, letters to friends and family, and diaries, Irish-American Unionists insisted that secession imperiled the political and civil liberties afforded to foreigners by the Constitution. Others emphasized that the United States was a haven for the oppressed peoples of Europe, especially Ireland. Only if its system of constitutional democracy was preserved, they asserted, could the American Republic continue to offer hopes of political liberty to future generations of immigrants. The prospects of Irish nationhood also hung in the balance of the American war, or so many Irish Americans claimed. Some Irish nationalists in America filled the ranks of the Union army in the hopes of gaining valuable military training and experience that they could one day put to use against the Crown's forces in Ireland. Then, too, Irish nationalists on both sides of the Atlantic were apoplectic that a weakened American Republic would necessarily strengthen the might of the British Empire. For all of these reasons, restoring the Union was paramount to most Irish Americans in 1861, even if it meant siding with antislavery Northerners who allegedly bore much responsibility for fracturing the Union in the first place.

However enthusiastic Irish Americans were about restoring the Union, the antebellum Irish-American critique of antislavery rendered them skeptical of the newly inaugurated Republican president and the Republican-majority Congress that would oversee the Union war effort. In the first year of the war, Irish-American editors and soldiers detected signs that Republican politicians and military officers were treating Irish immigrants unfairly in the Union's armed forces, including a prominent Irish-born general. Moreover, Union armies generally fared poorly in 1861 and 1862, especially in the Eastern Theater, where most of the best-known Irish-American Union regiments served. It seemed at times as if Confederate forces were on the cusp of securing the Confederacy's independence. At the same time, the steady erosion of slavery in the war's first year was unmistakable, as enslaved men and women seized the opportunity afforded by the tumult of war to strike out for freedom. When viewed collectively, these developments confirmed critical elements of the Irish-American critique of antislavery. As the Republican Party—an antislavery party—took the reins of government, nativism, disunion, and abolition appeared to run rampant. By the end of 1862, the Irish in the North still overwhelmingly desired the restoration of the Union, but many were convinced that such an outcome was impossible if Republicans continued to implement their anti-Irish, antislavery agenda.

Yet a growing number of Irish-American soldiers arrived at a starkly different conclusion by the fall and winter of 1862. The conflict, these soldiers believed, was not being waged as an abolition war. On the contrary, Irish-American soldiers' experiences in the army taught them that freed people, especially those whose freedom was aided and abetted by Union soldiers, could hasten the Union's restoration. But for that to happen, soldiers had to help enslaved people secure their freedom, a process enslaved men and women set in motion by fleeing to Union lines. Irish-born soldiers' support for emancipation as a means of advancing the Union cause was a remarkable development in the early stages of the war, one that defies a deeply ingrained narrative of Irish-American disillusionment with the war's emancipatory turn. Irish-American Unionists who assisted enslaved people in their attempts at self-liberation early in the conflict demonstrated that their belief in the American Union's destiny as a haven for Irish immigrants and an ally to Ireland could override their long-standing contempt for abolitionism and the politics of antislavery.

Irish-American Unionism in 1861–62

Most Irish Americans in the loyal states rallied in support of the federal cause in April 1861 because they held three key assumptions about the conflict's meaning, each built on a tenet of antebellum Irish-American Unionism. First, Irish immigrants across the loyal states argued that all "adopted citizens" had a particular obligation to defend the nation that gave them refuge and to uphold the Constitution that afforded political and civil liberties to foreigners. Second, many also maintained that the sectional crisis of the 1850s and the secession movement were the fruits of a sinister British plot to stamp out republican government and expand the British Empire. Seen in this light, to fight for the Union was, in effect, to fight against Britain, a calculation that took on a hint of reality as Anglo-American relations soured during the first year of the war. Third, and related to the Anglophobic interpretation of the Civil War, was the belief that the restoration of America's Union was essential to Ireland's hopes for independence, especially since Irish-American soldiers who gained military experience in the United States could augment what seemed to be a dearth of willing revolutionaries in Ireland itself. In these ways, Irish Americans who met the Lincoln administration's call for volunteers to put down the Confederate rebellion or who voiced their support for the Union war effort continued to interpret the core issues of the national crisis through a transatlantic lens. Deeply knowledgeable of and fully immersed in the politics of their adopted country, Irish-American Unionists remained invested in the social, economic, and political future of their homeland, and their perspective on the American conflict necessarily took into consideration its implications for Ireland and its people.[2]

A full treatment of precisely which Irish Americans enlisted in the Union war effort in 1861–62 or joined up later in the war is not in the purview of this study. However, to understand the ideas that informed many Irish-American soldiers' enlistment and service, it is necessary to dispel certain commonly accepted tropes about Irish immigrants in the Union's armed forces. The stereotype of the young, jobless, and bewildered Irishman "fresh off the boat" who enlisted for the promise of steady pay and a bounty has proven remarkably durable in both popular culture and academic treatments of the Civil War, bestowing an air of inevitability on Irish Americans' involvement in the conflict. Careless of the cause for which he fought and aggrieved by the war's emancipatory turn in 1862–63, the story goes that the typical Irish-American soldier grew disillusioned with the Union war effort. Such a sketch of Irish-American soldiering will not suffice. Using anthropometric, demographic, and military data gleaned from the regimental descriptive books of four predominantly Irish-American units, Jim Zibro has compiled the largest sample of Irish-born Union soldiers of any study. Through sophisticated analysis of that data, Zibro arrived at a rough sketch of "Paddy Yank" that upends long-standing assumptions of Irish-American soldiers' poverty, lack of skill in the labor market, recent arrival in the United States, and youthfulness. The typical Irish-born soldier was several years older than his American-born comrades, was occupied in skilled labor or white-collar work before the war, and had lived in the United States for a decade by the time of Lincoln's election. He most likely enlisted in 1861 or 1862 before the Lincoln administration and state governments turned to using bounties to entice recruits. Paradoxically, he was both more likely to desert and more likely to be killed in battle than his native-born comrades. In short, as Zibro concludes, Irish-American soldiers constituted a "petty elite" among the American Irish. This is not to discount the experiences or perspectives of the many unskilled, young, impoverished, and recently arrived Irish who enlisted in the Union Army, especially as the war dragged on into 1863, 1864, and 1865.[3] However, recognizing that most Irish-American soldiers did not fit that bill opens up new perspectives on the ideas and backgrounds that shaped their participation in the war.

Across the loyal states in 1861, Irish Americans reacted to the secession crisis and outbreak of war by insisting that they had a singular duty to uphold the

Constitution. A speaker at a Union rally in Boston's heavily Irish North End declared two weeks after the attack on Fort Sumter that "we—the foreign-born citizens of Boston, who have sworn allegiance to the Constitution and the country" must demonstrate "our bona-fide intention to maintain and abide by the Constitution and the laws." B. S. Treanor, a prominent Irish American in Boston who later enlisted in the 9th Massachusetts Regiment, also spoke at the North End rally. He declared that his countrymen in the North would "stand by the Union, the Constitution, and the President, whom the people have Constitutionally elected." When journalists in Ireland questioned why Irish people should support a war for the Union that seemed from afar to deny Southerners their aspirations to nationhood—much as the much-despised Act of Union denied Ireland its sovereignty—Patrick Donahoe of the *Pilot* quickly dismissed the analogy. "It is for the Constitution the North is up," Donahoe insisted, ". . . it is against unjustifiable rebellion . . . that the Northern states are martially arrayed. The aim of the North is not to *conquer*, but to reconstruct." The language that Irish Americans used to describe the war's relationship to the Constitution—"maintain," "stand by," and "reconstruct"—illustrates their conception of the Union cause in 1861 as a conservative one to be fought in the name of established political principles and relationships.[4]

Such support for a conservative, restorative war was echoed by Irish-American Catholic leaders in the spring and summer of 1861. Southerners' rebellion against the Constitution, some Irish-American clergymen reasoned, held out the prospect that bigoted nativists could run roughshod over constitutional safeguards for religious liberty. In Cincinnati, Edward Purcell, the Cork-born editor of the *Catholic Telegraph and Advocate*, initially opposed restoring the Union by force because holding a nation together through coercion was unchristian, and Catholics could maintain spiritual ties across national lines. But one day after the attack on Fort Sumter, Purcell published a letter to the editor whose author argued that because the Confederacy was nothing more than a "slave oligarchy," and under oligarchy, "all forms of government are nothing," Catholics were obliged to defeat "armed treason and rebellion against the best form of government ever framed by human wisdom." From the author's perspective, the Confederate rebellion posed a grave threat to the rights enshrined by the Constitution, including religious liberty. Purcell was convinced, declaring it to be Catholics' "solemn duty, as good and loyal citizens, to walk shoulder to shoulder with all our fellow citizens in support of the laws and national honor." A Catholic editor in Philadelphia similarly advised his coreligionists to sustain the government that "protects them in their civil rights, and secures to them and their posterity, the blessings of liberty and equality." Fearing that Confederates' wanton rebuke of constitutional law presented a slippery slope toward the loss of religious freedoms, these Irish Catholic journalists rallied to the Union cause. Additionally, with the anti-Catholic hysteria of the 1850s a recent memory, some Irish-American Catholic soldiers viewed military service, especially in visibly Catholic units, as a means of proving that their faith was not an encumbrance on their patriotism. In this sentiment, they were joined by leading clerics from across the loyal states, as clergymen in New York City, Cincinnati, Pittsburgh, Milwaukee, and Philadelphia rushed to raise the American flag over their cathedrals. Most prominent in the Catholic hierarchy's initial embrace of the war to restore the Union was Archbishop John Hughes of New York. In response to Southern bishops who questioned how their Northern peers could support an antislavery administration after having sanctioned slavery, Hughes pointed out in August 1861 that neither Congress nor the Lincoln administration gave any indication of waging a war of emancipation. To his Southern coreligionists, Hughes argued that "the Constitution having been formed by the common consent of all the parties engaged in the framework and approval thereof, . . . no state has a right to secede." Hughes and the Catholic hierarchy in the loyal states proudly evinced their fealty to the Union in 1861.[5]

Specific references to Constitutional safeguards and religious liberty reflected a more general sentiment among Irish-American Unionists that the American Republic had to be preserved because it gave immigrants liberties and privileges unavailable in Ireland. An Irish-born soldier from New York, William Dennis, exemplified how Irish Americans conceived of the political freedoms they enjoyed in the United States through the prism of their backgrounds in Ireland. Writing to his brother John in Ireland, William noted that he had enlisted in the Union army. His service would be for "A Gloureous Cause the Cause of Freedom And Liberty We Came Here to Enjoy Liberty And Wee ought to Be Ready to Maintain the Flag that Wee Swore to Protect to the Best of our Ability." Dennis's support for the forceful restoration of the Union resulted from his distinct experience as an Irish immigrant who "Came Here [America] to Enjoy Liberty," the implication being that such liberty was nonexistent in Ireland. Precisely that belief was stated more baldly in a January 1861 editorial in the *Irish Pictorial Weekly*, a newly established Irish-American newspaper in Boston edited by James Sullivan. It was "the mission of America," Sullivan opined, to be "a sure asylum for the oppressed and exiled of the world." After the Confederate bombardment of Fort Sumter in April, the newspaper declared that Irishmen would defend "the government and the country which has been an asylum and a home to the oppressed of every nation." A May 1861 letter to the *Irish-American* averred that Irish Americans must keep America under one flag, "the flag of the free—one which exiles cannot afford to lose." "The Irish-American Song," printed in the *Cincinnati Catholic Telegraph and Advocate* in July 1861, celebrated the "Flag of the Free" [i.e., the United States flag] as a symbol of the protection that America provided when "Famine swept o'er our land" and let loose "the tyrant's hand" on the Irish. Memories of oppression in Ireland served as the basis of these Irish Americans' reasons for fighting to protect constitutional democracy in the United States.[6]

The second-generation Irish-American judge Charles Patrick Daly explained precisely why the Irish could understand better than anyone else the terrible fate of a disunified, factionalized nation. Before presenting the 69th New York with its green battle flag, Daly gave the regiment's officers a poignant lesson in Irish history. According to Daly, the regiment's green flag symbolized "the period when Ireland was a nation." At the turn of the first millennium, Daly continued, the Irish high king Brian Boru had conquered "the petty princes who ruled separate parts" of the island, turning Ireland into the thriving nation of bards' lore. But the island's "ambitious leaders, the Jefferson Davises of that period, overthrew the fabric of the national government." Because of "internal weakness and clashing interests," Ireland was then "brought under the power of that stalwart English monarchy which has since held her in its grasp." Though far-fetched, Daly's analogy between medieval Ireland and the United States in 1861 had an important point. If Americans succumbed to sectional division and internal discord, they left themselves prone to the oppressive clutch of foreign powers.[7]

Ironically, Irish opinion itself was divided over whether Confederates had a legitimate claim to independence and whether loyal Americans' efforts to restore the Union by force were justifiable. This split in Irish public opinion was evident in the writings of the Reverend Dr. Daniel William Cahill, an Irish priest and lecturer who, by 1861, was one of the most widely respected Catholic intellectuals in Ireland. As the secession crisis unfolded in the winter and spring, the Reverend Dr. Cahill happened to be on a lecture tour of the United States. Cahill's "Letters from America" during these crucial months were picked up by several leading Irish newspapers and helped to shape Irish opinion on the outbreak of civil war across the Atlantic. Writing from Boston in January—perhaps with the memory of Father Mathew's 1850 visit to the city in mind—the Reverend Dr. Cahill reiterated an earlier pledge not to meddle in American politics, preferring instead to describe the perspectives on each side of what he cheekily termed "the Repeal of the Union." But as Cahill realized the direness of the American situation and its implications for Irish people, his letters to Ireland took on a Unionist hue. In February, Cahill predicted that the dynamics of the slavery debate embedded in the secession crisis would lead England to side with the Union. England, he conjectured in a riff on the famine-era Irish critique of abolitionism, "puts herself forward on paper as the advocate of liberality, or toleration, of liberty all over the world, while her own subjects in Ireland are the victims of intolerance not surpassed, perhaps not equalled in any country in Europe." Cahill's Anglophobia ran deep, and if his prediction had borne fruit, there can be little doubt that he would have counseled Irish neutrality of opinion if not outright support for the Confederacy. But by April, Confederates' pursuit of British support and British policymakers' apparent willingness to entertain the prospect of recognizing Confederate belligerency caused Cahill to fret over the prospect of British imperialists establishing a foothold in North America. A potential Anglo-Confederate alliance, he foretold, could only result in the "British Union Jack on the graves of Washington and Jackson! All the freemen all over the globe," Cahill continued, "and all the Irish victims that abhor the perfidy and tyranny of England will, alas! Mourn over this fatal American secession." Cahill also predicted that the economic decline produced by the secession crisis would affect prospective Irish emigrants. "On this disastrous topic," he wrote, "my counsel to you is very brief—namely, you wretched victims of misrule in Ireland must not think of emigrating at present to America." For Cahill, a steadfast proponent of Irish immigration to the United States before the secession crisis, the damaging effects of secession on the prospects of would-be Irish emigrants combined with British policymakers' readiness to entreat with Confederate diplomats could only mean that Ireland's interests were invested in the restoration of the Union.[8]

Cahill's "Letters to America" established two key frameworks through which Irish newspaper editors interpreted developments in the American war. First, Irish perspectives on the conflict were filtered through nationalist lenses. Moderate nationalists—those who supported a peaceable, constitutional resolution to Anglo-Irish tensions that would keep Ireland as part of the British Empire—tended to sympathize with and even cheer on secessionists. A. M. Sullivan, editor of the Dublin *Nation*, spoke on behalf of this faction when, in 1862, he lamented the dissolution of the Union but opined that "as a number of the States, large enough to constitute a powerful nation, wish for a separate existence as such, their right to choose their own rulers is clear, and it should not be denied to them," a sentiment that was supported by the *Cork Examiner*. Conversely, P. J. Smyth, editor of the Dublin *Irishman*, conveyed the views of republican nationalist journals like the *Dundalk Democrat* and *Galway American* in echoing Cahill's argument that the triumph of the Union would weaken British global power. After the *Irishman* initially threw its support behind the Confederacy,

Smyth quickly reversed course after finding English journals openly supported the Confederacy. "When we Irish are side by side with England in any quarrel," Smyth pronounced only a week after having blessed the Confederate rebellion, "we *must* be in the wrong." In the coming months and years, Smyth and other republican nationalists grew more convinced that the war to restore the Union aligned with their aims. As a July 1862 editorial in the *Dundalk Democrat* counseled, "Weaken America and England becomes strong; and whilst that strength lasts, Ireland will be obliged to suffer from insult and injustice. Ireland's best policy is to advocate the union of all Americans, and the wisest course for the Irish in America is to aid in destroying the rebellion." The second framework by which Irish journalists evaluated the war in America followed from his speculations on how the American conflict would impact Irish immigrants, both those who had already crossed the Atlantic and those who might do so one day. Whereas Cahill had pointed to the secession-induced spike in unemployment as a reason why immigrants and prospective emigrants should mobilize in support of the Union, Southern sympathizing editors at the *Nation* and *Cork Examiner* raised the prospect of desperate, unemployed immigrant laborers being used as cannon fodder in the Union armed forces to argue for an immediate cessation of hostilities. Pro-Union Irish journals disputed such claims, arguing instead that too many Irish men and women depended on the United States to act as a haven for the oppressed and impoverished for it to be as weakened as it was by secession. The material and political prosperity of the Irish people, they concluded, was intertwined with a robust American Union.[9]

Indeed, such an image of the United States as a refuge for liberty-deprived Irish immigrants proved remarkably durable between 1861 and 1862. A year after the Confederate attack on Fort Sumter, setbacks in the Union war effort and concerns on the part of Irish-American editors and military leaders that Republican legislators and commanders were slighting their countrymen in the army dampened some of the initial Irish-American enthusiasm for the war. Yet both Irish-American soldiers and editors maintained that fighting to preserve the Union was an almost sacred duty for immigrants who had escaped oppression in Ireland. In April 1862, Colonel John McCluskey of the 15th Maine Regiment received his unit's flag, which included a harp and shamrock on one side in recognition of the many Irish-American soldiers in the regiment. McCluskey, who had come to the United States at the age of nineteen during the famine, expounded on what he and his fellow Irish-born soldiers were fighting for. It was, he contended, "especially . . . the duty of Irishmen to sustain this[,] the only free government to which they can look for protection of that liberty which they have been cruelly deprived for centuries" in Ireland. After mounting death tolls in mid-1862 led some newspaper editors in Ireland to question immigrants' enlistment in the Union army, the Boston *Pilot* answered with a question: "If the Union disappears, where will [the Irish] escape to from the dire oppression of Britain?" Even one soldier who expressed his frustration with nativists in the army reminded a correspondent that America was still "the home of the Exile, and refuge for the oppressed." As if to himself, he exhorted, "We must keep it so, and then demand all its priviledges [*sic*] guaranteed to all citizens alike."[10]

British policy early in the conflict seemed to legitimize Irish and Irish-American Unionists' claims that monarchists sought to cripple the American Republic. To deny the Confederacy belligerent status under international law, the Lincoln administration announced in May 1861 that the Confederate rebellion was an internal "insurrection." But British statesmen argued that by also declaring a blockade of Southern ports, Lincoln had committed an act of war that bestowed the Confederacy with belligerent status. Through a proclamation by Queen Victoria, Great Britain claimed neutrality between the two American belligerents, thereby granting Confederates the right to secure British loans, purchase British arms, and commission cruisers to search and seize Union vessels in international waters. The Queen's Proclamation of Neutrality was not a recognition of Confederate nationhood, but many loyal Americans, following the lead of Secretary of State William Seward, perceived it as a pretext for such recognition and an act of open hostility to the Union.[11]

To some Irish Americans, British policymakers' eagerness to recognize Confederate belligerency confirmed that they desired the disintegration of the United States. In the Queen's Proclamation of Neutrality, the *Irish-American* saw nothing less than a conspiracy hatched by English imperialists to "perpetuate and embitter the struggle in which she [Britain] fondly hopes to see the power, glory, and liberty of this nation shattered and wrecked for ever." More than a year later, an Irish-American soldier camped near Harper's Ferry, Virginia, echoed the *Irish-American*, arguing in the *Pilot* that England had used "the Abolition Question as the wedge" to splinter the nation. Such claims were reminiscent of Irish immigrants' protests against the visiting English abolitionist George Thompson in 1851. They could even be traced back to Irish-American nationalists' abandonment of the Irish Repeal movement in 1845 when Irish nationalist leader Daniel O'Connell threatened to side with Great Britain in an Anglo-American dispute over Texas. Irish immigrants had warned that Britain would subvert America's republican experiment, and they rallied in support of the Union when that scenario seemed to be playing out in 1861.[12]

Fears of British policymakers using the Civil War to thwart the spread of democratic governance swelled in December 1861 when a Union navy officer's seizure of two London-bound Confederate diplomats nearly led to a third Anglo-American war. The so-called *Trent* Affair, named for the British mail ship on which the Confederate diplomats were captured, provoked bloodlust and fear among Irish Americans. Philadelphia's Ancient Order of Hibernians resolved that if England declared war on the Union, "the Irish element, not only here but throughout the world, will write the history of her injustice in letters of blood at the point of the sword." Before the threat of war passed in January 1862, the *Catholic Telegraph and Advocate* warned that if England allied with the Confederacy, Irish Americans would be "again within sight of that pestilent [British] flag, from which we had hoped the breadth of the Atlantic had saved us forever." From Miners Hill, Virginia, in December 1861, Irish-born Michael Leary of the 9th Massachusetts Regiment predicted that "we will not only have to Fight the Rebels But John Bull also" as a result of the *Trent* Affair. Though a peaceful settlement of the incident was obtained, the *Trent* Affair further convinced Irish Americans that by breaking up the Union, Southerners had exposed America to the anti-republican designs of British imperialists.[13]

The Anglophobic element of Irish-American Unionism in 1861–62 was bolstered by a widely held belief that American battlefields could serve as training grounds for future Irish republican revolutionaries. When the Civil War began, nationalists in Ireland were in a state of disarray. Indeed, only a few years earlier, former Young Irelander Charles Gavan Duffy quipped that the chances for the Irish national cause were equal to those of "the corpse on the dissecting table." True, the revolutionary Irish Republican Brotherhood was established in Dublin in 1858 and maintained close ties with its American counterpart, the Fenian Brotherhood. But since the early 1850s, nationalist MPs in Ireland had concentrated their energies on tenant rights and, to a lesser degree, the constitutional reform of the Anglo-Irish relationship, eschewing the type of militant republicanism that Irish Americans tended to gravitate to in the 1850s. A fascinating chapter of Irish-American nationalism that played out during the first year of the Civil War illustrates the disorganized state of revolutionary nationalism in Ireland at the start of the conflict and how Irish-American nationalists helped revive it. On January 15, 1861, the exiled Young Ireland rebel Terrence Bellew McManus died in San Francisco. Seeing an opportunity to stoke the coals of Irish-American nationalism, the city's chapter of the Fenian Brotherhood led a nationwide and eventually transatlantic Fenian endeavor to return his body to Ireland. Shipped in a metallic coffin across Central America and up the East

Coast, McManus's corpse was mourned by Fenians in several cities before it crossed the Atlantic, most triumphantly in New York. There, on September 15, Archbishop Hughes conducted a funeral mass for McManus at which Thomas Francis Meagher, soon to be commissioned as a brigadier general and given command of the Irish Brigade, fondly remembered his fellow former rebel and exile. In Dublin, meanwhile, the fecklessness of the Irish Republican Brotherhood was such that its leader, James Stephens, worried the arrival of McManus's body would trigger an uprising he could not control. Ultimately, McManus's Irish funeral was held in Dublin's Glasnevin Cemetery in November 1861 with much pomp and circumstance before some thirty thousand mourners who heard an American Fenian deliver the graveside oration. The McManus funeral—conceived of and primarily carried out by Irish-American nationalists—breathed new life into the militant republican strain of Irish nationalism just as tens of thousands of Irish immigrants were trained and armed in the Union army.[14]

In this atmosphere of renewed transatlantic coordination between Irish nationalists, Irish-American editors and soldiers predicted their countrymen's successful prosecution of the war to restore the Union would redound to the benefit of Irish nationhood. The *Pilot* cited the prospect of battle-hardened Irish-American veterans leading the liberation of Ireland as a reason why readers should remain optimistic after the disastrous Union defeat at the Battle of Bull Run in late July of 1861. A prolonged war, Donahoe predicted, would fuel American Anglophobia, stir the passions of nationalists in Ireland, and, most of all, train Irish-American soldiers who could one day fight in Ireland. Thus, the Union war effort was "certain to have much splendid effect upon Irish liberty and independence." More than a year later and in the wake of a calamitous string of defeats for Union soldiers in the Eastern Theater, Donahoe commented favorably on the growth of the Fenian Brotherhood within the Union army in an article optimistically titled, "America Freeing Ireland." Americans' disdain for Britain had only increased as a result of the *Trent* Affair, Donahoe pointed out, and few would be inclined to stand in the way of the hundreds of thousands of Irish-born soldiers who dutifully donned the Union blue. Among those men were many who had joined the "Fenian Society" and desired nothing more than "the freedom of their native country." Under these circumstances, Donahoe prophesied, Irish Americans could look forward to a day when they would see "emigrants—expatriated—exterminated emigrants, returning over the ocean to free their native land."[15]

Throughout 1862, Irish-American recruiters and soldiers routinely connected the successful prosecution of the Union war effort with the prospects of Irish nationhood. Speaking in July to a crowd of prospective recruits for the Irish

Brigade in New York City, General Thomas Francis Meagher proclaimed that Union soldiers were "battling in the cause of a nation with whose existence and prosperity the hopes of Ireland are inseparably connected." In Boston, a group of self-described "Irish Nationalists" greeted the famous ex-colonel of the 69th New York Regiment, Michael Corcoran, in September as he arrived to drum up recruits for a new Irish-American unit, Corcoran's Legion. The Boston delegation endorsed Corcoran's recruitment efforts in the city, asserting that the "future freedom, not only of Ireland, but of Europe, depends on the contest in which this government is now engaged. The last hope of mankind is centered upon the perpetuity of republican institutions here." Perhaps the most striking alignment of the Union war effort and Irish national cause in 1862 played out in March as soldiers in the 9th Massachusetts Regiment steamed down the Potomac River aboard *The State of Maine* en route to Fortress Monroe at the mouth of the Chesapeake Bay. To honor the Irish-American regiment, the ship's captain raised the green flag of Ireland on the main mast. At that moment, "hundreds of Irish throats" cheered, according to a soldier in the regiment, for the flag-raising was "emblematic of the lifelong desire of their hearts, *i.e.*, 'freedom for Ireland.'" Irish-born Hugh McDermott, who captained a company of Irish-American soldiers in the 17th Wisconsin, experienced a similar thrill in the summer of 1862. In a letter to the Chicago *Western Tablet* that was copied into an Irish newspaper, McDermott wrote fondly of his men marching to patriotic Irish songs like "The Green Flag," "The Boys of Tipperary," and "Garryowen." And, he confessed, "the rebellious thought will cross my mind sometimes, 'Oh! for such an opportunity for the old sod [i.e., Ireland].'" For these and the tens of thousands of other Irish-American Union soldiers who marched and fought under an Irish flag within the Union's armed forces, it was easy to envision a correlation between the Union war effort and Irish independence.[16]

Incidents of the war in 1861–62, like the one that unfolded aboard *The State of Maine*, suggest that Irish immigrants' interpretation of the Union cause both meshed with and departed from general perceptions of the war in the loyal states. After the war erupted in April 1861, many loyal Americans explained their determination to restore the Union by force with reference to a belief that the United States was uniquely capable of proliferating democracy and republican institutions around the globe. That sentiment was captured in March 1862 by a Union regimental newspaper from a non-Irish unit that predicted the collapse of "Republican Liberty and self-government throughout the world" should Confederate forces prevail. No doubt many German, Scottish, English, or other immigrants would have agreed with this sentiment, but Irish Americans' global conception of the Union's importance had a specific transatlantic dimension. The historian Gary Gallagher points out that an "unequivocally exceptionalist reading of America's role in the world aligned perfectly with how loyal citizens explained the importance of the Union." The Irish in the North legitimized Northerners' "exceptionalist reading" of America's global influence and offered an immediate possibility for where Americans should exert their influence: Ireland.[17]

Not all Irish Americans believed that the Union cause served the interests of Irish immigrants. James McMaster, editor of the *New York Freeman's Journal*, was not Irish, but thousands of Irish immigrants read his Catholic newspaper. From August 1861 until the conflict ended, McMaster lambasted the Lincoln administration's prosecution of the war and alleged disregard for the Constitution. Other Catholic newspapers popular with Irish Americans, including New York's *Metropolitan Record* (which served as an unofficial newspaper of record for Archbishop John Hughes), Iowa's *Dubuque Herald*, and the *Cincinnati Enquirer*, similarly alleged that the Lincoln administration had violated the Constitution in its prosecution of the Union war effort. Editors of these newspapers, led by McMaster after his six-week imprisonment on federal charges of disloyalty, warned that Republicans' disregard for the Constitution opened the door to anti-Catholic policies. Other Irish Americans rejected the notion that their service in the Union army would advance the aims of Irish nationalists. Patrick Dunny, an immigrant living in Philadelphia, lamented to a brother in Ireland that Irish-born soldiers had fought one another at the Battle of Bull Run in July 1861. According to Dunny, the 69th New York and a Confederate Irish regiment whose members he supposed to be "as good Irish as anyone and with as much love for Ireland" had met on the battlefield. Such a cruel fate led Dunny to conclude that a war in which immigrants killed one another was "grievous to every Irishman." Some newspaper editors and nationalist leaders in Ireland continued to question if the war to restore the Union aligned with Irish nationalist principles of self-determination and independence. The former Young Ireland leader William Smith O'Brien's influence was greatly diminished by 1862, but his voice still carried weight with some Irish Americans. In July, the *Pilot* ran an article from the Dublin *Daily News* in which O'Brien objected to Irish immigrants' involvement in the Union war. Referring to the thousands of Irish immigrant soldiers in the Union army, O'Brien fumed that "many of our countrymen in America are . . . violating those rights of self-government which they wish to apply in Europe, not only to Ireland, but also to Poland, to Hungary, to Venetia, and even to the Ionian Isles."[18]

Generally, however, Irish-American editors and soldiers maintained through the summer of 1862 the initial enthusiasm for the Union they had displayed in April 1861. Rallies in support of the war continued to attract Irish immigrants in Cincinnati, New York, Boston, and elsewhere, and Irish-American military units continued to draw recruits. While 1861 saw little substantive Union military success, the *Trent* Affair at the end of the year fanned the flames of Irish-American hostility toward Great Britain and lent credence to the notion that the Old World—Britain, especially—awaited the American Republic's demise. Over the first few months of 1862, a string of Union military victories in Tennessee, North Carolina, Arkansas, New Orleans, and Virginia bucked up Unionists and was only interrupted by the Confederates' successful defense of Richmond in June. Following victories by the newly ascendant Confederate General Robert E. Lee and Thomas "Stonewall" Jackson in the summer months, Northern morale was revived again when Union general George B. McClellan, a particular favorite of Irish Americans, returned in early September to command of the Army of the Potomac.[19]

A New Birth of Anti-Abolitionism

Even as Irish-American Unionists demonstrated over the first year and a half of the war that they were not the tools of the Slave Power that many abolitionists and Republicans believed them to be, they also sharpened the antebellum Irish-American critique of antislavery. During the secession winter of 1860–61, Irish Americans had argued that if the Union crumbled, antislavery politicians would share just as much blame as Southerners. "The spirit of black republicanism is simply abolitionism, and means war upon the South and South-west," the *Pilot* warned in its coverage of the 1860 presidential campaign. Shortly after so-called Black Republicanism triumphed at the polls, the *Pilot* lamented South Carolinian secessionists' hot-tempered extremism but declared that "all the tumult about disunion . . . must be laid to the charge of Northern abolitionism." Following the secession of South Carolina on December 20, an Irish immigrant in Philadelphia wrongly claimed that because Lincoln had "declared he will free all slaves in southern states," those states "will not give up their propurty by no means without war in stead." Well before the secession crisis unfolded, Irish Americans had come to see the Republican Party as synonymous with abolitionism, and they viewed its political ascent in 1860 as the chief cause of secession. Even as most Irish Americans threw their support behind the Union war, they clung to the belief that Republicans' antislavery agenda was to blame for the Union's crisis.[20]

On the one hand, Irish-American charges that Republicans provoked proslavery Southerners to secede echoed those of Northern Democrats who aimed to capitalize on the tumult that ensued from Lincoln's election. Like the *Pilot*, another Boston-based Irish-American newspaper, the *Irish Pictorial Weekly*, connected the dots between abolitionism and mainstream antislavery politics amid the secession crisis. Editor James Sullivan opined in January 1861 that abolitionism was "not a debatable question" for it was "an open and wanton violation of the LETTER of the Constitution; and, therefore, is treason. . . . Every Abolition speech, or other act interfering with Slavery, is an act of war against the Constitution." Even Cincinnati's *Catholic Telegraph and Advocate*, one of the few Irish-American newspapers to editorialize against slavery before the war, argued that "Southern people have had grounds of complaint" in the sectional crisis over slavery. While the *Telegraph* opposed secession and pointed out that abolitionists were not a decisive influence in the free states, it denounced abolitionists' sanctimoniousness nonetheless. "Essentially a fanatic," from the *Telegraph*'s perspective, an abolitionist knew "but one vice, and one virtue." Such conflations of abolitionism and Republicanism, of calls for immediate, unconditional emancipation and opposition to slavery's expansion in the West, were echoed in Democratic editorials and speeches throughout the loyal states.[21]

On the other hand, within the blanket Democratic rejection of "Black Republicanism" was a distinctive Irish-American thread that was spun out of the Irish critique of abolitionism during the famine years and woven into the Irish-American critique of antislavery in the 1850s. That singular stitch was on full display at Brookes' Hall in the Bowery section of Manhattan, where, in January of 1861, a "Meeting of Workingmen of New York" passed a series of resolutions regarding the secession crisis. Declaring that secessionists were engaged in a struggle to "preserve the Constitution from being overthrown by Abraham Lincoln" and proclaiming that they, too, would "[uphold] the Constitution and the Union," the workingmen stated that they viewed "slaveholders as the natural allies of the Northern laborers." Tellingly, the attendees denounced the Republican Party as a "British antislavery party." Republicans' electoral success, they posited, was proof that "Great Britain has conquered the North with the pen, having abolitionized the press and the pulpit." "[W]hile the heel of her [i.e., Britain's] oppression is upon the white men in Ireland, England, and Scotland," the men continued, "she tries to divert attention from her sins at home by false philanthropy for negroes in America even while oppressing the poor of Ireland, Scotland, and England." That the anonymous New York workingmen who passed these resolutions gathered in the heavily Irish Sixth Ward of Manhattan suggests an Irish-American influence. More significantly, the convention's characterization of the Republican Party as a "British antislavery party" and its claim that British abolitionists neglected poverty at their doorstep in Ireland were unmistakably rooted in the famine-era Irish critique of abolitionism. Indeed, while constitutional and republican nationalist editors in Ireland disagreed over how Irish people's interests aligned with the warring American sections, they shared the belief that disingenuous antislavery reformers on both sides of the Atlantic were the architects of disunion. Characterizing the "attitude of the North" in May 1861 as "insolent and intolerable," Dublin's *Irishman* likened the conduct of antislavery Northerners to "that coarse and brutal fanaticism, which in England (and peculiarly to England), under the outraged name of freedom, assails religious and social liberty." Editor P. J. Smyth insisted that he abhorred Black chattel slavery yet faulted the "Northern Republican party" for having "formed a coalition with the Abolitionists and a Native American [i.e., nativist] party" to capture the White House. The Irish critique of abolitionism and its corollary in the Irish-American critique of antislavery were alive and well on both sides of the Atlantic Ocean in 1861, exerting a powerful influence on how Irish Americans construed the root cause of secession and the rise of the Republican Party in the North.[22]

Yet Irish Americans' overt displays of support for the Union war effort after the bombardment of Fort Sumter indicate that their critique of antislavery was subservient to their Unionist sentiments. Through the end of 1861, Irish-American editors, soldiers, and orators directed more of their attention to restoring the Union than harping on the alleged misdeeds of antislavery Northerners. Even though his *Pilot* blamed abolitionists and antislavery politicians for causing secession, editor Patrick Donahoe regularly provided the antislavery Republican governor of Massachusetts, John A. Andrew, with suggestions for how to recruit for and commission officers in the state's Irish regiments. Prominent Irish-American recruiters like Thomas Francis Meagher similarly downplayed long-standing grudges against abolitionists to mobilize Irish immigrants for a war they would fight alongside antislavery Northerners. In an October 1861 recruitment speech for the Irish Brigade, Meagher conceded that abolitionists were "mainly instrumental in producing that fearful inflammation of the Southern mind." But not even "the most indulgent Democrat," he countered, could blame them for the Confederates' "desperate attempt . . . to wrest from the Stars and Stripes the forts and frontiers south of the Potomac." Although splenetic editors like James McMaster of the *Freeman's Journal* attacked abolitionists throughout 1861, other influential editors, such as Donahoe, and prominent Irish-born soldiers like Meagher, placed the Union's preservation above their disdain for antislavery, rendering McMaster's voice marginal in 1861.[23]

Two developments in the war in 1862, however, invigorated the Irish-American critique of antislavery and generated concern from Irish-American Unionists over the Republicans' handling of the war. The first revolved around General James Shields, an Irish-born Californian who had risen to the rank of major general during the Mexican-American War. Many Irish Americans revered Shields for his political clout and military heroism. In 1847, while leading a charge at the Battle of Cerro Gordo in Mexico, Shields suffered what was initially thought to be a mortal wound when grapeshot punctured his right lung and nearly severed his spine. He not only survived the wound but also went on to win election to the US Senate in both Illinois and Minnesota before moving to California. Shields seemed to be a promising candidate for command of a division in the Union army when war erupted in 1861. He was so confident of his appointment that he even declined command of the newly formed Irish Brigade, which was being organized and recruited under the stewardship of Meagher and other veteran officers of the 69th New York State Militia. Having obtained the rank of major general during his service in Mexico, Shields viewed a brigadier's commission as tantamount to a demotion.[24]

Much to Shields' chagrin, a divisional command in the Union army remained elusive, convincing the Democratic stalwart that abolitionists in Congress were to blame. In a letter to New York judge Charles Patrick Daly, who helped to recruit and fundraise for the Irish Brigade's New York regiments, Shields complained that the Senate held up his commission as major general because it wanted "Abolition instruments in the army—or Democrats who have not the power or influence." Shields believed that Senate Republicans' expulsion of Indiana Democrat Jesse D. Bright on charges of treason had effectively destroyed any hopes that a former Democratic senator like himself would receive his due rank in the army. To his surprise, the Senate quickly gave him command of a division, but at the rank of brigadier general. Shields' division experienced fleeting success but was promptly defeated by Confederate forces under Stonewall Jackson in the Shenandoah Valley. After being injured at the Battle of Kernstown in March of 1862, Shields was nominated by Lincoln as a major general, after which the Senate added insult to injury by refusing to grant the promotion. Disgruntled, Shields resigned from the army on March 28, 1863.[25]

Irish-American reactions to the Shields commission fiasco in the first half of 1862 echoed the general's belief that antislavery politicians squashed his promotion. After the Senate denied Shields his promotion, a correspondent of Judge

Daly lamented that the "Hero of Mexico is at last 'Disgraced' and through him, irish bravery and valor." As to why Shields had been mistreated, the author blamed "the bigotry of the North, [which] places the Irish lower than the black slaves of the South," a complaint that smacked of the antebellum Irish-American critique of antislavery. In late June 1862, an Irishman from Boston wrote to the *Irish-American* to lament that the "august Senate" had erred in refusing to commission Shields, for the denial would be "resented by every Irishman in the country" and thereby weaken the Union war effort. The Boston Irishman's prediction proved prescient, for when the now-Brigadier General Thomas Francis Meagher returned to New York to recruit soldiers to fill the thinned ranks of the Irish Brigade, he found his countrymen deeply resentful of Shields' treatment. As Meagher informed President Lincoln, "The Irish-born residents not only in this city, but throughout all the loyal states are fiercely indignant at the action of the Senate in regard to their gallant countryman [Shields]." By October, Colonel James Mulligan, a fellow Irish-American Democrat from Illinois who commanded the Irish 23rd Illinois Regiment, still held out hope that Shields, the "true Irish military representative in America," would receive another divisional command. But he predicted that "Politics will prevent the 'Powers' from" organizing an Irish division under Shields. To Mulligan, a virulent anti-abolitionist and opponent of emancipation, "Politics" meant antislavery war policies, and the "Powers" were abolitionists in Congress. These Irish-American commentators saw the Shields' case as further proof of antislavery politicians' disdain for the Irish.[26]

While the Shields controversy breathed new life into the charge that antislavery and nativist politics were one and the same, signs that Republican legislators were jettisoning their initial hands-off approach to slavery also raised Irish Americans' suspicions as the war to restore the Union dragged on with no end in sight. Like most Americans in both the Union and Confederacy, Irish Americans went to war in 1861 believing that victory would come quickly and easily. Initial Union successes in 1862 seemed to portend the victory that had been elusive in 1861, especially in late June as Union soldiers fought their way up the James Peninsula to the outskirts of the Confederate capital in Richmond. But by September, a summer's worth of tenacious fighting found Union forces reeling and Confederate soldiers singing "My Maryland" as they splashed across the Potomac into Union territory. As the war to restore the Union floundered, Congress passed a series of measures designed to cripple the Confederacy's war-making capacity. These measures marked a dramatic shift in the relationship between the restoration of the Union and the future of American slavery. They included a flurry of antislavery bills, and according to the historian Eric Foner, the highly publicized debate around those laws "helped to educate the northern public about the relationship of slavery to the rebellion." In March, army and navy officers were forbidden from returning fugitives from slavery to Confederate enslavers, effectively undermining the Fugitive Slave Law. Congress abolished slavery in the District of Columbia in May, encouraging escapees from Virginia and Maryland to seek freedom in the capital. June saw slavery abolished in the Territories, fulfilling a founding principle of the Republican Party. And when Lincoln signed the Second Confiscation Act into law on July 17, enslaved people became forever free if they were owned by a Confederate enslaver and came within Union lines, signaling both the most sweeping Congressional antislavery measure to date and the most hard-handed Union war policy to that point in time.[27]

Amid this shift in Republican politicians' strategy for restoring the Union, Irish-American editors, politicians, and soldiers argued throughout the first half of 1862 that abolitionists had hijacked the war to restore the Union to its detriment. Reacting to the abolition of slavery in US Territories in May, the New York *Freeman's Journal* decried "the crazy fanaticism [of] New England Abolitionism" and charged that the ban was unconstitutional. General Shields echoed the *Journal*'s complaint in a letter to Judge Charles Patrick Daly. Shields had recently visited Washington as part of the campaign to regain his major generalship and spoke with President Lincoln about the progress of the Union war effort. While Shields was satisfied by Lincoln's recent approval of the Militia Act, the Irish-born general was perturbed by the conduct of antislavery congressmen he encountered at the White House. Expressing his contempt for the "Abolition arrogance" of congressmen who "ventured to lecture the . . . Pres[iden]t in his presence," Shields concluded that abolitionists were "insane and their insanity will be the ruin of us." Shields' sentiments echoed those of rank-and-file Irish-American soldiers whose spirits were sunk in the summer of 1862 by the disastrous Seven Days battles on the outskirts of Richmond. Two weeks after the string of battles that forced Union soldiers to beat a retreat back down the James Peninsula, a soldier in the Irish Brigade's 69th New York wrote to a friend back home, observing that he had seen Richmond's steeples. However, thanks to "the damned abolitionists in Congress," he claimed, the Army of the Potomac was denied the additional soldiers necessary to finish the job. An Irish-American priest and friend of Judge Daly, Father Bernard O'Reilly, shared this soldier's perspective, claiming late in July that Lincoln's "abolitionist Knights . . . have given victory to the Slave-Power." McMaster's *Freeman's Journal*, reacting to the Seven Days battles, the Second Confiscation Act, and Union General David Hunter's proclamation of emancipation in the Department of the South, argued that antislavery policies led Confederates to fight harder and pushed the South into the welcoming arms of Great Britain. "Is not this the very thing the Abolition traitors are aiming at?" the *Freeman* asked. "We believe it is."[28]

Long before emancipation became a defined policy in the Union war effort, many Irish Americans had decided that abolitionists in power were delaying the Union's restoration to ensure the destruction of slavery. This perspective had its origins in the Irish-American critique of antislavery that took shape in the 1850s, which held in part that all types of opposition to slavery were necessarily detrimental to the preservation of the Union. But the facts of the war in 1862 added new and more tangible meanings to that critique. Many congressmen were antislavery, some radically so; an Irish-American military hero had been unable to obtain the command he desired from a Republican-led Congress; a series of antislavery measures had come out of the Capitol; and, most importantly, Republicans were growing bolder in their use of political power to undermine slavery, even as the nation itself was more divided than ever.

This was the backdrop to the preliminary Emancipation Proclamation of September 22, 1862. Issued by Lincoln after a strategic Union victory at the Battle of Antietam, the preliminary proclamation declared "then, thenceforward, and forever free" enslaved people residing in Confederate states who did not return to the Union by January 1, 1863. Influential Irish Americans saw the Emancipation Proclamation not as an asset to the Union cause but as confirmation that the Union cause was being subordinated to a war for abolition. The editor of the *Irish-American* pointed out that before the proclamation, antislavery newspapers like Horace Greeley's *Tribune* had denounced Union general George B. McClellan's overly cautious prosecution of the war. But because enslaved people in states that remained in rebellion would now be declared free on January 1, 1863, the *Tribune* and other abolitionist tracts seemed content to let the war drag on. Richard O'Gorman, an exiled Young Irelander turned New York lawyer and Democratic powerbroker, declared in a speech to the Democratic Union Association of New York that the proclamation was indicative of how "abolitionists were doing more to destroy the country than any one else." The *Pilot* argued that the antislavery strain of "New England politico-religious fanaticism" was now "the real arbiter of the fate of this nation," for abolitionists had taken hold of the war's prosecution. Republicans had "no wish that there should be a cessation of hostilities," the *Pilot* claimed, for they were not only "filling their pockets" through war-profiteering, but also relishing the chance to enact their program of "whiggery, know-nothingism and abolitionism." Of course, Irish Americans were just one subset of Northern Democrats who vehemently registered their opposition to

Lincoln's proclamation. Across the Union, Democrats who had cautiously supported Lincoln during the first year and a half of the war denounced the proclamation as unconstitutional and counterproductive. But the *Pilot*'s insistence on connecting the preliminary Emancipation Proclamation with nativist politics reveals the durability of the Irish-American critique of antislavery.[29]

In Ireland, Confederate-sympathizing editors struggled to reconcile their admiration of Southern separatism with their self-proclaimed desire to see the extinction of slavery. Early in the war, constitutional nationalist weeklies like the Dublin *Nation* and *Cork Examiner* pointed to the absence of a federal antislavery policy as proof that the Union war effort was one of conquest over a people seeking to rule themselves. With no apparent irony, the *Nation* insisted as late as September 13, 1862, that Unionists were engaged in "an endeavor to enslave a people determined to be free." The preliminary Emancipation Proclamation of September 22, 1862, forced the *Nation* and provincial newspapers like the *Cork Examiner* and *Tipperary Advocate* to confront the fact that the war to restore the Union was also now a war to hasten slavery's demise. The *Nation* raised specious constitutional objections to the policy and parroted Democratic organs in predicting that the proclamation could only lead to a bloody servile insurrection. This was a baldly racist conjecture that, ironically, was also amplified by the *Nation*'s perpetual antagonist, the *Times* of London. Still, the *Nation* dug in its heels and condemned Irish editors for having bought into "Exeter Hall [i.e., British abolitionist] arguments" by endorsing the proclamation.[30]

Though temporarily broken at Antietam, the string of Union military setbacks that led many Irish-American observers to see a cause-and-effect relationship between antislavery war policies and Confederate victories continued through the end of 1862. In mid-December at Fredericksburg, Virginia, Union soldiers suffered their most demoralizing defeat to that point in the war, with the Irish Brigade alone reporting 545 of its 1,300 soldiers dead, injured, or missing after the battle. Lincoln's promulgation of the final Emancipation Proclamation on January 1, 1863, came on the heels of that devastating defeat, one that was especially grievous for Irish-American Unionists. For some Irish-American editors, workers, and even soldiers, the prospect of Union soldiers enforcing emancipation as the Union war effort teetered on the brink of collapse and Irish-American units were cut to pieces was too much to bear. The tenets of Irish-American Unionism, it seemed to them, were being undercut by an abolitionist crusade. This understanding of the Union war effort in late 1862 fulfilled Irish Americans' warnings about the dire consequences that would result from antislavery politicians taking hold of the federal government. But this anti-war perspective was far from dominant among

Irish immigrants in the loyal states, for over the first year and a half of the war, a new influence on how Irish Americans conceived of slavery, emancipation, and the Union had emerged. Increasingly, the actions of enslaved people showed that the causes of the Union and Black freedom were mutually supportive.[31]

"It is only negroes that will be at work on it soon": Contrabands and Emancipation

The first rumblings of a seismic shift in Irish Americans' perspectives on American slavery and its relationship to the Union came in the form of enslaved men and women's hushed planning and quieted footsteps as they fled from those who claimed them as property. Mere weeks after the attack on Fort Sumter, three enslaved men tasked with building Confederate fortifications on the Virginia shoreline appropriated a rowboat and paddled across the mouth of the James River to Union-occupied Fortress Monroe. There, General Benjamin Butler justified his refusal to return them to Confederate colonel Stephen Mallory on the grounds that the men were "contraband" whose labor would aid the Confederate war effort. Within days, a steady stream of fugitives from slavery appeared at the fort, and over the coming weeks and months, ever greater numbers of enslaved Black men, women, and children attempted to exploit the chaotic conditions produced by war to become free. From 1861 to 1862, Union commanders like General Butler and eventually politicians in Congress and bureaucrats in the War Department wrestled with the legal, military, and ethical implications of their decisions to protect—or sometimes subvert—the freedom of those who fled to Union lines. But it was the rank and file of the Union Army who met escapees at picket lines; provided them with rations; ordered them to cook, clean, and dig; harassed or berated them; or labored and marched alongside them. Throughout the war, relations between Union soldiers and fugitives from slavery who worked behind Union lines or lived in hastily constructed "contraband camps" were tenuous at best. Enslaved African Americans' paths to freedom were frequently obstructed by disease, abuse at the hands of white Union soldiers, and separation from loved ones. For the Irish-American soldiers who, in many ways, aided them along that path, the world was turned upside down. Instead of arguing or acting on behalf of enslavers' claims to ownership of Black people, more and more Irish immigrants in the Union Army found themselves approving of and even abetting slave emancipation.[32]

Almost as soon as Irish-American soldiers arrived at the seat of war in 1861, they found a warm reception from enslaved and free Black Southerners alike.

James Turner, an officer in the Irish Brigade, wrote privately to his family in May 1861 that there were "plenty of negros" around his unit's camp who washed soldiers' shirts and drawers for "six cents a piece." On another occasion, Turner noted that one of the women who did his laundry was formerly enslaved and had been freed by the man who claimed her as property, a cousin of the mayor of Georgetown. To be sure, Irish-American soldiers' descriptions of enslaved men and women continued to reflect an inveterate racism common among many white Americans but especially among Irish immigrants in Northern cities. Arthur O'Keefe, the son of Irish immigrants and a member of the 34th New York, described marching through Baltimore in early July 1861. "We saw about 10,000 niggers," O'Keefe wrote to his parents, "and they were waving their pocket hankerchiefs and cheering us as we marched with fixed bayonets through the streets." William McCarter, an Ulster immigrant serving in the Irish Brigade as a member of the 116th Pennsylvania, had a similar experience when in September 1862, some "negroes going through the ranks" provided him and his fellow soldiers with much-needed "good, fresh, clear drinking water" as they passed through Baltimore. Daniel Finn, an Irish-born musician who served in a predominantly Irish-American regiment from Ohio, awoke one morning in Parkersburgh, Virginia, to find that "a little 'darkie'" had polished his and his fellow soldiers' boots "all for five cents." These types of exchanges between enslaved or free Black Southerners and Union soldiers abounded in 1861 and 1862. The demeaning and nakedly racist language used by O'Keefe and Finn to describe African American men, women, and children indicates that such exchanges did not erase soldiers' belief in white supremacy. But in the crucible of war, there was no mistaking that Black Southerners looked favorably on the success of Union arms.[33]

While petty commercial transactions and provisions for thirsty soldiers were undoubtedly appreciated, military intelligence provided to Union soldiers by enslaved and free Blacks offered more substantial proof that emancipation could bolster the Union war effort. For soldiers in the Irish-American 9th Massachusetts, that realization came early in the regiment's first campaign. In a July 1861 letter to his wife, Nellie, Private Michael Leary of Boston described how the unit's colonel had been "told by a Nigger" that "there was 200 Rebel Cavalry with in 3 miles of our camp" on Arlington Heights, Virginia. That warning allowed the Union troops to prepare a "warm welcome" for the Confederate attack. Two weeks later, Leary and about a hundred other Irishmen from the 9th went on a scouting mission that came under Confederate fire, wounding the man next to Leary. The next day, men from the 9th attempted another scouting mission but were "told by some free niggers that if we went into the next wood ahead of us that we would either get shot or taken prisoners," at which point the undermanned force returned to its post. Leary's accounts of freedmen aiding the 9th Massachusetts with military intelligence illustrate what one rebel officer termed the "omnipresent spy system" that African Americans developed in the war. As is evidenced by Leary's blithe use of the term "niggers" regarding the Black men who helped to protect his unit, African Americans' military assistance to Irish-American soldiers did not stop the soldiers from speaking or acting as racists. Yet considering that dozens of the men in the regiment had taken part in the reenslavement of Anthony Burns a few years earlier, the encounters described by Leary in 1861 constituted a remarkable turnabout.[34]

Enslaved men and women who sought freedom behind Union lines, bringing with them the capacity to labor and useful military intelligence, forced Union officials to develop clear policies on how the army would treat runaways. In August 1861, Congress followed the lead of General Butler by passing the First Confiscation Act, a measure that instructed soldiers to protect the freedom of any enslaved person who came within Union lines if that individual had been employed "in any military or naval service whatsoever" on behalf of the Confederate war effort. Because Union soldiers could not be expected to have direct knowledge of how a fugitive from slavery had been employed before they reached Union lines, the War Department instructed commanders to accept and guard the freedom of all fugitives until civil authorities determined the loyalties of their presumptive owners. Congress pressed the issue further in March 1862 by passing a law that barred Union military personnel under any circumstances from capturing and then returning fugitives to those who claimed possession of them. Then, in July, the Second Confiscation Act broadened the category of enslaved people whose freedom Union soldiers were legally obligated to protect by clarifying that all disloyal Americans had forfeited their right to claim possession of enslaved men, women, and children. By the summer of 1862, then, all enslaved people whose enslavers were loyal to the Confederacy were freed upon reaching Union lines, or so the Republican-led Congress ordered. Many of these so-called contrabands dug trenches, erected fortifications, and even diverted bodies of water in support of the Union army. Others continued to provide invaluable information on Confederate positions, troop movements, and morale. Not only did this work benefit the Union war effort, but also it deprived the Confederacy of invaluable labor.[35]

Even as Irish-American editors and more illustrious Irish-born soldiers like James Shields groused about "Black Republican" antislavery measures like the First and Second Confiscation Acts, Irish-American soldiers in the field dutifully enforced these measures. Of course, as enlisted men or junior officers, they had virtually no other option. But scattered evidence from letters written to Irish-American newspapers, private correspondence, diaries, and postwar regimental histories suggests that Irish-born soldiers embraced their new emancipatory duties, albeit with varying levels of enthusiasm. Amid the Peninsula Campaign in April 1862, Lieutenant-Colonel Patrick Guiney of the 9th Massachusetts welcomed five enslaved women into Union picket lines by proclaiming, "In the name of old Ireland and Massachusetts, I set you free." As an Irish immigrant who had voted the Republican ticket prior to the war out of a long-held aversion to Black slavery, Guiney was a rarity among Irish-American soldiers. Perhaps at least partly for this reason, several junior officers in his regiment staged a futile protest against his promotion to colonel several months later, in 1862. Guiney's lofty sentiment to liberate enslaved women in "the name of old Ireland and Massachusetts" was likely not shared by many of his subordinates. But as Lieutenant Michael Finnerty of the 9th Massachusetts pointed out to readers of the *Pilot*, Irish-American soldiers had good reasons for welcoming the women into Union lines. Finnerty observed that they "seemed . . . anxious to give us every possible information," meaning that they likely provided knowledge of the local roads or even Confederate positions. For soldiers in the 9th Massachusetts who might not have shared Patrick Guiney's abhorrence of enslavement, sheltering escapees could mean nothing more or less than aiding the Union war effort.³⁶

Other Irish-American soldiers' views on Black freedom and their willingness to protect it evolved as they encountered African American men and women with greater frequency. On May 28, 1862, the 10th Ohio musician Daniel Finn recorded in his diary that he and a few other soldiers in the mostly Irish-American unit had "sent our nigger home to his master, with a letter stating we were no abolitionists."³⁷ Finn's use of the phrase "our nigger" not only reveals his white supremacist views but also implies that the man had spent at least some time with the unit, likely as a cook or laborer within the 10th Ohio's encampment. Yet Finn and his comrades had, for one reason or another, decided that they would no longer protect the man's freedom. However, only a month and a half later, Finn noted in his diary that "[t]he Band's contraband 'Charles' is seeking refuge in our tent from his master who is prowling about the camp in search of him." The nearly day-by-day entries in Finn's diary reveal that between these two radically different interactions with contrabands in the 10th Ohio's camp, Finn had visited a Black church, watched the marriage of a Black couple, and received some pies from a Black woman for whom he had done a favor. Finn did not explain why he let one fugitive from slavery hide in his tent after he had essentially helped to reenslave another man only weeks before. But his experiences indicate that regular interactions with African Americans in the countryside of western Virginia led him, like other Union soldiers, to recognize their humanity and the inhumanity of their enslavement.[38]

Freed people's productive capacity provided yet another incentive for Irish-American soldiers to welcome fugitives from slavery to their lines. By the spring of 1862, few soldiers who had served for a significant length of time retained romantic notions of soldiering. Not only had an ever-growing casualty list robbed many soldiers of dear friends and even family, but also the drudgeries of soldiering in between battles had become inescapable. Soldiers from the 28th Massachusetts Regiment, which later joined the Irish Brigade, learned this firsthand in March 1862 when the unit's daily detail included 200 men to dig entrenchments, 100 men to cut trees, and 50 men to unload supplies at Hilton Head. A few months later, as the Peninsula Campaign reached its climax outside Richmond, a soldier from the brigade fumed over civilians and newspaper editors who criticized the slow pace at which the army advanced on the Confederate capital. "Those people that complain should come out here and do what we have to do here both day and night," the soldier vented; "they would then realize the labor that has been performed and is to be performed before we can attack the enemy by a general engagement." As this soldier learned, war meant pickaxes, saws, and shovels, not just guns and drums. With casualties mounting and their non-combat duties more grueling by the day, Irish-American soldiers realized that contrabands could lighten their workloads. James P. Sullivan, an Irish-American Wisconsinite in the Union's famed "Iron Brigade," recalled after the war that in June 1862, an officer in his regiment convinced the soldiers to accept the cooking services of a contraband named William. William cooked for Company K, Sullivan's unit, until an artillery bombardment sent him running from a Virginia battlefield, never to return. The Irish Brigade's James Turner informed his sister in July 1862 that his "Negro boy Billy" not only cooked for him but also had assembled a comfortable bed from four posts, some branches, leaves, and "a red blanket which looks very well & sets if off." Thomas Cahill of the 9th Connecticut, a substantially Irish-American regiment, observed in July 1862 that freedmen's labor held vital military importance to the Union war effort. In the stifling summer heat of Mississippi, Cahill and his unit were part of a contingent of Union troops tasked with diverting the Mississippi River to dislodge the Confederate stronghold at Vicksburg, Mississippi. "[W]e have not yet got the ditch cut through . . . to turn the Missippi [sic] River out of its Course," Cahill wrote to his wife. "It is only negroes that will be at work on it soon as we are collecting them from all around have some 800 or 1,000 of them at work on it now so will not want the Soldiers to work on it soon." Under these circumstances, Irish-American soldiers realized that contrabands' paid labor for the Union was infinitely more beneficial to them than defending enslavers' rights to extract labor from enslaved Blacks.[39]

The military logic of aiding enslaved people in their acts of self-liberation was clear to many Irish-American soldiers by September 1862, as it was throughout the Union's armed forces, in Congress, and across much of the North. It was at this critical juncture that Lincoln issued the preliminary Emancipation Proclamation. As we have seen, some Irish-American editors and soldiers viewed the preliminary proclamation with deep suspicion, believing that it was indicative of Republicans' willingness to wage a war of abolition even if that meant further alienating white Southerners from the Union. But in reality, the proclamation constituted a multi-pronged strategic attack against the Confederate war effort. Not only did it aim to deprive Confederates of a massive portion of their labor force, but also it portended to transfer much of that productive capacity to the Union as growing numbers of freed people labored behind Union lines. Moreover, by once and for all signaling that emancipation was central to the Union war effort, Lincoln hoped to stave off any attempted mediation in the war on the part of the British or French governments. The measure also struck a delicate balance between transforming the Union war effort into an all-out campaign against slavery and retaining the loyalties of enslavers and proslavery residents in the Border States by exempting those states, along with specific areas controlled by Union forces, from its provisions. Still, there was no mistaking that by enacting emancipation as a war policy, Lincoln had turned Union soldiers into agents of slavery's demise. When Lincoln signed the final Emancipation Proclamation on January 1, 1863, the measure retained much of the preliminary proclamation's language while adding a provision that allowed Black men to enlist in the armed services and an order for the Union Army and Navy to protect the freedom of newly emancipated people.[40]

Gauging Irish-American soldiers' reactions to the preliminary and final Emancipation Proclamation between September 1862 and the winter of 1862–63 is problematic. Almost certainly, many concurred with Colonel James Mulligan of the 23rd Illinois, whose opinion of the measure was recorded in his diary entry for January 1, 1863. "President's Proclamation published: something about freeing Niggers," Mulligan wrote with evident bitterness. "We have forgotten Washington to exalt Fred. Douglass." A similar perspective was exhibited by an Irish-born soldier in the 7th Rhode Island, who informed the *Pilot* in January that soldiers were disgruntled because "we all believed we were fighting for the restoration of our once glorious Union, and not for 'nigger emancipation' and its almost certain dissolution." But to suggest that these and a handful of other sources revealing an individual Irish-American soldier's opposition to emancipation were indicative of an "overwhelmingly negative response" to the proclamation by Irish-born soldiers is shortsighted. Publication of the final Emancipation Proclamation came at a nadir in the Union war effort. After their victory at Antietam in September, Union forces in the Eastern Theater once again found themselves mired in quagmire, and in November, Lincoln sacked the Army of the Potomac's commander, General George B. McClellan, in favor of General Ambrose Burnside. The rank and file of the army deeply admired McClellan, and while Burnside initially seemed poised to lead Union troops back to Richmond, he blundered spectacularly in Fredericksburg, Virginia, just days before Christmas. The Battle of Fredericksburg was a stunning victory for Robert E. Lee's Army of Northern Virginia, and as we have seen, it cost the Union's Irish Brigade dearly. It would be months before Union morale recovered from this disastrous defeat, especially since the spring saw Lee's army in Virginia achieve an even greater victory at the Battle of Chancellorsville. At the same time, Union forces in the Mississippi River Valley struggled to make headway in their efforts to capture the vital Confederate stronghold of Vicksburg, Mississippi. Amid these demoralizing developments, Irish-Americans who entered the war believing all forms of antislavery were detrimental to the preservation of the Union blamed Lincoln's proclamation for the disastrous direction in which the Union war effort seemed headed.[41]

Yet there is evidence that Irish-American soldiers' reactions to the Emancipation Proclamation were not as lopsided as most historians have assumed. For starters, Irish-American desertion rates did not spike around the time of the proclamation. In his study based on a sample size of 3,600 Irish-born soldiers, Jim Zibro found that although Irish immigrants deserted at a significantly higher rate than native-born or other foreign-born soldiers, that rate declined significantly after 1862. In comparison, Irish-American desertion rates peaked in August 1862 before the preliminary proclamation was issued. Additionally, Irish-American desertion rates in 1863 peaked in June, long after the enactment of the final proclamation. Data on the Irish-American 9th Massachusetts is especially instructive, for many of the soldiers in that unit came from Boston's notoriously anti-abolitionist Irish-American community. The unit itself was organized around a former Irish-American militia company whose involvement in the reenslavement of Anthony Burns in 1854 was well known. For the entirety of the war between 1861 and 1865, Union soldiers deserted at a rate of about 12 percent, making the 9th's total desertion rate of 13.7 percent for the war slightly above average. About a third of the 9th's total deserters left the army in 1862, but importantly, most of these desertions took place before Lincoln issued the preliminary Emancipation Proclamation. A mere 6.3 percent of Irish-American soldiers in the regiment who deserted in 1862 did so between late September and December, the period that preceded the official enactment of emancipation. Of course, some soldiers may have been waiting to see if the proclamation would go into effect. But only 5.3 percent of all the 9th's desertions for 1863 occurred the month after Lincoln signed the final Emancipation Proclamation on January 1, 1863. In short, the Emancipation Proclamation caused no significant spike in desertions among Irish-American soldiers in the 9th Massachusetts. Nor did it produce anything approaching a steep rise in desertions by Irish-born soldiers generally.[42]

A more fruitful line of inquiry regarding Irish-American soldiers' reactions to the Emancipation Proclamation may be why so many continued to fight in a war that now linked the preservation of the Union to the destruction of slavery. Encounters between Irish Americans and fugitives from slavery after Lincoln issued the preliminary Emancipation Proclamation reveal how the unpredictable fortunes of war led formerly proslavery soldiers to see emancipation as necessary for the Union cause to prevail. "J. D.," a soldier in Corcoran's Irish Legion, apprised readers of the *Irish-American* in November 1862 that the "poor negroes have the worst of it so far in this war." He described "two runaways from Richmond" who were "tolerably intelligent" and gave a full account of the condition of Confederate hospitals, the scarcity of provisions in Richmond, and the progress of Confederate efforts to build an ironclad vessel. Two weeks later, J. D. wrote again to the *Irish-American*, relating how "fugitive slaves" had gathered furniture for soldiers from abandoned houses, including the "excellent spring-chair" in which he penned his letter. By no means did J. D. or most other Irish-American soldiers come to see freed people as their equals, as his blithe descriptions of one fugitive being "black as the King of Spades" and officers in the unit as "slave-dealers" suggest. Yet his letters to the *Irish-American* in the interlude between the preliminary and final proclamations are remarkable when one considers that since its first issue in 1850, the newspaper had consistently railed against any outside interference with slavery. As loyal Americans debated whether emancipation would help or hinder the Union war effort, J. D. and other Irish-American soldiers gave tangible proof to Irish-American Unionists on the home front that freed people shared their interests in restoring the Union by force.[43]

Even more instructive are the experiences of the Irish Brigade's James Turner. The author of dozens of letters to the *Irish-American* during the war, Turner wrote his missives under the nom de plume "Gallowglass," a reference to mercenary

Scottish warriors who fought alongside Gaelic chieftains against the Anglo-Norman colonizers of parts of Ireland between the twelfth and fourteenth centuries. In one of Turner's letters, written on the eve of the disastrous Union loss at Fredericksburg, he dwelt at some length on the plight of Harry, the contraband teamster who drove a covered wagon for the Irish Brigade. Harry was a valuable enslaved man on a Culpepper, Virginia, plantation until he escaped to Union lines in 1862, leaving a wife and seven children behind. In Turner's tongue-in-cheek phraseology, Harry "[stole] away himself from his lawful and constitutional master." Moreover, Turner continued, Harry was "contemplating another robbery. He talks glibly to us of stealing his own wife and seven children, if he can only get the chance." The situation gave Turner pause for reflection. "Here we are in this wagon, three of us, ultra-proslavery Democrats, listening to this disciple of Wendell Phillips (who never heard of Phillips in all his life), and giving heed to his plans for running the underground railroad." A few days after the Battle of Fredericksburg, Turner returned to Harry and the Irish Brigade's other contrabands in another letter to the *Irish-American*. He observed that "notwithstanding the general opinion of their stolidity and stupidity," there was "an abundant philosophy crammed away somewhere in the brain of the negro." In modern parlance, Turner was using racist language to describe his and his comrades' anti-racist course of action, which was, in all likelihood, a calculated ploy to justify that course of action to the *Irish-American*'s rabidly anti-abolitionist readership.[44]

As an Irish immigrant from a wealthy, well-educated family, James Turner was exceptional. As an Irish-American soldier who demonstrated a willingness to risk life and limb for the Union cause when a bullet shattered his arm at Antietam, where 540 other members of the Irish Brigade became casualties of war, he was not. As similar examples show, Turner was also unexceptional as an Irish-American soldier who realized that preserving the Union would require new answers to the question of slavery's future in the United States. As the 9th Connecticut's Thomas Cahill, writing from New Orleans in late December 1862, realized of his Confederate foes, "These fellows will die for the nigger for he has a real and practical value for them and they mean to fight for him." The corollary to this, of course, was that depriving Confederates of the people they claimed as property had practical effects on Southerners' abilities to fight and to subvert the Union that Irish Americans cherished.[45]

Fenian-sympathizing editors in Ireland quickly picked up on the practical benefits that emancipation afforded the war to restore the Union, which they continued to evaluate in terms of its potential to weaken Britain's global standing and strengthen the prospects of Irish nationhood. Leading the pro-emancipation

Irish nationalist press was James Roche, a Fenian, a former writer for the Democratic *Irish News* of New York, and, as of April 1862, editor of the newly established *Galway-American*. In May, Roche asserted that the future of American slavery could "only be considered in reference to its bearing on the paramount question of the restoration of the Union." Roche left no doubt as to where the *Galway-American* stood on the matter: "[I]f slavery stand in the way of a speedy restoration of the Union, then away with it." Upon learning of the preliminary proclamation in October, the Dublin *Irishman*'s editor, P. J. Smyth, celebrated the policy as one that "inseparably identifies the cause of the Union with the cause of freedom." English "hypocrites and liars" who had supported the Confederacy while professing their "hostility to slavery" would have no choice but to switch their allegiances, Smyth gleefully predicted. Likewise, the *Dundalk Democrat* read the proclamation through an Anglophobic lens. "That the English government desires to see the rebellion successful," the *Democrat* averred, "there cannot be the slightest doubt. We think this fact should convince every Irishman that to dissolve the American Union would not be beneficial to either Ireland or America." Emancipation would not only hasten the restoration of the Union but also, according to the *Democrat*, reveal that Britons' "talk about freedom is mere hypocrisy."[46]

By the time Lincoln enacted the Emancipation Proclamation on January 1, 1863, Irish Americans in the loyal states had arrived at two starkly different visions of emancipation's relationship to the restoration of the Union. From one perspective, restoring the Union and preserving its promises of political liberty, economic betterment, and nationhood to Irish people on both sides of the Atlantic Ocean remained as paramount as ever, necessitating a heavy-handed approach to dealing with Confederates. James Turner, writing to the *Irish-American* as "Gallowglass" in August 1862, perfectly captured this perspective in a description of Union soldiers burning to the ground the house of the arch-secessionist, proslavery fire-eater Edmund Ruffin. Burning Ruffin's house was, in Turner's words, "a sort of offering to the outraged National spirit and instinct." So, too, he might have added, was the ongoing assault on the institution of slavery that Irish Americans had once believed to be the nation's keystone. For Turner and other Irish-American soldiers in the first two years of the war who embraced their role as emancipators, Irish-American Unionism proved to be a remarkably compelling set of ideas.[47]

Conversely, the other Irish-American perspective on the Union war effort would have seen the destruction of Ruffin's house as a detestable step down the path of abolitionism. From this perspective, the Union cause had been subverted by radical abolitionists who would stop at nothing—not even the permanent division of the nation—to free enslaved Blacks. Leading that fight were the "Black Republicans," politicians whose nativist bigotry and willingness to jeopardize the restoration of the Union to abolish slavery were thought to go hand in hand. James McMaster's *Freeman's Journal* illuminated this perspective in a chilling July 1862 editorial. "[W]ere half a dozen abolitionists of the press and pulpit to be hanged in New York for their rascalities," McMaster mused, "and three or four in Pennsylvania and Ohio, . . . who will doubt that half a dozen of the border states would be ready to come back under a re-united Constitution." The restoration of the Union, in other words, depended upon wooing Confederates back by showing them that Northerners would repudiate abolitionism, just as they had before hostilities commenced. For McMaster and a particular segment of the Irish-American home front, the course of the war had affirmed the Irish-American critique of antislavery.[48]

Both Irish-American perspectives on the war reflected the unique lens through which Irish immigrants saw the slavery question in their adopted country. Irish Americans shared a broader Northern belief that America's survival as a nation was essential to the future of humanity and constitutional democracy. But when Irish immigrants articulated their reasons for supporting the Union war effort in 1861 and 1862, they focused on the particular role that the United States had played and would continue to play in the lives of Irish people on both sides of the Atlantic. Unlike native-born Northerners, Irish Americans' backgrounds and connections to Ireland gave them a lived experience of how the United States had exercised its influence abroad and how it might do so in the future. Additionally, while white, native-born Unionists rallied in 1861 to preserve the practice of constitutional democracy passed down to them by their parents and grandparents, Irish-American Unionists pointed to their own experiences in Ireland and the political oppression their countrymen and women continued to endure as they explained the necessity of restoring the American Republic and its promise of liberty—at least to white Americans. Finally, the deterioration of Anglo-American relations as a result of the *Trent* Affair and British recognition of Confederate belligerency, as well as the ascent of Fenianism among the Irish in the loyal states in 1861 and 1862, offered new hope to Irish-American nationalists who, since the 1840s, had clung to the belief that the United States would play an essential part in their quest for Irish sovereignty. In these respects, Irish-American Unionists who embraced emancipation took a separate path from Northerners who vaguely championed America's global destiny or the superiority of free labor when justifying emancipation early in the war.[49]

Irish-American opposition to the Union's antislavery war policies in 1861 and 1862, meanwhile, also revealed singularly Irish concerns. The combined effects of the Shields commission episode, a series of antislavery war measures, and a concerning list of military blunders had ominous portents to many Irish immigrants. Because these three developments played out simultaneously under a Republican administration, it seemed that the antebellum Irish-American critique of antislavery had been justified. The triumph of antislavery politics in the election of 1860 had produced disunion, antislavery politicians were allegedly discriminating against the Irish in the armed forces, and antislavery policies appeared to have taken precedence over reuniting the country. As the war dragged on and changed course over the coming year, Irish-American adherents to the pro-emancipation and anti-emancipation perspectives on the Union war effort would find more evidence for their respective views in the form of new military measures and changes in Irish society and politics.

6   Unionism and Emancipation on the Home Front and Battlefield

At several pivotal junctures between the winter of 1862 and the fall of 1863, the restoration of the Union seemed a forlorn hope. Resounding Union defeats in Virginia—one at Fredericksburg in December 1862 and the other at Chancellorsville in May 1863—became inflection points for loyal Americans' frustrations over the costliness and indecisiveness of the war. In July 1863, Lee's Army of Northern Virginia marched again over Union soil, this time in southern Pennsylvania. Military affairs in the West were more promising, but a Confederate offensive in Kentucky was turned back only with significant loss of life. As the war entered its second full year, the long-anticipated opening of the Mississippi River had failed to materialize. Loyal Americans on the home front, meanwhile, were left aghast by grizzly photographs of the bloated battlefield dead at Antietam that illustrated the costs of the war in gruesome detail. The enactment of the Emancipation Proclamation on January 1, 1863, caused growing numbers of heretofore loyal Americans—especially Democrats—to withdraw their begrudging support for the Lincoln administration and the Union war effort itself. As the dog days of summer neared, military-aged men and their families waited in angst-ridden anticipation for the first round of a military draft that aimed to fill the Union's depleted ranks.[1]

While many Irish-American newspaper editors, military commanders, and rank-and-file soldiers insisted that restoring the Union was worth any cost, some immigrant laborers on the home front reacted to these developments by taking the Irish-American critique of antislavery to its most extreme, violent conclusion. As Republican politicians enacted a slew of antislavery measures that culminated with the Emancipation Proclamation, Irish immigrant laborers reacted with a brutal wave of racist violence against Black Americans. Irish-American violence against Black communities in Northern cities was hardly a new problem, but a web of interconnected developments in 1862–63 brought it to unprecedented levels. Democratic editors and politicians fanned the flames of racist paranoia by predicting that newly freed people would rush to Northern cities, accept lower wages, and push white workers out of the labor market. On the levees of the Ohio River, the banks of Lake Erie, and the East River waterfront, this fear-mongering seemed prescient in 1862 as employers used Black workers to break strikes by Irish-American laborers. In the summer of 1863, the prospect of a federal draft deepened Irish-American workers' opposition to emancipation and the war to restore the Union to which it was now linked. Fearing that conscription would force them to give up their tenuous position in the labor market to fight a war of emancipation, Irish immigrants in New York City forcefully resisted the first round of the federal draft in July 1863. Their protests against conscription degenerated into an outright assault on the Union war effort itself, one that was directed most violently against the Black New Yorkers whom they alleged would benefit from the twin policies of emancipation and conscription.

Yet Irish Americans' prominence in the New York City Draft Riots belied continued support for the Union war effort—including emancipation—among Irish-American soldiers. Irish-born Union soldiers combatted their countrymen during the riots, and many Irish-American soldiers condemned the rioters and dismissed their grievances. Soldiers' reactions to the draft riots were symptomatic of their support for restoring the Union by any means possible, including freeing enslaved people and enlisting them in the Union army. Throughout 1863, Irish-American soldiers continued to embrace emancipation, with some even going so far as to seek positions in newly raised African American regiments. Soldiers' support for emancipation ran the gamut from begrudging to enthusiastic. However, no matter its quality, their support demonstrated a monumental change from the virtually unanimous antebellum Irish-American opposition to all forms of antislavery.

Events on the battlefield and army encampments created the practical environment for Irish-American soldiers to support emancipation, but Irish-American Unionism provided the impetus to continue waging war. Events on both sides of the Atlantic in 1863 reinforced Irish-American soldiers' belief that a robust American republic was paramount to the Irish. Over the course of the year, Irish-born Union soldiers and Irish-American civic leaders in Northern cities raised money to aid victims of a food shortage in Ireland. Simultaneously, immigration to the United States from Ireland rose considerably after an initial lull early in the war, while more and more Irish-American soldiers joined the ranks of the Fenian Brotherhood in the hopes of securing Irish independence upon the conclusion of the American war. Cumulatively, these developments left many with a reinvigorated commitment to reuniting the nation that afforded a haven to destitute Irish men and women and a potential ally for Irish nationalists. As

Irish-American soldiers redoubled their efforts in 1863 to restore the Union by force so that it could continue to serve Irish interests, many grew more receptive to eliminating the root cause of the American conflict: slavery. Thus, even as Irish Americans continued to think about Union and American slavery from their transatlantic perspective, many drew starkly different conclusions than they had in the antebellum period on how to resolve the tension between those issues.

"If the Negro comes North, he comes to meet extermination"

Even as Irish-American soldiers at the front realized the potential for slave liberation to bolster the Union war effort, many Irish immigrants on the home front in the latter half of 1862 were alarmed by the prospect of freedmen competing against them for wages and jobs. In the antebellum period and especially in the 1860 presidential race, Democratic newspapers like the *New York Herald* and politicians like Fernando Wood of New York had conjured up images of newly freed Black men descending on Northern cities to take jobs from white workers. But even in 1860, mass emancipation was inconceivable to most Americans. However effective the *Herald*'s or Wood's demagoguery might have been, the antebellum Irish-American critique of antislavery rarely dwelled on the fate of immigrant workers in a post-emancipation labor market. But during the spring and summer of 1862, the combined effects of Republican antislavery war policies and labor unrest in Ohio and New York gave rise to what might be called a labor competition critique of emancipation. This viewpoint augmented the Irish-American critique of antislavery by construing emancipatory war policies as intended to weaken the position of working-class Irish immigrants. Many Irish Americans adopted the labor competition critique at precisely the same time that emancipation became a Union war policy.[2]

By the summer of 1862, Cincinnati's proximity to the Union-occupied slave state of Kentucky had rendered it a tinder box for anti-emancipation labor unrest among its sizeable immigrant workforce on the wharves of the Ohio River. The first spark came in July when, according to the *Catholic Telegraph*, vessels that previously employed "many white hands in loading, unloading, porterage, and other laborious duties of river freightage" replaced white workers with Blacks. While the antislavery *Cincinnati Gazette* claimed that the newly hired Black workers replaced Irish-American dockhands who left for higher wages in Illinois and Missouri, it also pointed out that Black workers took only $30 per month as opposed to the $40 per month prevailing wage on Ohio riverboats. Some historians have claimed that the shift to Black employment on the wharves resulted from the mostly Irish-born dockworkers having gone on strike, but there is no mention of a strike in the *Catholic Telegraph and Advocate*, the *Cincinnati Gazette*, or the *Cincinnati Enquirer*. Whatever the circumstances of the changes to the riverfront labor force, Irish longshoremen took swift and brutal action against African Americans in Cincinnati. Gangs of Irishmen descended on the levees, attacked Black workers, and, on July 15, burned homes in the predominantly African American Thirteenth Ward. A Black observer informed readers of the *Christian Recorder* that "no *colored* man could pass along the streets without being assaulted by from five to fifty most loyal citizens, armed with clubs and boulders, and shouting as they came, 'Kill the *dam nagur!*'" The author blamed "*Celts*, the most turbulent race" for the violence. After receiving no help from the city's police, some Black Cincinnatians took the law into their own hands and attacked Irish neighborhoods, killing at least one man. A truce lasted only until late August when another white mob assaulted Black dockworkers.[3]

Though supportive of the Union cause and averse to slavery, Cincinnati's *Catholic Telegraph* pointed to the July riots as evidence of the war's damaging effects on immigrant labor. Regretting the rioters' "hard feeling against inoffensive colored people," the newspaper described Irish-born workers' replacement on the docks as "a question of bread and butter or starvation to thousands." Editor Edward Purcell also reprinted an article from the antislavery *Gazette* that requested "any laboring man who fears (negro) competition" to "present himself at one of our recruiting offices and he can at once procure permanent employment." Such language played directly into the Irish-American critique of antislavery, as it amounted to an already despised Republican adversary taunting immigrants with the prospect of being replaced by Black workers as they risked their lives in the army. As self-emancipated men and women from central and northern Kentucky boosted Cincinnati's relatively small African American population of 3,731 before the war (a little more than 2 percent of the city) and hundreds of Irish Cincinnatians continued to serve as Union soldiers, the events of July 1862 generated nervous speculation over how the war's continuation would affect Irish-American labor.[4]

Elsewhere in the Old Northwest, Irish immigrant workers similarly channeled the labor critique of emancipation as they attacked Black workers. One week before the Cincinnati riots, the *Chicago Tribune* reported that Irish stevedores on strike for higher wages in Toledo were replaced by "negroes employed at the old prices." The Irish strikers "tried to prevent negroes from working, attacking them with stones, clubs, etc." on Toledo's wharves and in the city's Black neighborhoods. In mid-July, the *Tribune* reported Irish-American violence against African

Americans in its own backyard. On July 14, Richard Kelly, an Irish-born omnibus driver, refused passage to a Black man named W. E. Walker. The two men nearly fought before Walker gave in and Kelly drove off. But news of the incident spread across the city, thanks in no small part to Kelly gathering "a small crowd of men from the . . . cattle yards." By the afternoon, "several colored men were assaulted, and it was hardly safe for them to appear upon the street at all." Kelly was brought to trial for his actions and acquitted. He capitalized on his sudden notoriety by recruiting dozens of Irish-American soldiers into the newly formed 90th Illinois Regiment, earning himself an officer's commission.[5]

Irish-American violence against Blacks in Western cities did not go unnoticed back east, where Democratic editors stoked white workers' fears of post-emancipation labor competition. In a short but devastatingly effective article on August 2, 1862, James McMaster's *Freeman's Journal* pointed to the Cincinnati and Toledo riots, along with a similar incident in Evansville, Indiana, as proof that "White and Black labor are incompatible." "The Blacks are courted and employed by a certain short-sighted class, on the Ohio river towns," McMaster asserted, occasioning "bloody riots" in Cincinnati and elsewhere. "This is but the beginning of the end," McMaster predicted. "Miserable Cuffy will be the chief sufferer. If the Negro comes North, he comes to meet extermination." As this last sentence indicated, the perception that freedmen were heading north gave new immediacy in August 1862 to the question of emancipation.[6]

New York's unskilled immigrant workers along the East River responded to McMaster's race-baiting by lashing out at Black workers in their community. Irish-born workers' hostility to their Black counterparts had intensified since June when merchants replaced hundreds of predominantly Irish longshoremen with Black workers who took lower wages. On August 4, two days after the *Freeman's Journal* predicted the "extermination" of freed slaves in the North, an Irish-American mob surrounded Watson's tobacco factory on Sedgwick Street by the Brooklyn waterfront. The factory's white workers had gone home for the noon-hour supper, leaving two dozen or so Black employees (mostly women with their children) who did not live in the neighborhood eating inside. Led by Patrick Keenan, a thirty-year-old Irish-born grog shopkeeper on neighboring Columbia Street, the mob pelted the factory's windows with paving stones, beat one worker severely, and chased Black employees to the third floor before policemen arrived and forced the crowd outside. Keenan directed the mob to set the building aflame, with African American women and children taking shelter on the third floor, an act that policemen prevented by extinguishing the fire as the crowd pelted them with stones and brickbats.[7]

Determining who made up the Watson tobacco factory mob and why the mob assembled is important, for answers to these questions reveal how the labor competition critique of emancipation fueled Irish-American violence against Black Northerners in 1862 and 1863. Testimony from the factory's owner, who had demanded police protection of his property before August 4, suggests that the mob was not organized spontaneously. Of the eight members of the mob brought to trial, seven were Irish-born, and three of these were laborers, while descriptions of the mob's size ranged from a few hundred to more than two thousand. Newspaper reports portrayed the mob as Irish, and reports of rioters' accents ("burn the naygurs" and "turn out the nagers") also suggest a strong Irish-American presence. In sum, Patrick Keenan, the grog shopkeeper who led the mob, rallied hundreds of Irish immigrants as New York's Democratic press predicted the "extermination" of African Americans in the North.[8]

Only by following coverage of labor violence from 1862 to 1863 can a full explanation of why Irish immigrants attacked the Watson tobacco factory in August 1862 emerge. Thomas Watson had employed Black and white workers without trouble since the mid-1850s. Contemporaries were therefore baffled by the suddenness of the riots, with some blaming excessive drinking at nearby grogshops and others claiming that Confederate agents were responsible. Yet a brief article in the *New York Times* on June 14, 1863, reveals that the August 1862 scene on Sedgwick Street was likely little different from similar violence in the West. "Longshoremen," the *Times* reported in June 1863, were "congregat[ing] in large numbers about the docks and street corners" of Brooklyn, and "as the colored women were leaving Lorrilard's tobacco factory in Sedgwick-street, they were attacked by a gang" of idle dockworkers. An identical scenario had no doubt occurred in August 1862 when longshoremen's work was uncertain at best and jobless immigrant laborers convened in groggeries along the Brooklyn docks. With Union war policies and self-liberated men and women eroding slavery and Democrats raising the prospect of labor competition, Patrick Keenan likely had little trouble whipping up a mob of unemployed Irish-born dockworkers in the grogshops near the East River.[9]

Amid the spate of Irish-American labor violence in the summer of 1862, editors and prominent Irish Americans doubled down on the labor competition critique of emancipation. The *Freeman's Journal* observed on August 16 that the "commotions that have followed a very trifling interference with Southern labor, show what would follow on a more general emancipation." The *Pilot* still backed the war to restore the Union. However, it also embraced the labor competition argument in a mid-August article entitled "Rights of White Labor over Black."

The article asserted that the Union cause was of the utmost importance, but so was preventing freed people from competing against immigrants in the Northern labor market. Archbishop Hughes did not explicitly address the issue of freed people in the labor market in an August 1862 statement on war mobilization. But he cast scorn on factory owners who allegedly shuttered their doors early in the war "to compel Irish and Catholic operatives to enlist," only for these workingmen to find that "other operatives" had filled their former jobs. Hughes surely knew that most Irish-American workers would interpret "other operatives" to mean Black men and women.[10]

To what extent newly emancipated African Americans moved into competition with Irish-American workers in the loyal, free states is not altogether clear. Whatever the number of freed people who left the South during the war, they were never a threat to the position of white laborers. Yet rumors still swirled that Northern industrialists were systematically replacing workers with freed people and European immigrants who would accept depressed wages; by February 1863, the laboring classes of New York City were referring to such men and women as "contrabands." As the Emancipation Proclamation gave the Union war effort a clear-cut antislavery thrust between September 1862 and early 1863, a combination of inflation, semi-employment, and sinking wages yielded still more strikes along the New York waterfront. All the while, antislavery editors inadvertently inflamed the labor critique of emancipation. Horace Greeley's *Tribune*, for instance, tried to assuage workers' concerns by claiming that emancipation would "benefit no class so much as that whose tasks they [freed slaves] assume and whose toils they relieve." For the thousands of Irish immigrants who could barely muster three days of dock work per week and were unacquainted with occupational mobility, such promises no doubt smacked of abolitionist sophistry, as newspapers like the *Freeman's Journal* and virulently anti-emancipation *Metropolitan Record* claimed they were.[11]

Thus, by 1863, the labor competition critique of emancipation was firmly established within the broader Irish-American critique of antislavery. For the considerable number of Irish immigrant laborers who had not enlisted in the Union army or otherwise supported the Union war effort to this point in the conflict, the labor critique of emancipation no doubt offered a compelling case for continuing to withhold their services and sympathies. When the prospect of conscription was added to the equation, resistance became an all too attractive option. But a curious endnote to the Watson tobacco factory fracas reveals the possibility that even some of the most inveterate Irish-American opponents of emancipation in 1862 soon found themselves practically, if not ideologically, aligned with antislavery Unionists. In September, all charges against Patrick Keenan and his co-rioters were dismissed after neither the complainants in the case nor their lawyers appeared at a court hearing. The *New York Times* ended its coverage of the rioters' trial by noting that "the most active participants have since enlisted and are now at the seat of war." This meant that by late September, Irish immigrant laborers who had tried to burn Black workers alive in Brooklyn were fighting for an army whose rank and file had practically become agents of emancipation and under an administration that had signaled the Union's restoration would be accomplished through the destruction of slavery. This ironic conclusion to the Watson tobacco factory riot was a harbinger of even greater changes in how Irish Americans viewed and increasingly took part in the demise of slavery.[12]

Draft Riots and Reaction

In hindsight, the wave of Irish-American violence against Black workers across the loyal states in 1862 was a dress rehearsal for the New York City Draft Riots of July 1863. Between July 13 and 17, 1863, mobs of mostly unskilled Irish laborers responded to the first round of the federal draft by demolishing draft offices, wreaking havoc on war-related infrastructure and symbols of the Republican Party, and butchering Black New Yorkers. The historian Iver Bernstein has argued that the New York City Draft Riots were the most violent episode of a longer conflict in which not just Irish immigrants but also native-born workers and the city's "best men" struggled to instill their various visions of order over a rapidly changing metropolis. Bernstein's long-term perspective on the riots masterfully disentangles a vortex of urban change in nineteenth-century America, but it can also obscure contemporary reactions to what was essentially an anti-war mob. Many Irish Americans in the Union's armed forces, along with some leading Irish-American journalists and politicians, publicly and privately condemned their riotous countrymen. Soldiers' reactions to the riots, especially, suggest that by mid-1863, the demands of prosecuting the Union war had left Irish Americans divided over immigrants' obligations to and interests in their adopted country.[13]

The catalyst for the New York City Draft Riots was the inauguration of federal conscription of civilians into the military. Following the devastating defeat at Fredericksburg in December 1862, Union recruitment had dwindled by early 1863, leading Congress to pass the Enrollment Act in early March in the hope that the threat of a draft would boost volunteering. The law required states that failed to meet assigned quotas for volunteers to draft men between the ages of twenty and forty-five to fill their vacant ranks. All men in that age group were subject to conscription, including foreigners who had declared their intent to naturalize. A draftee who reported when called and was needed to meet his state's quota could still avoid service by demonstrating a physical or mental disability or proving that he was the sole means of support for a dependent relative. If still liable to be held to service, he could also hire a substitute to fill his quota spot or pay a $300 fee to commute his service. About 46,000 of approximately 776,000 Northern draftees were held to military service, and immigrants, especially those from Ireland, were underrepresented within this class. But working-class Irishmen and their families were privy to none of this knowledge in the spring and summer of 1863. Instead, Democratic editors and the so-called Copperhead, or anti-war, faction of the Democratic Party pointed to the $300 commutation clause as proof that the conflict was a rich man's war but a poor man's fight. Even worse, they claimed, was that draftees fighting in a war of emancipation would hasten their own demise in the labor market by enabling newly freed people to fill their vacant positions.[14]

As the draft riots unfolded across five hellish summer days, the combination of immediate and long-standing circumstances that produced them became clearer. Early on Monday, July 13, gangs of mostly native-born workers closed down shops, factories, and other places of work before a fire company stormed the provost marshal's headquarters, where the selection of names had just commenced, and set the building ablaze. Monday's rioting began primarily as an overt reaction to the draft and a general assault on anything associated with Republican rule, as Seymour Walton, an accountant visiting New York, recorded in his diary. The motley assemblage of rioters "burned all the houses of many of those connected with the obnoxious draft," Walton observed. "They have killed several policemen and as to negroes woe be to the unlucky darkey that falls into their hands." Walton astutely noticed that as Monday's violence progressed, some rioters directed their fury at Blacks and policemen while others, whose sole grievance was the draft's iniquities, helped to repress this newer violence.[15]

From the second day of the riots until their denouement, racist violence carried out by young Irishmen prevailed. Monday's rioters had razed the Colored Orphans' Asylum on Fifth Avenue, a physical symbol of abolitionists' concern for African Americans. But on Tuesday and thereafter, roving gangs of Irish laborers beat, mutilated, and lynched Black men they encountered in the streets or whom they regarded as a threat to the local social order. On Tuesday night, for instance, twenty-one-year-old James Best, an Irish-born laborer, dragged Alfred

Derrickson from his Worth Street home. Derrickson, the son of a Black laborer at a local train depot, was "brutally beaten about the head and breast with an axe until he was feeble" and would have been lynched had a group of Germans in the neighborhood not interceded. Distinct patterns of violence emerged throughout the week. Irish laborers targeted African Americans whom they saw as a threat in the workplace or neighborhood, while skilled, industrialized workers attacked African Americans whom they associated with the draft and its Republican overseers.[16]

While the brutal racist violence carried out by Irish Americans during the draft riots had a long history, its manifestation in July 1863 is best understood in the context of the war. Longshoremen led the carnage, and their attacks on Blacks around the waterfront and surrounding neighborhoods continued a pattern evident since the summer of 1862. Irish longshoremen went on strike, merchants hired Black workers as substitutes, and the strikers attempted to drive Black men and their families from the wharves. Such violence had important antecedents in antebellum Manhattan, but since the summer of 1862, racist Irish-American labor violence had escalated there and across the North. In the weeks preceding the riots, Irish-American newspapers reported on Irish-led violence against African Americans in Newburgh and Buffalo. This surge in anti-Black violence between the summer of 1862 and the summer of 1863 tracked with the antislavery thrust of the Union war effort. Irish-born stevedores and cartmen could see just as well as Irish-American editors and Democratic operatives that the war was ushering in slavery's demise. When those editors and operatives told them time and time again that white laborers would end up on the losing end of this dramatic shift in the national labor market, thousands of Irish-American workers lashed out against both the visible manifestations of the Union war effort and the Black men, women, and children who they had been told would soon supplant them. The *Freeman's Journal*'s August 1862 threat of "extermination" was brought to its logical conclusion.[17]

Yet many Irish Americans outside of New York City, and more than a few Irish-born New Yorkers, saw things from a different perspective than their riotous countrymen. Rather than perceiving the Union war effort's emancipatory shift as an existential threat, Irish-American Unionists maintained that reuniting the nation was worth any cost or sacrifice, up to and including the destruction of slavery. Irish-American soldiers, especially, remained steadfast in their devotion to the prosecution of the war and restoration of the Union. The stories of Colonel Robert Nugent, a provost marshal whose home was ransacked during the riots, and Colonel Henry O'Brien, who was murdered while battling the rioters, reveal fissures among the American Irish over these issues. Irish-American soldiers' reactions to the riots indicated that immigrants who opposed the draft were fundamentally at odds with their countrymen in the army over the war's meaning.

A native of Kilkeel in County Down, Colonel Nugent began the war as an officer in the 69th New York and commanded the regiment when he was shot in the groin at Fredericksburg late in 1862. The War Department assigned him to the unenviable position of acting assistant provost marshal during his recuperation in New York, leaving Nugent responsible for enforcing the draft in Manhattan and Long Island. When rioting began on Monday, Nugent's duties expanded to restoring law and order. Both of Nugent's tasks made him an enemy to the discontented, and on the first night of the riots, a furious mob looted his Eighty-Sixth Street apartment. The mostly Irish-born rioters threw the tattered flag of the 69th New York out a window, stole a sword given to Nugent by an antebellum Irish-American militia unit, and ran knives through photographs of Nugent and Irish Brigade commander Thomas Francis Meagher in their Union army uniforms. Had Nugent been at his apartment, he would have shared the fate of his portrait, but he escaped the mob's fury and later assumed command of the Irish Brigade in November 1864.[18]

Colonel O'Brien, born in Ireland around 1823, was less fortunate than his comrade and countryman, Colonel Nugent. While little of O'Brien's background other than his Irish birth can be gleaned from surviving sources, by July 1863, he was a veteran officer and newly appointed colonel of the 11th New York. The first day of the riots found O'Brien home in New York to recruit men for his regiment. When the second day of violence erupted on Tuesday, O'Brien volunteered himself and 150 of his recruits to subdue the rioters; he was sent to Second Avenue and Thirty-Fourth Street to do so. Details of O'Brien's pacification efforts are murky, but as he dispersed the Second Avenue mob, an errant shot from one of his soldier's guns killed two-year-old Ellen Kirk and possibly her mother. In response, the mob descended on O'Brien's home, ransacking much of its contents. As he inspected the damage to his house later in the day, O'Brien was confronted by straggling vigilantes and, after brazenly walking into a crowd that gathered around him, beaten to death over the course of six hours. At various points, O'Brien was bludgeoned about the head with a paving stone, dragged by the legs through the streets, and hanged from a lamppost. Though his face was "nearly one mass of gore, while the clothes were also saturated with the crimson fluid of life," he continued to draw labored breaths. An Irish-American priest, Father Clowry, convinced the mob to let him bring O'Brien indoors for the rite of extreme unction, but the mob dragged O'Brien's mangled body back out into an alley and tried to burn it. Only Father Clowry's efforts saved the colonel's corpse from the fire.[19]

What happened to Colonels Nugent and O'Brien was the result of their respective roles in the Union war effort and its relationship to emancipation. As New York's provost marshal, Nugent was empowered by the Conscription Act to force immigrant workers into an army that many believed would flood the labor market with freedmen. By looting icons of the Union war effort, such as the 69th New York's flag, a sword, and photographs of officers in uniform, the rioters were, in essence, absconding with the instruments and mementos of an antislavery army. Given that O'Brien and his soldiers directly targeted the rioters and that they very likely killed innocent bystanders, explaining the mob's brutal treatment of him requires less abstraction. Yet the rioters' handling of O'Brien was also eerily similar to the ritualistic violence inflicted upon Black New Yorkers. It was no coincidence that O'Brien's fate mirrored that of lynch-mob victims during the riots, for in the mob's eyes, a Union soldier fighting a war for emancipation was just as much a threat to the unskilled worker's position in the labor market as a Black man himself. While Robert Nugent and Henry O'Brien were exceptional in terms of Irish Americans' overwhelming involvement in the draft riots as rioters, their stories serve as reminders that while the riots unfolded in New York, tens of thousands of Irish-American soldiers remained under arms as practical agents of emancipation.

Some Irish-American soldiers had come out in favor of the draft well before the first names were pulled in July 1863, and in the days, weeks, and months after the riots, many Irish-American soldiers and civilians scorned the rioters. Some simply wished to avoid being tainted by the stain of disloyalty, one that nativists were quick to apply to the entirety of Irish America in the aftermath of the draft riots. Yet many Irish Americans who expressed their bewilderment and chagrin over the actions of Irish-born rioters in New York simultaneously affirmed their support for the Union war effort, including both emancipation and conscription. Rarely registering in standalone works on Irish Americans in the Civil War era and unmentioned in broader treatments of the war, loyal Irish Americans' condemnations of the draft riots were indicative of a persistent Unionist sentiment within the ranks. In official resolutions, private letters to friends and family, and published letters in Irish-American newspapers, Irish-born soldiers insisted that conscription was a necessary policy that would help restore the Union.[20]

Reactions to the draft riots from officers in the 69th New York illuminate efforts by soldiers to reassert Irish Americans' support for the Union cause in mid-1863. A distinguished antebellum militia unit, the 69th New York consisted almost entirely of Irish immigrants or second-generation Irish Americans. When the news of the riots reached the unit in Baltimore, a group of officers in the regiment drew up resolutions in response. They acknowledged that blame for the riots had been "imposed on the citizens of Irish birth, with whom this regiment as a body . . . is proud to be identified." But, they continued, Irish Americans had "shown themselves to be earnest, fearless, and self-sacrificing supporters of the laws and institutions of these United States." The charge that the rioters represented immigrants as a whole, they continued, was "unjustly made by the enemies of our race and ourselves." The officers asked to be "ordered to New York to . . . aid in repressing the violence and disorder which now afflict the people of that (our own) city." Although the 69th's colonel formally requested that his men be sent home to aid in the suppression of the riots, that request was turned down by the regiment's departmental commander. Still, the 69th's officers had made their point. Irish-American soldiers would continue to fight to reunite the country, even if it meant combatting fellow Irishmen in the streets of Manhattan.[21]

Crucial Union victories at Gettysburg and Vicksburg only days before the draft riots sharpened Irish-American soldiers' criticisms of the rioters. Writing from his camp with the 1st Connecticut Heavy Artillery in Virginia on July 14, Country Leitrim native John O'Brien presumed that "all are overjoyed at the news from our armies" but noted bitterly that "New York is acting a part which does not reflect much credit on its law-abiding citizens. I sincerely hope," O'Brien concluded, "that the leaders in those riots will suffer death and that none of the guilty wretches will be shielded from justice." Peter Welsh of the Irish Brigade's 28th Massachusetts argued that "even the disaffected of New York" would have to admit Union armies' progress after victories at Gettysburg, Vicksburg, and Port Hudson. "A pretty time they are getting up," Welsh wrote of the rioters, "when one unanimous efort might finish up this accursed war in a few weeks. . . . every leader and instigator of those riots should be made an example of. . . ." Welsh knew that Irish Americans were responsible for the riots but still advocated the use of "grape and canister" to mow the rioters down. Like John O'Brien, Welsh was disgusted by the rioters' attempt to hinder the Union war just as it gained momentum on the battlefield.[22]

Irish-American soldiers continued to denounce draft resisters in the months after the riots, an indication that these initial reactions emanated from a deep commitment to prosecuting the war rather than a fleeting sense of outrage or embarrassment. Michael Donlon, a famine immigrant whose family settled in Groton, Massachusetts, in 1849, was chagrined to read reports of draft resistance in Boston that also involved Irish immigrants. As his unit replenished its diminished ranks after months of hard fighting, Donlon inquired of a brother whether "they take the draft good at home" and closed his letter with a postscript: "Please write soon and enforce the draft." More expansive in his support for conscription was County Limerick native Edmund O'Dwyer, another famine immigrant whose family had settled in Rochester, New York, in the early 1850s before Edmund made his way to Chicago before the start of the war. O'Dwyer had been one of the first soldiers to enlist in the Irish-American 23rd Illinois; in September 1863, he asserted in a letter to his brother, Thomas, that "[e]very government has the right to compel its citizens to bear arms for the common welfare." O'Dwyer excoriated Democratic New York governor Horatio Seymour for "doubting the constitutionality of the draft, for there should be no such questions raised." Other Irish-American soldiers were more vindictive in prescribing solutions to draft resistance. Michael MacNamara, one of two brothers who helped to organize the Irish-American 9th Massachusetts Regiment in 1861, claimed that when his comrades learned of New York's riots, "how heartily [they] wished for a chance to . . . show them how the Irish Ninth could charge." The men contented themselves instead with "maledictions to the copperheads." For these Irish-American soldiers, the draft not only carried legal sanction but also merited physical enforcement if necessary.[23]

By mid-1863, earlier divisions among Irish Americans over how to subdue the Confederate rebellion had materialized into two distinct positions on whether or not the war should be continued. Critically, both perspectives were rooted in particularly Irish-American concerns, even if they meshed with broader Northern opposition to and support for the war to restore the Union. Most anti-war Democrats, or Copperheads, came to oppose the war in 1863 and thereafter on the grounds that Republican-initiated war measures—namely, Lincoln's suspension of *habeas corpus*, the Emancipation Proclamation, and conscription—exceeded constitutional bounds and therefore delegitimized the Union war effort. By contrast, Irish Americans who came out in opposition to the Union war effort in 1863 tended to focus more on how it had exacerbated their circumstances as unskilled, low-paid workers. Conversely, many loyal Democrats insisted that the war had to be prosecuted to a successful conclusion but maintained that victory—defined as the restoration of the Union—was only desirable if attained through a limited war that could engender a speedy reunion. But especially in the wake of the draft riots, as nativists rushed to brand Irish Catholics as traitors, Irish-American Unionists perceived that they did not have the luxury of qualifying their loyalties. The rioters, New York lawyer and diarist George Templeton

Strong recorded, were "lousy, blackguardly Irishmen." It was no wonder, Strong mused, that St. Patrick drove the snakes out of Ireland, for "its biped mammalia supply that island its full average share of creatures that crawl and eat dirt and poison every community they infest." Responding to such criticisms on behalf of its many Irish-American readers, the Democratic *Chicago Times* insisted that "Roman Catholics have been among the most steady and faithful adherents and supporters of the Union cause. None of our people," the *Times* protested, "have volunteered more freely or fought more bravely than Catholics." Similar sentiments poured forth from the pulpits and presses of Irish-American communities in the summer of 1863 as clergymen and editors joined Irish-born Union soldiers in distancing themselves and their compatriots from the actions of the Irish in New York. In so doing, they emphasized the necessity of an unqualified obedience to federal authority, one that was encapsulated in a post-draft riot pastoral written by the Bishop of Buffalo: "submit to law and God will protect you."[24]

Ireland and the War for the Union in 1863

Yet it would be a mistake to interpret Irish Americans' denunciations of the draft riots and professions of support for conscription strictly as a rearguard action against accusations of disloyalty. After two years of war, Irish-American Unionists were just as convinced as they had been in 1861 and 1862 that preserving the American Republic was vital to the political and economic welfare of Irish people on both sides of the Atlantic and to their hopes for Irish nationhood. On the one hand, this fervent sense of American nationalism was a holdover from the 1850s, when immigrants argued against any interference with slavery lest the nation that gave refuge to the famine immigrants and stood as a potential ally for Irish nationalists be irreparably divided by the slavery issue. On the other hand, developments in Ireland and across the loyal states gave Irish-American soldiers and civilians new reasons to think that the American Republic was truly the last, best hope of the Irish on both sides of the Atlantic. From 1861 to 1863, famine once again stalked the Irish countryside, and relief efforts led by prominent Irish-American civilians found ample support from Irishmen in the Union army. Partly because of such food shortages, immigration to the United States from Ireland rose sharply in 1863, with both the Lincoln administration and the Republican-led Congress signaling their intentions to facilitate this transatlantic movement. Most important to Irish-American soldiers was the rapid growth of the Fenian Brotherhood within the Union's ranks, which convinced many that the day of Ireland's liberation was fast approaching. For these reasons, Irish-American

Unionism was reinvigorated in 1863, a development that proved crucial to Irish-American soldiers' embrace and enforcement of emancipation.[25]

As Northerners braced for the first round of conscription in the spring of 1863, tens of thousands of Irish peasants, along with many of the island's scattered pockets of industrial workers and even some of its more prosperous commercial farmers, wondered where their next meal would come from. After an exceptionally dry year in 1859, prolonged periods of rain in 1860 caused extensive crop failures, especially in hay. Lacking sufficient feed, cattle and sheep herds perished over the winter of 1860-61, dealing a tremendous blow to many strong farmers. Heavy rains returned during the harvest season of 1861, especially in the south and west of Ireland, causing rivers to spill over their banks and submerging fields of potatoes and oats. A mild winter in 1861-62 portended some relief, but although flooding was minimal in 1862, excessive rainfall continued to plague crops. Potatoes were especially vulnerable, for blight thrived in the cool, damp conditions. As if to mock the waterlogged island, dry conditions in the spring of 1863 heralded the return of drought. In that year, yields of oats, wheat, barley, and flax were less than half of what they had been on average between 1856 and 1858, while yields of potatoes, turnips, and hay were down by 40-50 percent. As a group of Irish-American philanthropists said, "Every crop has failed, and there is no part of the country which can be said to be exempt from causes which have been general in their effect." Theirs was no exaggerated lament, for as the historian James Donnelly, Jr., points out, "[M]emories of the ghastly nightmare of the late 1840s were still fresh enough in the early 1860s that when the potato crops failed repeatedly, loud cries of impending mass starvation were quickly raised." In between coverage of the raging conflict in their adopted country, Irish-American editors apprised their readers between 1861 and 1863 of the appalling conditions in their native land.[26]

Responding to reports of economic distress and a looming famine in Ireland, prominent Irish-American jurists, editors, and exiled nationalists mobilized between 1862 and 1863 to organize a relief campaign. The Irish Relief Society was established in Manhattan on May 21, 1862, "to take into consideration the present destitute condition of the Irish peasantry, and the steps properly to be taken for their relief." Some of the organizers of the Irish famine relief campaign that took shape over the coming year were veterans of the 1846-47 famine relief endeavors, and others had come to the United States as exiles from the failed 1848 Young Ireland rebellion. They also represented a curious cross-section of Irish-American opinion on the war to restore the Union. An initial call for relief was put forth in April 1862 by Richard O'Gorman, who had capitalized on his status as an exiled

Young Irelander to win acclaim as a New York lawyer. While O'Gorman parlayed his juridical notoriety into heroic status among anti-war Democrats as a vocal critic of the Lincoln administration, he was joined at the helm of the Irish Relief Society by the Irish-American judge Charles Patrick Daly, whose fundraising for and assistance in recruiting the three New York regiments of the Irish Brigade indicated his deeply Unionist sentiments. O'Gorman's skepticism of the Union war effort paled in comparison to another key figure in the Irish Relief Society, John Mullally. A Belfast native, Mullally edited the vehemently anti-war *Metropolitan Record*; later, in 1863, he was arrested on allegations that he incited participants in the New York City Draft Riots. Counterbalancing O'Gorman and Mullaly's presence on the committee's leadership were John Savage and Patrick Meehan. Like his fellow exile O'Gorman, Savage dodged the hangman's noose in 1848 by going to Manhattan. But unlike O'Gorman, Savage remained a hardened republican nationalist, and when war broke out in 1861, he joined the 69th New York, hoping to acquire military training and experience to put to use in Ireland. By 1863, Savage had returned to civilian life to devote his energies to the affairs of the Fenian Brotherhood. Patrick Meehan, editor of the solidly Unionist *Irish-American*, also took a leading role in New York's famine relief endeavors. In short, Irish famine relief in New York City between the spring seasons of 1862 and 1863 brought together leading Irish-American critics of the Lincoln administration with ardent Irish-American Unionists.[27]

The bulk of the Irish Relief Society's labors unfolded in the winter and early spring months of 1863, a time frame that historians typically interpret as a nadir in Irish-American support for the Union war effort. In late March, the executive board of the Irish Relief Society circulated a call for aid in New York's leading newspapers, one that was picked up by editors across the Union. It detailed the causes of the "impending famine" in Ireland and concluded with an urgent appeal that tugged at the patriotic heartstrings of Irish- and native-born Unionists alike. "We can hope for no response to this appeal," the committee pointed out, "except from that part of the United States now engaged in an earnest struggle to maintain the territorial unity of the nation against the attempt that has been made to dismember it." In other words, only Unionists could rescue Ireland, just as only Unionists could reunite the American Republic. This association between Irish famine relief and the preservation of the Union was a central theme of speeches delivered a few weeks later during a fundraiser sponsored by New York's Knights of St. Patrick. Presided over by the Republican mayor of New York, George Opdyke, the fundraiser was attended by some seven thousand New Yorkers, most of them Irish immigrants, who paid fifty cents each to gain admission. Richard

O'Gorman, a favorite of New York's Peace Democrats, featured prominently in the lengthy lineup of scheduled speakers, and attendees were especially delighted to coax an impromptu speech from George McClellan, the deposed commander of the Army of the Potomac who, over the coming months, would flirt with the anti-war wing of the Democratic Party. Given the depressed state of Irish Americans' morale concerning the war, O'Gorman and McClellan might have been expected to avoid the subject altogether and to urge the crowd to focus its sympathies and energies on the suffering poor in Ireland. Instead, both speakers drew direct connections between preserving the Union and Irish relief. "What is it that enables us now to extend our hands in succor to your brethren across the Atlantic?" McClellan queried before answering his own question. Previous generations, he continued, had established "upon this broad continent one nation, one free government, that might be a refuge for all from foreign lands." To "great cheering," McClellan ended his speech with a line that might have doubled as a recruitment call: "All our energies, all our thoughts, all our means, and if necessary, the last drop of our blood must be given to uphold that unity, that nationality." O'Gorman's speech similarly played up the interdependence of the United States and Ireland. "The union between Ireland and America," he declared, "increases day by day; there is not a ship that crosses the ocean from an Irish to an American port, but is as the shuttle weaving in closer and firmer ties the destinies of these two nations, now and forever united." Only weeks before the draft riots, these two critics of the Union war effort—one a famed Irish-American exile and the other a darling of Irish-American soldiers and newspaper editors—tapped into key elements of Irish-American Unionism as they tried to stir the passions of a predominantly Irish-born crowd in Manhattan.[28]

It should be no surprise to find that Irish-American soldiers attached great importance to the cause of famine relief in 1863. In response to the *Irish-American*'s pleas for donations, soldiers and sailors sent contributions to the Irish Relief Society that typically ranged between $1 and $5, with some larger donations, like the $1,240 collected by the Irish Brigade's chaplain, Father William Corby, arriving on behalf of entire units. At least 870 Union soldiers and sailors, the majority of them Irish Americans, contributed directly to the famine relief campaign in the spring and early summer of 1863. Additionally, two colonels of Irish-American regiments sold pamphlets containing the Irish Relief Society's appeal for donations, allowing the rank and file to learn about the causes of Ireland's food shortage and reminding them that relief could only come from "that part of the United States now engaged in an earnest struggle to maintain the territorial unity of the nation." The Irish famine relief campaign of 1863 gave Irish-American servicemen further proof that the United States was singularly capable of giving succor to Irish men and women. In turn, their donations confirm the judgment rendered by the Irish Brigade's commander, General Thomas Francis Meagher, at the Academy of Music fundraiser. On leave as he battled a bout of rheumatism, Meagher's speech extolled the accomplishments of the men under his command and emphasized that their devotion to Ireland was part and parcel with their allegiance to the Union. "[T]he Irish soldier, fighting the battles of the United States," Meagher thundered to great applause, "never ceases to think of the land that bore him, and the claims which her misfortunes, as well as her grand aspirations, have sacredly and eternally imposed upon him."[29]

A significant uptick in immigration to the United States from Ireland in 1863 also shored up Irish-American Unionists' vision of the American Republic as a haven for oppressed and impoverished Irish people. After the crop failures of 1860, 1861, and 1862, a comparatively stronger harvest in 1863 afforded many prospective immigrants the funds they needed for the transatlantic passage. Added to this was the introduction of a new line of Cunard steamships whose voyages between Liverpool and New York included a stop in Dublin's port, Kingstown, and whose fares were competitive. As a result, more than 94,000 Irish immigrants disembarked at northern ports in 1863, nearly tripling the roughly 33,000 arrivals of the previous year. From Connaught, one of the most severely affected regions, the *Western Star* reported in August that "large numbers are still leaving this country for America, notwithstanding the disturbed state of society beyond the Atlantic." American consuls in Ireland were flooded with requests for draft-exempt certificates, indicating that many emigrants saw the potential to find economic stability in the loyal states without depending on enlistment bounties or military pay. To be sure, cases in which unscrupulous Union agents duped Irishmen into the army with promises of high pay and exorbitant bounties were widely reported in the Irish press, especially by Confederate-sympathizing newspapers like the Dublin *Nation* and the *Cork Examiner*. But in the pages of the *Galway-American*, *Dundalk Democrat*, and Dublin *Irishman*, Union-supporting editors attempted to squash such accounts, whether real or fictional. Early in 1864, the *Irishman* published President Lincoln's recent message to Congress in which he pledged that newly arrived immigrants would not be pressed into military service.[30]

This surge in wartime immigration bolstered Irish-American soldiers' belief that the American Union served as a haven for the Irish poor. Take, for example, the 28th Massachusetts's Peter Welsh, who enlisted in the Union army in 1862 to avoid the wrath of his wife and father-in-law after a drunken "spree" in Boston.

Despite the ignoble circumstances of his enlistment, Welsh wrote with immense pride about his service in letters home to his wife, Margaret, and her father, often making an explicit connection between his soldiering and the fate of his countrymen and women in Ireland. In a February 1863 letter to Margaret, Welsh shuddered to think of "the condition to day of hundreds of thousands of the sons and daughters of poor oppressed old erin if they had not a free land like this to emigrate." Moreover, Welsh continued, "the same may be said of thousands from other lands and especialy of the opressed states of jermay [sic]." The thought of the Union's permanent severance, Welsh concluded, left him convinced that "there is yet something in this land worth fighting for." O'Dwyer of the 23rd Illinois similarly thought it impossible in late 1863 for Irishmen to be "idle spectaters [sic]" in the war. "[T]his country afforded us an asylum and facilities for improving our conditions unobtainable in our unhappy country, then, would we be not very ungrateful did we not stand idly by and not assist in defending the flag and the integrity of the country," O'Dwyer queried.[31]

Welsh and O'Dwyer wrote from the perspective of immigrants, making their assessment of the Union's importance to the Irish all the more revealing, but they were by no means alone in this opinion. Recall that the former commander of the Army of the Potomac, George B. McClellan, offered the same sentiments in his speech at the Knights of St. Patrick famine relief fundraiser in New York. "It is unfortunate . . . for Ireland," McClellan told the crowd, "that laws, with the making of which her people had so little to do, and a government in which they have been so little represented, should have compelled so many of them to leave their native land and seek refuge in foreign climes." But, he pivoted as loud cheers erupted in the hall, "the loss of Ireland has been the gain of America." In these lines, the native-born, Protestant, West Point-educated McClellan articulated the importance of the Union in terms that Irish immigrants could readily grasp. Only a few weeks after McClellan's speech, one of the most popular news publications in the Union, *Harper's Weekly*, dedicated its editorial column to the recent increase in immigration. Solidly Republican in its politics, *Harper's* interpreted the phenomenon as a sign that the "working-men of Europe" were throwing their support behind "popular government" and "the cause of the working-man." It was an exaggeration to claim, as the *Harper's* editorial did, that immigrants were animated primarily by an opposition to "the oligarchs of Europe" in their decisions to emigrate. But in associating the interests of "the [European] working-man" with the Union, the magazine was on firmer ground, a fact that President Lincoln and many Republicans had come to recognize by 1863. In his annual message to Congress that year, Lincoln urged lawmakers to provide "essential, but very cheap, assistance" to prospective immigrants, whom he described as a "source of national wealth and strength." Observing that there were "tens of thousands of persons, destitute of remunerative occupation . . . thronging our foreign consulates," the president argued that Congressionally appropriated funds to assist such men and women could fill the "deficiency of laborers in every field of industry, especially in agriculture and in our mines." Thus, as Irish-American soldiers justified their continued devotion to the Union cause by emphasizing its importance to prospective immigrants, Lincoln justified federal funding for prospective immigrants by emphasizing their importance to the prosperity of the Union.[32]

Lincoln's encouragement of immigration in 1863 was more than a symbolic about-face for the Republican Party. Throughout the war, most Irish-American editors continued to push a key element of the antebellum Irish-American critique of antislavery by insisting that Republicanism and nativism were synonymous. But early in the conflict, Republicans realized immigration could compensate for the shortage of agricultural production that resulted from farmers' enlistments. In response, lawmakers sought to attract Europeans to land west of the Mississippi. After Lincoln urged lawmakers to devise "a system for the encouragement of immigration" in the December 1863 message to Congress, the Republican-majority body responded. On July 4, 1864, Lincoln signed the "Act to Encourage Immigration," which made oceanic transportation for immigrants more affordable and less hazardous. The act stood in sharp contrast with some Republicans' nativist roots and, crucially, encouraged immigration to augment agricultural production rather than to channel immigrants into the Union military. Returning to the subject of immigration in his annual message to Congress in December 1864, Lincoln eloquently described immigration as "one of the principal replenishment streams which are appointed by Providence to repair the ravages of internal war, and its waste of national strength and health."[33] One of the key tenets of antebellum Irish-American Unionism was the notion that the United States was a haven for the oppressed and impoverished of Europe, especially Ireland. The pro-immigration rhetoric and policies put forth by Republican lawmakers in 1863-64 affirmed that notion even as the nation itself remained imperiled.

Perhaps the most consequential development for Irish-American Unionists in 1863, especially for those in the army, was the proliferation of the Fenian Brotherhood. Many Irish-American soldiers had marched off to war in 1861 and 1862, believing their military service would prepare them to take part in Ireland's liberation, an idea often suggested to them by Irish- and native-born recruiters. Of the 115 members of the Fenian Brotherhood circle in Milford, Massachusetts, for example, 80 enlisted in a single company of the 9th Massachusetts Regiment in 1861. Until 1863, the potential for a postwar Irish-American-led rising in Ireland or some other military strike against the British Empire, like an invasion of Canada, seemed remote at best. Fenian leaders on both sides of the Atlantic worried the American conflict would deplete the ranks of republican nationalists, a concern that, for some, grew more intense as casualties piled up with no end to the war in sight. But by 1863, it was undeniable that the Union army not only afforded Irish-American nationalists military training and experience but also the opportunity for recruitment and disciplined organization. For these reasons, and to keep alive the possibility that a reunited American Republic would back Irish-American veterans' plans to liberate their native land, the New York-based leadership of the Fenian Brotherhood threw its support behind the Union war effort. In turn, Irish-American soldiers flocked to the revolutionary organization. By November 1863, the 80 Fenians who originally enlisted in the 9th Massachusetts had grown to some 300 men who intended to end British rule in Ireland, at least according to the head of the Brotherhood's Rappahannock Circle. As the example of the 9th Massachusetts suggests, companies with significant numbers of Irish Americans were readily convertible to Fenian circles. Corcoran's Legion, an Irish-American brigade organized by the Fenian ex-colonel of the 69th New York after his release from Richmond Prison in 1862, became another hotbed of recruitment for the Brotherhood. Perhaps for this reason, John O'Mahony, the Head Centre of the Fenian Brotherhood in America and another key player in the Irish Relief Society of New York, eventually gained a commission as the colonel of a three-month regiment from the Empire State. Late in 1863, the Brotherhood scored another coup when Thomas Francis Meagher, who had resigned his command of the Irish Brigade in May, took the Fenian pledge to "labor . . . for the liberation of Ireland from the yoke of England and for the establishment of a free and independent government on Irish soil." While the American Fenians' backing of the Union war effort was met skeptically in Dublin by the Irish Republican Brotherhood's leader, James Stephens, it generated tremendous excitement among Irish-American nationalists.[34]

Outraged over reports of food shortages and starvation in Ireland and confident their military training and growing numbers had increased their chances of success, some Fenians in the Union army believed 1863 would be a year of action. Among them was Colonel Bernard Mullen of the largely Irish-American 35th Indiana, who was stationed with his unit in Madison, Indiana, to guard against a potential Confederate invasion from Kentucky. Mullen was a leading Fenian, and when in mid-August rumors swirled that his unit would soon be dispatched to the front, members of the Fenian circle that formed around the 35th Indiana requested that he remain in Madison to recuperate from a bout of illness. They also had another thinly veiled agenda. "There is trouble brewing in Ireland," one soldier in the regiment wrote to Indiana governor Oliver Morton, and Mullen's "Irish friends" wanted the colonel ready for action in his native land. Other leading figures in Madison's Fenian circle who were not Union soldiers stated the matter more bluntly. "We are selfish and confess his position in the Fenian Brotherhood is such as to be considered of much importance to us," they informed Governor Morton. "We are as devoted to the Land of Our Adoption, as we will be faithful to the Land of our Birth, the time is near at hand when every Irish Arm and Irish Musket will be required to maintain the American Union and strike for the Nationality of Ireland, and if possible let Colonel Mullen remain with us for the present." Ultimately, the 35th Indiana was deployed to southeast Tennessee, where it sustained heavy casualties at the Battle of Chickamauga in September. While such losses were disheartening to some Fenians, they also demonstrated that many of the tens of thousands of Irish-American Union soldiers in the Brotherhood would be hardened and battle-tested by the war's end. "The bone and sinew are here," Irish Brigade officer David Powers Conyngham informed readers of the *Irish-American* in September. "We have thousands of trained and tried soldiers, whose hearts are full of an undying hatred for England." Other Fenian Union soldiers observed that the British government's dalliance with recognizing Confederate sovereignty left many loyal, native-born Americans with similarly Anglophobic sentiments. Felix Brannigan, an Irish-born soldier from New York, predicted in an 1863 letter to his father in Ireland that after the Union's restoration, the "American Eagle" would "pitch into the hide of the British lion." Brannigan's hopeful prediction of postwar Anglo-American hostilities was shared by Fenian-supporting Irish newspapers like the Dublin *Irishman* and *Dundalk Democrat*.[35]

While Fenian soldiers who anticipated a rising in Ireland in 1863 were to be disappointed, the Brotherhood's continued growth aligned it even more closely with the cause of the Union. In early November 1863, an inaugural convention held in Chicago brought together some 300 delegates representing 63 Fenian circles spread out over twelve states, Washington, D.C., and three federal armies. As the historian Christian Samito points out, the constitution these delegates drafted "consciously tracked tenets of American republicanism," and the resolutions they passed conjoined "America and Fenianism in a global struggle for republicanism." One resolution denounced the "hostile attitude" toward the Union displayed by "the English oligarchy, merchants, and the press" and called for young Fenians to acquire military training in the event of an Anglo-American war. Another resolution declared that American Fenians pledged their "ENTIRE ALLEGIANCE, TO THE CONSTITUTION AND LAWS OF THE UNITED STATES," even though the membership pledge they adopted required new inductees to "labor with earnest zeal for the liberation of Ireland from the yoke of England, and for the establishment of a free and independent government on Irish soil." Rather than an incongruity, the American and Irish allegiances professed by Fenian inductees indicated how the ongoing war had cemented a core tenet of antebellum Irish-American Unionism. Ireland's freedom, Fenians concluded, was inextricably bound up with the fate of the United States. Further evidence of Irish-American Unionism's influence on Fenianism can be found in the more mundane business of the organization's leadership structure. The five-man Central Council elected at the Chicago convention included two officers in the Army of the Potomac, while five of the newly elected state centres also came from the commissioned ranks of the Union army.[36]

Collectively, the famine relief campaign, a steep rise in immigration from Ireland, and the maturation of the Fenian Brotherhood in 1863 gave Irish-American Unionists fresh evidence of the American Republic's importance to Irish men and women on both sides of the Atlantic. Consequently, many Irish-American soldiers grew more determined to subdue the rebellion that threatened to sever permanently their adopted country, even in the face of morale-sapping defeats between December 1862 and May 1863. Writing to Judge Daly in January, the Fenian leader and soon-to-be Brigadier General Michael Corcoran admitted that he was "dispirited on account of the results of late battles" but resolved that his conduct as a soldier was "the same now as I always desired it to be from the commencement of the war." Besides, Corcoran added, his newly raised brigade of Irish-American soldiers was "everything its most ardent friends could desire" and would "do honor to their name and race" when committed to battle. "Fenian," a soldier in the 164th New York and a regular correspondent to the *Irish-American*, informed readers of that newspaper in January that his comrades in Corcoran's Legion "wished to avenge the death of their brothers at Fredericksburgh [sic]." The Irish-American 23rd Illinois Regiment's colonel, James Mulligan, was more downtrodden than Corcoran; the war, he recorded in his diary in January 1863, was being grossly mismanaged by the Lincoln administration. Yet he also expressed a firm resolve to fight on to victory and insisted that adding an entire division of Irish-born soldiers under an Irish-American general could bring about a "Fontenoy . . . upon the Fields of America." Here, Mulligan referenced a 1745 battle in which a brigade of Irish troops fighting under Louis XV played a crucial role in defeating their British foes. Several weeks later, Mulligan again vented in his diary about corruption and ineffective leadership in the capital before reaffirming his commitment to "glorify the purity and the heroism of Washington & his companions" by defeating the rebellion. From the ranks of the 29th Wisconsin at Friar's Point on the Mississippi River, an Irish-born soldier wrote in January that the men in his regiment—a fifth of whom were Irish-born, he claimed—were "very anxious for even a skirmish." Thousands of Irish-American soldiers' spirits were lifted in March when General Meagher organized a massive St. Patrick's Day festival in Falmouth, Virginia. Soldiers chased a soaped pig and competed with each other in wheelbarrow races, potato sack races, and Irish dance contests before enjoying a sumptuous feast that included thirty-five hams, a pig stuffed with boiled turkeys, eight baskets of champagne, ten gallons of rum, and twenty-two gallons of whiskey. A few weeks later, Major John Mahan of the Irish-American 9th Massachusetts wrote to his commanding officer after being slighted for what he believed was an overdue promotion in rank. Mahan requested that he be allowed to serve in a different regiment if his promotion was not forthcoming in the 9th, for he was "determined to remain until this foul Rebellion against the best Government that was ever known was forever crushed."[37]

Even after another disastrous defeat in Virginia at the Battle of Chancellorsville in May, soldiers in Irish-American units continued to express their devotion to the cause for which they fought. Darwin Hickley, an Irish-born surgeon in the 90th Illinois, thanked his state's adjutant general in June for sending another "Surg[eon] for the 90 Reg (Irish Legion) he is not a copper head but gives his whole soul for the prosecution of the war to a successful termination[.]" A few months later, County Leitrim native John O'Brien explained his decision to re-enlist in the army to a correspondent in his hometown of New Haven. O'Brien pointed out that he was owed some $1,200 in combined federal and state bounties, but he saw himself as no mere mercenary. "I have an interest in the cause," O'Brien averred. "I always advocated the great principles of freedom—the idea for which we are fighting—how would it look for me to leave the contest before it was finished. I could not do it." Recent studies that detail desertion rates in Irish-American units bear out the sentiments expressed by individual Irish-American soldiers in their private and published correspondence. One, a study of three "mixed" regiments with large numbers of Irish-born soldiers, found that the overall desertion rate within those regiments was lower than the average Union regimental rate of 10 percent. Soldiers in these units who enlisted or were drafted between May 1862 and May 1864 were less likely to desert than their comrades who had enlisted earlier in the conflict. The latter finding is supported by the second study, which shows that 6 out of every 10 desertions of Irish-born soldiers occurred prior to 1863. Indeed, as the war continued into 1864 and 1865, desertion rates among Irish-born soldiers dropped precipitously. For Irish-American soldiers who remained under arms by the fall and winter of 1863, the necessity of restoring the Union by force was as evident as ever.[38]

Emancipation's Unlikely Advocates

This rejuvenated commitment to reuniting their adopted country led Irish-American soldiers to press for a more vigorous prosecution of the Union war effort throughout 1863. Many not only supported conscription but also enthusiastically enforced the Emancipation Proclamation and welcomed Black men to the Union's ranks. To be sure, these sentiments were shared by most loyal Americans. Dual triumphs at Gettysburg and Vicksburg in early July put much-needed wind in the sails of Unionists' morale. Still, the escape of the Army of Northern Virginia from Pennsylvania, as well as the slumbering volcano that erupted on the home front in the form of the draft riots only days later, revealed that neither Confederate soldiers nor Northern opponents of the war were vanquished. No sooner than they had subsided, concerns over the Union war effort rose in late July and August as reports of a daring raid through Kentucky, Indiana, and Ohio by Confederate cavalryman John Hunt Morgan grabbed headlines. Although Morgan was captured, reports that he and his men were aided by Copperhead sympathizers in Indiana and Ohio outraged loyal Americans. Over the coming weeks and months, the loyalties of Buckeye State residents, in particular, remained in question as the notorious anti-war Democrat Clement Vallandigham made a highly publicized bid for governor. Vallandigham was trounced in the mid-October election, but his candidacy revealed that some unknown but significant portion of the Union's populace desired an end to the war at all costs. A growing segment of native-born, Protestant Union soldiers interpreted these developments and the prolongation of the war as a punishment from God for the sin of slavery, one that could only be expiated through emancipation. Few Irish-American soldiers interpreted events in 1863 through this evangelical Christian prism, but as a result of the reinvigoration of Irish-American Unionism, they arrived at the same conclusion: Slavery, the source of the nation's woes and the cause for which Confederates fought, had to be abolished for the Union to be restored. Throughout the year, then, the Irish in the Union army learned to embrace emancipation and even the more revolutionary measure of Black soldiering as policies that would ultimately hasten the restoration of the Union.[39]

Serving as agents of emancipation was a role that few, if any, Irish-American soldiers envisioned when they enlisted and one that some tolerated only to serve Irish ends. "Fenian," a member of the Corcoran Legion, informed the *Irish-American* in a January 1863 letter from Suffolk, Virginia, that "[t]hirty niggers in a body came here a few days ago, and were delivered to the Provost Marshal. They ran away from their masters on hearing of the millennium Proclamation of the President." This soldier was almost certainly opposed to emancipation, for he signed his letter as "the nigger-government hating, Fenian." Yet his *nom de plume*, "Fenian," suggests that he shared the Brotherhood's belief that the Union's restoration would hasten Irish independence. He therefore accepted and even enforced emancipation only insofar as it aided the Union war effort and, from his perspective, allowed Irish immigrants to redirect their efforts toward the liberation of their homeland. Other Irish-American soldiers who initially feared emancipation would imperil the Union's restoration continued to fight the war. "P.J.D." wrote in February 1863 that the mostly German- and Irish-born soldiers in his regiment enlisted solely for the purpose of "crushing the rebellion and restoring and maintaining the Union in its integrity." He believed the Emancipation Proclamation hindered soldiers' abilities to achieve those tasks but concluded that "not only the men of the 61st, but the entire Army of the Potomac" would continue to "endure all and more than all they have endured." Similar in this regard was Captain Patrick Flynn of the Irish 90th Illinois, who was surprised in March 1863 to read in the *Chicago Post* that he had resigned his commission in protest of the Emancipation Proclamation. Flynn informed the *Rockford Register* that he had not resigned and would not publicly disagree with emancipation, stating he had "raised no issue on that question." "I will faithfully endeavor to do my duty to my country," Flynn declared, "by fulfilling every obligation I owe as an officer and a soldier." Soldiers like P.J.D. and Captain Flynn knew by 1863 that their martial duties required them to enforce the Emancipation Proclamation, regardless of their personal views.[40]

As these examples suggest, many Irish-American soldiers were initially skeptical of emancipation. After all, the vast majority entered the war convinced that any interference with slavery would alienate Southerners from the Union, and for that reason, few were enthusiastic at first about their new roles as de facto emancipators. An incident in the 90th Illinois Regiment in March 1863 reveals that military officials sometimes mistook this skepticism of emancipation as resistance, an understandable reaction in light of Irish Americans' overwhelming opposition to all forms of antislavery before the war. As part of his efforts to raise recruits for the newly formed United States Colored Troops (USCT) regiments, Adjutant General Lorenzo Thomas lectured soldiers under the command of General Ulysses Grant, including soldiers in the 90th Illinois, on the strategic importance of emancipation and Black soldiering. When Thomas called for "*three cheers* for the President's 'war policies' with regard to the negroes," many soldiers in the regiment were conspicuously silent. Outraged, Thomas "ordered every man opposed to [emancipation] to step to the front." Sergeant Michael Meehan stepped forward and declared that he had "never disobeyed an order of my superior officers, and never shall; but I cannot cheer for principles which I—" before Thomas cut him off. While Captain Thomas Barrett was dismissed from the regiment for disparaging Adjutant General Thomas in a published letter that described the incident, the 90th went on to fight in the Vicksburg and Jackson campaigns, while Barrett tried unsuccessfully to regain his commission. For soldiers in the 90th Illinois, emancipation could be tolerated as part of the fight to restore the Union, even if officials like Thomas remained dubious about Irish Americans' commitment to the war.[41]

However, as the war progressed in 1863, Irish Americans with misgivings over liberating enslaved African Americans discovered that enforcing emancipation crystallized the divisions between loyal Americans and traitorous Confederates. James Sullivan, an Irish-born soldier in the 6th Wisconsin, reached this conclusion after helping to free "some thirty-five or forty" enslaved men, women, and children hidden in the garret of three Virginia sisters who had been entertaining Union soldiers. When Sullivan and his comrades raised a ladder to escort the group to the protection of Union soldiers, the sisters' hospitality turned into contempt: "Out of this house, you Northern mudsills," one woman cried, "you infernal Yankee Nigger thieves; you desecrators of southern soil; you cowardly hirelings." Such incidents led Sullivan and other Irish-American soldiers to the realization that the Confederates' war against the Union hinged on their claims to ownership of Black Americans. Indeed, slavery's centrality to Southern society and the Confederate economy was unmistakable to the myriad Irish-born Union soldiers who had never ventured south of New England or New York before 1861. John Dee, a famine immigrant who enlisted in Company I of the 50th Massachusetts Regiment in August 1862, saw firsthand in the summer of 1863 how vital enslaved labor was to the Confederacy's ability to wage war. After his unit helped seize control of Port Hudson in July, Dee's company, which included a handful of Irish-born comrades from the small town of Westborough, Massachusetts, was assigned to bring some 1,000 rebel prisoners upriver to Natchez. There, the Confederate captives were offloaded, and around 1,200 contrabands returned with Dee's unit to the encampment of the 19th Corps. Two weeks later, Dee and his Irish-American comrades in Company I returned to Natchez to "clear out the plantations on both sides of the river. This being effectually done," Dee related after the war, "we again returned, having a boat full of freed negroes."[42]

As the experiences of James Sullivan and John Dee suggest, it was by 1863 obvious to even the most hardened Irish-American critics of abolitionism that slavery was the backbone of the Confederate rebellion. Peter Welsh of the Irish Brigade's 28th Massachusetts Regiment acknowledged in a letter to his wife in February 1863 that many of his fellow Irish-American soldiers remained skeptical of the Emancipation Proclamation. But Welsh, whose letters home brimmed with disdain for abolitionists, had concluded that "if slavery is in the way of a proper administration of the laws and the integrity and perpetuity of this nation then I say away with both slaves and slavery sweep both from the land forever rather then [sic] the freedom and prosperity of a great nation such as this should be destroyed." Moreover, many Irish-born soldiers who had few interactions with African Americans before the war had by now dealt personally with Black men and women as they pushed deeper into the heart of the Confederacy or seen firsthand African American soldiers. For some, these interactions cemented antislavery convictions. Marching with the 9th Massachusetts Regiment near Culpepper, Virginia, in September 1863, Michael MacNamara met an eighty-year-old freedman who told the soldiers that he had been "turned . . . out to graze" by his master upon growing too old to work. MacNamara described the encounter in a postwar history of his regiment, observing that it led him and his comrades to feel "more than ever, in heart and principle, an uncompromising enmity to human slavery." One of those comrades was First Lieutenant Nicholas Flaherty. In 1848, Flaherty and his family left Cork and settled in Boston, where in 1853, at the age of fifteen, he joined the Sarsfield Guards, an Irish-American militia unit. In 1854, Flaherty had turned out with his unit to help return the fugitive from bondage Anthony Burns to a Virginia enslaver. When the war broke out in 1861, Flaherty gave up an opportunity to study law—a rarity for an Irish immigrant in antebellum Boston—in order to enlist in the 9th Massachusetts. Writing to his former legal mentor in September 1863, Flaherty observed that while the Emancipation Proclamation had received "the sanction and approval of the vast majority of the Army," it had less support among soldiers in the "Democratic Ninth." But Flaherty believed that

Irishmen in the 9th could be won over by "a few more exhibitions of bravery and devotion, such as that displayed by the gallant 54th [Massachusetts]," an African American regiment. Such demonstrations would "lead people to the conclusion that after all, a Negro is a <u>human</u>, and has a <u>right</u> to that freedom for the enjoyment which he has <u>proved</u> himself so willing to sacrifice his life." Tellingly, each of the Irish-American converts to antislavery highlighted above also conveyed through their wartime writing or actions a desire to see Ireland gain its independence. Irish-American Unionism exerted a powerful influence on these soldiers' embrace of emancipation.[43]

Nicholas Flaherty's hopes that the valor of Black soldiers might win more converts to antislavery revealed another powerful dynamic in the Irish-American debate over emancipation. By the fall of 1863, tens of thousands of Black men had donned Union blue, and approximately 180,000 African Americans had enlisted by the war's end. Most of them were recently liberated men, and depending on when and where they enlisted, the federal government also promised freedom to their families. Black soldiering accelerated the demise of slavery by not only conferring freedom upon enlistees and their families but also turning freedmen into agents of emancipation as Union soldiers. But it was far from certain that white soldiers would look as favorably on African American soldiering as they had on contrabands working behind Union lines. A letter to the *Irish-American* from an Irish-born soldier in the 164th New York Regiment captured the racist beliefs behind many white soldiers' objections to serving in the same army as freedmen: "A slave your equal!—a negro your superior!—The black man to receive the same pay, the same grub . . . Oh, Mr. Lincoln . . . Retire gracefully to the quiet shades of your home in Illinois." To some Irish Americans, the admission of Black men to the ranks of the Union army strained the limits of their loyalty to the Union cause.[44]

While there were doubtless many Irish-American soldiers who shared the sentiments of the soldier from the 164th New York, there were also dozens—virtually absent from the ample body of scholarship on Irish Americans in the Civil War—who requested or secured commissions in African American regiments. Knowing that Black enlistment would provoke a fierce backlash from racist white Unionists, Union officials decided initially that only white men would be commissioned as officers in Black regiments, the vast majority of which were organized under the purview of the USCT branch of the army. Starting in March 1863, Adjutant General Thomas sought enlisted men and commissioned officers from the field to staff the officer corps of USCT regiments. In Massachusetts, Governor Andrew solicited suitable candidates and fielded dozens of requests from white soldiers eager to be commissioned in one of the state's three African American regiments. The Union's political and military establishment assumed that officers in these regiments would need to be exceptionally well-qualified to account for what they believed to be the inherent deficiencies of Black men as soldiers. Because many of these same officials also had doubts about the qualities of Irish-born soldiers, they eschewed recruiting Irish-American soldiers as officers for Black regiments. Nevertheless, dozens of Irish Americans in the Union army sought commissions in either a USCT regiment or one of the Massachusetts "colored" regiments—the 54th and 55th Massachusetts Volunteer Infantry (Colored) and the 5th Regiment, Massachusetts Cavalry (Colored). Of the 386 white commissioned officers in Joseph Glatthaar's study of the relationship between officers and enlisted men in Black regiments, 6 were born in Ireland. If the ratio of Irish-born to non-Irish-born officers holds true for all of the roughly 7,700 commissioned officers in the Union's Black regiments, then well over 100 Irish immigrants served as officers in these units.[45]

Irish-American soldiers' eagerness to serve as officers in Black regiments came as a pleasant surprise to some contemporaries. Colonel Thomas Wentworth Higginson, who commanded a regiment of freedmen recruited in Florida and South Carolina, informed Governor Andrew in January 1863 that despite "the prejudices which have too often made the Celt and the Negro appear antagonistic races . . . three of my best lieutenants are of Irish birth." Some Irish-American newspaper editors had long suspected Andrew himself of harboring anti-Irish proclivities, and perhaps Higginson's observation aimed to convince the governor that Irishmen could be effective commanders of Black soldiers. His commentary was prescient, for Andrew fielded several requests in 1863 from Irish-American soldiers seeking commissions in one of the state's two African American infantry regiments. From his Bowery Street home in Manhattan, a disabled Irish-American soldier named M. A. Morrissey wrote to Andrew in April, seeking employment as a recruiter for Black soldiers in Boston. That same month, two Irish-born officers from the 164th New York wrote Andrew "on behalf of many others" in the regiment. They asked the governor if he would commission them to raise a regiment of freedmen in Virginia. The officers told Andrew they were impressed by the freedmen's "appearance and soldierly qualities . . . endurance, ready obedience, great tact and their Knowledge of the Country And of the Rebels their late Masters And above all for their unflinching Courage." While their requests were denied, these Irish-American soldiers were evidently more than receptive to Black soldiering, as were several other Irish-born soldiers who wrote to Andrew in 1863, hoping to secure a commission in a Black regiment. This was true even for those who came from Democratic neighborhoods and served in units alongside other soldiers who loathed the thought of having Black comrades.[46]

While there was an element of opportunism in Irish-American soldiers' attempts to gain commissions in African American regiments, their readiness to serve in Black units signaled a fundamental shift in how some Irish Americans perceived slavery's relationship to the Union. That shift is strikingly evident in the story of Christopher Plunkett. In December 1860, the Irish-born Boston resident organized a mob to disrupt a memorial service held to commemorate the one-year anniversary of John Brown's hanging. Plunkett's mob stormed the stage of Boston's Tremont Temple, interrupting a speech by Frederick Douglass with chants of "Down with the nigger!" But by January 1864, Plunkett was a first lieutenant in the 9th Massachusetts Regiment, having served with the unit since the first months of the war. With several other junior officers, Plunkett wrote to Governor Andrew to obtain "command of a mounted regiment of colored men," perhaps hoping that Andrew would form a second Black cavalry unit to complement the 5th Massachusetts Colored Cavalry. Eager for Andrew to assent to their request, the men procured an endorsement from Senator Henry Wilson. While there is no conclusive evidence regarding Plunkett's views on race and equality at this point in the war, indirect evidence can be found in postwar regimental histories written by two brothers who joined him in seeking commissions from Governor Andrew. Michael and James MacNamara's accounts of the 9th Massachusetts Regiment are replete with the elements of Irish-American Unionism in their descriptions of soldiers' motivations and the unit's identity. If Plunkett's views in any way resembled those of his comrades, his commitment to the Union war effort stemmed in large part from a belief that the American Republic was singularly capable of uplifting Irish men and women. Thus, the leader of an anti-abolitionist mob in 1860 could, by 1864, seek the opportunity to march into battle alongside formerly enslaved Black men.[47]

Yet even the most zealous Irish-American proponents of emancipation had grown accustomed to a society in which their skin color conferred power over Black Americans, a dynamic that was all too apparent in the case of Jacob Moore. A dark-haired, gray-eyed laborer who emigrated from Waterford in 1850, Moore joined the 23rd Kentucky Regiment in October 1861 under the alias John Kingston to avoid detection by his father, who opposed the war. According to Kingston, his antislavery convictions subjected him to verbal abuse from his Kentuckian comrades. As a result, he sought a place in one of the two Black regiments organized in Massachusetts. Writing in April 1863 to one of

Governor Andrew's aids, Kingston claimed to see in the enlistment of African Americans "the hope of peace, and Union (on the only grounds on which peace and Union are worth preserving) for my beloved Country on the principles of equal rights to all men." Kingston even claimed that it "matters not to me whether the man who command be of darker hue than I am" and promised his "cordial and prompt obedience" to his superior officer regardless of skin color. The War Department was not about to open the commissioned ranks to Black men, so Kingston gained his sought-after commission as a second lieutenant in the 55th Massachusetts in May. But like many other white officers in Black regiments, Kingston believed that the men under his command required severe discipline to be turned into an effective fighting force. During a training exercise south of Boston in July, Private Benjamin Hayes refused to follow an order from Kingston. Determined to make an example of Hayes, Kingston shot him on the spot, severely wounding the private. Hayes's comrades were outraged and "determined to revenge the shooting," prompting Kingston to flee from the regiment's training ground while the soldiers pelted him with rocks. Realizing his position in the regiment was untenable, Kingston tendered his resignation to Colonel Nathaniel Hallowell, though he insisted that he remained committed to the "advancement of the cause of Freedom, [and] the elevation of an injured and despised race." Hallowell informed Governor Andrew that Kingston "did what he had a right to do" as an officer reprimanding an insubordinate soldier and would not face a court-martial, but he accepted the resignation because Kingston was "a rough, swearing fellow and withal an Irishman which in the eyes of colored men is a crime."[48]

Given the long history of Irish-American violence against African Americans—a history that was fresh in mind in July 1863 in the aftermath of the New York City Draft Riots—the Black men who trained under Kingston were understandably suspicious of the Irishman's regard for their well-being. When Kingston shot one of their brothers in arms, that suspicion turned into outrage; whatever possibility there was for the Irish-born Kingston to lead the Black rank and file in the 55th Massachusetts vanished the moment he pulled the trigger on Private Hayes. While it is tempting to frame this incident squarely within a history of antagonistic relations between Irish immigrants and African Americans, doing so would leave the picture incomplete. Kingston's Unionist sentiments were genuine—he went on to serve in another unit for the duration of the war—and there is no indication that his professed opposition to slavery was false. His shooting of Private Hayes stemmed partially from a widely shared racist assumption among white officers in Black units that discipline had to be severe to be effective, but it was also a horrific manifestation of Moore's intertwined hopes of restoring the Union and ending slavery. Like the dozens of other Irish-born soldiers who sought commissions in African American regiments, Kingston concluded that Black soldiering could turn the tide of the war for the Union—but only if the soldiers themselves were disciplined and obedient to their commanders. Under the influence of this mixture of racism and patriotism, Kingston—an Irish-born abolitionist from a slave state—shot Private Hayes in a vain attempt to intimidate the Black men under his command and make them more effective Union soldiers and emancipators.

By the end of 1863, many Irish-American soldiers had redoubled their support for the Union cause and embraced emancipation, albeit with various degrees of enthusiasm. These developments resulted from a combination of events within the war itself, like victories at Gettysburg and Vicksburg or resistance to conscription, and circumstances that uniquely shaped Irish immigrants' perspectives on the war, including the reports of an impending famine in Ireland, increased immigration from the island, and the growth of Irish-American nationalism in the army. Irish-American opponents of the war also acted based on how the war's effects blended with their concern as immigrants that unskilled labor was besieged by newly freed Black men. Although they reached drastically different conclusions, Irish-American workers in Northern cities and soldiers in the Union army gauged the war's meanings and consequences from an immigrant's perspective. While the Irish-American critique of antislavery reached its dreadful conclusion in the New York City Draft Riots, Irish-American Unionism spurred growing numbers of soldiers to embrace any and all measures to subdue the rebellion and restore the Union, including both emancipation and Black soldiering.

It remained to be seen how Irish-American newspaper editors, clergymen, and politicians would respond to and try to frame the actions of their countrymen who rioted in the streets of New York or welcomed their newfound roles as emancipators in Southern climes. Unlike the wage earners in New York who feared that emancipation would rob them of their tenuous position in the labor market or the soldiers in Virginia or the Mississippi River Valley who witnessed firsthand the transformative effects of emancipation on the war effort, these influential figures in the Irish-American community had few intimate experiences with the process of emancipation. Instead, they considered how Irish immigrants' long-standing opposition to all types of antislavery and the more immediate Irish-American resistance to the Union war effort in New York might affect the status of the Irish in America in light of the fact that the restoration of the Union was now seemingly contingent on the destruction of slavery. Many of these influential Irish Americans on the home front came around to support emancipation, concurring with Irish-born soldiers who viewed it as nothing more and nothing less than a measure that would redound to the benefit of the Union. But given their distance from the war and their elevated status among the American Irish, the Irish-born journalists, clerics, and politicians who embraced emancipation in the latter half of the war did so for different reasons than their countrymen under Union arms.

7   "All true Republicans": Irish-American Leaders and Emancipation

Mass emancipation and the abolition of American slavery were never guaranteed outcomes of a war that the vast majority of loyal Americans fought to reunite the nation. Freedom was contingent on the progress of Union armies whose victories allowed wartime emancipation to take effect and who, by eventually vanquishing their Confederate foes, ensured that the abolition of slavery could be enforced. Between January 1, 1863, when the Emancipation Proclamation went into effect, and April 1865, when the Army of Northern Virginia surrendered, were several critical junctures at which the Union faced the distinct possibility of defeat, even as late as the summer of 1864. But by mid-1863, emancipation was part and parcel with the war to restore the Union, and it was increasingly difficult for white Unionists to envision the war's end without some form of emancipation. In short, emancipation was of secondary importance to restoring the Union for most loyal Americans during the Civil War. But the longer the war continued, the harder it was to conceive of that Union with slavery intact.[1]

While most white Unionists had to be convinced that the preservation of the republic was incompatible with the preservation of chattel slavery, Irish Americans' transatlantic perspective on the fate of the American Union led them to embrace emancipation for singular reasons. Irish-American soldiers first realized the utility of emancipation as a strategic advantage in their war against the Confederate rebellion. Expressed in private and public correspondence, their change of opinion influenced Irish Americans on the home front whose commitment to restoring the Union was no less palpable than that of soldiers. Especially after the New York City Draft Riots of July 1863, in which Irish immigrants demonstrated the extremes to which anti-emancipation sentiment could take them, Irish-American clergymen, editors, and nationalist leaders followed the lead of Irish-American soldiers who learned to accept and even abet the liberation of enslaved African Americans. However, as these Irish-American leaders explained to their immigrant countrymen and women, as well as newspaper editors and nationalist leaders in Ireland, how and why they found themselves in agreement with abolitionists and antislavery legislators, they focused less on military logic and more on how Irish interests might be served by embracing emancipation.

Between 1863 and 1865, three influential arguments emerged as Irish-American Unionists explained why they had abandoned a long-standing opposition to all varieties of antislavery. One line of reasoning came from Irish-American Catholic clergymen and laymen who claimed their faith had a lengthy history of opposition to slavery, allowing Irish immigrants to come around on emancipation based on their religious beliefs. Second, to convince the laboring classes of emancipation's benefits, Irish-American journalists pointed out that the absence of slavery in the South could open up the region's land to Irish immigrants and their descendants who would otherwise be confined to the North's urban slums. Finally, Irish-American nationalist leaders argued that emancipation would help to once and for all reunite the American Republic so that the Irish in America could devote their energies to establishing an Irish Republic, one whose liberation from Great Britain might be aided by sympathetic and grateful loyal Americans. Some went so far as to argue that ending slavery would make the United States an even more worthy model for would-be republics like Ireland.

While no single Irish-American argument for emancipation was decisive, each one rested on the assumption that the intertwined fates of American slavery and the American Union had unique and transatlantic repercussions for the Irish. Because the Irish were Catholics, because Ireland would continue to send large numbers of poor, unskilled laborers to the United States, and because Irish independence hinged on America's survival as a nation, Irish Americans should support the end of American slavery. By 1865, Irish-American Unionists had reached a starkly different conclusion about the future of American slavery in their adopted country than that which they held for most of the preceding two decades. But the dénouement to Irish Americans' involvement in the slavery debate was also marked by continuity. Immigrants' backgrounds in and connections to Ireland, as well as their distinctive circumstances in the United States, continued to influence what they thought about the future of American slavery. As a critical mass of loyal Americans and enslaved men and women themselves resolved that a more perfect Union would emerge from the nation's internecine conflict, Irish-American religious, civil, and nationalist leaders maintained that the Union was singularly capable of uplifting their countrymen and women in both the United States and Ireland.

"Facts, just or unjust, are against us":
Irish-American Catholics and Emancipation

The Emancipation Proclamation confronted Irish Catholics in the North with two critical questions: could they justify support for emancipation when Church leaders had so forcefully opposed abolitionism, and if so, how? Led by the Reverend Edward Purcell, an Irish-born editor of the Cincinnati *Catholic Telegraph*, many Irish-American Catholics responded to the emancipatory shift in the Union war effort by recovering an antislavery tradition within the Roman Catholic Church. These writers generally ignored Irish-American Catholics' overwhelming support for slavery before the war or explained away this past by arguing that the American Catholic hierarchy had acted in the interests of preserving the Union. Still, Irish Americans who, in newspaper columns and from Northern pulpits, celebrated a tradition of emancipatory Catholicism gave faithful Irish immigrants who were otherwise skeptical of emancipation reason to support the Union war effort from 1863 onward. This was a critical development that has been largely ignored by historians of the American Irish in the Civil War.[2]

By the time the Emancipation Proclamation took effect, leading Irish-American clergymen and Catholic journalists were sharply divided over not only the future of American slavery but also the prolongation of the war itself. Prominent clerics like Archbishop Hughes of New York had initially supported the Union war effort because secession was an act of defiance against an established, legitimate source of authority. Irish-American Catholics' military service and support for the restoration of the Union, they reasoned, might also dull the edges of anti-Catholicism. But by 1863, some questioned if the Lincoln administration had exceeded constitutional limits of power. Irish-born John Mullaly's *Metropolitan Record*, the official newspaper of the Archdiocese of New York, lampooned emancipation as an illegal abolitionist folly and prophesied the collapse of the Union war effort through 1865. While Mullaly was the most stridently anti-war Irish-American Catholic journalist, others like Patrick Donahoe of the *Pilot* and the Sadlier brothers of the *New York Tablet* occasionally joined him in denouncing measures like conscription or charging that a hidden abolitionist agenda hindered the progress of Union arms. Still, Irish-American bishops were leery of stoking the coals of anti-Catholic nativism; anxious to avoid charges of disloyalty, they offered only tepid criticisms of the Union war effort and were more likely to pray for peace than a Confederate victory. Moreover, a pro-war, anti-Republican segment of Irish-American Catholic editors attempted to maintain their Unionist credentials. The influential Donahoe, for example, was a War Democrat who wavered between stinging rebukes of Lincoln and the Republican Congress's handling of the war and fervent expressions of Unionism—sentiments echoed by the Sadliers in New York. Importantly, a minority but not an insubstantial segment of the Irish-American Catholic press urged its readership to see the war to restore the Union through to the end, even if that meant endorsing a policy of mass emancipation.[3]

A first step toward reconciling Irish Americans with emancipation was dissociating their faith from the traitorous, proslavery deeds of draft rioters. Archbishop Hughes's reaction to the riots provided a prominent example for Irish-American Catholic critics of the rioters, for Hughes chastened the rioters for their lawlessness soon after the riots began. He also delivered a speech as the riots tapered off that dwelled on immigrants' miserable backgrounds in Ireland, urging listeners to reflect on the comparative bounties they found in America and to support Unionists' efforts to reunite the country that took in the impoverished Irish. Other Irish Americans pointed out that the Church had sided with the government during the riots and that several New York clergymen had come to the aid of Black New Yorkers. The Sadliers' *New York Tablet* proudly noted that several Irish Catholic priests prevented rioters from burning buildings near churches. A Father Treanor, in particular, "saved a whole family of coloured people whom the mob were about to hang" by hiding them in the basement of the Transfiguration Church in Manhattan's Five Points neighborhood. "Gotham," a New York City Irishman and contributor to the Cincinnati *Catholic Telegraph*, reported that clergy members had helped prevent destruction of property. At least one Irish-born nun, Sister Ulrica O'Reilly, confronted rioters as they attempted to raze a hospital in Central Park. "Gotham" also noted that "[s]everal of the unfortunate negroes found a refuge in our churches" during the riots. Even Mullaly's avowedly racist and anti-emancipation *Metropolitan Record* tried to distance Irish-American Catholics from the racist violence perpetrated by the rioters, blaming abolitionists for bringing African Americans "out of their proper sphere" and then abandoning them to an unruly mob. Other Irish-American Catholic reactions to the draft riots dwelled on Irish-born policemen's and soldiers' efforts to suppress the riots. They argued that Irish Catholic rioters had been unwitting tools of nativists who sought to fan the flames of anti-Catholicism.[4]

Beyond their particular role in the draft riots, the service of Irish-American priests and nuns on behalf of the Union war effort set an example for some immigrants who were skeptical of emancipation. University-based religious orders sent dozens of priests to serve as chaplains in the Union army, while hundreds of nuns worked in Union military hospitals. As nuns mended soldiers' bodies and nurtured souls whose faith had been tested by the vices of army life and the strains of combat, Catholic chaplains bolstered soldiers' morale and discipline by conducting Mass, hearing confessions, and, in some cases, granting them absolution before battle. Nuns, especially, bore witness and fell victim to the gruesome vicissitudes of the war, and the steadfast devotion with which they labored impressed the native-born Protestant men and women who, respectively, came under their care and labored alongside them. Meanwhile, priests who served as chaplains in Union regiments exerted a powerful influence on Irish-American Catholic soldiers, especially since they were relatively few in number. For every 3,773 Catholic soldiers, only one Catholic chaplain was available. With their services in high demand, some Irish-American priests became influential supporters of emancipation, as is evidenced by the wartime ministry of the Reverend Thaddeus Butler of the 23rd Illinois. Irish-born and educated at All Hallows in Dublin and the Propaganda Fide in Rome, Butler ministered to congregants of St. John the Evangelist Church in Chicago before the war. Like other Irish Catholic priests in Chicago, Father Butler was an ardent supporter of the Union war effort and, in mid-June 1861, was commissioned as chaplain in the 23rd Illinois. A prominent Chicagoan convert to Catholicism described Father Butler's wartime preaching as "true to the training of the Propagandist, which always declares equality without distinction of race or color, and a horror of slavery." Until he was forced to resign his commission in March 1863 because of disability, the openly antislavery Father Butler shared his tent with Colonel James Mulligan, a virulent anti-abolitionist who filled his wartime journal with denunciations of emancipation.[5]

Though the tentmates held conflicting views on emancipation, Father Butler and Mulligan found common ground in their devotion to Catholicism. Mulligan's diary is replete with criticisms of the Lincoln administration, especially in the weeks after Lincoln promulgated the Emancipation Proclamation on January 1, 1863. His February 12, 1863, entry is typical: "The same desolation of activity; the same dreaminess everywhere. Tumbling, goes the Republic. Nobody heads it. Negroes and parties & contracts are the staples of the day." As a commissioned officer, Mulligan could have resigned, yet he continued as colonel of his regiment until he was killed in battle in July 1864. One of Mulligan's last letters summarized his beliefs: "I am a soldier and obey my general. I am a Catholic and obey my bishop." Thaddeus Butler was no general or bishop, but he shared Mulligan's willingness to risk death to restore the Union and had the devout colonel's respect. Mulligan almost certainly went to his grave with doubts over emancipation, but in all likelihood, Butler, who officiated at the colonel's funeral, counseled him to at least tolerate slavery's end as a necessary consequence of reuniting the country. Other soldiers in the 23rd Illinois admired Butler as much as Mulligan did while sharing Mulligan's anti-abolitionism, suggesting that Butler's chaplaincy enabled him to allay Irish-American soldiers' concerns about emancipation.[6]

By the summer of 1863, Irish-American clergymen and Catholic journalists were on the defensive about their coreligionists' loyalties, even as scores of Irish-born priests and nuns ministered to the tens of thousands of Irish-American Catholic soldiers under Union arms. It was in this context that the Purcell brothers of Cincinnati emerged as leading Irish-American Catholic proponents of emancipation outside of the Union army. Natives of Mallow, County Cork, the Purcells arrived in the Queen City decades before the vast majority of Irish-born Cincinnatians came as part of the famine migration. Before the war, both Purcells had avoided direct support for emancipation and joined their compatriots in condemning abolitionism. But in August 1862, John Purcell—now the Archbishop of Cincinnati—returned from a visit to Europe that included a meeting with Bishop Felix Dupanloup, a liberal French cleric and outspoken abolitionist. In the months and years ahead, the brothers grew noticeably more pronounced in their opposition to African American slavery. At a public lecture in Cincinnati shortly after his return from Europe, Archbishop Purcell charged that proslavery extremism had caused the war and delivered pointed criticisms of enslavers. As yet another indication of how Irish-American Union soldiers pushed their countrymen on the home front to embrace emancipation, the archbishop was joined on stage by Father William O'Higgins, the Irish-born Catholic chaplain of the 10th Ohio Regiment. While Archbishop Purcell could not have known that Lincoln would issue a preliminary proclamation of emancipation only weeks later, he predicted that such a measure would bring the conflict to a swift conclusion. Although the Reverend Edward Purcell's *Catholic Telegraph* did not explicitly endorse Lincoln's proclamation, Archbishop Purcell did so publicly in October. For its part, the *Telegraph* endorsed a pastoral letter written by Bishop Dupanloup that condemned slavery as antithetical to the teachings of the Church.[7]

During the winter and spring of 1863, the Purcells wrote and spoke more frequently and enthusiastically in support of emancipation, provoking a war of words with conservative Catholic editors. Within this intra-Catholic feud, Rev. Edward Purcell pushed readers to recover and emulate the Roman Catholic Church's emancipatory tradition. The editorial exchange began in March when the *Telegraph* ran an editorial lauding the emancipation of serfs in the Russian Empire. In response, James McMaster's fiercely conservative *Freeman's Journal* argued that slavery and Catholicism were perfectly compatible. In an April 8, 1863, shot across the bow at McMaster and other American Catholic apologists for slavery, the *Telegraph* asserted that "a great change is at hand in the political welfare of the country, and . . . it is of some consequence to Catholics to decide wisely what part to take." Purcell called for Catholics to reconcile themselves with emancipation, for "slavery is extinguished in the United States, and all that we have to do is to decide how we shall accommodate ourselves 'to coming events.'" Though wildly optimistic in his decree that emancipation was a fait accompli, Purcell perceived correctly that Catholics could no longer both support the Union war effort and openly resist the end of slavery.[8]

Having accepted emancipation's inevitability, the *Telegraph* devoted numerous articles over the ensuing weeks to the Catholic Church's history of antislavery teachings and deeds. Purcell aimed to show Irish-American Catholics, in particular, that they could "accommodate" themselves to the changes wrought by the war. The April 8, 1863, editorial in response to the *Freeman's Journal*, for instance, called attention to various popes who had denounced slavery, including Pius II in 1462, Paul III in 1537, Urban VIII in 1639, and Gregory XVI in 1839. Subsequent articles elucidated the theological underpinnings of Catholic antislavery teachings and gave historical examples of the Church having ameliorated the harshness of slavery or conferred freedom on enslaved people. Two examples provided by Rev. Purcell were of particular importance to Irish-American readers. One appeared in an April 22, 1863, article on the history of the Council of Armagh, a conference of Catholic prelates in Ireland that met in 1171. According to Purcell, the Council decreed "the emancipation of *all* English slaves then in Ireland." Purcell likely hoped the Council of Armagh's example would show Irish Americans that their Church had recognized the immorality of enslaving even the most ancient enemies of the Irish. For a second and more recent example of an Irish Catholic antislavery tradition, the Purcells instructed their Irish-born readers and congregants to look no further than Daniel O'Connell. Archbishop Purcell paid for an antislavery pamphlet written by O'Connell in 1843 to be reprinted for mass distribution, while Rev. Edward Purcell displayed a copy of the pamphlet signed by O'Connell himself in the window of the *Telgraph*'s offices. By the end of May, two months into his Catholic antislavery campaign, Purcell wrote of his astonishment at the "immense and most persevering efforts made by the Church for the suppression of domestic slavery."[9]

Throughout 1863, the *Telegraph*'s campaign against Catholic proslavery apologists brought Irish-American proponents of emancipation out of the woodwork. One immigrant writing from New York City in June thanked the *Telegraph* for providing Irish-American Catholics with their first antislavery periodical, for he had feared that "some future Bancroft writing the history of this rebellion" would characterize Catholics as a "proslavery body." Another Irishman in New York, Patrick Murphy, wrote to Purcell in October to convey his disgust with John Mullaly's proslavery *Metropolitan Record*. "If I could be persuaded," Murphy declared, "that our holy mother, the Church, took sides with this bellowing editor and slavery against the brightest bon [sic] of God to man on earth—Human Liberty—I would be in a week without a religion, as I am now without a country." Purcell claimed that letters poured into the *Telegraph*'s offices from across the country, all of them expressing gratitude, in the words of one reader, for a "Catholic-Church-paper . . . not afraid to raise its voice in favor of the most oppressed people on earth." "Matha," another Irish-American correspondent to the *Telegraph*, observed in July that while it was "hard for our people at once to realize the somersault that public affairs have taken by the operation of the war," the *Telegraph* was forcing Irish Catholics to confront the new reality of emancipation. Orestes Brownson, the North's most admired Catholic theologian and a leading Catholic advocate of emancipation, called Purcell the "first priest to bear a clear, distinct, and unmistakable testimony in public against slavery."[10]

With the *Telegraph*'s standing as the nation's leading Catholic antislavery journal cemented by the fall of 1863, its subscriber list continued to grow, a fact that Rev. Purcell never missed a chance to point out. In September, several "working-men, who had had little time for reading" on the subject of slavery wrote to Purcell, asking that the *Telegraph* devote even more space to the topic. The following month, Rev. Purcell published a speech by his elder brother in which the archbishop made his most forceful argument to date for the incompatibility of Catholic teaching and human bondage. "The Catholic Church," Archbishop Purcell asserted, "has ever been the friend of human freedom. It was Christ's mission to make men free," he continued, and Catholics who sought to "uphold or perpetuate involuntary human servitude" had cast aside "his precepts and principles and example." While the brothers' efforts to align the Catholic Church with Republican antislavery policies certainly turned off some *Telegraph* readers, Rev. Purcell insisted that new subscribers more than made up for such losses. In November, an Irish immigrant in Dubuque, Iowa, named John O'Meara, submitted subscriptions for "27 new subscribers for [Purcell's] truly patriotic and Christian paper." Two months later, Irish-born Thomas Farrell requested ten copies of the *Telegraph* for readers in New York City who were "getting emancipated slowly but surely" from "baneful and destructive teaching and degrading and unchristian sentiment" on the slavery question. "Josephus," an Irish Catholic in Philadelphia, wrote to Purcell in

January 1865, offering to report regularly on Philadelphia Catholics' "adherence to the exalted principles of union and freedom" in the *Telegraph*'s columns. This anecdotal evidence of the *Telegraph*'s influence was confirmed in December 1864 when the newspaper notified readers that its subscriber list had doubled over the past three years. In short, Rev. Purcell's labors to recast the Catholic Church as an antislavery institution turned the *Telegraph* into a hotbed of Irish-American antislavery sentiment.[11]

At first, Purcell's arguments encountered an overwhelmingly hostile reception from other widely read Irish-American newspapers, especially self-styled Catholic journals. The timing of Purcell's campaign perturbed some fellow Catholic editors, for it coincided with an uptick in Irish-American anxieties over growing numbers of casualties of war, conscription, and the consequences of emancipation for unskilled workers. Even as Purcell laid before Irish-American Catholics their Church's supposedly timeless antislavery credentials, the *Freeman's Journal* and the *Metropolitan Record*, the two leading Catholic journals of New York, exhorted readers to resist the draft and predicted dire consequences for Irish-American workers in the wake of emancipation. Purcell had little hope of winning over such staunchly anti-war Catholic editors. The *Freeman's Journal*'s vehement dissent from the Lincoln administration's policies had already led to the arrest of its editor, James McMaster, on the specious and ultimately unsubstantiated charge of treasonous sedition. Even after his release from prison, McMaster championed the perpetuation of Black slavery, using the *Freeman's Journal* to counter the *Telegraph*'s Catholic antislavery argument by claiming that Purcell was trying to make Irish Americans "bacon-on-Friday Catholics" by reading selectively into the Church's past. Patrick Donahoe's *Pilot* was less severe in its opposition to emancipation and chided McMaster for his overtly proslavery views. Yet it, too, reviled the *Telegraph*. "Does our friend of the Telegraph desire to make Abolitionists of his readers?" a *Pilot* editorial asked in late July of 1863. Answering the question, Donahoe declared, "He cannot taint his Irish readers."[12]

Yet over the coming weeks and months, *Pilot* editorials on slavery and emancipation assumed a nearly identical substance and style to the *Telegraph*'s lessons on the Catholic Church's emancipatory tradition. This was no small matter, for the *Pilot* remained the most widely read and influential weekly among the American Irish. Not only was it the official newspaper of the Archdiocese of Boston, but also it boasted a subscriber list in the tens of thousands; through reading rooms and secondhand readership, the *Pilot* likely reached well over fifty thousand individual readers. Throughout the war, editor Patrick Donahoe's influence rendered the *Pilot* solidly Unionist, as is evidenced by an April 1865 editorial that celebrated Irish-American soldiers who had fought for "the preservation of the Union; for the perpetuity of Constitutional Republican Government over the Union, and for all the rights, blessings and duties which such a government confers and imposes upon every one of her citizens." However, for much of 1862 and 1863, its enthusiasm for the Union war effort waned as Irish-born casualties increased and the Emancipation Proclamation was enacted. On the one hand, the *Pilot* continued to promote Irish-American enlistment in the Union army, supported conscription, and, in 1862, started a weekly column that ran for the duration of the war entitled "Records of Irish-American Patriotism" to highlight the service of soldiers of Irish birth or extraction. On the other hand, Donahoe was sometimes despondent over the prospects of a Union victory. Just weeks before Lincoln issued the final Emancipation Proclamation, the *Pilot* called for an armistice. Always consistent in its paramount desire to see the Union restored, the *Pilot*'s coverage of the war in 1863 conveyed a sense of doom, one that its authors unfailingly connected to the allegedly disastrous consequences of emancipation. In this way, the *Pilot*'s dilemma encapsulated one that confronted countless Irish-American Unionists in 1863: Having argued for two decades that the perpetuation of slavery was an evil necessary for the survival of the American Republic, how would the *Pilot* fare in a Union whose restoration was accomplished through the destruction of slavery?[13]

Under these circumstances, Donahoe and his staff at the *Pilot* found utility in Purcell's invocation of a Catholic antislavery tradition. In September 1863, only two months after it criticized the *Telegraph* for portraying the Church as antislavery, the *Pilot* asserted that the "Church in its own good time will embark on the matter" of emancipation. As the phrase "in its own good time" suggested, the *Pilot* envisioned the Catholic hierarchy overseeing a gradual process of emancipation. Only through the conversion of enslavers to Catholicism, the *Pilot* argued, could that outcome be achieved. In what was surely a line aimed at Rev. Purcell, the *Pilot* asserted that it knew "as well as any negrophilist can tell us . . . that the voice of the universal church, has always been against slavery." But the restoration of the Union had to precede emancipation: "If the Union is irretrievably divided," an October 1863 editorial queried, "is not the continuation of slavery in America certain?" As it had done before the war, the *Pilot* conceded that the abolition of slavery was desirable but maintained that the political restoration of the nation-state be given top priority.[14]

By December 1864, however, the Union was on the verge of restoration, and emancipation was an indisputable factor in the triumph of Union arms. These circumstances forced the *Pilot* to travel further down the Catholic antislavery path blazed by the *Telegraph*. To counter claims made by the *New York Tribune* and the *New York Times* that proslavery sentiment led Irish Catholics to sympathize with the Confederacy, the *Pilot* reprinted a recent *Telegraph* article. That article dismissed Republican newspapers' claims that Catholics favored slavery and therefore supported the Confederacy. "[T]he whole history of the Catholic Church has been against slavery," the *Pilot* quoted from the *Telegraph* in its retort to the *Tribune* and *Times* accusations. The *Pilot*'s use of the *Telegraph*'s Catholic antislavery argument was remarkable. In 1862, the *Pilot* had argued that "emancipation of the slaves would render it utterly impossible to restore the Union." Now, it quoted from the nation's most zealous antislavery Irish-American Catholic editor as proof that Irish Americans were not proslavery Confederate sympathizers. This about-face was not lost on attentive Irish-American readers. D. Downing, a County Cork native from St. Louis, wrote to congratulate Purcell for having "enlightened the vision of the Editor of the *Boston Pilot*, and enabled him to see the handwriting on the wall, as he is forced to see that slavery is wrong."[15]

The circumstances that led the anti-abolitionist *Pilot* to tout Irish-American Catholics' purported antislavery credentials were pinpointed in a February 1864 editorial in the Philadelphia *Universe*. "We, Irish Democrats," the *Universe* author admitted, "may not like this complexion of things, and we may abuse till we burst, the abolitionists as principal instigators of the Southern revolt; but facts, whether just or unjust, are against us." Evidently, the Irish-American critique of antislavery was hard to let go. But as the *Universe*'s reference to changed "facts" acknowledged, slavery was not the necessary evil that the vast majority of Irish immigrants had believed it to be. "As it is justice to the nation to destroy slavery," the *Universe* concluded, "let us be just to the nation; and as the future peace of the country demands the ruin of slavery, let us secure the future peace of the country." Securing the Union and emancipation had become mutually dependent goals, and unearthing the Catholic Church's antislavery past allowed Irish-American Catholics to embrace emancipation on their own terms.[16]

"Let them come in thousands": Immigration, Labor, and Emancipation

While Purcell's campaign to recover a Catholic antislavery tradition struck a chord with some Irish-American Catholics between 1863 and 1865, many Irish-American laborers would have scoffed at the idea that a decision by the Council of Armagh in 1171 should dictate their perspective on emancipation. Plain to see in their resistance to the draft, many Irish-born unskilled workers felt by 1863 that the war's emancipatory turn imperiled their tenuous position in the

Northern labor market. To these men and their families, it seemed like the antebellum Irish-American critique of antislavery had come to fruition. As a Republican administration and Congress bestowed freedom upon enslaved African Americans, immigrant laborers fretted over being conscripted into an army of emancipation only to see newly freed men replacing them on the docks or in factories and mines. Ignorant of the fact that New York's Black population declined during the war, Irish-born laborers were swayed by Democratic politicians like New York governor Horatio Seymour and Ohio congressman Samuel Cox, who foretold the demise of the white working class in Northern cities as a consequence of emancipation. Such demagoguery undergirded a labor critique of emancipation that was accepted as fact by conservative Democratic politicians and editors and propagated by the likes of the exiled Young Irelander Richard O'Gorman and the *Metropolitan Record*'s John Mullaly. Faith alone would not convince Irish-born laborers in New York and other Northern cities to come to terms with emancipation.[17]

Thus, from the summer of 1863 onward, some Irish-American leaders turned the labor critique of emancipation on its head by arguing that the end of slavery would open up new prospects for current and future Irish laborers in America. The *Catholic Telegraph* was once again at the fore of this distinctively Irish-American case for embracing emancipation as a necessary and beneficial element of the Union war effort. Instead of flooding the Northern labor market and cheapening wages, Purcell argued, emancipation would open the fertile fields of the South to white immigrants whose superior work ethic would command higher wages than those paid to freed people. While the premises of Purcell's vision aligned neatly with Republican free labor thought, his hypothetical scenario was tailored to appeal to the masses of unskilled immigrant laborers whose experiences of tenuous employment, poverty, and—from Purcell's point of view—moral decay had jaded their perspective on wage labor. By moving to a post-emancipation South, the Irish cartman, coal heaver, or ditch digger who lived in a ramshackle hut or a musty cellar might one day earn enough money to purchase land and take his rightful place within the nation's yeomanry. Better still, the dispersal of Irish immigrants across the South and Southwest would free them from the vices of teeming Northern cities and spread the Catholic faith across what was, to this point in time, an overwhelmingly Protestant section of the nation. Purcell's immigrant labor hypothetical evolved between 1863 and 1864. But its core proposition—that emancipation could improve the condition of Irish-American labor—remained intact. Meanwhile, Irish-American soldiers offered a twist on the immigrant labor hypothetical for the many Irish-American workers who were likely dubious of their prospects for success in postwar Southern climes. Rather than dwell on the possibility that emancipation would yield a socioeconomic windfall for unskilled Irish workers, Irish-American soldiers pointed to the reality that emancipation was bringing thousands upon thousands of freedmen into the Union army as laborers and soldiers. Whether digging entrenchments that white soldiers would have otherwise dug or facing down a Confederate rifle that a white soldier might have otherwise confronted, freedmen were performing the monotonous, murderous labor of soldiering.

The *Telegraph* first articulated the immigrant labor hypothetical in the spring of 1863, just as relief efforts for a presumptive impending famine in Ireland were in full swing. This was no coincidence; Rev. Purcell had followed reports in Irish newspapers of repeated crop failures on the island and rightly predicted that "the distress which prevails in Ireland" would soon swell the ranks of emigrants. The timing of this migration was propitious, Purcell argued, for labor was bound to be in high demand in states like Kentucky, Missouri, and Tennessee. "Free labor in free states will be the result of this civil war," Purcell declared confidently. No small part of Purcell's confidence in the prospects for immigrant labor in the postwar South emanated from his belief in white supremacy. "The negro . . . cannot compete with the white man," Purcell claimed. "It is not in his blood or muscle or brain." From this assumption of white supremacy, Purcell parried the counterargument that white landowners would simply employ freedmen in some version of a wage labor system. He also assuaged the anxieties of white workers in Northern cities who feared their potential replacement by newly freed Black migrants. Claiming "personal knowledge" that "the most extensive landholders in Kentucky and Tennessee" had in the past tried unsuccessfully to recruit Irish immigrants to work their lands, Purcell argued that the demise of slavery would make such offers much more attractive in the years to come. Besides, he reasoned, agricultural work in the South would liberate immigrant laborers from "that demoralization which so often overtakes them in the crowded towns." Purcell's concern for immigrants' "demoralization" in cities was literal. He envisioned Irish laborers, their morals bolstered by the uplifting effects of honest labor and freedom from the degradation of cities, spreading their Catholic faith throughout the South. Thus, Purcell wrote of potential Irish emigrants, "Let them come in thousands. There is enough for all."[18]

While the immigrant labor hypothetical was slow to gain traction in the spring and early summer of 1863, Irish-born laborers' notoriety in the draft riots seems to have motivated Rev. Purcell to make his case with greater gusto. In a July 15 editorial that was published as the carnage in Manhattan unfolded, Purcell addressed the grievances that animated Irish-American opponents of emancipation. "Our hostility to the restoration of slavery is not so much for the emancipation of the blacks," Purcell declared, "as for the social elevation and independence of our white brethren." This statement flew in the face of several recent *Telegraph* articles that assailed the immorality of slavery and urged Irish-American readers to see the theological incompatibility between slavery and Catholicism. But as Purcell admitted later in the July 15 article, moral and theological reasoning had done little to assuage the concerns of immigrant laborers: "The great argument constantly used against our position is this—If slavery be abolished we will be overrun by colored people, who will compete with the white laborer, and finally supplant him." The labor issue was impossible for Purcell to ignore if he hoped to win over Irish-American workers.[19]

With the Union cause ascendant in the aftermath of victories at Gettysburg and Vicksburg, the *Telegraph* dismissed fears of emancipation by assuring workers that once free, African Americans' labor power could be neutralized. "We do not wish to see the black man in competition with the white," Purcell asserted in the July 15 editorial. Once slavery was abolished, he continued, Blacks would not seek work in the North but instead return en masse to the South, removing the potential for labor competition in Northern cities. Moreover, Southern planters would be ruined without an enslaved labor force, turning their plantations into "small farms, like sunny spots" that would "dot the land in the free States." To Purcell, the question of who would work and reap the fruits of those "sunny spots" was easily answered. "Abolish [slavery]," he concluded, "and the native power of the white man will be instantly developed." Here, from the pen of an Irish-American Catholic priest and amid the New York City Draft Riots, was a bald recapitulation of Republican free labor ideology.[20]

Purcell's vision of immigrant labor thriving in a post-emancipation Southern economy drew immediate criticism from Irish-American editors. Newspapers like the *Freeman's Journal*, which was still attempting to prove that enslaved African Americans were content in their bondage, railed against Purcell, but more moderate editors also critiqued his argument. After admitting that slavery was "an evil" and acknowledging the appeal of Purcell's hypothetical, the *Pilot* disputed Purcell's logic by questioning how immigrants could acquire land in the South if freed people remained and Northern Blacks emigrated there. The *Pilot* found it impossible to believe that Blacks and whites could live amicably alongside one another if whites took possession of the land, as Purcell had envisioned. The solution was "plain and inevitable," according to the *Pilot*: Blacks could live only "in the servile condition." Ironically, as Purcell's recovery of a

Catholic antislavery tradition seemed to win over the *Pilot* on religious grounds, his immigrant labor hypothetical pushed the Boston weekly back into the camp of Irish-American editors who clung to the belief that emancipation could only produce social upheaval.[21]

Throughout the rest of 1863 and into 1864, Rev. Purcell refined his argument in favor of emancipation based on its potential benefits to immigrant laborers. Aided by readers who furnished him with anecdotal and statistical evidence, Purcell insisted that slavery was the sole obstacle to Irish and German immigrants obtaining remunerative employment on Southern farmland. A September 1863 article quoted an anonymous Tennessean's observation that an Irish immigrant laborer commanded $1.50 per day, a sum that would amount to $1,500.00 in three years. For that amount, the anonymous source continued, "we can buy a nigger, who will work—not for three years but all his life—without any wages." In January 1864, the *Telegraph* published a letter to the editor from Paducah, Kentucky, as further proof that slavery shut out immigrant labor from the South. "I have to pay them nothing, and they have to work," the Kentuckian wrote of the two men he claimed as property. "What they make is mine, which would not be if I had to have Irishmen or Germans." This and similar anecdotes not only furnished immigrant laborers with hard figures for their potential pay but also harped on an inherent injustice within slavery that Purcell believed even the staunchest foes of emancipation would grasp: Enslavers denied working people the fruits of their labor. A November editorial returned to this theme as Purcell once again refuted the claim that freed Black workers would "cheapen free labor by competition." That claim was preposterous, Purcell argued, for Irish immigrants had found precious few opportunities for gainful employment in slave states. "We tell you, Irish and German working men," Purcell concluded, "the theory of slavery is not that black men should be slaves, but that *labor*, white or black, should be *owned by capital*."[22]

Purcell and his allies evinced a sense of empathy for the plight of the Irish immigrant that was often lacking in antebellum antislavery appeals to Irish-American self-interest. For instance, Purcell acknowledged that Ireland's inequitable tenantry laws had yielded yet another wave of evictions amidst the repeated crop failures of the early 1860s. With this in mind, the *Telegraph* tapped into the exiled sensibilities of famine immigrants and new immigrants alike over the latter half of 1863 and into 1864. In response to the *Metropolitan Record*'s incessant proslavery screeds, Purcell wryly observed in September that it was "a very strange thing to see the man who was oppressed *at home*, the very loudest on the side of oppression here!" Having singled out editor John Mullaly, a Belfast-born famine immigrant, Purcell broadened his scope, arguing that it was "a strange thing to see the man who was compelled to labor *at home* for so small a pittance that his family was on the verge of starvation, crying out lustily in this country to make men work, under the lash, for which they receive no pay at all!!" In these lines, Purcell wove a thinly veiled critique of Irish landlordism into a more standard-fare denunciation of slavery, a tactic that he and other *Telegraph* contributors employed over the coming months. From East Tennessee in March 1864, a *Telegraph* reader recounted the history of conquest in Ireland that had given way to the island's present suborned state, querying how Irishmen "who have themselves been in thraldom [sic] for centuries" could tolerate the existence of chattel slavery. A similar line of inquiry informed speeches at a Meadville, Pennsylvania, St. Patrick's Day celebration, where a local priest reminded his Irish-born audience of the infamous penal laws that, for more than a century, circumscribed Irish Catholics' civic, social, and economic freedom. By conflating the deeds of Irish landlords, Cromwellian soldiers, and Crown authorities in Ireland with the oppressive conduct of American enslavers, the *Telegraph*'s trumpeting of free labor sounded a distinctively Irish tune. While it is impossible to gauge precisely how Purcell's readers responded to this campaign, letters from Irish-born correspondents suggest that his arguments hit the right note. "Matha," an Irish-born Cincinnatian, asked rhetorically in the summer of 1863 if "you, Irish Catholic, free laborer" would "go before God stained with guilt of oppressing the poor—the crime that cries to Heaven for vengeance against England?" "Gotham," an Irish immigrant living in Manhattan, offered a similar perspective in a March 1864 letter to the *Telegraph* that chided proslavery Irish-American editors like Mullaly. "It is a shame and a disgrace to find Irishmen, who were persecuted at home, and who came here to escape it and make a living, the greatest enemy the poor persecuted negro has got in this country," Gotham lamented.[23]

In its most robust form, Purcell's immigrant labor hypothetical—tinged by self-interest and white supremacy—was situated as the cornerstone of a transatlantic political ideology of republicanism. In July 1864, after a botched attempt by *New York Tribune* editor Horace Greeley to negotiate terms of surrender with Confederate agents in Canada, Purcell pointed out that Confederates were unwilling to negotiate for peace without a guarantee slavery would be left intact. This was proof, he asserted, of the driving animus behind the rebellion, being that "*labor*, white or black, should be *owned by capital.*" Even as immigrants arrived daily from Europe, Purcell fumed, Confederates fought for a system of labor that excluded Irishmen from the lucrative farmlands of the South and contributed to the degradation of the "poor white man." "Hence," he concluded, "the anxiety of the English government that the South may triumph, both being solicitous to see Republicanism destroyed." By preventing immigrants from achieving the status of free laborers who could enjoy the fruits of their labor, in other words, Confederates threatened a form of government whose lifeblood was an independent, incoercible labor force. To Purcell, this was precisely what English authorities desired, for the demise of republicanism in America would stifle the rise of republicanism in Ireland.[24]

Purcell's immigrant labor hypothetical caught the attention of the exiled Young Irelander turned Confederate propagandist John Mitchel, who attempted to refute the Cincinnati clergyman's arguments with claims that Union agents were conning young Irishmen to emigrate. Since Mitchel's move from New York City to East Tennessee in 1854, he had remained a vigorous proponent of slavery's expansion; in the late 1850s, Mitchel also endorsed the reopening of the African slave trade. He relocated to France in 1860 to fundraise for the Fenian movement, but he soon soured on the organization's leadership and, in 1862, ran the Union blockade of the Confederate coastline to return to the South. An impassioned secessionist, Mitchel spent the rest of the war in Richmond, where he deployed his editorial talents in the *Richmond Enquirer* and *Richmond Examiner* to marshal support for the Confederate war effort. Even after losing two of his three sons who donned Confederate grey, Mitchel urged on the rebellion, often by drawing a parallel between Britain's subjugation of Ireland and the attempted conquest of the Confederacy by the Union. Increasingly, he worried that Irish immigration was strengthening the Union's manpower, and in late 1863, he penned a letter to the editor of the Dublin *Nation*, a Confederate-sympathizing weekly, discouraging prospective emigrants from crossing the Atlantic. The "fraudulent operations of Yankee agents in Ireland," Mitchel alleged, had duped young Irishmen into believing they would be awarded "grants of land" in the South if they enlisted in the federal armed forces. Even if the rebellion was crushed, Mitchel continued, his countrymen should have no illusions about their prospects for prosperity. "They are to be made use of precisely as the poor negroes are," Mitchel predicted, "thrust to the front in every fight, and thrown aside afterwards as broken tools." Mitchel's charges of duplicitous and possibly illegal federal recruiting in Ireland were echoed by the *Nation* and other leading constitutional nationalists in Ireland, including the former Young Irelanders John Martin and William Smith O'Brien.[25]

Mitchel's charges of illicit Union recruitment gained substance as reports of such nefarious affairs made headlines in 1863 and 1864. On November 3, 1863, a Union sloop of war, the USS *Kearsarge*, docked in Queenstown, Ireland, to resupply. When the vessel sailed out of port two days later, sixteen Irishmen from Queenstown and surrounding towns had either stowed away on the vessel or enlisted in its service. Alerted to the incident by Confederate agents in Queenstown, British officials protested that the *Kearsarge*'s captain had violated the Foreign Enlistment Act, which prohibited recruitment for and enlistment in foreign service on British soil. While the men were returned to Queenstown the next month, a subsequent incident lent further credence to allegations that Union recruiters operated illegally in Ireland. In March 1864, reports surfaced in Boston of more than one hundred Irishmen from the vicinities of Dublin and Galway who were enticed by a Massachusetts-based labor recruiting agent with promises of employment. However, upon arriving in Portland, Maine, some of the men were plied with liquor and pressured to enlist in the Irish-American 20th Maine Regiment. Of the more than eighty immigrants from the group who made it to Boston, several enlisted in the army after they were told that no employment was available. Tales of similar incidents on a smaller scale appeared in the pages of several Irish-American newspapers throughout 1864, and in the summer, Parliament opened an inquiry into the role of illicit federal recruitment in the past year's rise in emigration from Ireland. Simultaneously, a proclamation from Dublin Castle, the seat of British authority in Ireland, warned prospective emigrants of employment offers that might inveigle them into the service of the Union's armed forces.[26]

Ultimately, editorials in Union-sympathizing Irish newspapers and testimonies from immigrants themselves substantiated the Lincoln administration's claim that immigrants were not being coerced or deceived into enlisting in the Union armed forces. In answer to Mitchel's argument that emigrants who left Ireland for the Union were lending their brawn to a war of conquest, the Dublin *Irishman* pointed out repeatedly in 1864 that, unlike Irish nationalists, Confederates fought for "the establishment of a Slave Empire." A September 1864 letter to the *Irishman* concurred and pointed out the false equivalence upon which Mitchel's analogy between Ireland and the Confederacy rested. If Irish nationalists' aim was to "separate from England for the purpose of putting our peasantry more completely under foot of the landlords," the author commented, then "there might be some similarity; but our cause has no such damning stain upon it." Instead, nationalists in Ireland sought "to free the land from the vestiges of feudal serfdom . . . and to make all our people the free, educated, and enlightened citizens of a free state." Those aims, the author contended, were nearly identical to those of Irish-American Unionists across the Atlantic. While few nationalists in Ireland were enthusiastic about young Irishmen risking their lives in the

American conflict, they were equally as desirous to emphasize that emigration was an inevitable consequence of economic stagnancy and bad governance. Jeremiah O'Donovan Rossa, an Irish Fenian whose two brothers served in the Union army, argued that "the landlord and English interest" in Ireland used allegations of illicit Union recruiting to "blind the world to the patent fact that this emigration is solely attributable to the blighting effect upon our people of landlord and English rule." James Roche, an Irish immigrant who had returned to Ireland to edit the Fenian, pro-Union *Galway-American*, went a step further than O'Donovan Rossa. In response to reports of illicit Union recruiting, the *Galway-American* encouraged prospective emigrants to "become citizens of a more favored land" in the United States. While the *Galway-American*'s promotion of emigration drew scorn even from Union-sympathizing revolutionary nationalists in Ireland, it resonated with the contents of letters written by prospective emigrants to American consuls in Dublin, Galway, Cork, Belfast, and Derry. William B. West, a US Vice-Consul stationed in Dublin, was so impressed by the volume of letters his office received from prospective emigrants that he proposed the creation of a new territory to be governed by the former Irish Brigade commander Thomas Francis Meagher. In this western clime, Irish immigrants could "regenerate themselves in a Country and on a soil they could really call their own: under a government as free as the air they breathe." Thus, as Purcell lobbied immigrant laborers to see that the demise of slavery might open up the vast agricultural lands of the South for them, republican nationalists in Ireland reminded audiences on both sides of the Atlantic that they, too, sought to overthrow a powerful and oppressive landed class.[27]

Meanwhile, as the war ground on in 1864, Irish-American soldiers embraced a twist on the immigrant labor hypothetical. Over the past year, Purcell's vision of immigrants obtaining employment on farmland formerly worked by enslaved Black men and women took shape in response to Irish-American fears that freedmen would replace unskilled white workers in the Northern labor market. Now, with tens of thousands of Irish-American soldiers still under arms and having endured months, if not years, of hard service, some acknowledged their willingness to let newly freed Black men replace them in the ranks or behind a shovel. In January 1864, Patrick Maher, a veteran of the 24th Connecticut, wrote to a friend in the 9th Connecticut, Captain Lawrence O'Brien, with an update on recruiting in New Haven. Maher, an Irish-born common laborer, acknowledged that there had been "a great excitement here among the Lads that don't want to go to war the last two months for fear they would be drafted." But, he continued, New Haven's quota was met thanks to the enlistment of Black men, about seven hundred of whom were now enrolled in the 29th Connecticut, an African American regiment from the Nutmeg State. Even though he was skeptical of Black soldiers' capabilities, Maher was content to let them take up the fight. The Union army's deployment of freedmen also released white soldiers from some of the most labor-intensive elements of campaigning. One Irish-American soldier's account of Sherman's "March to the Sea" in Georgia noted how "slaves of all ages and both sexes left homes at a moment's preparation . . . in search of freedom" to march with the Union soldiers. "The able-bodied men were put to work as pioneers," the soldier noted satisfactorily, "and really did good service with the shovel and axe, in many cases." In Virginia, "Garryowen," a correspondent for the *Irish-American* who accompanied an Irish-American regiment up the James River in November 1864, marveled at the work of Black laborers employed by the Union army. A canal dug by laborers from the Roanoke Island Freedman's Colony met "the most sanguine expectations of its promoters," Garryowen observed. Whether as soldiers or ditch diggers, Black men's labor on behalf of the Union war effort steadily eroded Irish-American resistance to emancipation.[28]

No pithier encapsulation of Irish-American soldiers' views on Black soldiering during the later stages of the war can be found than that conveyed by the Irish-born journalist-turned-soldier, Charles G. Halpine. Better known by his *nom de plume*, Private Miles O'Reilly, Halpine was born in County Meath, Ireland, in 1829. After graduating from Trinity College in Dublin, Halpine flirted with the Young Ireland movement in the late 1840s before immigrating to New York in 1850. Witty and well-educated, Halpine threw himself into the world of New York City journalism, and by 1861, he had held positions at the *New York Times, New York Herald,* and *New York Leader*. Upon the outbreak of war, Halpine was commissioned as a lieutenant in the Union army's most prestigious Irish-American unit, the 69th New York. After the unit's initial three-month term of service expired, Halpine transferred to General David Hunter's staff and accompanied Hunter to Hilton Head, South Carolina, in 1862. As the first of the Sea Islands captured by Union forces, Hilton Head was a vital node in Union operations along the Atlantic seaboard. From there, Union troops pushed deeper into the South Carolina and Georgia Lowcountry. Four out of every five residents of the region were enslaved African Americans, and throughout much of 1863, the Lowcountry was the setting for Union forces' efforts to beef up their control over a coastline whose northeasterly curvature led to the prize of Charleston, South Carolina. Halpine's position on Hunter's staff made him instrumental to the formation of the African American 1st South Carolina Regiment and the deployment of the African American 54th Massachusetts Regiment in the summer of 1863.[29]

Having taken part in the Union's earliest efforts to recruit and deploy Black soldiers, Halpine used his acerbic pen and elevated status among Irish-American soldiers to convince his comrades of the merits of Black enlistment. Throughout the war, Halpine published satirical poetry and short stories under the pen name Private Miles O'Reilly, a fictitious Irish-born soldier in the 47th New York Regiment whose caricatured Irish brogue and biting sarcasm served as a comedic veneer for commonly held views on the conflict. Of the dozens of poems and stories Halpine published under O'Reilly's name, not one was more popular than "Sambo's Right to Be Kilt." First circulated among the troops under Hunter's command in the Department of the South in 1863, "Sambo's Right to Be Kilt" was sung to the tune of a popular song, "The Low-Backed Car." Written from the fictitious Private O'Reilly's point of view and in his exaggerated brogue, its upshot was brutally simple: White soldiers should be happy to let Black soldiers take their place in the ranks of fallen soldiers. "Some say it is a burnin' shame / To make the naygurs fight / And that the thrade of bein' kilt / Balongs but to the white," Private O'Reilly muses in the poem's most barbed verse, "But as for me, upon me sowl / So liberal are we here / I'll let Sambo be murthered in place myself / On every day in the year." Halpine later wrote that the poem "at once won over the Irish, who had been the bitterest opponents of the measure [Black soldiering], to become its friends." While this claim was almost certainly exaggerated, there is good evidence to indicate the popularity and effectiveness of Halpine's poem among Irish-American soldiers. "Sambo's Right to Be Kilt" gained notoriety outside the army in January 1864 when it was performed at a banquet honoring the surviving members of the Irish Brigade. Badly depleted by casualties, the remnants of the brigade's three New York regiments had limped home to enjoy the thirty-five-day furlough awarded to eligible soldiers who reenlisted over the winter of 1863–64. While the Peace Democrats in the city's governing chambers refused to honor the returning veterans, the brigade's officers, wounded veterans, and local Irish-American supporters organized a banquet at Irving Hall on January 16 to honor their service. Several hundred enlisted men joined the brigade's former and current officers, along with wounded veterans, for an afternoon of speeches and toasts, one of which was delivered by a Captain Daly of the 47th New York. Called on for a song, Daly introduced "Sambo's Right to Be Kilt" by commenting that it was "very popular in the department he came from" and "had done much to reconcile the soldiery . . . to the institution it referred to." He then proceeded to sing Halpine's poem, eventually arriving at its paradoxically racist yet egalitarian concluding verse: "The men who object to Sambo / Should take his place and fight; / And it's better to have a naygur's hue, / Than a liver that's wake an' white / Though Sambo's black as the ace of spades, / His finger a thrigger can pull / And his eye runs sthraight on the barrel sights / From under its thatch of wool!" Over the coming weeks, "Sambo's Right to Be Kilt" was published in several leading Irish-American newspapers, including the *Pilot*, *Catholic Telegraph*, and *Irish-American*, as well as the Dublin *Irishman*, each of whom gave extensive coverage to the Irish Brigade banquet.[30]

By 1864, Irish-American leaders like Rev. Purcell and Irish-American soldiers like Halpine had honed their arguments to convince Irish-American workers of the benefits of emancipation. Purcell's immigrant labor hypothetical, a distinct strain of free labor thought that accounted for the circumstances of Irish labor on both sides of the Atlantic Ocean, made emancipation palatable in the aftermath of the New York City Draft Riots. Simultaneously, Irish-American soldiers' receptiveness to Black laborers and soldiers joining the Union army set an example for Irish-American Unionists on the home front. It bears emphasis that these arguments in favor of emancipation rested, respectively, on Purcell's belief in the inherent supremacy of white labor and a cold-blooded willingness on the part of Irish-American soldiers to give Black men an equal opportunity to kill and be killed. Though far from a move in the direction of racial egalitarianism, Irish-American leaders' embrace of a labor-based argument in favor of emancipation during the latter stages of the war was nonetheless a remarkable turn of events from the racial violence perpetrated by Irish-born laborers in the New York City Draft Riots.

"Stars and Stripes and Erin go Bragh": Irish-American Nationalism and Emancipation

As Rev. Purcell spelled out the religious and economic reasons why his countrymen in the United States might welcome slavery's demise, the war raged on. In April 1864, Halpine's Miles O'Reilly commemorated the third anniversary of the 69th New York's formation in a poem entitled "April 20, 1864." "Of the thousand stalwart bayonets / Two hundred March today," Halpine lamented, "Hundreds lie in Virginia Swamps / And hundreds in Maryland clay." Over the next two months, hundreds more Irish-born soldiers in the 69th New York and the four other Irish Brigade regiments were added to the list of the fallen. Under the command of newly appointed Lieutenant General Ulysses S. Grant, the Army of the Potomac and the Army of the James inaugurated the Overland Campaign, an unprecedented stretch of sustained fighting in eastern Virginia. Having replenished its ranks during the January 1864 furlough in New York, the Irish Brigade lost fully one-third of its manpower between May and June. By mid-June, Grant's armies were locked in what was to be a protracted siege at the vital railroad juncture of Petersburg, Virginia, some two dozen miles south of the Confederate capital. Meanwhile, from May through September, more than one hundred thousand Union soldiers under the command of General William Tecumseh Sherman probed for a path to another crucial Confederate railroad juncture, this one at Atlanta. Though ultimately successful, the Atlanta campaign stood at an impasse for much of the summer, and in July, the New York *Tribune* editor Horace Greeley wrote privately to Lincoln to express his despair over the war's continuation. "Our bleeding, bankrupt, almost dying country longs for peace," Greeley warned, "shudders at the prospect of fresh conscriptions, of further wholesale devastations, and of new rivers of human blood." Little wonder that on August 23, Lincoln demanded that the members of his cabinet sign blindly a memorandum pledging their support for the president-elect in the event that Lincoln lost his bid for reelection.[31]

Under these circumstances, the heretofore Union-sympathizing leadership of the Fenian Irish Republican Brotherhood, including its head centre, James Stephens, spoke out against further enlistments of Irish-born soldiers in the Union army. In the pages of his newly established newspaper, the *Irish People*, Stephens heaped scorn on emigrants who left Ireland with the intention of joining the Union army, going so far as to brand them as traitors to Ireland. He also criticized two pro-Union Fenian newspapers in Ireland—the *Galway-American* and Dublin *Irishman*—for their praise of Irish-American soldiers. As for Irish-American soldiers who had enlisted earlier in the war, Stephens had a mixed opinion. On the one hand, the *Irish People* expressed Stephens's optimism that these "battle-trained exiles" would fulfill their vows to the Fenian Brotherhood by fighting for Ireland's liberation. "We look for help," Stephens admitted, "to our countrymen in America." On the other hand, Stephens grew impatient with the American war and the Unionist leadership of the Fenian Brotherhood in the United States, especially its head centre, John O'Mahony. In a thinly veiled attempt to convince would-be Irish revolutionaries in the United States to return to Ireland, Stephens published in December 1863 a poem entitled "An Irish maiden to her American soldier." "Come home with the heart you bore away— to your kindred and home and sire-land," the poem beckoned, "But stay away if you bear not back your manhood's resolve for Ireland." In 1864, Stephens's frustration with what he perceived as a lack of "resolve for Ireland" within the American Fenian Brotherhood led him to make a personal recruiting tour in the Union's armies. Although he came away impressed by the strength of Fenianism within the ranks, he remained skeptical of O'Mahony's leadership, especially because O'Mahony, the ostensible head of an Irish revolutionary organization, had elected to accept a commission in an American army.[32]

Amid this transatlantic Fenian dispute over Irish-American soldiering, some nationalist leaders in Ireland resurrected the Irish critique of abolitionism in 1864 as part of their campaign to discourage further Irish enlistments. The moderate, constitutional nationalist faction, whose views were reflected in the pages of the *Nation* in Dublin, had already dismissed the antislavery thrust of the Union war effort because "the slaves were better cared for than the peasantry of Ireland," a line that bore an uncanny resemblance to arguments made by Young Irelanders during the 1840s. Throughout the war, the *Nation* and like-minded journals like the *Cork Examiner* charged that the Republican leadership of the Union was anti-Irish to their core. Significantly, in 1864, Stephens's *Irish People* joined its rival *Nation* in proclaiming that Irish nationalists should have nothing to do with a war of emancipation. Stephens, too, rehashed key elements of the famine-era Irish critique of abolitionism, claiming in a December 1864 editorial that Daniel O'Connell's embrace of antislavery in the 1840s had "divided the American-Irish, and paralyzed their exertions in behalf of their native land." Now, Stephens warned, Irish Americans who took up the Union's emancipatory crusade similarly threatened the unity of the Irish national cause.[33]

Faced with the prospect of an Irish revolt against their involvement in or support for a war whose aims now included the destruction of slavery, Irish-American Unionists looked to square their hopes for Irish independence with the imperatives of the Union war effort. Once again, Rev. Purcell of Cincinnati's *Catholic Telegraph* stepped into the breach by leading a transatlantic campaign to convince Irish nationalists that the war's emancipatory turn aligned with their interests. Ironically, as the *Nation* and *Irish People* in Ireland revived the famine-era Irish critique of abolitionism in 1863-64, Purcell turned to the very figure whose antislavery rhetoric in the 1840s had allegedly driven a wedge between nationalists at that time: Daniel O'Connell. On August 5, 1863, the *Telegraph* printed an 1843 letter from O'Connell to the Irish Repeal Association of Cincinnati, in which O'Connell berated Queen City repealers for defending slavery. According to Purcell, the letter had been "concealed for twenty years by a well-known Democrat" who now brought it to the *Telegraph* editor's attention in the hopes that it might convince Irish immigrants to abandon their opposition to antislavery once and for all. Purcell not only printed the letter in its entirety but also displayed the original, signed copy in the offices of the *Telegraph* for skeptics to behold. "It was not in Ireland you learned this cruelty," O'Connell's 1843 letter had remonstrated.

Continuing, O'Connell had taken Irish Americans who defended enslavers or even so much as equivocated on the question of slavery's perpetuation to task for defying a supposedly innate Irish contempt for oppression and betraying the principles of the Declaration of Independence. O'Connell deemed America unworthy of Ireland's admiration while it upheld slavery and told Irish immigrants that, by defending slavery, they ceded claims to Irish identity and American values. In addition to reprinting O'Connell's 1843 letter in the *Telegraph*, Rev. Purcell sold it in pamphlet form for three cents per copy or two dollars for one hundred copies.[34]

Purcell's publication of the O'Connell letter came at an inflection point for Irish-American opposition to emancipation—the draft riots had subsided less than three weeks earlier—and provoked the indignation of some Irish-American newspapers. The *Freeman's Journal* predictably dismissed the letter on the grounds that O'Connell never laid eyes on American slavery and ignored "the canons of the Church, which forbid stealing or seducing slaves away from their masters." The *Pilot* was more admiring of O'Connell, but it also condemned him and those responsible for bringing the 1843 letter to light. O'Connell's letter far surpassed anything written by American abolitionists, according to the *Pilot*, but it had come to light because its owner, "under the disease of 'nigger on the brain,'" foolishly passed it along to the abolitionist Purcell. As to the letter itself, it "*disregards the Constitution of the United States*" by asking Irishmen to become abolitionists—the same people who were responsible for "*the rupture of the grandest Republic ever formed.*" In this statement, the *Pilot* repeated a core tenet of the Irish-American critique of antislavery, which held abolitionists and antislavery politicians alike responsible for secession.[35]

While it was condemned by the *Freeman's Journal* and *Pilot*, the O'Connell letter quickly circulated among Irish Americans in the loyal states and struck a chord with some. Serving in the largely Irish-American 23rd Illinois as the regiment campaigned in Virginia, Edmund O'Dwyer read what he referred to as "a great letter of O'Connell's" in the *Wheeling Intelligencer*. O'Dwyer sent the article to his brother in New York and asked that he send it to a friend after reading it, a chain likely mimicked by many other soldiers who used newspapers to keep informed on current events and share their perspectives on the war. Irish-American soldiers, especially, relished the opportunity to keep up on the news not only in their home communities but also in Ireland; the reappearance of the O'Connell letter in the *Telegraph* in 1863 no doubt created a stir among them. A similar dynamic played out among Irish Americans removed from the battlefield. In late November 1863, Father John Hogan, an Irish-born priest in Chillicothe,

Missouri, thanked his correspondent, Thomas O'Reilly, for sending him a copy of O'Connell's Cincinnati letter. The letter had invigorated his memory of "the Great Liberator, in whose presence I once stood," Hogan recalled, and he wished that its "few and instructive pages will be read by every lover of true liberty, and especially by those for whose sole benefit it was written—the author's countrymen in America." O'Reilly forwarded the priest's letter to the *Missouri Democrat* and, in an aside, asserted that "every page of the history of Ireland is filled with the evidences of how deeply the Irish race abhor slavery." As soldiers and civilians, Irish Americans used the O'Connell letter to justify emancipation's role in restoring the Union.[36]

Native-born Protestant Unionists also welcomed the opportunity to remind Irish immigrants that their most revered national hero had once condemned their opposition to emancipation. In mid-October 1863, Sinclair Tousey, a vice president of New York's Union League Club and later the founder of the American News Company, included excerpts from O'Connell's letter on a placard entitled "Dan'l O'Connell on Democracy!" During the draft riots, Tousey had plastered the streets of Manhattan with posters that warned rioters of the public's outrage over their actions; in all likelihood, he similarly plastered the "Dan'l O'Connell on Democracy" placard across New York buildings in the fall of 1863. Tousey's poster played up O'Connell's characterization of slavery as unchristian. Primarily, however, O'Connell's words were a starting point for Tousey's portrayal of slavery as "anti-democratic because it is a war on the interests and rights of the workingman." Even Tousey's inclusion of "A Democratic Workingman" as a signatory to the poster indicated his intent to reach Irish-American laborers in Manhattan by channeling O'Connell's memory. Other antislavery Unionists, like Joseph Medill of the *Chicago Tribune*, similarly drew attention to the Cincinnati Repeal letter after Purcell republished it in 1863, indicating that at least some native-born Americans believed Irish Americans' perspectives on the future of slavery were finally subject to change.[37]

It is difficult to determine the extent to which the publication and circulation of O'Connell's 1843 letter reflected Irish-American support for emancipation in 1863. But the fact that Irish Americans across the loyal states and in the Union army were reading, buying, and urging one another to reconsider O'Connell's scathing indictment of chattel slavery is itself revealing. Twenty years earlier, O'Connell's letter and similar transatlantic antislavery exhortations to the Irish in America were met with resounding defiance and contempt. Now, amidst a war that brought O'Connell's hopes for abolition tantalizingly close, some Irish Americans were eager to listen to the Liberator. In October 1864, sensing that change was afoot across the Atlantic, several of O'Connell's former allies in the Irish antislavery movement organized a pro-Union rally at the Mechanics' Institute in Dublin. James Haughton, Richard Davis Webb, and Isaac Varian—all veteran HASS leaders—delivered lectures alongside P. J. Smyth, editor of the Fenian *Irishman* newspaper. Adopting an O'Connellite tactic, the organizers concluded the meeting by composing a transatlantic missive entitled, "Address of the Workingmen of the Capital of the Fatherland to their Kindred of their own order in the Loyal States of the Republic." Much of the address dwelled on the impending presidential election and urged the Irish in America to vote the Republican ticket, while other sections bore the influence of Rev. Purcell's immigrant labor hypothetical by extolling the benefits of a free labor economy in the postwar South. While its contents reflected the historical moment in which it was composed, the acts of composing and shipping across the Atlantic an antislavery address from Ireland were inspired by O'Connell's numerous transatlantic antislavery communiques. Unionist sympathizers in Ireland realized that the vicissitudes of war had finally created an opening for O'Connell's distinctively Irish antislavery views to gain traction among Irish Americans. This turnabout was perhaps the clearest indication yet that the war had altered how Irish Americans perceived the relationship between American slavery, the American Union, and Irish freedom.[38]

Still, O'Connell's decades-old appeals went far to match the moment in which Irish-American Unionists found themselves. It was left to one of O'Connell's former allies-turned-adversaries from the repeal movement, the exiled Young Irelander Thomas Francis Meagher, to drive home to Irish nationalists in Ireland and America the intertwined stakes of the Union war effort and emancipation. Meagher took an improbable path to championing emancipation during the latter stages of the war. To be sure, his renown as an orator and wordsmith was well established by 1863. But during the sectional crisis, Meagher strove to appease the largely Democratic readership of his newspaper, the *Irish News*, and as late as 1861, he evinced sympathy for secessionists. Ever eager for glory, Meagher joined the 69th New York in 1861 and, through political maneuvering, won command of the Irish Brigade early in 1862. Over the next year, the brigade suffered severe losses, and in May 1863, Meagher threatened to resign if its five regiments were not removed from the front while their manpower was restored. The War Department called Meagher's bluff, and he was removed from command. Allegations that Meagher imbibed to excess on the field of battle and that his men suffered from his vainglorious willingness to commit them to battle dogged him throughout the war. So, too, did the charge from some Irish-American editors that Meagher had abandoned his Democratic allies in favor of the nativist-backed

Republican Party. In light of these facts, some historians have argued that Meagher's influence over the Irish in the loyal states had diminished by 1863.[39]

Yet Meagher remained devoted to the Union war effort after resigning from the Irish Brigade and was undeniably popular among the tens of thousands of active and veteran Irish-born soldiers. The soldiers of the Irish Brigade found his departure from command a bitter pill to swallow. Meagher had acted honorably, they argued, in demanding that the War Department bring the Irish Brigade back up to full strength. Hearty cheers greeted Meagher when he visited with the Irish-American soldiers of Corcoran's Legion at their winter encampment in Virginia in December 1863, and his soaring oratory roused the veterans of the Irish Brigade a few weeks later at a banquet in New York City. Not content to sit out the remainder of the war, Meagher had already visited President Lincoln in November of 1863 to seek out a new command, and in September of 1864, Meagher took command of a detachment of troops tasked with guarding a vital Union supply train that stretched from Nashville to Atlanta. In Nashville that fall, Meagher stumped for Lincoln's reelection. But his efforts to convince his compatriots in Ireland of the merits of emancipation proved to be an even greater service to the cause of the Union.[40]

In the interval between his resignation from the Irish Brigade in May 1863 and his efforts to be reinstated in the army, Meagher penned letters to the editors of two Union-sympathizing Irish newspapers, the *Citizen* and *Irishman*. Each appeared in print in the respective newspapers, as Meagher surely knew they would, allowing not only prospective emigrants but also Irish immigrants in the United States to mull over the famed exile's perspective on the Union war effort. Meagher himself had obtained copies of both Dublin weeklies while in command of the Irish Brigade, and Irish-American newspapers continued the long-standing practice of clipping stories from the Irish press into their own publications. By the end of 1863, the Loyal Publication Society of New York had packaged the two letters together into a pamphlet, giving Meagher a broad, transatlantic audience. At least one Irish-American soldier, First Lieutenant Thomas W. Wildes of the 23rd Illinois, believed that Meagher's influence was great enough to "educate Irish sentiment as regards the true nature of this contest." Fearing that "Irishmen . . . will land in this country, thousands yearly, open enemies of the North and its free institutions" if Meagher and other "distinguished Irishmen" did not write and speak publicly in support of the Union war effort, Wildes must have been elated to see Meagher's letters published in the *Citizen* and the *Irishman*. Between their circulation in the Irish press, reprinting in Irish-American newspapers, and inclusion in the Loyal Publication Society's pamphlet series, Meagher's *Letters* were almost certainly read by tens of thousands of Irish Americans and thousands of prospective emigrants in Ireland.[41]

While Meagher's *Letters* no doubt served his aim to regain a commission in the Union army, they also provided a powerful explanation for why Irish Americans must embrace emancipation. Meagher first explained why he, like virtually all Irish immigrants in the free states, had opposed all varieties of antislavery during the 1850s. "I was not in favor of slavery," Meagher wrote, "but was devoted to the Union; and . . . as the Union involved slavery. . . I had to accept the latter to befriend and serve the former." Enslavers' claims to ownership of Black men and women were protected by the Constitution that naturalized citizens swore to uphold, Meagher observed, and abrogating that oath would make them unworthy of the nation's beneficence. Irish Americans, he claimed, had "stood as a wall of granite between the South and the New England neophytes and crusaders of Exeter Hall." The reference to Exeter Hall, the heart of Britain's antislavery movement, tipped off Meagher's belief, or at least his acknowledgment that many of his compatriots believed, that British abolitionists fomented disunion, a staple of the Irish-American critique of antislavery. Like most Irish Americans, he viewed the sectional crisis through that distinctively Irish lens.[42]

Yet, as Meagher argued, the war profoundly altered Irish immigrants' obligations in the sectional conflict. Secession, in particular, had "emancipated all true Republicans from their complicity with an ordained system of bondage, which . . . neutralized the glory of a Republic, which otherwise was unexceptionable and incomparable." The rebellion, in other words, allowed all lovers of democratic self-government to stop defending a practice they found repulsive. Meagher's use of the phrase "all true Republicans" is noteworthy. Many of his contemporary rivals no doubt took the phrase as confirmation that he now affiliated with the Republican Party and had embraced its antislavery principles and policies. But as Meagher used the term, "true Republicans" were first and foremost those who fought to preserve and perpetuate republican institutions of government. Meagher embraced emancipation as a "true Republican" in 1863 because his background as an Irish nationalist invested him in the survival of republican governance, an outcome that now necessitated the end of slavery.[43]

Just as Meagher explained Irish immigrants' antebellum opposition to emancipation within a transatlantic context of anti-abolitionism, so too did he interpret the significance of Irish-American Unionists' involvement in the war with reference to the Old World. In Meagher's analysis, Irish-American soldiers had joined the Union war effort to thwart the ambitions of an aristocratic order that knew no national bounds. The Confederacy, Meagher surmised in the *Citizen*, threatened to make America "the laughing-stock of the slave-owners and cattle-breeders of Europe generally, and Ireland in particular." It was for this reason that Irish-American soldiers formed "the life, the heart, the soul" of the armies that mobilized to snuff out Confederate nationhood. In P. J. Smyth's *Irishman*, Meagher compared the "dense mist of misery and humiliation" in Ireland with the bright prospect of citizenship and mobility that awaited them in the United States. Devoid of slavery, Meagher asserted, immigrants' adopted country would be "stronger, worthier, nobler than ever" as the reunited nation resumed its place as "the sanctuary and renovation of the impoverished and oppressed of Europe." Having seen the nation nearly meet "the fate of Mexico," politicians would replace the partisanship and quarrelsomeness of the 1850s with a culture of fairness and courage "from the Ward Committee-room to the Halls of Congress." To Meagher, wiping the stain of slavery from the Union was an essential step toward making America an internationally robust, internally unified republic. Doing so would make the country "worthier" of emulation around the world and better able to improve the lives of those who sought refuge from oppression in their land of birth. What Meagher termed the "inexorable logic of war" had transformed emancipation from the Union's gravest threat to its panacea, and as the Union went, so did the fate of the Irish.[44]

While Meagher's *Letters* and his contemporaneous public support of the Lincoln administration and emancipation cost him some admirers among the Irish in America, they also shored up his reputation among Irish-American soldiers. They even provoked begrudging respect from some otherwise antagonistic quarters. In New York, the *Irish-American* claimed that Meagher had sided with the abolitionists who inaugurated and prolonged the war. Meagher's "unprovoked attack upon our people," a reference to Meagher's criticisms of Irish-American Democratic voters, was one thing, but an all-out embrace of the Republican platform was unforgivable. His calls for Irish Americans to embrace emancipation cost Meagher significant influence among the New York Irish. Yet outside and even within New York City, Meagher's star retained its luster. Although his letters to the *Irishman* and *Citizen* outraged constitutional nationalists in Ireland like William Smith O'Brien, who had cast their lots with the Confederacy, Meagher found defenders among his compatriots in America. One wrote to the *Irishman* early in 1864 to declare that if ever there was a cause more deserving of "the prayers of the lovers of freedom throughout the world," it was the Union, which could no longer coexist with slavery. "Irishmen, above all other people ... cannot afford to let the Union go to pieces," the author wrote in concurrence with Meagher. The *Catholic Telegraph*'s correspondent in New York, "Gotham," wrote in

November 1863 to upbraid Meagher's critics, especially those like O'Brien, who questioned the Union's commitment to following through with emancipation. An Irish-American political club in San Francisco that mobilized to support the reelection of President Lincoln in 1864, reportedly numbering more than five thousand, referenced Meagher in an appeal to the Irish in California that linked Ireland's fate with that of the Union and reviled proslavery immigrants. Even the *Pilot* reported positively on an April 1864 speech in which Meagher pointed to slavery as the cause of the war and declared that the institution had to be "utterly destroyed" lest Americans be forced to fight the conflict again and again.[45]

Soldiers offered the most revealing commentary on Meagher's efforts to convince Irish-American nationalists of the need to embrace emancipation to save the Union. Edmund O'Dwyer of the 23rd Illinois agreed with Meagher that Irish Americans had a singular obligation to fight for the nation that provided them refuge and afforded them opportunities unmatched in their native land. An August 1864 poem in the *Catholic Telegraph* about the Irish Brigade put soldiers' perspectives to verse: "A planet of Heaven is hailed in Meagher! / And the airs is rent with a wild huzzah, / For the Stars and Stripes and Erin go Bragh." Though he had long since resigned his command of the unit, Meagher led an open-air celebration near Petersburg, Virginia, for the third anniversary of the Irish Brigade's founding in September 1864. After receiving "a rapturous burst of cheering, such as Irishmen know how to give," Meagher spoke about the upcoming presidential election and urged soldiers to vote for Lincoln, receiving "loud cheers." Collectively, Meagher's *Letters*, his stumping for Lincoln, and his outspoken support for emancipation lost him the support of some Irish-American newspaper editors but enhanced his standing in the eyes of many Irish-American soldiers.[46]

Meagher's earnestness has been treated with deep skepticism by historians. Some point to allegations that he drank in excess while in command and abandoned his first wife and only son as evidence of deficiency in his character. He was unquestionably a political schemer, and his loquaciousness can easily be mistaken for false bravado. But fundamentally, he was someone who spoke in the vernacular of his time, even if he did so more elegantly than most, and who matched his words with actions. Meagher fought to restore the Union in which he saw the fulfillment of his personal ambitions, the improvement of his compatriots in America, and the redemption of the homeland that, in a certain sense, he never left behind. He had defended the interests of enslavers—even justified human bondage—out of a deep-seated belief that a politically unified and economically vibrant United States would elevate the condition of the Irish on both sides of the Atlantic. The war taught him that emancipation was necessary for the states to be reunited, but Meagher also saw Civil War emancipation as a chance to right a wrong. The near destruction of the nation forced Meagher and a great many other Irish Americans to realize the incompatibility of slavery and freedom.

Just as there was no neat and tidy conclusion to the Civil War, there was no definitive resolution to Irish Americans' involvement in the debate and conflict over the future of American slavery. As the embers of war burned down in the form of a string of surrenders by Confederate generals in the spring and summer of 1865, thousands upon thousands of Irish-born Union soldiers returned home with fundamentally changed views on African American slavery and its effects on the politics, economy, and society of their adopted country and their native Ireland. Many of the Irish-American journalists, clergymen, and nationalist leaders who celebrated the soldiers' return had arrived at a similar realization that slavery was incompatible with their transatlantic interests in preserving the American Union. Passage on January 31, 1865, of the 13th Amendment, which abolished slavery and involuntary servitude in the United States and its territories except as punishment of a crime, rendered mute the dissent of what was likely a great many Irish Americans who remained opposed to emancipation. Even as the last Confederate forces fought futilely to maintain their toehold on independence, questions pertaining to the reconstruction of the nation, including how formerly Confederate states would be readmitted to the Union and what was to become of the roughly four million newly freed African Americans, dominated national discourse. Seen in this light, Irish Americans' general acceptance by 1865 of the necessity of wartime emancipation appears as but a trifle in the saga of the Civil War.[47]

Yet the fact that a significant, if indeterminate, number of Irish Americans had not only accepted but also, in many cases, embraced and even hastened the demise of African American slavery *was* meaningful to contemporaries. It was not lost upon James Gordon Bennett's *New York Herald*, one of the most widely circulated newspapers in the loyal states. "Previous to the Rebellion," the *Herald* recounted in an April 1864 article, "our citizens of Irish birth were to be found . . . among the most active and unscrupulous of the Pro-Slavery propagandists. They were in favor of the institution of Slavery, and their opposition to every party that avowed any desire to ameliorate the condition of the negro might be counted upon as a foregone conclusion." However, the war had wrought previously unimaginable changes in how Irish Americans thought and acted with respect to the question of slavery's future. "What could not be done with these people by argument," the *Herald* opined, referring to the tortured relationship between the American Irish and antislavery reformers, "the slow teachings of time and rough schoolings of this war are fast accomplishing." Pointing to prominent Irish-American proponents of emancipation like Charles Halpine and Fenian Head Centre John O'Mahony, the *Herald* envisioned a radically different future concerning relations between the American Irish and African Americans. "Let us hope," the article concluded, "that the old jealousy or dislike of the negro will soon be a forgotten prejudice in the minds of all classes of our citizens; and, indeed, that it is fast becoming so in the minds of our Irish-born fellow-citizens, we have good reason to believe." Unfortunately, the author mistook a pendulum swing in Irish Americans' views on the enslavement of African Americans for a broader revolution in American race relations. But given that less than a year earlier, thousands of Irish-born New Yorkers had amassed in lynch mobs in the streets of Manhattan, his optimism is understandable. The examples of Halpine, O'Mahony, and hundreds, if not thousands, of other Irish Americans who had written, spoken, or acted on behalf of Black freedom over the past few years must have seemed a miraculous turnabout.[48]

"This war has been a great educator," an Irish immigrant in New Haven, Connecticut, began in a May 1864 letter to the *Catholic Telegraph*. The pupil that he had in mind was Colonel Thomas Cahill of the 9th Connecticut, an Irish-American infantry regiment from the author's hometown. Cahill departed from New Haven "a DOUGLAS Democrat," according to the author, and the colonel's letters to his family and friends reveal that, as late as July 1862, he had little sympathy for enslaved African Americans. But when he returned in May 1864, Cahill had become "a Democrat in the legitimate and only true sense of that much-abused word; an earnest believer in the equal rights of men, an advocate of universal freedom." He had never truly been a "pro-slavery man," but neither had he allowed his inborn dislike for slavery to override a commitment to preserving his adopted country. The war, though, had "made his thoughts words, and his words deeds," meaning Cahill now spoke and acted against slavery. While he had not needed these invigorated antislavery convictions to make him fight harder, Cahill's New Haven friend concluded, they provided "even a holier purpose to that which first inspired him to take up arms for the preservation of the Union."[49]

*Conclusion:
Irish America and Ireland
after the Civil War*

Irish Americans like Thomas Cahill who were proud "Douglas Democrats" before the Civil War had insisted then and throughout the duration of the conflict that their views on and involvement in the debate over the future of American slavery emanated from a desire to protect and strengthen the American Union. Many of them perceived a tension between nationalism and antislavery before they arrived in the United States. In the 1840s, the transatlantic antislavery movement's position that abolition took precedent over Irish sovereignty and even the amelioration of famine-stricken peasants led nationalists in Ireland to develop an Irish critique of abolitionism. The Irish critique of abolitionism found fertile ground in antebellum America, especially because the famine migration, American donations to Irish famine relief, and the proliferation of Irish revolutionary societies inspired a uniquely transatlantic spirit of nationalism among the American Irish. The United States was destined to play a singular role in the betterment of Irish emigrants and in the liberation of Ireland, or so influential Irish-American journalists and exiled nationalists claimed. Any threat to the republic's system of constitutional democracy, its flawed but ultimately uplifting economy, or its capability to aid aspiring republics was therefore inimical to the interests of Irish people on both sides of the Atlantic. Abolitionism was one such threat, they insisted, for not only had it divided Irish nationalists during the famine, but it also pushed proslavery Southerners to go to extreme lengths to maintain and perpetuate African American slavery, even potentially breaking apart the nation itself. Not far removed from the abolitionists were antislavery politicians whose anti-Irish proclivities took center stage during the Know-Nothings' ascent and who, under the umbrella of the Republican Party in the late 1850s, turned a blind eye to the misfortunes of Irish immigrants and irreparably divided the nation. For Cahill and many other Irish Americans like him in the 1840s and 1850s, the pillars of anti-abolitionism were anchored securely to a foundation of nationalism.

But as the "education" of Thomas Cahill suggests, the circumstances of war, which for Irish Americans included not only what happened on Southern battlefields and Northern docks but also on Irish farms and in Dublin newspaper offices, reversed the dynamic between nationalism and antislavery. Developments in both the United States and Ireland affirmed Irish Americans' conviction that the Union's survival was vital to the interests of prospective emigrants and the ultimate success of the Irish national cause. Secession not only threatened to render toothless the Constitution that bestowed the rights and privileges of American citizenship upon Irish immigrants but also dealt a potentially lethal blow to the principles of democracy itself, thereby opening the nation's door to "Old World" systems of power. Meanwhile, revolutionary Irish nationalism in the form of the Fenian Brotherhood found a congenial climate in the Union, especially within its armed forces. For contemporaries, it was a distinct possibility that the restoration of the American Union would be followed by an American-backed liberation of Ireland led by battle-tested Irish-American veterans. Irish republican nationalist editors cheered on the loyal citizenry who mobilized to fight on behalf of democratic principles and lauded Unionists' ability to send relief to suffering Irish farmers even while continuing to wage war. The fact that many Irish faced the prospect of famine again was another indication that future generations of prospective emigrants would look to the United States for socioeconomic stability and improvement. Even as these developments reinforced the tenets of Irish-American Unionism, the actions of enslaved people and their interactions with Irish-American soldiers in the Union army disproved a long-standing assumption that the perpetuation of slavery was an evil necessary for the Republic's survival. Enslaved men and women who laundered Irish-American soldiers' clothes, drove their supply wagons, provided them with military intelligence, and eventually donned the same uniforms as them were unquestionably Unionists. As the war continued, the cause-and-effect relationship between enslaved African Americans' acts of self-liberation and the Confederates' weakened capacity to wage war was difficult to ignore. While not all Irish-American soldiers came to adopt Thomas Cahill's belief in "the equal rights of men," most came to understand that emancipation hastened the restoration of the Union and uprooted the source of its internecine conflict. By 1865, their views were echoed by a growing number of Irish and Irish-American journalists and nationalist leaders who counseled Irish people on both sides of the Atlantic to embrace emancipation.

For the vast majority of Irish-American Unionists, emancipation was a cudgel with which to beat back an armed rebellion against America's constitutional democracy. To be sure, that motive led many native- and non-Irish, foreign-born Unionists to support emancipation during the war. But Irish-American perspectives on American nationhood arose from a singular, transatlantic confluence of events that, cumulatively, tied the economic, political, and national aspirations of Irish people to the perpetuity of a robust American Republic. When the vicissitudes of war proved that the republic's survival hinged on the demise of slavery, Irish-American Unionists figuratively and at times literally admitted their error in having spoken, voted, and acted in opposition to the antislavery movement. If, as the present work has argued, Irish-American Unionism ultimately trumped Irish-American opposition to antislavery, then did its promises of economic security, political empowerment, and national belonging for future generations of Irish hold true?

In addition to the roughly 2 million Irish-born men, women, and children who lived in the United States in 1865, the next three and a half decades witnessed the arrival of nearly 3 million more immigrants from Ireland. By 1900, the United States was home to some 1.6 million people born in Ireland and nearly 3.4 million of their American-born children. Those 5 million Irish Americans outnumbered the total population of Ireland. While immigration from Ireland made up a diminishing share of immigration totals in the late 1800s, it was still impressive. In the 1870s, 15.5 percent of all immigrant arrivals came from Ireland—a figure that dropped to 12.5 percent in the 1880s, and to 10.5 percent in the 1890s. While no part of Ireland was left untouched by emigration, those who departed for the United States after the Civil War were disproportionately from the western province of Connaught, and many of these (half in the 1880s) were Irish speakers. Their decisions to leave Ireland resulted from a combination of depressed agricultural prices, the eviction of small farmers and landless tenant laborers, and the absence of an urban industrial base where displaced rural dwellers could find work. After the famine, agricultural land was increasingly consolidated by so-called strong farmers who evicted smallholders and cottiers and converted the land from tillage to pasture. This process of consolidating and commercializing Irish agriculture unfolded over decades, ensuring a steady stream of displaced rural poor with few options other than emigration. In 1875, 75 percent of departing emigrants were classified as either laborers or servants, a percentage that rose to a startling 91 percent at the turn of the twentieth century.[1]

For the millions of unskilled, displaced rural Irish in search of new homes in the latter third of the nineteenth century, America's booming industrial economy, combined with the relative ease of transatlantic travel and the presence of an established Irish-born community, made settlement in the United States a logical choice. Irish Americans sent hundreds of millions of dollars to Ireland in the second half of the nineteenth century, much of which took the form of prepaid transatlantic ship fare. While several attempts were made to establish Irish farming colonies deep in the American interior, none succeeded on a replicable scale. Instead, post–Civil War Irish immigrants continued to settle disproportionately in established urban Northern enclaves, especially in the mid-Atlantic, New England, and the Midwest. There, they remained much more likely than native-born residents and other immigrant groups to receive charitable aid, to be arrested for drunk and disorderly conduct, and to be institutionalized. The disproportionately high numbers of post–Civil War immigrants who came from Irish-speaking communities and owned little or no land before their departure were especially vulnerable to the vices of urban-industrial America. Many of those who maintained steady work and lived as "good Christians" still did so for pittance wages and amid squalid living conditions in the nation's poorest slums.[2]

Yet the late-nineteenth century also saw considerable improvement in the socioeconomic prospects of the Irish in America, even if that improvement was, in the words of one historian, "slow, halting, and incomplete." In the Irish case, economic improvement was not of the "rags to riches" variety but was marked by a transition from unskilled, common labor to semi-skilled or skilled work. By the end of the century, 35 percent of Irish Americans were employed in white-collar or farming work, with an additional 50 percent employed in skilled trades. The significance of these figures is that they were virtually identical to those for white Americans of native birth and parentage. Correspondingly, Irish Americans became just as likely as their white, native-born peers to own property, even if wages from adolescent children were often necessary for Irish-American families to join the propertied ranks. While immigrants typically experienced smaller degrees of occupational and socioeconomic mobility, their children fared much better. For example, one out of every ten Irish-born Bostonians in 1890 worked in white-collar occupations, but four out of every ten American-born children of Irish immigrants in the city did the same. Irish Americans made up 6 percent of the nation's population in 1900, but they made up 20 percent of all teachers in Northern cities. Teaching was one of a handful of white-collar professions, including secretaries, stenographers, and nurses, into which Irish-American women entered in greater numbers by the 1880s and 1890s. Most striking to contemporaries was that Irish women dominated the ranks of domestic service in the second half of the nineteenth century. To be sure, that line of work was, in a basic sense, servile and potentially exploitative, especially as it left women vulnerable to the unwanted sexual advances and abuses of the fathers and sons whose houses they toiled and lived in. But it also offered hundreds of thousands of Irish women and their children an eventual path to middle-class respectability. That path simply did not exist in Ireland, where the alternative was a far less remunerative life of domestic servitude under the watchful and judging eyes of a father or elder brother. Indeed, regardless of gender, Irish Americans in late-nineteenth-century America found socio-economic stability and generational upward mobility, the likes of which were difficult, if not impossible, to come by in their native land.[3]

In the political realm of the late nineteenth century, Irish-American men experienced a similar combination of persistent marginalization and steady upward progress. On the one hand, the Irish in post–Civil War America suffered from their long-standing association with the Democratic Party, which, in the eyes of myriad voters and legislators, was the party of slavery and treason. The democratizing impulse behind the extension of voting rights to Black men during Reconstruction also animated Republicans' efforts to ensure fair and free elections—efforts that targeted Democratic political machines like Tammany Hall, whose Irish-American base willingly took part in election-rigging schemes. Provisions of the Naturalization Act of 1870, passed by a Republican-dominated Congress, aimed to crack down on false voter registration, double voting, and ballot rigging. In particular, the Naturalization Act's six-month extension of the period before which newly naturalized citizens could vote and its centralization of naturalization records were thinly veiled attempts to limit immigrants' political clout, which punched overwhelmingly in favor of the Democratic Party. The Naturalization Act of 1870, when seen from a global perspective, was an attempt by Congress to assert its authority over a growing and increasingly cosmopolitan foreign-born population that, led by Irish-born Fenians, demanded protections from the designs of Old-World sovereigns who refused to recognize their departed subjects' American citizenship. However, viewed from Tammany Hall, the Naturalization Act was a message to Irish Americans that their influence on national politics was unwelcome.[4]

However, at the local level, Irish Americans found in late-nineteenth century urban political machines the perfect vehicle for meeting the needs of their Irish-born constituencies and enabling some of them to gain access to municipal and state chambers of power. With tens of thousands of newly arrived Irish adding annually to the already inflated numbers of Irish-born and second-generation Irish-American urban dwellers, many cities saw their school boards, city councils, and mayoral chambers come under varying degrees of Irish-American influence if not outright control. New York's Tammany Hall was only the most infamous of the dozens of Irish-dominated political machines that ushered in an era of Irish-American urban political power. Machines like Tammany offered money, jobs, physical protection, and even a shortcut to citizenship to Irish immigrants in exchange for their promises to cast ballots for machine-backed candidates.

They also functioned as springboards to elected office for the American-born children of Irish immigrants. Fourteen-year-old Michael Curley came to Boston in 1864 from a small farm in County Galway with his two half-brothers, Daniel and Patrick. He found work as a hod carrier in the City of Boston's paving department thanks to the beneficence of P. James "Pea-Jacket" Maguire, a ward boss in nearby Roxbury where Michael lodged alongside other Galway natives. The work was grueling, but it supported Michael enough to allow for marriage and children, including a son named James, born in 1874; soon after his father's death in 1884, James adopted Michael as a middle name. Whereas Michael, a teenage Irish immigrant, relied on the deeply personal ward politics of post–Civil War Boston to find work, James Michael Curley would come to control the politics of the ward itself by the time he was twenty-five—but only after he latched onto one of its two rival machine factions to secure a seat on the Boston Common Council in 1900. Two years later, Curley was elected to serve as a representative in the state legislature. As if to cement his status as a force to be reckoned with, he established a new machine headquartered in what Curley playfully dubbed the "Tammany Club." It would serve as the base of his storied and often scandalous political career over the next half-century.[5]

To be sure, James Michael Curley was a singular figure in American political history, let alone the history of the Irish in America after the Civil War. And it says something of the continued plight of Irish-born laborers in late-nineteenth-century America that Curley's father died as the result of a jobsite accident. Still, the outward signs of Irish Americans' socio-economic and political ascent were unmistakable by the time that Curley took his seat on Boston's Common Council. Ironically, Irish-American Union veterans in the 1880s and 1890s worried that this more prosperous generation had forgotten the sacrifices they and their fallen comrades made during the war. From their perspective, the hundreds of thousands of Irish Americans who helped to defeat the Confederate rebellion had bequeathed to Michael Curley the ability to find remunerative work and raise a family and to James Michael Curley the ability to climb the political ladder afforded by America's system of constitutional democracy. With greater frequency around the turn of the century, many of these former soldiers published regimental histories or personal war memoirs and organized or contributed to campaigns to erect monuments and statues for prominent Irish-American units or individual soldiers. A common theme in these acts of memory-making was that the socioeconomic stability and political liberties enjoyed by Irish Americans today would be distant dreams if not for the soldiers' wartime sacrifices.[6]

If, on the one hand, Irish-American Unionism held out promises of economic stability and political liberty for the Irish in America and prospective emigrants, then on the other hand, it celebrated the American Union as a champion of Irish sovereignty and model republic for the Irish people to emulate. Thus, even as Irish-American veterans looked back in time to keep the memory of their service to the Union alive, many joined hundreds of thousands of other Irish-American nationalists after the Civil War in looking forward to Irish independence. Indeed, by the time the war ended in 1865, the revolutionary Fenian Brotherhood claimed fifty thousand members, many of whom were Union veterans. Rumors swirled that these American Fenians planned to infiltrate Ireland and lead tens of thousands of members of the Irish Republican Brotherhood (IRB) in an armed rebellion. A contingent of American Fenians established operations in Dublin soon after Lee's surrender at Appomattox and set in motion plans for a rising. But in September 1865, British authorities preemptively imprisoned key leaders of the IRB, along with a handful of Irish-American Union veterans suspected of fomenting revolution. Still, Irish-American Unionists who believed the United States was destined to help secure Irish independence had good reason to be optimistic. Initially, Fenianism enjoyed an unusual level of support from influential editors at the New York *Herald* and *New York Tribune*. That support was due in no small part to the British government's dalliance with recognizing Confederate sovereignty during the war and stubborn refusal to compensate the federal government for damage to American naval vessels inflicted by British-built Confederate ships. Perhaps most promisingly, high-ranking officials in Washington—including President Andrew Johnson—praised the Fenians and spoke in favor of Irish independence.[7]

Over the next five years, the Fenian movement suffered a series of setbacks that threatened to dash Irish-American Unionists' dreams of an American-backed Irish independence movement. British authorities' crackdown on the IRB in Dublin prompted competing factions of American Fenians to redirect their armed revolutionary activity at Canada. Britain's North American colony, they argued, might be taken hostage by a Fenian invasion force and surrendered only in exchange for Irish independence. Although thousands of Fenians participated in numerous invasions of Canada in 1866, the organization's hopelessly divided leadership made coordinated action impossible. Worse still, when push came to shove, the Johnson administration condemned Fenians' violation of American neutrality and directed federal forces to intercept Fenian raids on New Brunswick and Quebec. Their Canadian schemes dashed, Fenians led by Union veteran John O'Mahony once again focused their efforts on Ireland by pressuring embattled IRB leader James Stephens to call for a rising. Stephens reluctantly complied, and on March 5, 1867, hundreds of IRB members instigated skirmishes at more than a dozen sites around Dublin and in the south of the island. But the 1867 rising was little more than a loosely coordinated series of shootouts that led to hundreds of arrests and lengthy prison terms for its leaders. Adding insult to injury, an American Fenian filibustering expedition aboard the optimistically re-christened vessel *Erin's Hope* arrived off the Atlantic coast of Ireland several weeks too late for its cargo of rifles, canons, and ammunition, along with dozens of Irish-American Union veterans, to be of use in the rising. Frustrated by their American counterparts' overeagerness and internecine squabbling, IRB leaders in 1868 severed relations with the Fenian Brotherhood. Two years later, Union army veteran John O'Neill led a band of die-hard American Fenians in another failed Canadian invasion. Shortly after his men exchanged fire with Canadian militia, O'Neill was arrested and charged with violating the American Neutrality Act. O'Neill's arrest came on the heels of an agreement between American and British officials that exempted British-born American citizens from perpetual allegiance to the Crown, dealing yet another blow to Fenians' hopes of precipitating an Anglo-American war. For all intents and purposes, the Fenian Brotherhood's plan to liberate Ireland at the hands of revolutionary Irish-American nationalists had collapsed.[8]

Yet Fenianism bore a lasting influence on Irish nationalism, one that aligned neatly with a core tenet of Irish-American Unionism in the Civil War era: Nationalists in Ireland continued to rely on the American Irish for ideological, strategic, and financial support. Fenians' plans to foment a concerted transatlantic armed struggle against British rule in Ireland were shunned by late-nineteenth and early-twentieth-century nationalists. But the numerical strength, organizational prowess, and ideological clarity with which Fenianism operated in the 1860s left nationalists on both sides of the Atlantic convinced that Irish-American strategizing, money, and political capital would be critical factors in future nationalist endeavors. Even as the Fenian movement collapsed, it was succeeded in the United States by a more secretive revolutionary society, Clan na Gael, whose New York City–based leadership in 1877 reestablished ties to the IRB in Dublin via a seven-member Joint Revolutionary Directory. Led by John Devoy, an IRB veteran who emerged as a prolific journalist after immigrating to New York in 1871, Clan na Gael became the preeminent militant nationalist organization in the Irish diaspora. Funding from its tens of thousands of members and Devoy's organizational prowess proved crucial to the 1916 Easter Rising in Dublin that set the stage for a war of independence in 1919–21.[9]

Irish Americans' influence on Irish politics and society extended beyond physical force republicanism, whose devotees by the late 1870s were in the minority among nationalists in the diaspora. In 1878, Devoy pledged Clan na Gael's support for Irish MPs' efforts to secure domestic autonomy, or Home Rule, for Ireland through constitutional means, a campaign led by the County Wicklow landlord and son of an American mother, Charles Stewart Parnell. Simultaneously, IRB Supreme Council member Michael Davitt convinced Devoy to champion the cause of Irish land reform amid an escalating agrarian conflict between tenants and landlords across the island. Dubbed the New Departure, the now intertwined causes of militant republicanism, Home Rule, and land reform united otherwise disparate segments of Irish society and Irish America. In 1879–80, Parnell toured the United States, where he delivered speeches in sixty-two cities, raised hundreds of thousands of dollars to support embattled Irish tenant farmers, and lectured a joint session of Congress on the justice of Home Rule while also aiding in the establishment of the American Land League before his departure. Within two years, the Land League boasted more than one thousand branches across the United States. These branches contributed money to support Irish Home Rule MPs and the many tenant farmers who battled the Irish landlord system figuratively and, at times, literally. The Land League also served as a vehicle through which Irish Americans could address problems of labor and economic inequality in the United States. Best encapsulated by *Irish World and American Industrial Liberator* editor Patrick Ford's dictum that the "cause of the poor in Donegal is the cause of the factory slave of Fall River," these intersecting efforts to attack socioeconomic injustice in Ireland and the United States saw thousands of Irish Americans step to the forefront of American radicalism. Increasingly, however, the essentially political concerns of the militant Republicans led by Devoy and constitutional nationalists led by Parnell pushed the fundamentally economic grievances of reformers like Davitt and Ford to the margins. Ultimately, Parnell's infamous part in a scandalous divorce case and sudden death in 1891 scuttled the Home Rule campaign, while Devoy redirected Clan na Gael's energies back to plotting the violent overthrow of British rule in Ireland.[10]

The transatlantic ties that bound Irish and Irish-American nationalists were again on display amid the culminating events of the Irish independence movement from 1916 to 1921. The proclamation of an independent Irish Republic set forth outside Dublin's Grand Post Office by leaders of the Easter Rising on April

24, 1916, noted that the rebellion was "supported by [Ireland's] exiled children in America," and with good reason. Still in command of Clan na Gael, John Devoy was brought into the planning of the rebellion by leaders of the IRB, who relied on Devoy for much-needed funds and for plans to procure German arms amid the ongoing world war. Simultaneously, Devoy and other Clan na Gael leaders organized a new organization, the Friends of Irish Freedom (FOIF), in anticipation of the rising. After British forces suppressed the rebellion and executed sixteen of its leaders, the FOIF whipped up Irish-American support for the rebels. By 1919, the FOIF claimed some three hundred thousand members, most of whom had formerly supported Home Rulers' peaceful approach to Irish independence. This sudden and virtually unanimous shift to physical-force nationalism among Irish Americans was mirrored in Ireland by the rapid political ascent of Sinn Féin, which captured 73 out of Ireland's 105 seats in Parliament in the December 1918 elections. Refusing to sit in a legislative body whose authority they refused to recognize, Sinn Féin delegates met instead in Dublin in January 1919, where they declared Ireland's independence. Over the next two and a half years, the newly established Irish Republican Army (IRA) waged a brutal guerilla war against British forces sent to bring Ireland back into the fold of the British Empire.[11]

During the Irish War of Independence (1919–21), Irish Americans waged a campaign on two fronts to secure Irish sovereignty. On the one hand, hundreds of thousands of Irish-American voters and scores of Irish-American elected officials lobbied President Woodrow Wilson to make Irish independence a condition of the peace settlement in Europe. After Wilson balked and the Treaty of Versailles did not recognize the Irish Republic, Irish Americans lobbied the Senate to reject the treaty. In 1920, Irish-American women led picket line protests outside the British embassy in Washington, D.C., and convinced Irish-American longshoremen in New York to refuse to handle the cargo of British ships docked on Manhattan's West Side. On the other hand, Irish Americans continued to send enormous sums of money to the republican cause in Ireland, amounting to some $10 million in the five years between the Easter Rising and the conclusion of the War of Independence. Additionally, Americans purchased more than $5 million in bond certificates issued by *Dáil Éireann*, the new Irish parliament. The bond certificate drive was a key feature of an eighteen-month tour of the United States by Éamon de Valera, a participant in the Easter Rising whose life was spared by British authorities on account of his American birth. Newly elected as the first president of the Irish Republic, de Valera returned to the land of his birth not only to raise money for the fledgling Irish government but also to strategize with the likes of Devoy and other FOIF leaders. Ultimately, de Valera chafed at the FOIF's insistence that Irish sovereignty depended on recognition by the international community. In 1920, he joined dissident Irish-American nationalists in a new organization, the American Association for Recognition of the Irish Republic (AARIR), whose membership quickly ballooned to seven hundred thousand.[12]

The AARIR's meteoric rise in 1920–21 was to be a high point for Irish-American nationalism. In December 1921, Irish and British leaders signed the Articles of Agreement, a Treaty between Great Britain and Ireland. The treaty effectively ended the War of Independence even as it set the stage for an even bloodier civil war in Ireland. While the 1921 treaty served as official recognition by the British government of Irish independence, that independence took the form of an Irish Free State within the British Commonwealth whose legislators would swear an oath of allegiance to the British Crown. To hardline republicans like de Valera, the treaty constrained Irish sovereignty and maintained a detestable connection to the monarchy. Vocalizing his objections to the treaty during a January 1922 debate in the *Dáil*, de Valera drew from Lincoln's Gettysburg Address. "I believe fundamentally in the right of the Irish people to govern themselves," the Irish president stated. "I believe fundamentally in government of the people by the people and, if I may add the other part, for the people. That is my fundamental creed." Critics of the treaty also lamented its silence on how the six Ulster counties that remained part of Great Britain, recently recognized by Parliament as Northern Ireland, would ultimately become part of the Free State. These objections notwithstanding, the *Dáil* approved the treaty by a narrow margin in January, prompting anti-treaty legislators led by de Valera to walk out in protest. By April, anti-treaty "Irregular" forces occupied government buildings in Dublin in defiance of the Free State government; their occupation continued even after a pro-treaty mandate in June elections secured Free State leaders' control of the *Dáil*. Given the choice by British Prime Minister David Lloyd George to subdue the anti-treatyites himself or face a British invading force to accomplish the same, Free State leader Michael Collins ordered his forces on June 28 to attack the Irregulars who occupied Dublin's Four Courts building. The Irish Civil War had commenced.[13]

By the time the Irish Civil War ended in 1923 with the victory of pro-treaty Free State forces, the virtual unanimity that once characterized Irish-American support for the republican cause had succumbed to a mixture of pro- and anti-treaty partisanship and melancholy over the bloodshed in Ireland. Irish Americans whose interests in Ireland centered on issues of social and economic equality had long since abandoned hopes of effecting their visions of revolution there.

Indeed, the Irish Free State that emerged in 1923 was a far cry from the Irish Republic envisioned by John Devoy, and the nagging poverty that continued to push rural Irish dwellers to seek new homes abroad proved a disappointment to the ideological heirs of Michael Davitt and Patrick Ford. As the Irish Free State settled into a stable yet uninspiring existence in the 1920s and 1930s, former Irish-American nationalists once deeply invested in the Irish republican cause redirected their energies into the American labor movement or electoral politics in the United States.[14]

Despite Irish Americans' ambivalence concerning the politics of the Irish Free State, by 1923, there was no denying that both the Irish in America and the United States itself had played consequential parts in the decades-long campaign to establish a sovereign Irish nation. More than any living individual, John Devoy embodied the transatlantic Irish nationalist movement. In the summer of 1924, Devoy made only his second trip back to Ireland since he was exiled in 1871. During a six-week sojourn, Devoy received a hero's welcome across the island, including a dockside welcoming committee headed by the distinguished Irish poet William Butler Yeats and a visit with President William T. Cosgrave. In announcing Devoy's impending arrival, the *Freeman's Journal* lauded the Clan na Gael founder and New Departure architect for his persistence in the cause of Irish independence. "Each opportunity as it offered," the Dublin newspaper recounted, "he seized to advance the cause that he had at his heart as far as it might be advanced in the circumstances of the hour." Observing that Devoy had first joined the Fenian movement as a young man in Dublin in 1861, the *Journal* pointed out the remarkable fact that Devoy was a principal player in the events of 1916, some fifty-five years later. Above all else, the article emphasized, Devoy had an unrivaled ability to "muster all the sympathetic forces that existed in the Greater Ireland of the West." In that pithy phrase—"the Greater Ireland of the West"—the *Journal* perfectly encapsulated a spirit of transatlantic nationalism that had sustained Irish Americans' efforts to marshal their money, intellect, and political capital, as well as their adopted country's international influence, in support of an independent Ireland.[15]

In the final analysis, Irish Americans in the decades after the Civil War seized the opportunities for economic security, political empowerment, and national belonging that Civil War–era Irish-American Unionists had fought to preserve in the form of a robust American Republic. Of course, it is impossible to know what would have become of the Curleys and countless other emigrant families or when and on what terms Ireland would have gained its sovereignty if the Union war effort had failed. The main point here is that the intertwined histories of

Irish America and Ireland in the half-century after the Civil War bore out Irish-American Unionists' core belief that the perpetuity of the American Union held intrinsic benefits for Irish people on both sides of the Atlantic Ocean. As this study has argued, that belief animated Irish-American opposition to all varieties of antislavery before the Civil War just as much as it eventually pushed many Irish Americans to embrace emancipation for the sake of restoring the Union.

The interdependence of American nationhood, American slavery, and the future of Irish people in the United States and Ireland was not lost on Patrick Ford, who, from 1870 until the early twentieth century, edited the nation's most widely read Irish-American newspaper. Having settled in Boston with his family during the famine, Ford obtained a position as a printer's devil at William Lloyd Garrison's *Liberator* in the 1850s. The stint under Garrison primed him for a lifelong battle against injustice and inequality, most of which unfolded in newspaper columns. His career in journalism was only interrupted by the outbreak of the Civil War in 1861, at which time the twenty-four-year-old Galway native enlisted in the 9th Massachusetts Regiment and, in that capacity, became an agent of emancipation. Upon the war's conclusion, Ford relocated to South Carolina, where, over the next few years, he oversaw two newspapers whose chief concerns were equal rights for African Americans and the cause of Irish independence. Finding a limited readership and ample hostility for promoting Black voting rights, Ford moved to New York City in 1870, where he established the *Irish World*.[16]

Ford's stewardship of the *Irish World* ensured that Irish Americans in the late nineteenth and early twentieth centuries could not forget their economic, political, and national ambitions were interwoven with those of other injured and oppressed peoples, not the least of whom were African Americans. During its first two decades of publication, the *Irish World* (amended in 1879 to the *Irish World and American Industrial Liberator*) displaced the Boston *Pilot* as the mouthpiece of Irish America. The newspaper's circulation reached 50,000 by 1878 and doubled by 1884. When Ford handed control of the *Irish World* to his son, Patrick, in the early twentieth century, the newspaper boasted a circulation of 125,000, including 20,000 in Ireland. On the one hand, the *Irish World*'s success was owed to Ford's masterful fusion of the cause of Irish sovereignty with the cause of the Irish poor in Ireland and the United States. Ford argued that Irish independence would materially improve conditions for the people of Ireland only if it were accompanied by radical changes in the island's landholding system that would turn peasants into proprietors of the land they worked. But Ford did not stop there, pointing to the condition of working-class Irish Americans as symptomatic of the need to redress the structural inequalities inherent in American capitalism.

He instructed his Irish-American readers to see trade unionism, the eight-hour workday, and the breaking up of monopolies as part and parcel with Irish tenant farmers' rent strikes and boycotts of land agents. In this way, Ford built upon an established transatlantic and increasingly diasporic conception of Irish identity. On the other hand, Ford used the pages of the *Irish World* to champion the cause of Ashantis who fought against British colonialism, Native Americans who fought against American imperialism, and especially African Americans who fought to maintain hard-won rights of citizenship and, for men, suffrage. Ford demanded that his Irish-American and Irish readers see the common plight they shared with African Americans, especially because racism remained ingrained in Irish-American life. The "factory slave" of Fall River, the landless peasant in Donegal, and the sharecropper in the Mississippi Delta were all, in Ford's vision, "defrauded workingm[e]n." Thus, Ford encouraged African Americans to join the Land League in the 1880s and advocated for working people to organize across the color line. Ford's views won him admiration from former leading lights of the abolitionist movement like Wendell Phillips and James Redpath, as well as from Black reformers like T. Thomas Fortune and Frederick Douglass.[17]

It bears emphasis that Ford's promotion of interracial cooperation and his belief that race had no influence on national belonging were rare among late-nineteenth-century Irish Americans. But here we must recall the unanimity with which Irish Americans had stood in opposition to reformers and politicians who championed the basic condition of Black freedom only a decade before Ford printed the first issue of the *Irish World*. Seen in this light, the fact that the most popular Irish-American newspaper in the half-century after the Civil War championed economic justice, voting rights, and civil rights for African Americans becomes all the more remarkable. His newspaper's circulation figures suggest that Ford struck a chord with a significant segment of Irish America, one that had the potential not only to foster a transatlantic movement of Irish working people but also to transcend the color line in the United States. Perhaps the origins of Ford's vision are to be found in his time as a soldier in the 9th Massachusetts, where he had marched, bunked, and fought alongside formerly proslavery Irish Americans whose commitment to restoring the Union led them to embrace emancipation. Then, preserving the American Republic had provided sufficient motivation for Irish Americans to aid and abet the emancipation of enslaved African Americans. Was it possible, then, that Irish people who sought an Irish nation where they earned the fruits of their labor on their soil might make common cause with freed men and women whose aims were essentially the same?

Acknowledgments

Any work that takes this long to come to fruition necessarily incurs many debts. I can't thank enough my peers, colleagues, and family who have, in countless ways, supported me personally and professionally (and often both) along the way.

For the better part of two decades, I've benefited from the encouragement, intellect, and friendship of two teachers and mentors. At Bridgewater State College, Tom Turner's class on the Civil War lit a spark in me that hasn't died out. I became fascinated with Irish immigrants' involvement in the Civil War when I first encountered the Irish Brigade's monument at Gettysburg during the spring break of that semester in Tom's Civil War class. Without his encouragement to pursue graduate studies in history, my life would be very different.

When I started at Boston College, Kevin Kenny saw in my scholarship something that I didn't know was there. More importantly, he also saw what was lacking. I didn't fully appreciate the value of his handwritten, painstakingly precise editing of seminar papers and dissertation chapter drafts until I tried to provide it to my own students. In that feedback, and in countless conversations in between, I learned what it is to be a historian.

I also had the great fortune to study nineteenth-century American history and the Civil War era under Cynthia Lynn Lyerly and Heather Cox Richardson, both of whom served on my dissertation committee and thereby improved this book. Lynn added the much-needed point of view of a historian of the American South, while Heather pushed me to clarify many convoluted ideas and sentences.

As this project took shape, languished, and came back to life, I benefited from feedback, words of encouragement, and models of exemplary scholarship from Rachel Ball, Catherine Bateson, David Brundage, Pete Cajka, Tom Chaffin, Adam Chill, Mimi Cowan, Jim Downs, David Gleeson, Eli Janis, Matt Karp, Ryan Keating, Brian Kelley, Will Kurtz, Niamh Lynch, Caleb McDaniel, Gráinne McEvoy, Julie Mujic, David Quigley, Edward Rugemer, Chris Samito, Rob Savage, Aaron Sheehan-Dean, Damian Shiels, Cathal Smith, Owen Stanwood, Chris Staysniak, Susannah J. Ural, Kid Wongsrichanalai, and Jim Zibro. Hidetaka Hirota has always inspired me to be a better historian, while conversations over beers and baskets of wings with Seth Meehan and Clayton Trutor have been a constant source of support. Angela Murphy talked through ideas about this project with me when it was a dissertation and then gave a thoughtful review of the manuscript. I'm forever grateful to Andy Slap for waiting out long overdue revisions to this manuscript and for twice providing a careful reading of it. Fred Nachbaur and his team at Fordham University Press steered the manuscript to its conclusion, and Mildred Sanchez performed herculean copyediting work.

As exemplary teacher-scholars, colleagues at Springfield College inspired me to get this to the finish line. Thanks to Tom Carty, Laurel Davis-Delano, Justine Dymond, Bob Gruber, Rebecca Lartigue, Francesca Spina, and Paul Thifault. Every historian should be so lucky to work with an archivist like Jeff Monseau, who lets them tinker in, design lessons, and bring entire classes of students into their collections. And I'm especially grateful for the collegiality and friendship of Kate Dugan and Susan Joel.

In Simi Valley, Dallas, Sacramento, and Tucson, I've found Ericksons, who welcomed me into their families and homes, and I'm grateful for their support. Paul and Kathleen—hopefully, there's room for this book somewhere on the shelves of the office.

To the Lees—Aunt Barbara, Uncle Greg, Tim, Brendan, Lauren, Ben, and Ally—thanks for always taking an interest in my work and making family get-togethers fun and meaningful.

My sister, Leigh, inherited any creative storytelling ability that exists in our family, so the reader has her to thank for any deficiencies in that regard. Fortunately, my parents, Connie and Brian, handed down more than enough argumentative capability for me to make this book lively and well-reasoned (I hope). Any merits in the writing can be attributed to my mom. My dad will lay claim to anything that passes for wittiness. For my part, I'm just grateful to have them as parents.

Monica, Patrick, and Catherine have all left their imprint on this, far more so than I can put into words. Marie—you've always asked what I'm thinking about, and I've never given a good answer. Maybe this is halfway there. This book is for you, with all of my love.

Notes

Introduction

1. *Irish-American*, April 18, 1863.

2. *Irish-American*, April 18, 1863; Cincinnati judge quoted in Kerby Miller, *Emigrants and Exiles: Ireland and the Irish Exodus to North America* (New York: Oxford University Press, 1985), 337–38.

3. Robert McElderry to Thomas McElderry, May 31, 1854, T2414/16, Public Records Office of Northern Ireland (hereafter cited as PRONI); William McElderry to "Uncle Moore," December 1854.

4. For the emphasis on labor competition, see Albon P. Man, Jr., "Labor Competition and the New York City Draft Riots of 1863," *Journal of Negro History* 36, no. 4 (October 1951): 375–405; Albon P. Man, Jr., "The Irish in New York in the Early Eighteen-Sixties," *Irish Historical Studies* 7, no. 126 (September 1950): 87–108; Willis H. Lofton, "Northern Labor and the Negro during the Civil War," *Journal of Negro History* 34, no. 3 (July 1949): 251–73; Carl Wittke, *The Irish in America* (Baton Rouge: Louisiana State University Press, 1956), 125–26. For the emphasis on the American Catholic hierarchy, see especially Wittke, *Irish in America*, 128–30; Madeline Hooke Rice, *American Catholic Opinion in the Slavery Controversy* (Gloucester, MA: Peter Smith, 1964), 11–24, 86–109; Jay Dolan, *The Immigrant Church: New York's Irish and German Catholics, 1815–1865* (Baltimore: John Hopkins University Press, 1975), 122–27; Kevin Kenny, *The American Irish: A History* (New York: Pearson Education, 2000), 77–80, 85–86, 124–25. For the emphasis on the Democratic Party, see especially Florence E. Gibson, *The Attitudes of the New York Irish Toward State and National Affairs, 1848–1892* (New York: Columbia University Press, 1951), 86–110; Wittke, *Irish in America*, 130–34; William V. Shannon, *The American Irish* (New York: Macmillan, 1963), 54–59; Andre M. Fleche, *The Revolution of 1861: The American Civil War in the Age of Nationalist Conflict* (Chapel Hill: University of North Carolina Press, 2012), 29–30. For the "whiteness" explanation, see David R. Roediger, *The Wages of Whiteness: Race and the Making of the American Working Class* (New York: Verso, 1991); Noel Ignatiev, *How the Irish Became White* (New York: Routledge, 1995). For representative inter- and transnational studies of Irish migration, see Kevin Kenny, *Making Sense of the Molly Maguires* (New York: Oxford University Press, 1998); Victor A. Walsh, "A Fanatic Heart: The Cause of Irish-American Nationalism in Pittsburgh during the Gilded Age," *Journal of Social History*, no. 15 (1981): 187–204; Cian T. McMahon, *The Global Dimensions of Irish Identity: Race, Nation, and the Popular Press, 1840–1880* (Chapel Hill: University of North Carolina Press, 2015); and Ely Janis, *A Greater Ireland: The Land League and Transatlantic Nationalism in Gilded Age America* (Madison: University of Wisconsin Press, 2015). For studies of Irish-American views on slavery in the early to mid-1840s that adopt a

transatlantic perspective, see Angela F. Murphy, *American Slavery, Irish Freedom: Abolition, Immigrant Citizenship, and the Transatlantic Movement for Irish Repeal*. Baton Rouge: Louisiana State University Press, 2010; Bruce Nelson, *Irish Nationalists and the Making of the Irish Race* (Princeton, NJ: Princeton University Press, 2012).

5. For general treatments of the Civil War era, see James McPherson, *Battle Cry of Freedom: The Civil War Era* (New York: Oxford University Press, 1988), 609–10; Harry S. Stout, *Upon the Altar of the Nation: A Moral History of the Civil War* (New York: Penguin, 2007), 245–47. For more focused works on Irish Americans, see Bryan McGovern, *John Mitchel: Irish Nationalist, Southern Secessionist* (Knoxville: University of Tennessee Press, 2009), especially 133; Susannah Ural Bruce, *The Harp and the Eagle: Irish-American Volunteers in the Union Army, 1861–1865* (New York: New York University Press, 2006), especially 136–40; Kenny, *American Irish*, especially 123–26. For notable exceptions, see Christian G. Samito, *Becoming American Under Fire: Irish Americans, African Americans, and the Politics of Citizenship during the Civil War Era* (Ithaca, NY: Cornell University Press, 2009), 131–32; and McMahon, *Global Dimensions*, 4 and 132–33.

6. Edward Rugemer, *The Problem of Emancipation: The Caribbean Roots of the American Civil War* (Baton Rouge: Louisiana State University Press, 2009); Fleche, *Revolution of 1861*; Don H. Doyle, *The Cause of All Nations: An International History of the Civil War* (New York: Basic Books, 2017). Other exemplary transnational studies of the Civil War era include Thomas Bender, *A Nation Among Nations: America's Place in World History* (New York: Hill and Wang, 2006), 116–81; Caleb McDaniel, *The Problem of Slavery in the Age of Democracy* (Baton Rouge: Louisiana State University Press, 2013); Aaron Sheehan-Dean, *Reckoning with Rebellion: War and Sovereignty in the Nineteenth Century* (Gainesville: University Press of Florida, 2020). For the emphasis on immigrants' loyalties, see William L. Burton, *Melting Pot Soldiers: The Union's Ethnic Regiments* (New York: Fordham University Press, 1998); Bruce, *Harp and the Eagle*; Samito, *Becoming American*; David T. Gleeson, *The Green and the Grey: The Irish in the Confederate States of America* (Chapel Hill: University of North Carolina Press, 2016); Ryan W. Keating, *Shades of Green: Irish Regiments, American Soldiers, and Local Communities in the Civil War Era* (New York: Fordham University Press, 2017).

7. James L. Huston, "Interpreting the Causation Sequence: The Meaning of Events Leading to the Civil War," *Reviews in American History* 34, no. 3 (September 2006): 324.

8. Cian T. McMahon, "Ireland and the Birth of the Irish-American Press, 1842–61," *American Periodicals: A Journal of History, Criticism, and Bibliography* 19, no. 1 (2009): 5–20; Francis R. Walsh, "Who Spoke for Boston's Irish? The Boston *Pilot* in the Nineteenth Century," *Journal of Ethnic Studies* 10, no. 3 (Fall 1982): 21–36.

9. First Lieutenant Nicholas Flaherty, 9th Massachusetts Infantry, to John L. Whiting, Esq., September 6, 1863, Letter Book, 9th Massachusetts Volunteer Infantry Regiment, G01/Series 567X, Massachusetts Governor Executive Department letters, 1853–1893, 9th Regt. Infantry 1861–1865: vol. 25, Massachusetts State Archives (hereafter cited as 9th MA Letterbook, MSA). Emphasis in original. For the risks and rewards of researching in Civil War soldiers' letters, see Ian Delahanty, "Soldiers' Diaries and Letters," *Essential Civil War Curriculum*, accessed November 3, 2022, https://www.essentialcivilwarcurriculum.com/soldiers-diaries-and-letters.html.

1. "We want no slave lecturing here": The Irish Critique of Abolitionism

1. Kevin Kenny, *The American Irish: A History* (New York: Pearson Education, 2000), 45–54; Kerby A. Miller, *Emigrants and Exiles: Ireland and the Irish Exodus to North America* (New York: Oxford University Press, 1985), 74–81; Cian T. McMahon, *The Global Dimensions of Irish Identity: Race, Nation, and the Popular Press, 1840–1880* (Chapel Hill: University of North Carolina Press, 2015), 3.

2. Angela F. Murphy, *American Slavery, Irish Freedom: Abolition, Immigrant Citizenship, and the Transatlantic Movement for Irish Repeal* (Baton Rouge: Louisiana State University Press, 2010); Douglas C. Riach, "Richard Davis Webb and Antislavery in Ireland," in *Antislavery Reconsidered: New Perspectives on the Abolitionists*, ed. Michael Fellman and Lewis Perry (Baton Rouge: Louisiana State University Press, 1979).

3. For O'Connell and antislavery, see Murphy, *American Slavery, Irish Freedom*, passim; Bruce Nelson, *Irish Nationalists and the Making of the Irish Race* (Princeton, NJ: Princeton University Press, 2012); Christine Kinealy, *Daniel O'Connell and the Anti-Slavery Movement* (London: Pickering and Chatto, 2011); Patrick Geoghegan, *Liberator: The Life and Death of Daniel O'Connell* (Dublin: Gill and Macmillan, 2010), especially 197–211; John F. Quinn, "Expecting the Impossible? Abolitionists Appeals to the Irish in Antebellum America," *New England Quarterly* 82, no. 4 (December 2009): 667–710; Angela F. Murphy, "Daniel O'Connell and the 'American Eagle' in 1845: Slavery, Diplomacy, Nativism, and the Collapse of America's First Irish Nationalist Movement," *Journal of American Ethnic History* 26, no. 2 (2007): 3–26; Nini Rodgers, *Ireland, Slavery, and Anti-Slavery: 1612–1865* (New York: Palgrave Macmillan, 2007), 259–77; Maurice J. Bric, "Daniel O'Connell and the Debate on Anti-Slavery, 1820–50," in *History and the Public Sphere: Essays in Honour of John A. Murphy*, ed. Tom Dunne and Laurence M. Geary (Cork: Cork University Press, 2005), 65–82; Douglas C. Riach, "Daniel O'Connell and American Anti-Slavery," *Irish Historical Studies* 20, no. 77 (March 1976): 3–25; Gilbert Osofsky, "Abolitionists, Irish Immigrants, and the Dilemmas of Romantic Nationalism," *American Historical Review* 80, no. 4 (1975): 889–912. For the HASS, see Riach, "Webb and Antislavery," 151.

4. Murphy, *American Slavery, Irish Freedom*, 27–30; Roy Foster, *Modern Ireland, 1600–1972* (New York: Penguin Press, 1988), 308–17; Richard Davis, *The Young Ireland Movement* (Totowa, NJ: Barnes and Noble, 1987), 9–36; Lawrence J. McCaffrey, *Daniel O'Connell and the Repeal Year* (Lexington: University of Kentucky Press, 1966); Robert Kee, *The Green Flag: A History of Irish Nationalism* (London: Weidenfield and Nicolson, 1972), 202–11; D. George Boyce, *Nationalism in Ireland*, 3rd ed. (New York: Routledge, 1995), 147.

5. Murphy, *American Slavery, Irish Freedom*, 54–72; David Brundage, *Irish Nationalists in America: The Politics of Exile, 1798–1998* (New York: Oxford University Press, 2016), 57–68; David Sim, *A Union Forever: The Irish Question and U.S. Foreign Relations in the Victorian Age* (Ithaca, NY: Cornell University Press, 2013), 14–16.

6. Daniel O'Connell, "Speech at the Loyal National Repeal Association, Corn Exchange, Dublin. May 9, 1843," and "Speech before the Loyal National Repeal Association, Conciliation Hall, Dublin. September 29, 1845," in *The Irish Patriot: Daniel O'Connell's Legacy to Irish Americans* (Philadelphia: 'Printed for Gratuitous Distribution,'

n/d), 24–30, P. 9257, National Library of Ireland, Dublin [herafter cited as NLI]; Cian T. McMahon, "Did the Irish 'Become White'? Global Migration and National Identity, 1842–1877" (PhD diss., Carnegie Mellon University, 2010), 21–79; *Liberator*, September 12, 1845; Christine Kinealy, "The Liberator: Daniel O'Connell and Anti-Slavery," *History Today* 57, no. 12 (December 2007): 2.

7. Miller, *Emigrants and Exiles*, 48–51; Kenny, *American Irish*, 46–49; 90–91; William McFeely, *Frederick Douglass* (New York: W. W. Norton, 1991), 126; Douglas C. Riach, "Ireland and the Campaign against American Slavery, 1830–1860," (PhD diss., University of Edinburgh, 1975), 520.

8. Riach, "Webb and Antislavery," 156–58; Richard Davis Webb to Edmund Quincy, April 14, 1846, Boston Public Library, Anti-Slavery Collection, Rare Books and Manuscripts Division (hereafter cited as BPL); Richard Davis Webb to Caroline Weston, March 25, 1849, Ms.A.9.2.24.69, BPL; Richard Allen to Maria Weston Chapman, July 29, 1845, Ms.A.9.2.21.39, BPL; Richard Allen to Maria Weston Chapman, November 16, 1847, Ms.A.9.2.23.75, BPL.

9. Riach, "Campaign against American Slavery," 335; *Liberator*, October 17, 1845; Davis, *Ireland Movement*, 123–24.

10. Richard Allen to Maria Weston Chapman, November 16, 1847, Ms.A.9.2.23.75, BPL; Richard Davis Webb to Caroline Weston, March 25, 1849, Ms.A.9.2.24.69, BPL.

11. Annie Allen to Maria Weston Chapman, June 2, 1844, Ms.A.9.2.20.36, BPL; Isabel Jennings to Maria Weston Chapman, August 2, 1847, in *British and American Abolitionists: An Episode in Transatlantic Understanding*, ed. Clare Taylor (Edinburgh: Edinburgh University Press, 1974), 319, (emphasis in original); Richard Davis Webb to William Lloyd Garrison, June 2, 1845, Ms.A.9.2.32.40, BPL; McFeely, *Frederick Douglass*, 121; Riach, "Webb and Antislavery," 164; Richard Davis Webb to Caroline Weston, March 25, 1849, Ms.A.9.2.24.69, BPL; Parker quoted in John T. McGreevy, *Catholicism and American Freedom: A History* (New York: W. W. Norton, 2003), 63. For Webb's anti-Catholicism, see Riach, "Webb and Antislavery," 164–65; Riach, "O'Connell and American Anti-Slavery," 8–9.

12. Mary Ireland to Maria Weston Chapman, January 24, 1846, Ms.A.9.2. 22, 14, BPL; Jane Jennings to Maria Weston Chapman, November 1, 1846, Ms.A.9.2 22, 113, BPL; *The North Star*, October 27, 1848; Clare Taylor, ed., *British and American Abolitionists: An Episode in Transatlantic Understanding* (Edinburgh: Edinburgh University Press, 1974), 4. See also Ellen M. Oldham, "Irish Support of the Abolitionist Movement," *Boston Public Library Quarterly* (October 1958): 175–87.

13. Tom Chaffin, *Giant's Causeway: Frederick Douglass's Irish Odyssey and the Making of an American Visionary* (Charlottesville: University of Virginia Press, 2014); McFeely, *Frederick Douglass*, 119–30; Rodgers, *Ireland, Slavery, and Anti-Slavery*, 278–86; Fionnghuala Sweeney, "The Republic of Letters: Frederick Douglass, Ireland, and the Irish Narratives," in *New Directions in Irish-American History*, ed. Kevin Kenny (Madison: University of Wisconsin Press, 2003).

14. *Cork Examiner*, October 13, 1845.

15. *Cork Examiner*, October 20, 1845; *Liberator*, November 28, 1845; McFeely, *Frederick Douglass*, 124; *Liberator*, December 26, 1845; Chaffin, *Giant's Causeway*, 74–75.

16. Paul A. Townend, *Father Mathew, Temperance, and Irish Identity* (Portland, OR: Irish Academic Press, 2002), 1–8; Colm Kerrigan, *Father Mathew and the Irish Temperance Movement, 1838–1849* (Cork: Cork University Press, 1992); *Galway Vindicator and Connaught Advertiser*, October 4, 1845; Rodgers, *Ireland, Slavery, and Anti-Slavery*, 281.

17. Mary Ireland and Hannah Witt to Maria Weston Chapman, January 24, 1846, Ms.A.9.2.22.14. BPL; Marry Mannix to Maria Weston Chapman, October 24, 1846, Ms.A.9.2.22.104, BPL; Richard Davis Webb to Maria Weston Chapman, October 31, 1846, Ms.A.9.22.109, BPL; Oldham, "Irish Support of the Abolitionist Movement," 175–87.

18. Ralph Varian to William Lloyd Garrison, November 10, 1845, printed in the *Liberator*, December 12, 1845; *Cork Examiner*, November 7, 1845; Rodgers, *Ireland, Slavery, and Anti-Slavery*,

19. Marie-Louise Legg, *Newspapers and Nationalism: The Irish Provincial Press, 1850–1892* (Dublin: Four Courts Press, 1999), 23, 65–66; James Grant, *Impressions of Ireland and the Irish* (Philadelphia: G. B. Zieber, 1845), 200–201, 289–93; H. F. Kearney, "Father Mathew: Apostle of Modernisation," in *Studies in Irish History Presented to R. Dudley Edwards*, ed. Art Cosgrave and Donal McCartney (Dublin: University College, Dublin, 1979), 171–72; *Cork Examiner*, January 24, 1849; Roy F. Foster, *Modern Ireland: 1600–1972* (New York: Viking, 1988), 311. See also Kevin B. Nowlan, "The Origins of the Press in Ireland," in *Communications and Community in Ireland*, ed. Brian Farrell (Dublin: Mercier Press, 1984), 16.

20. Michael Keyes, *Funding the Nation: Money and Nationalist Politics in Nineteenth-Century Ireland* (Dublin: Gill and Macmillan, 2011), 101.

21. W. Caleb McDaniel, "Repealing Unions: American Abolitionists, Irish Repeal, and the Origins of Garrisonian Disunionism," *Journal of the Early American Republic* 28, no. 2 (Summer 2008): 243–69; William Lloyd Garrison to George W. Benson, March 22, 1842, Ms.A.1.1.3.87, BPL; James Haughton to Daniel O'Connell, April 6, 1843, Ms. 13, 649: Letters to Daniel O'Connell, 1840–1846, NLI, Dublin. Haughton also raised the issue at Repeal meetings. See Dublin *Freeman's Journal*, May 10, 1842; Samuel Haughton, *Memoirs of James Haughton, with Extracts from His Private and Published Letters, by His Son, Samuel Haughton* (Dublin: E. Ponsoby, 1877), 59–60; O'Connell, "Speech at the Loyal National Repeal Association . . . May 9, 1843," in *Irish Patriot*, 24–28.

22. Riach, "O'Connell and American Anti-Slavery," 14; Dublin *Nation*, August 9, 1845; James Haughton to Samuel May, May 28, 1846, in Taylor, *British and American Abolitionists*, 264; Murphy, *American Slavery, Irish Freedom*, 155–56, 158; Geoghegan, *Liberator*, 206.

23. Dublin *Nation*, January 13, 1844 and March 23, 1844 quoted in O'Connell, "O'Connell, Young Ireland, and Negro Slavery," 132.

24. O'Connell quoted in Kee, *Green Flag*, 222; Kevin B. Nowlan, *The Politics of Repeal: A Study in the Relations between Great Britain and Ireland, 1841–50* (London: Routledge & Kegan Paul, 1965), 74–77; Ian Delahanty, "'A Noble Empire in the West': Young Ireland, the United States and Slavery," *Britain and the World* 6, no. 2 (2013): 178–79.

25. Kee, *Green Flag*, 226–31; Peter Karsten, "Irish Soldiers in the British Empire: 1792–1922: Suborned or Subordinate?" *Journal of Social History* 17 (Fall 1983): 36; Thomas Bartlett, "The Irish Soldier in India, 1750–1947," in Michael Holmes and Denis Holmes,

eds., *Ireland and India: Connections, Comparisons, Contrasts* (Dublin: Folens, 1997), 12–17; Kevin Kenny, ed., "The Irish in the Empire," in *The Oxford History of the British Empire*, Companion Series, *Ireland and the British Empire* (New York: Oxford University Press, 2004), 90–123.

26. Murphy, *American Slavery, Irish Freedom*, 193–94; Matthew Karp, *This Vast Southern Empire: Slaveholders at the Helm of American Foreign Policy* (Cambridge, MA: Harvard University Press, 2016), 82–86.

27. April 5, 1845; Murphy, *American Slavery, Irish Freedom*, 197–98; Thomas Steele to Daniel O'Connell, April 4, 1845. Ms. 22, 481, NLI, Dublin (emphasis in original).

28. Murphy, *American Slavery, Irish Freedom*, passim; Murphy, "Daniel O'Connell and the 'American Eagle,'" passim, but especially 4.

29. John Blake Dillon to Thomas Davis, n/d, quoted in Charles Gavan Duffy, *Young Ireland: A Fragment of Irish History, 1840–50* (London: T. Fisher Unwin, 1896), 746; Dublin *Nation*, April 12 and May 31, 1845.

30. Dublin Nation, August 9, 1845. Thomas Mooney, *A History of Ireland, from Its First Settlement to the Present Time* (Boston: Self-published, 1845), 1605–7.

31. Dublin *Nation*, August 9, 1845; Davis, *Ireland Movement*, 210. Readership estimate can be found in Kee, *Green* Flag, 194–95; Foster, *Modern Ireland*, 311. Foster notes that the actual circulation numbers may have been far less than the number of readers. Kevin B. Nowlan lists a daily circulation in 1843 of 10,700 copies. Nowlan, "Origins of the Press in Ireland," 16.

32. Davis, *Ireland Movement*, 37–81, 208–11; Geoghegan, *Liberator*, 212–27; Foster, *Modern Ireland*, 313–15; Patrick Geoghegan, "Daniel O'Connell and the Campaign against Slavery," *History Ireland* 18, no. 5 (September–October 2010): 23; Maurice O'Connell, "O'Connell, Young Ireland, and Negro Slavery: An Exercise in Romantic Nationalism," *Thought* 64 (June 1989): 130–36.

33. Geoghegan, *Liberator*, 233; Kenny, *American Irish*, 89–90; Miller, *Emigrants and Exiles*, 281–84.

34. Murphy, *American Slavery, Irish Freedom*, 213–14; Kee, *Green Flag*, 242–44; New Orleans *Daily Delta*, December 17, 1845; Dublin *Nation*, February 20, 1847; Merle Curti, *American Philanthropy Abroad: A History* (New Brunswick, NJ: Rutgers University Press, 1963), 57; *National Anti-Slavery Standard*, January 14, 1847; Charleston (SC) *Mercury*, January 15, 1847.

35. Curti, *American Philanthropy Abroad*, 64, for quote, and 56–61 for description of contributors.

36. *Cork Examiner*, April 7 and April 14, 1847; articles from the Dublin *Freeman's Journal* and *Kilkenny Journal* quoted in *Cork Examiner*, April 12, 1847; Curti, *American Philanthropy Abroad*, 49; Robert F. Forbes, *An Interesting Memoir of the Jamestown Voyage to Ireland* (Boston: James B. Cullen, 1890), 5; Francis Costello, "The Deer Island Graves, Boston: The Irish Famine and Irish-American Tradition," in *The Meaning of the Famine*, ed. Patrick O'Sullivan (London: Leicester University Press, 1997), 115–17; Christine Kinealy, *The Great Irish Famine: Impact, Ideology, and Rebellion* (New York: Palgrave, 2002), 77–79; Stephen Puleo, *Voyage of Mercy: The USS Jamestown, the Irish Famine, and the Remarkable Story of America's First Humanitarian Mission* (New York: St. Martin's Press, 2020).

37. James Haughton to Editor of the *Nation*, April 3, 1847, printed in the Dublin *Nation*, April 10, 1847; James Haughton to the Rev. Samuel May, March 29, 1847, in Taylor, *British and American Abolitionists*, 310; Henry C. Wright to the Central Relief Committee of the Society of Friends in Ireland, April 4, 1847, printed in the *National Anti-Slavery Standard*, May 13, 1847; Richard Davis Webb to Sidney Howard Gay, May 30, 1847, printed in the *National Anti-Slavery Standard*, June 24, 1847; Richard S. Harrison, *Richard Davis Webb: Dublin Quaker Printer (1805–72)* (Cork: Red Barn Publishing, 1993), 61–63; Richard Davis Webb to Sidney Howard Gay, January 3, 1847, printed in the *National Anti-Slavery Standard*, February 4, 1847; *National Anti-Slavery Standard*, February 25, 1847.

38. Charleston, South Carolina, *Mercury*, March 2 and 3, 1847; Dublin *Nation*, April 3, 1847, reprinted in Charleston, South Carolina, *Mercury*, April 28, 1847; Dublin *Nation*, March 20, 1847; Charleston, South Carolina, *Mercury*, July 26, 1847. For other *Mercury* articles on Irish famine relief, see February 8, 10, 11, and 25; March 6 and 29; April 16, 27, and 28; May 26; June 1, 1847.

39. James Adger et al. on behalf of the Irish Relief Committee, Charleston, South Carolina, to the Central Relief Committee of the Society of Friends, February 19 and February 23, 1847; Hugh Jenkins on behalf of the Irish Relief Committee, Baltimore, to the Central Relief Committee of the Society of Friends, February 25, 1847, in *Transactions of the Central Relief Committee of the Society of Friends during the Famine in Ireland, in 1846 and 1847* (Dublin: Hodges and Smith, 1852), 231, 232–33; Richard Allen to the Central Relief Committee of the Society of Friends, March 29, 1847, printed in the *National Anti-Slavery Standard*, May 6, 1847; Henry C. Wright et al. to the Central Relief Committee of the Society of Friends, n/d, printed in the *National Anti-Slavery Standard*, May 6, 1847; James Haughton to the Rev. Samuel May, August 30, 1847, Ms.b.1.6.3.38, BPL; Haughton to Rev. Samuel May, March 29, 1847, in Taylor, *British and American Abolitionists*, 310; Haughton to Maria Weston Chapman, April 1, 1847, Ms.A.9.2.23.20, BPL; Rob Goodbody, *A Suitable Channel: Quaker Relief in the Great Famine* (Bray, Ireland: Pale Publishing, 1995), 4–5.

40. *National Anti-Slavery Standard*, May 13, 1847 (emphasis in original); William Lloyd Garrison to Richard Davis Webb, July 1, 1847, Ms.A.1.1.4.54, BPL; Richard Davis Webb to Sidney Howard Gay, May 30, 1847, printed in the *National Anti-Slavery Standard*, June 24, 1847.

41. Richard Allen to William Lloyd Garrison, June 1847, printed in the *Liberator*, July 23, 1847; Rodgers, *Ireland, Slavery, and Anti-Slavery*, 288; Kinealy, *Great Irish Famine*, 66–69.

42. Riach, "Campaign against American Slavery," 334, 374–75; Rodgers, *Ireland, Slavery, and Anti-Slavery*, 287–89. Rodgers claims Allen did not "press home" his objection to the Charleston and Baltimore donations, but his March 29, 1847, letter to the Central Relief Committee argues otherwise.

43. Davis, *Young Ireland*, 82–117; Kee, *Green Flag*, 243–55; Brundage, *Irish Nationalists in America*, 78–83.

44. Dublin *Nation*, November 28, 1846; Haughton, *Memoirs of James Haughton*, 83–85; Davis, *Young Ireland*, 123–25. For more on Irish nationalists' views on the

Mexican-American War, see Murphy, "Daniel O'Connell and the 'American Eagle' in 1845"; Geoghegan, *Liberator*, 201; Bruce Nelson, "'Come Out of Such a Land, You Irishmen': Daniel O'Connell, American Slavery, and the Making of the 'Irish Race,'" *Éire-Ireland* 42 (2007): 76–77.

45. Dublin *Nation*, November 28, 1846, and January 16, 1847; Father John Kenyon to Editor of the *Nation*, January 19, 1847, printed in the Dublin *Nation*, January 30, 1847.

46. James Haughton to Editor of the *Nation*, February 1, 1847, printed in the Dublin *Nation*, February 6, 1847; Dr. R. R. Madden to James Haughton, February 1, 1847, printed in the Dublin *Nation*, February 6, 1847; Father John Kenyon to Editor of the Nation, February 9, 1847, printed in the Dublin *Nation*, February 13, 1847; James Haughton to Editor of the *Nation*, February 15, 1847, printed in the Dublin *Nation*, February 20, 1847.

47. Dublin *Nation*, April 10, 1847. Coverage of the April 7 meeting with varying degrees of completeness can also be found in the Dublin *Freeman's Journal*, April 8, 1847; *Cork Examiner*, April 9, 1847; Belfast *Vindicator*, April 10, 1847; Boston *Pilot*, May 22, 1847.

48. Dublin *Nation*, April 8, 1847; Haughton, *Memoir of James Haughton*, 84–85; James Haughton to H. C. Wright, November 3, 1848, printed in the *Liberator*, December 8, 1848.

49. Dublin *Nation*, April 10, 1847.

50. Dublin *Nation*, February 6, 1847, quoted in O'Connell, "O'Connell, Young Ireland, and Negro Slavery," 134; Bruce Nelson, "My Countrymen Are All Mankind," *Field Day Review* 4 (2008): 266. Recent and unfounded claims that Irish people were enslaved in the Caribbean in the seventeenth century are refuted in Matthew C. Reilly and Jerome Handler, "Contesting White Slavery in the Caribbean: Enslaved Africans and European Indentured Servants in Seventeenth Century Barbados," *New West Indian Guide* 91 (2017): 30–55.

2. "Over the broad Atlantic": Abolitionist Appeals to Emigrants and Immigrants

1. Carl Wittke, *The Irish in America* (Baton Rouge: Louisiana State University Press, 1956), 81; Kerby Miller, *Emigrants and Exiles: Ireland and the Irish Exodus to North America* (New York: Oxford University Press, 1985), 309–11; Cian T. McMahon, *The Global Dimensions of Irish Identity: Race, Nation, and the Popular Press, 1840–1880* (Chapel Hill: University of North Carolina Press, 2015), 42–43; Timothy Egan, *The Immortal Irishman: The Irish Revolutionary Who Became an American Hero* (Boston: Houghton Mifflin Harcourt, 2016), 65–84.

2. Kevin Kenny, *The American Irish: A History* (New York: Pearson Education, 2000), 45–46, 54–55; Angela Murphy, *American Slavery, Irish Freedom: Abolition, Immigrant Citizenship, and the Transatlantic Movement for Irish Repeal* (Baton Rouge: Louisiana State University Press, 2010), 7–8.

3. Richard Allen to William Lloyd Garrison, September 1, 1840, Ms.A.1.2.9.108, Boston Public Library, Anti-Slavery Collection, Rare Books and Manuscripts Division (hereafter cited as BPL); Maria Webb and Belfast Ladies Antislavery Association to Secretary of the Massachusetts Female Antislavery Society, June 17, 1846, in *British and American Abolitionists: An Episode in Transatlantic Understanding*, ed. Clare Taylor

(Edinburgh: Edinburgh University Press, 1974), 269; Richard Allen to William Lloyd Garrison, November 3, 1853, printed in the *Liberator*, November 25, 1853.

4. James Haughton to Editor of the Dublin *Nation*, December 28, 1846, printed in the Dublin *Nation*, January 9, 1847; James Haughton to "My Countrymen," printed in Drogheda *Argus*, September 19, 1853, reprinted in the *Liberator*, November 4, 1853; McMahon, *Global Dimensions*, 17–20.

5. Douglas C. Riach, "Ireland and the Campaign against American Slavery,1830–1860" (PhD diss., University of Edinburgh, 1975), 444–45. Riach attributes authorship to the Dublin Ladies' Anti-Slavery Society, but the pamphlet states explicitly that it came from simply the Dublin Anti-Slavery Society; Dublin Anti-Slavery Society, *To Irish Emigrants who are going to the United States of America* (Dublin: R. D. Webb, 1852); Maria Webb to Frederick Douglass, September 9, 1851, printed in *Frederick Douglass' Paper*, October 2, 1851; Deirdre M. Mageean, "Emigration from Irish Ports," *Journal of American Ethnic History* 13, no. 1 (1993): 19–21.

6. Dublin Anti-Slavery Society, *To Irish Emigrants*, 1–4 (emphasis in original); David R. Roediger, *The Wages of Whiteness: Race and the Making of the American Working Class*, rev. ed. (New York: Verso, 2000); Noel Ignatiev, *How the Irish Became White* (New York: Routledge, 1995).

7. Riach, "Campaign against American Slavery," 445.

8. James Haughton to Daniel O'Connell, January 11, 1840, Ms.13, 649, National Library of Ireland, Dublin (hereafter cited as NLI); Daniel O'Connell, "*Address from the People of Ireland to Their Countrymen and Countrywomen in America*," in *Daniel O'Connell upon American Slavery: With Other Irish Testimonies* (New York: American Anti-Slavery Society, 1860); David Brundage, *Irish Nationalists in America: The Politics of Exile* (New York: Oxford University Press, 2016), 71–73; Murphy, *American Slavery, Irish Freedom*, 50–53; John F. Quinn, "Expecting the Impossible? Abolitionists Appeals to the Irish in Antebellum America," *New England Quarterly* 82, no. 4 (December 2009): 689–701; Douglas C. Riach, "Daniel O'Connell and American Anti-Slavery," *Irish Historical Studies* 20, no. 77 (March 1976): 10–12; Gilbert Osofsky, "Abolitionists, Irish Immigrants, and the Dilemmas of Romantic Nationalism," *American Historical Review* 80, no. 4 (1975): 897–903.

9. William Lloyd Garrison to George William Benson, January 29, 1842, Ms.A.1.1.3.83, BPL; William Lloyd Garrison to Richard Davis Webb, February 27, 1842, Ms.A.1.1.3.85, BPL; Boston *Pilot*, August 30, 1845; Riach, "O'Connell and American Anti-Slavery," 10–11; Osofsky, "Abolitionists, Irish Immigrants," 75–84.

10. Riach, "Campaign against American Slavery," 192; Murphy, *American Slavery, Irish Freedom*, 121–23; Dublin *Nation*, October 14, 1843.

11. Brundage, *Irish Nationalists in America*, 75–76; Murphy, *American Slavery, Irish Freedom*, 212–13.

12. Miller, *Emigrants and Exiles*, 291–93; Kenny, *American Irish*, 89–90, 97–98; Cormac Ó Gráda, *Black '47 and Beyond: The Great Irish Famine in History, Economy, and Memory* (Princeton, NJ: Princeton University Press, 1999), 104–14.

13. Miller, *Emigrants and Exiles*, 295–97; Kenny, *American Irish*, 99, 105–6; David Noel Doyle, "The Irish as Urban Pioneers in the United States, 1850–1870," *Journal of American Ethnic History* 10 (Fall 1990–Winter 1991): 36–53.

14. Cian T. McMahon, "Ireland and the Birth of the Irish-American Press, 1842–61," *American Periodicals: A Journal of History and Criticism* 19, no. 1 (November 2009): 5–6; Neil Hogan, "The Famine Beat: American Newspaper Coverage of the Great Famine," in *The Great Famine and the Irish Diaspora in America*, ed. Arthur Gribben (Amherst: University of Massachusetts Press, 1999), 160–61; Charleston *Mercury*, February 8, 1847; Cincinnati *Catholic Telegraph*, April 22, 1847; *Irish-American*, December 16, 1849; Mary C. Kelly, *Ireland's Great Famine in Irish-American History: Enshrining a Fateful Memory* (New York: Rowman and Littlefield, 2014), 30–31.

15. McMahon, *Global Dimensions*, 40–43, 82–87; Egan, *Immortal Irishman*, 163.

16. Bryan McGovern, *John Mitchel: Irish Nationalist, Southern Secessionist* (Knoxville: University of Tennessee Press, 2009), 33–56; Mitchel quoted in Brundage, *Irish Nationalists in America*, 92–93; John Mitchel, *Jail Journal, or Five Years in British Prisons* (New York: Office of the "Citizen," 1854; repr., New York: Woodstock Books, 1996); John Mitchel, *The Last Conquest of Ireland (perhaps)*, ed. Patrick Maume (Dublin: University College Dublin Press, 2005).

17. Miller, *Emigrants and Exiles*, passim, but especially 280–344; Brundage, *Irish Nationalists in America*, 90–94 (McGee quoted on p. 94); David Sim, *A Union Forever: The Irish Question and U.S. Foreign Relations in the Victorian Age* (Ithaca, NY: Cornell University Press, 2013), 70–73.

18. "Outis" to Editor of the *Cork Examiner*, June 10, 1849, printed in the *Cork Examiner*, June 27, 1849 (emphasis in original); Timothy McCarthy to his mother, n/d, printed in the *Cork Examiner*, July 6, 1849 (emphasis in original); Patrick Hanlon to his father, May 10, 1851, D885/2, PRONI; "A New Song on Skibbereen" quoted in Miller, *Emigrants and Exiles*, 311.

19. *Liberator*, October 10, 1845 (emphasis in original); W. Caleb McDaniel, "Repealing Unions: American Abolitionists, Irish Repeal, and the Origins of Garrisonian Disunionism," *Journal of the Early American Republic* 28, no. 2 (Summer 2008): 245–47; *Liberator*, October 10, 1845 (emphasis in original); Richard Davis Webb to Editor of the *National Anti-Slavery Standard*, March 30, 1847, printed in the *National Anti-Slavery Standard*, May 6, 1847; Richard Davis Webb to Editor of the *National Anti-Slavery Standard*, November 16, 1849, printed in the *National Anti-Slavery Standard*, December 6, 1849.

20. *The North Star*, December 5, 1850, in *Frederick Douglass: Selected Writings and Speeches*, ed. Philip S. Foner (Chicago: Lawrence Hill Books, 1999), 169–70; James Brewer Stewart, *Holy Warriors: The Abolitionists and American Slavery*, rev. ed. (New York: Hill and Wang, 1997); James Brewer Stewart, *Wendell Phillips: Liberty's Hero* (Baton Rouge: Louisiana State University Press, 1986), 109–14; Richard Davis Webb to Editor of the *National Anti-Slavery Standard*, March 30, 1847, printed in the *National Anti-Slavery Standard*, May 6, 1847; Cathal Smith, "Second Slavery, Second Landlordism, and Modernity: A Comparison of Antebellum Mississippi and Nineteenth-Century Ireland," *Journal of the Civil War Era* 5, no. 2 (June 2014): 204–30; Angela Murphy, "Black Abolitionists in Ireland and the Challenge of Universal Reform," in *In Search of Liberty: African American Internationalism in the Nineteenth-Century Atlantic World*, ed. Ronald Johnson and Ousmane K. Power-Greene (Athens: University of Georgia Press, 2021), 279–96.

21. Frederick Douglass to Editor of the *Liberator*, February 26, 1846, printed in the *Liberator*, March 27, 1846; Tom Chaffin, *Giant's Causeway: Frederick Douglass's Irish*

Odyssey and the Making of an American Visionary (Charlottesville: University of Virginia Press, 2014), 102–6; Phillip S. Foner, ed., *The Life and Writings of Frederick Douglass*, vol. 1 (New York: International Publishers, 1952),138–42.

22. *National Anti-Slavery Standard*, November 8, 1849; Henry C. Wright to James Haughton, June 22, 1851, printed in the *Liberator*, July 4, 1851; "W. J. W." to Editor of the *Liberator*, July 29, 1851, printed in the *Liberator*, August 29, 1851.

23. *North Star*, December 3, 1847; *Frederick Douglass' Newspaper*, November 18, 1853.

24. Father John Kenyon to Editor of the Dublin *Nation*, February 9, 1847, printed in the Dublin *Nation*, February 13, 1847; Richard Davis Webb to Editor of the *National Anti-Slavery Standard*, March 30, 1847, printed in the *National Anti-Slavery Standard*, May 6, 1847; Boston *Pilot*, May 1, 1847 (emphasis in original).

25. New York *Nation*, August 4, 1849, reprinted in the *National Anti-Slavery Standard*, August 30, 1849; Boston *Pilot*, May 31, 1851; "Manhattan" to Editor of the *National Era*, April 24, 1852, printed in the *National Era*, April 29, 1852.

26. Christopher Leslie Brown, *Moral Capital: Foundations of British Abolitionism* (Chapel Hill: University of North Carolina Press, 2006); Edward Rugemer, *The Problem of Emancipation: The Caribbean Roots of the American Civil War* (Baton Rouge: Louisiana State University Press, 2009), 17–41; Matthew Karp, *This Vast Southern Empire: Slaveholders at the Helm of American Foreign Policy* (Cambridge, MA: Harvard University Press, 2016), 10–31 (Calhoun quoted on p. 21); Sim, *Union Forever*, 31–38; Elizabeth R. Varon, *Disunion! The Coming of the American Civil War, 1789–1859* (Chapel Hill: University of North Carolina Press, 2008), 166–67; "An Exile" to Editor of the Dublin *Nation*, July 1, 1845, printed in the Dublin *Nation*, July 26, 1845.

27. Rugemer, *Problem of Emancipation*, 222–57; W. Caleb McDaniel, *The Problem of Democracy in the Age of Slavery: Garrisonian Abolitionists and Transatlantic Reform* (Baton Rouge: Louisiana State University Press, 2013), 45–50, 62–64; McDaniel, "Repealing Unions," passim.

28. *Irish-American*, November 16, 1850; Henry C. Wright to James Haughton, June 22, 1851, printed in the *Liberator*, July 4, 1851; McDaniel, *Problem of Democracy*, 43–56.

29. James Haughton to Henry C. Wright, July 31, 1851, printed in the *Liberator*, August 29, 1851.

30. James Haughton to Henry C. Wright, July 31, 1851, printed in the *Liberator*, August 29, 1851; Kevin Kenny, "Twenty Years of Irish-American Historiography," *Journal of American Ethnic History* 28, no. 4 (Summer 2009): 67–69.

3. Irish-American Unionism and Slavery

1. Andre M. Fleche, *The Revolution of 1861: The American Civil War in the Age of Nationalist Conflict* (Chapel Hill: University of North Carolina Press, 2012), 11–16; Thomas Bender, *A Nation Among Nations: America's Place in World History* (New York: Macmillan, 2006), 122–23.

2. William V. Shannon, *The American Irish* (New York: Macmillan, 1963), 48–54; Kevin Kenny, *The American Irish: A History* (New York: Pearson Education, 2000), 118–21; 126–27; Robert Kee, *The Green Flag: A History of Irish Nationalism* (London: Weidenfield and Nicolson, 1972), 194; Tyler Anbinder, *Five Points: The 19th-Century New*

York City Neighborhood That Invented Tap Dance, Stole Elections, and Became the World's Most Notorious Slum* (New York: Plume, 2002), 145–71; Edward Pessen, *Jacksonian America: Society, Personality, and Politics*, rev. ed. (1969; repr., Chicago: University of Illinois Press, 1998), 35–38.

3. Kenny, *American Irish*, 82–83; Shannon, *American Irish*, 50–52; Michael F. Holt, *The Rise and Fall of the American Whig Party: Jacksonian Politics and the Onset of the Civil War* (New York: Oxford University Press, 1999), 207; Jean H. Baker, *Affairs of Party: The Political Culture of Northern Democrats in the Mid-Nineteenth Century* (New York: Fordham University Press, 1998), 317–52; *The Congressional Globe*, United States Senate, 29th Congress, 2nd Session, February 27, 1847, 534 (hereafter cited as *CG*, Cong., Sess.); *CG*, United States House of Representatives, 29th Congress, 1st Session, January 6, 1846, 146.

4. "Outis" to Editor of the *Cork Examiner*, June 10, 1849, printed in the *Cork Examiner*, June 27, 1849; Patrick Hanlon to his father, May 10, 1851, D885/2, Public Records Office of Northern Ireland (hereafter cited as PRONI); *Irish-American*, March 3, 1850; Dublin *Freeman's Journal and Daily Commercial Advertiser*, January 2, 1850.

5. *Galway Vindicator and Connaught Advertiser*, April 10, 1847; Dublin *Nation*, March 20, 1847; Merle Curti, *American Philanthropy Abroad: A History* (New Brunswick, NJ: Rutgers University Press, 1963).

6. Stephen Puleo, *Voyage of Mercy: The USS Jamestown, the Irish Famine, and the Remarkable Story of America's First Humanitarian Mission* (New York: St. Martin's Press, 2020), 58–62, 125–31; George Crosby to Bridget Crosby, March 28, 1847, Ms. 13.549, National Library of Ireland, Dublin (hereafter cited as NLI).

7. *Galway Vindicator and Connaught Advertiser*, April 10, 1847; Dublin *Nation*, March 20, 1847; Curti, *American Philanthropy*, 49–50; Jason H. Silverman, *Lincoln and the Immigrant* (Carbondale: Southern Illinois University Press, 2015), 3; Puleo, *Voyage of Mercy*, 135–37.

8. David Brundage, *Irish Nationalists in America: The Politics of Exile, 1798–1998* (New York: Oxford University Press, 2016), 84–87 (*Pilot* quoted on p. 86).

9. Brundage, *Irish Nationalists in America*, 94–99; David Sim, *A Union Forever: The Irish Question and U.S. Foreign Relations in the Victorian Age* (Ithaca, NY: Cornell University Press, 2013), 70–84; Thomas Reilly to John Kelly, June 19, 1848, and n/d, 1848 [written after June 19 and before late August], Ms.10.511, NLI.

10. W. Caleb McDaniel, "Repealing Unions: American Abolitionists, Irish Repeal, and the Origins of Garrisonian Disunionism," *Journal of the Early American Republic* 28, no. 2 (Summer 2008): 243–46 (quote on 246); W. Caleb McDaniel, *The Problem of Democracy in the Age of Slavery: Garrisonian Abolitionists and Transatlantic Reform* (Baton Rouge: Louisiana State University Press, 2013), 168–77; Elizabeth R. Varon, *Disunion! The Coming of the American Civil War, 1789–1859* (Chapel Hill: University of North Carolina Press, 2008), 15–16, 52–54.

11. Paul A. Townend, *Father Mathew, Temperance, and Irish Identity* (Portland, OR: Irish Academic Press, 2002), 1, 3–7; John F. Quinn, *Father Mathew's Crusade: Temperance in Nineteenth-Century Ireland and Irish America* (Boston: University of Massachusetts Press, 2002), 2–3; Colm Kerrigan, "Irish Temperance and US Anti-Slavery: Father Mathew and the Abolitionists," *History Workshop* 31 (Spring, 1991): 105–19.

12. *Cork Examiner*, July 27, 1849; Boston *Pilot*, September 15, 1849; New York *Herald*, July 3, 1849; *Boston Evening Transcript* article reprinted in the *Liberator*, August 24, 1849; *National Era* (Washington, D.C.), July 19, 1849; "Outis" to Editor of the *Cork Examiner*, n/d, printed in the *Cork Examiner*, August 1, 1849; Michael Rawson, *Eden on the Charles: The Making of Boston* (Cambridge, MA: Harvard University Press, 2010), 93–95; Ian R. Tyrell, *Sobering Up: From Temperance to Prohibition in Antebellum America, 1800–1860* (Westport, CT: Greenwood Press, 1979).

13. All quotes from the *Liberator*, August 10, 1849. See also John Quinn, "'The Nation's Guest?': The Battle between Catholics and Abolitionists to Manage Father Theobald Mathew's American Tour, 1849–1851," *U.S. Catholic Historian* 22, no. 3 (Summer 2004): 27–28; Kerrigan, "Father Mathew and the Abolitionists," 105–7; Henry Mayer, *All on Fire: William Lloyd Garrison and the Abolition of Slavery* (New York: W. W. Norton, 1998), 391–92.

14. *Liberator*, August 10, 1849; Wendell Phillips to James Haughton, August 20, 1849, printed in the *National Anti-Slavery Standard*, August 30, 1849; Roger B. Rogers to Editor of the *National Anti-Slavery Standard*, n/d, printed in the *National Anti-Slavery Standard*, August 24, 1849.

15. *Irish-American*, August 12, 1849 (emphasis in original); "Outis" to Editor of the *Cork Examiner*, August 14, 1849, printed in the *Cork Examiner*, August 29, 1849, (emphasis in original); Dublin *Nation*, December 22, 1849; New York *Nation* article reprinted in the Dublin *Nation*, October 27, 1849.

16. Boston *Pilot*, August 25 and November 10, 1849; "Outis" to Editor of the *Cork Examiner*, August 14, 1849, printed in the *Cork Examiner*, August 29, 1849; "Phileleutherias" to Editor of the *Irish-American*, August 12, 1849, printed in the *Irish-American*, August 19, 1849.

17. Stephen E. Maizlish, "Rehearsing for the Great Debate of 1850: The Controversy Over Seating Father Theobald Mathew on the Floor of the Senate," *Civil War History* 64, no. 4 (December 2018): 365–67; Kerrigan, "Father Mathew and the Abolitionists," 112; Quinn, "Nation's Guest?," 33; Boston *Pilot*, December 8 and December 15, 1849; *Irish-American*, December 12, 1849.

18. *Congressional Globe*, 31st Congress, 1st Session, 51, 52, and 57; Maizlish, "Rehearsing for the Great Debate," 369–70.

19. *CG*, 31st Cong., 1st Sess., 51, 52, 56, and 59.

20. *Irish-American*, February 10, 1850.

21. David Potter, *The Impending Crisis: 1848–1861* (New York: Harper and Row, 1976), 1–2, 18–23; James McPherson, *Battle Cry of Freedom: The Civil War Era* (New York: Oxford University Press, 1988), 48–60, 68; Bruce Levine, *Half Slave and Half Free: The Roots of Civil War*, rev. ed. (1992; repr., New York: Hill and Wang, 2002), 173–75, 180–83; Varon, *Disunion!*, 210–11.

22. Boston *Pilot*, January 5 and January 12, 1850; Cincinnati *Catholic Telegraph*, January 12, 1850; *Irish-American*, January 12, 1850.

23. *Irish-American*, February 10, 1850, and March 3, 1850; Boston *Pilot*, May 18, 1850; *Irish-American*, May 12, 1850; *Liberator*, May 17, 1850; Anbinder, *Five Points*, 141–44, and 166–67.

24. McPherson, *Battle Cry of Freedom*, 73–74, 86–87; "An Exile" to Editor of the Dublin *Nation*, March 4, 1850, printed in the Dublin *Nation*, March 23, 1850; Varon, *Disunion!*, 223–25; Don H. Doyle, *The Cause of All Nations: An International History of the Civil War* (New York: Basic Books, 2017); "Alpha" to Editor of the Boston *Pilot*, February 9, 1850, printed in the Boston *Pilot*, February 16, 1850; Boston *Pilot*, April 13, 1850.

25. Potter, *Impending Crisis*, 114; McPherson, *Battle Cry of Freedom*, 75–76.

26. William B. Kurtz, *Excommunicated from the Union: How the Civil War Created a Separate Catholic America* (New York: Fordham University Press, 2016), 93–94; Hughes quoted in James Canning Fuller to Daniel O'Connell, March 28, 1842, MS 13, 649, NLI, Dublin; Boston *Pilot*, November 2, 1850.

27. Thomas D. Morris, *Free Men All: The Personal Liberty Laws of the North, 1780–1861* (Baltimore: Johns Hopkins University Press, 1974), 1–106; Stanley W. Campbell, *The Slave Catchers: Enforcement of the Fugitive Slave Law, 1850–1860* (Chapel Hill: University of North Carolina Press, 1970), 5–14, 23–25; McPherson, *Battle Cry of Freedom*, 78–80; Chandra Manning, *What This Cruel War Was Over: Soldiers, Slavery, and the Civil War* (New York: Random House, 2007), 15–16, 232n–233n; John L. Brooke, *"There Is a North": Fugitive Slaves, Political Crisis, and Cultural Transformation in the Coming of the Civil War* (Amherst: University of Massachusetts Press, 2019), 78–79.

28. Sister Mary Alphonsine Frawley, S.S.J., *Patrick Donahoe* (Washington, D.C.: Catholic University of America Press, 1946), 8–45; Francis R. Walsh, "Who Spoke for Boston's Irish? The Boston *Pilot* in the Nineteenth Century," *Journal of Ethnic Studies* 10, no. 3 (Fall 1982): 21–24; Francis R. Walsh, "The Boston *Pilot* Reports the Civil War," *Historical Journal of Massachusetts* 8 (1981): 5–16; Kurtz, *Excommunicated from the Union*, 1.

29. Lewis Tappan, *The Fugitive Slave Bill: Its History and Unconstitutionality; With an Account of the Seizure and Enslavement of James Hamlet, and His Subsequent Restoration to Liberty* (New York: American Anti-Slavery Society, 1850), accessed January 9, 2020, https://www.loc.gov/resource/llst.076/?sp=2; Boston *Pilot*, November 2, November 23, and December 5, 1850.

30. Boston *Pilot*, November 2, 1850 (emphasis in original); *Catholic Mirror* article reprinted in the Boston *Pilot*, February 16, 1850; Susannah Ural Bruce, *The Harp and the Eagle: Irish-American Volunteers in the Union Army, 1861–1865* (New York: New York University Press, 2006), 29; Hughes quoted in Madeline Hooke Rice, *American Catholic Opinion in the Slavery Controversy* (Gloucester, MA: Peter Smith, 1964), 110–11, 118–121; John T. McGreevy, *Catholicism and American Freedom: A History* (New York: W. W. Norton, 2003), 52; Kenny, *American Irish*, 119, 125.

31. Gordon S. Barker, *The Imperfect Revolution: Anthony Burns and the Landscape of Race in Antebellum America* (Kent: Kent State University Press, 2010), 35–36; Boston *Pilot*, May 31, 1851.

32. McPherson, *Battle Cry of Freedom*, 84–88, 119–20; Barker, *Imperfect Revolution*, 13; Albert von Frank, *The Trials of Anthony Burns: Freedom and Slavery in Emerson's Boston* (Cambridge, MA: Harvard University Press, 1998), xviii, 67–68; Campbell, *Slave Catchers*, 124–27; *Boston Slave Riot, and Trial of Anthony Burns* (Boston: Fetridge and Company, 1854), 5, 10–12; Brooke, *"There Is a North,"* 227.

33. von Frank, *Trials of Anthony Burns*, 72, 212–13 (Higginson quoted on p. 32); *Boston Slave Riot*, 76–77, 84; Barker, *Imperfect Revolution*, 20; Boston *Pilot*, June 3, 1854; Thomas Wentworth Higginson, *Cheerful Yesterdays* (Boston: Houghton Mifflin, 1898), 148; *Independent* article reprinted in *Frederick Douglass' Newspaper*, June 16, 1854; *Liberator*, June 19, 1854; James Haughton to Editor of the Dublin *Freeman's Journal* reprinted in the *Liberator*, September 29, 1854.

34. Thomas Sweney to Editor of the Boston *Herald*, May 29, 1854, reprinted in the *Liberator*, June 19, 1854; von Frank, *Trials of Anthony Burns*, 136–37; Boston *Pilot*, June 17, 1854; *Citizen* article reprinted in the *Liberator*, June 19, 1854.

35. *Frederick Douglass' Newspaper*, June 2, 1854; James Brewer Stewart, *Wendell Phillips: Liberty's Hero* (Baton Rouge: Louisiana State University Press, 1986), 109–12; Theodore Parker, *The Material Condition of the People of Massachusetts* (Boston: Published by the Fraternity, 1860), 43–45; Theodore Parker to F. E. Parker, April 15, 1858, in *Life and Correspondence of Theodore Parker, Minister of the Twenty-Eight Congregational Society, Boston*, ed. John Weiss, 2 vols. (New York: Appleton, 1864), 1: 397–398; Boston *Pilot*, June 3, 1854; von Frank, *Trials of Anthony Burns*, 108–13, 248–49; Tyler Anbinder, *Nativism and Slavery: The Northern Know-Nothings and the Politics of the 1850s* (New York: Oxford University Press, 1992), 8–15, 103–27; Kenny, *American Irish*, 112–21; Jack Tager, *Boston Riots: Three Centuries of Social Violence* (Boston: Northeastern University Press, 2001), 126–33; Thomas O'Connor, *The Boston Irish: A Political History* (Boston: Northeastern University Press, 1995), 75–80.

36. *CG*, 33rd Congress, 1st session, 1716–17, 1848, 1958, and 2016; *New York Daily Times*, May 30 and July 20 1854.

37. Boston *Pilot*, June 17, 1854; Amos Adams Lawrence to Giles Richards, June 1, 1854, quoted in Jane J. Pease and William H. Pease, eds., *The Fugitive Slave Law and Anthony Burns: A Problem in Law Enforcement* (Philadelphia: Lippincott, 1975), 43.

38. Brian McGovern, *John Mitchel: Irish Nationalist, Southern Secessionist* (Knoxville: University of Tennessee Press, 2009), 96; Michael Toomey, "'Saving the South with All My Might': John Mitchel, Champion of Southern Nationalism," in *Thomas Francis Meagher: The Making of an Irish American*, ed. John M. Hearne and Rory T. Cornish (Dublin: Irish Academic Press, 2005), 123–38; David Gleeson, "Securing the 'Interests' of the South: John Mitchel, A. G. Magrath, and the Reopening of the Transatlantic Slave Trade," *American Nineteenth Century History* 11, no. 3 (2010): 279–98.

39. James Haughton to Thomas Francis Meagher, November 15, 1853, printed in the Dublin *Nation* and reprinted in the *Liberator*, December 23, 1853.

40. Quotes from the *Citizen*, January 14, 1854; Cian T. McMahon, *The Global Dimensions of Irish Identity: Race, Nation, and the Popular Press, 1840–1880* (Chapel Hill: University of North Carolina Press, 2015), 101–2. See also Mitchel's article reprinted in the *Liberator*, January 27, 1854, and in McGovern, *John Mitchel*, 130–31.

41. Potter, *Impending Crisis*, 163–65; James Brewer Stewart, *Holy Warriors: The Abolitionists and American Slavery*, rev. ed. (New York: Hill and Wang, 1997), 166–68; New York *Nation*, October 20, 1849. In contrast to this study, previous scholarship has emphasized the American origins of Irish-American anti-abolitionism. See especially David R. Roediger, *The Wages of Whiteness: Race and the Making of the American Working Class*

(New York: Verso, 1991); Noel Ignatiev, *How the Irish Became White* (New York: Routledge, 1995); Gilbert Osofsky, "Abolitionists, Irish Immigrants, and the Dilemmas of Romantic Nationalism," *American Historical Review* 80, no. 4 (1975), 889–912.

42. Richard Davis Webb to Maria Weston Chapman, June 12, 1847, Ms.A.9.2.23.29, BPL; Henry C. Wright to William Lloyd Garrison, January 23, 1854, printed in the *Liberator*, January 27, 1854; Parker Pillsbury to William Lloyd Garrison, February 8, 1854, printed in the *Liberator*, February 24, 1854; Richard Davis Webb to Sidney Howard Gay, February 8, 1854, printed in the *National Anti-Slavery Standard*, March 4, 1854; Samuel Haughton, *Memoir of James Haughton, with Extracts from his Private and Published Letters, by his son, Samuel Haughton* (Dublin: E. Ponsoby, 1877), 144–46; McGovern, *John Mitchel*, 130–32; James S. Donnelly, Jr., *The Great Irish Potato Famine* (Gloucestershire: Sutton Publishing, 2001), 217–19.

43. Potter, *Impending Crisis*, 145–76; McPherson, *Battle Cry of Freedom*, 121–24; D. S. Grandin to William Lloyd Garrison, July 22, 1854, printed in the *Liberator*, August 4, 1854; Henry C. Wright to William Lloyd Garrison, January 23, 1854, printed in the *Liberator*, January 27, 1854; New York *Tribune* article reprinted in the *National Anti-Slavery Standard*, January 28, 1854.

44. McMahon, *Global Dimensions*, 80–81; McGovern, *John Mitchel*, 133; Fleche, *Revolution of 1861*, 30–31.

45. Brundage, *Irish Nationalists in America*, 95–96; *Commonwealth* article reprinted in the Boston *Pilot*, January 28, 1854; *Independent* article reprinted in the *Liberator*, January 27, 1854; New York *Tribune* article reprinted in the *Liberator*, March 17, 1854.

46. *Citizen*, January 14, 1854; Boston *Pilot*, January 28, 1854; *American Celt* article reprinted in the Chicago *Western Tablet*, February 18, 1854 (emphasis in original); McGovern, *John Mitchel*, 111–15; Hughes quoted in McMahon, *Global Dimensions*, 180.

47. Doheny and the anonymous Young Irelander quoted in the Boston *Pilot* article reprinted in the *Galway Vindicator and Connaught Advertiser*, February 15, 1854; *Irish-American*, January 21, 1854; Carl Wittke, *The Irish in America* (Baton Rouge: Louisiana State University Press, 1956), 81; McMahon, *Global Dimensions*, 101–6; Timothy Egan, *The Immortal Irishman: The Irish Revolutionary Who Became an American Hero* (Boston: Houghton Mifflin Harcourt, 2016), 160–63.

48. Robert McElderry to Thomas McElderry, May 31, 1854, T2414/16, PRONI; *Citizen*, December 30, 1854, quoted in Cian T. McMahon, "Did the Irish 'Become White'? Global Migration and National Identity, 1842–1877" (PhD diss., Carnegie Mellon University, 2010), 163; McGovern, *John Mitchel*, 100.

49. McGovern, *John Mitchel*, 148–59; Gleeson, "Securing the 'Interests' of the South," 281; Toomey, "'Saving the South,'" 123–25; McGovern, *John Mitchel*, 142–43, 149.

50. McMahon, *Global Dimensions*, 103; Brooke, *"There Is a North,"* xi, 3–7.

51. Boston *Pilot*, January 12, 1850.

4. "As if I was a common Irishman": The Irish-American Critique of Antislavery

1. Kevin Kenny, *The American Irish: A History* (New York: Pearson Education, 2000), 104–6.

2. The reference to "hewers of wood and drawers of water" comes from Joshua 9:23 in the King James Bible; Joseph Brenan to Editor of the Dublin *Nation*, n/d, reprinted in the *Irish-American*, January 6, 1850 (emphasis in *Irish-American*); *Irish-American*, December 16, 1849.

3. Kenny, *American Irish*, 109–11.

4. Eric Foner, *Free Soil, Free Labor, Free Men: The Ideology of the Republican Party*, rev. ed. (1970; repr., New York: Oxford University Press, 1995), x–xiv, xxv, 11–39; Kevin Kenny, "Nativism, Labor, and Slavery: The Political Odyssey of Benjamin Bannan, 1850–1860," *Pennsylvania Magazine of History and Biography* 118, no. 4 (October 1994): 330; William E. Gienapp, *The Origins of the Republican Party, 1852–1856* (New York: Oxford University Press, 1987), 354–56; Bruce Levine, *Half Slave and Half Free: The Roots of Civil War*, rev. ed. (1992; repr., New York: Hill and Wang, 2002), 56–70.

5. Timothy McCarthy to his mother, n/d, printed in the Cork *Examiner*, July 6, 1849 (emphasis in the Cork *Examiner*); "Outis" to Editor of the Cork *Examiner*, June 10, 1849, printed in the Cork *Examiner*, June 27, 1849; Francis R. Walsh, "Who Spoke for Boston's Irish? The Boston *Pilot* in the Nineteenth Century," *Journal of Ethnic Studies* 10, no. 3 (Fall 1982): 27; Boston *Pilot*, June 24, 1854; Cahill quoted in Ryan W. Keating, *Shades of Green: Irish Regiments, American Soldiers, and Local Communities in the Civil War Era* (New York: Fordham University Press, 2017), 5; Kerby Miller, *Emigrants and Exiles: Ireland and the Irish Exodus to North America* (New York: Oxford University Press, 1985), 312–14.

6. For the lack of socioeconomic and occupational mobility for antebellum Irish immigrants, see Kenny, *American Irish*, 109–11; Miller, *Emigrants and Exiles*, passim, but especially 314; Oscar Handlin, *Boston's Immigrants: A Study in Acculturation*, rev. and enl. ed. (1941; repr., Cambridge, MA: Harvard University Press, 1959); Dennis Clark, *The Irish in Philadelphia: Ten Generations of Urban Experience* (Philadelphia: Temple University Press, 1973); Brian Mitchell, *The Paddy Camps: The Irish of Lowell, 1821–1861* (Urbana: University of Illinois Press, 1998); Robert Ernst, *Immigrant Life in New York City, 1825–1863* (New York: King's Crown Press, 1949). For abolitionists' views on free labor, see Eric Foner, ed., "Abolitionism and the Labor Movement in Ante-bellum America," in *Politics and Ideology in the Age of the Civil War* (New York: Oxford University Press, 1980), 59–64. For the decline of traditional artisanship and resultant rise in working-class consciousness in nineteenth-century America, see Sean Wilentz, *Chants Democratic: New York City and the Rise of the American Working-Class, 1788–1850* (New York: Oxford University Press, 1994); Peter Way, *Common Labour: Workers and the Digging of North American Canals, 1780–1860* (New York: Cambridge University Press, 1993).

7. David R. Roediger, *The Wages of Whiteness: Race and the Making of the American Working Class* (New York: Verso, 1991), 149; Noel Ignatiev, *How the Irish Became White* (New York: Routledge, 1995) 42; Carl Wittke, *The Irish in America* (Baton Rouge: Louisiana State University Press, 1956), 15. The provenance of the "common Irishman" quip within these sources is obscure. Roediger references an abbreviated version of this anecdote, quoting only the "common Irishman" part of it, but claims it was a story that drew nervous laughter from the Irishmen who repeated it. Roediger cites the New York *Freeman's Journal*, November 4, 1843. While the "My master is a great tyrant . . ." quote

does not appear in the *Freeman's Journal*, the same issue does include Daniel O'Connell's reference to Americans who claimed the Irish were "white negroes." Roediger's citation also includes Jay Rubin, "Black Nativism: The European Immigrant in Negro Thought, 1830–1860," *Phylon* 39, no. 3 (1978): 199. No reference to the quote was found in Rubin's article, which discusses nativism among African Americans. Ignatiev cites the *Irish-American* article as it appeared in Florence E. Gibson, *The Attitudes of the New York Irish Toward State and National Affairs, 1848–1892* (New York: Columbia University Press, 1951), 15. Joseph Brenan to Editor of the Dublin *Nation*, n/d, reprinted in the New York *Irish-American*, January 6, 1850; Maureen Murphy and James Quinn, "Cavanagh, Michael," in *Dictionary of Irish Biography*, ed. James McGuire and James Quinn (Cambridge: Cambridge University Press, 2010), accessed November 7, 2011, http://dib.cambridge.org/viewReadPage.do?articleId=a1571.

8. "Patrick" to Editor of the Chicago *Western Tablet*, n/d, printed in the Chicago *Western Tablet* November 20, 1852; Patrick Staunton and Patrick Roe to Editor of the Chicago *Western Tablet*, n/d, printed in the Chicago *Western Tablet*, March 19, 1853; Patrick Kennedy to Vere Foster, March 19, 1855, D3618/D/8/9, Public Records Office of Northern Ireland.

9. "A.O.Y." to Editor of the Boston *Pilot*, n/d, printed in the Boston *Pilot*, February 18, 1854; Jonathan Glickstein, "'Poverty Is Not Slavery': American Abolitionists and the Competitive Labor Market," in *Antislavery Reconsidered: New Perspectives on the Abolitionists*, ed. Lewis Perry and Michael Fellman (Baton Rouge: Louisiana State University Press, 1979), 195–218; Foner, "Abolitionism and the Labor Movement," 65–72; James Brewer Stewart, *Wendell Phillips: Liberty's Hero* (Baton Rouge: Louisiana State University Press, 1986), 113–16. Manisha Sinha has challenged the notion that abolitionists, especially Black activists, were uncritical of the nascent industrial capitalist system. See Sinha, *The Slave's Cause: A History of Abolition* (New Haven, CT: Yale University Press, 2016).

10. Kenny, *American Irish*, 132–34; Miller, *Emigrants and Exiles*, 347.

11. Dublin *Irishman*, November 26, 1859; William Lalor to Editor of the New York *Irish News*, n/d, reprinted in the Dublin *Irishman*, January 28, 1860; "J.M.E." to Editor of the *Irish-American*, March 10, 1856, printed in the *Irish-American*, March 29, 1856 (emphasis in original); *American Celt* article quoted in D. W. Mitchell, *Ten Years Residence in the United States* (London: Smith, Elder, 1862), 148 (emphasis in original); Jonathan Glickstein, *American Exceptionalism, American Anxiety: Wages, Competition, and Degraded Labor in the Antebellum United States* (Charlottesville: University of Virginia Press, 2002), 277–79.

12. Alvin F. Oickle, *Disaster in Lawrence: The Fall of the Pemberton Mill* (Charleston, SC: History Press, 2008); "J. G." to Editor of the Dublin *Irishman*, February 1, 1860, printed in the Dublin *Irishman*, February 25, 1860; *New York Times*, January 21, 1860; *Irish-American*, January 21, 1860.

13. James McPherson, *Battle Cry of Freedom: The Civil War Era* (New York: Oxford University Press, 1988), 121–25; David Potter, *The Impending Crisis: 1848–1861* (New York: Harper and Row, 1976), 158–64; Elizabeth R. Varon, *Disunion! The Coming of the American Civil War, 1789–1859* (Chapel Hill: University of North Carolina Press, 2008),

250–53; John L. Brooke, *"There Is a North": Fugitive Slaves, Political Crisis, and Cultural Transformation in the Coming of the Civil War* (Amherst: University of Massachusetts Press, 2019), 225–27.

14. Kenny, *American Irish*, 118–19; Tyler Anbinder, *Five Points: The 19th-Century New York City Neighborhood That Invented Tap Dance, Stole Elections, and Became the World's Most Notorious Slum* (New York: Plume, 2002), 156–58; William V. Shannon, *The American Irish* (New York: Macmillan, 1963), 55; Ignatiev, *How the Irish Became White*, 79; *CG*, United States House of Representatives, 33rd Cong., 1st Sess., May 19, 1854, 1232; Walsh's "You are slaves . . . " remarks quoted in Foner, *Free Soil*, xviii.

15. Potter, *Impending Crisis*, 175; Brooke, *"There Is a North,"* 227; *CG*, United States House of Representatives, 33rd Cong., 1st Sess., May 19, 1854, 1232. On Southerners' endorsements of slavery through denunciations of Northern "wage slavery," see Drew Gilpin Faust, ed., *The Ideology of Slavery: Proslavery Thought in the Antebellum South, 1830–1860* (Baton Rouge: Louisiana State University Press, 1981), 18–20; Manisha Sinha, *The Counterrevolution of Slavery: Politics and Ideology in Antebellum South Carolina* (Chapel Hill: University of North Carolina Press, 2000), 88–93, 140–42, 222–29; Eugene Genevese, *The World the Slaveholders Made: Two Essays in Interpretation* (New York: Pantheon Books, 1969), 129. The contemporary Southerner most associated with this argument, and indeed the focus of both Faust's and Genevese's analysis, is George Fitzhugh. See George Fitzhugh, *Cannibals All! Or, Slaves Without Masters*, ed. C. Vann Woodward (1857; Cambridge, MA: Harvard University Press, 1960).

16. Potter, *Impending Crisis*, 238–40, 247–50; Tyler Anbinder, *Nativism and Slavery: The Northern Know-Nothings and the Politics of the 1850s* (New York: Oxford University Press, 1992), 18; Matthew Karp, *This Vast Southern Empire: Slaveholders at the Helm of American Foreign Policy* (Cambridge, MA: Harvard University Press, 2016), 218–23.

17. The definitive account of the Know-Nothings' rise and fall is Anbinder, *Nativism and Slavery*. Other useful works include John Mulkern, *The Know-Nothing Party in Massachusetts: The Rise and Fall of a People's Movement* (Boston: Northeastern University Press, 1990); William E. Gienapp, "Nativism and the Creation of a Republican Majority in the North Before the Civil War," *Journal of American History* 72, no. 3 (1985): 529–59; Dale Baum, "Know-Nothingism and the Republican Majority in Massachusetts: The Political Realignment of the 1850s," *Journal of American History* 64, no. 4 (1978): 959–86; Michael F. Holt, *The Political Crisis of the 1850s* (New York: Wiley, 1978), 101–38.

18. Potter, *Impending Crisis*, 241–44; Kenny, *American Irish*, 99, 104–12; Anbinder, *Nativism and Slavery*, 20–21, 44.

19. Foner, *Free Soil*, 124–25; Boston *Pilot*, May 31, 1851 (emphasis in the *Pilot*); *Pilot* quoted in Wittke, *Irish in America*, 116. For similar claims in other newspapers popular with Irish Americans across the North, see Benjamin J. Blied, *Catholics and the Civil War* (Milwaukee: 1945), 63, 73–74.

20. Kenny, *American Irish*, 117; Kenny, "Nativism, Labor, and Slavery," 330–34; Anbinder, *Nativism and Slavery*, 130–36, 99–101; Kevin Kenny, *Making Sense of the Molly Maguires* (New York: Oxford University Press, 1998), 73–79.

21. Resolution of a Norfolk, Massachusetts, Know-Nothing meeting quoted in Gerald P. Fogarty, "Public Patriotism and Private Politics: The Tradition of American Catholi-

cism,'" *U.S. Catholic Historian* 4 (1984), 11; Kenny, *American Irish*, 117; John T. McGreevy, *Catholicism and American Freedom: A History* (New York: W. W. Norton, 2003), 63–63; James Haughton to Editor of the Dublin *Freeman's Journal*, March 1856, reprinted in the *Liberator*, May 9, 1856; Anbinder, *Nativism and Slavery*, 45–46. For anti-Catholicism in antebellum American nativism, see Ray Allen Billington, *The Protestant Crusade, 1800–1860* (Chicago: Quadrangle Books, 1938).

22. George McWhirk to Editor of the *National Era*, January 1, 1855, printed in the *National Era*, January 18, 1855; Anbinder, *Nativism and Slavery*, 87–94; Dale Baum, "Know-Nothingism," 959–86; Mulkern, *Know-Nothing Party*; "W" to Editor of *Frederick Douglass' Newspaper*, n/d, printed in *Frederick Douglass' Newspaper*, December 1, 1854.

23. Anbinder, *Nativism and Slavery*, 121, 135–42, 248–52; Thomas O'Connor, *The Boston Irish: A Political History* (Boston: Northeastern University Press, 1995), 76–77; John R. Mulkern, "Scandal Behind the Convent Walls: The Know-Nothing Nunnery Committee of 1855," *Historical Journal of Massachusetts* 11 (1983): 22–34; Mulkern, *Know-Nothing Party*, 94–96, 101–5.

24. *Cincinnati Enquirer*, July 29 and September 2, 1855; Salmon P. Chase to John Paul, December 27, 1854, quoted in Gienapp, *Origins*, 194; Letter from Chicago to the Editor of the *National Era*, March 7, 1856, printed in the *National Era* March 20, 1856; Letter from Genessee, IL, to Editor of the *National Era*, April 3, 1856, printed in the *National Era*, April 17, 1856; Anbinder, *Nativism and Slavery*, 174–80.

25. Abraham Lincoln to Joshua Speed, August 24, 1855, in *The Collected Works of Abraham Lincoln*, vol. 2, ed. Roy P. Basler (New Brunswick, NJ: Rutgers University Press, 1953), 323; Jason H. Silverman, *Lincoln and the Immigrant* (Carbondale: Southern Illinois University Press, 2015), 126–27; Potter, *Impending Crisis*, 253.

26. Foner, *Free Soil*, 258; McPherson, *Battle Cry of Freedom*, 145–53; Potter, *Impending Crisis*, 199–224; David Herbert Donald, *Charles Sumner and the Coming of the Civil War* (New York: Knopf, 1960), 289–97; William E. Gienapp, "The Crime Against Sumner: The Caning of Charles Sumner and the Rise of the Republican Party," *Civil War History* 25 (1979): 220–22; Brooke, *"There Is a North,"* 280–81.

27. Boston *Pilot*, June 14, 1856; "Dido" to Editor of the Boston *Pilot*, March 28, 1856, printed in the Boston *Pilot*, April 19, 1856; *Irish-American*, March 23, 1856; Adam Tuchinsky, *Horace Greeley's* New-York Tribune: *Civil War-Era Socialism and the Crisis of Free Labor* (Ithaca, NY: Cornell University Press, 2009), 156–68.

28. Boston *Pilot*, September 27, 1856; *Irish-American*, October 4, 1856.

29. Potter, *Impending Crisis*, 217–24; McPherson, *Battle Cry of Freedom*, 149–50, 160; Gienapp, *Origins*, 170–72, 298–99; John R. McKivigan, *Forgotten Firebrand: James Redpath and the Making of Nineteenth-Century America* (Ithaca, NY: Cornell University Press, 1998).

30. Boston *Pilot*, May 31 and July 19, 1856.

31. Quote from the *American Celt*, May 24, 1856; *National Era*, June 5, 1856; *New York Times*, July 14, 1856; *National Era*, July 31, 1856; *CG*, 34th Cong., 1st Sess., 1228–29.

32. Boston *Pilot*, June 14, 1856; *American Celt* article reprinted in the *National Era*, June 5, 1856; Charleston, SC, *Standard* article reprinted in the *National Era*, August 14, 1856.

33. Potter, *Impending Crisis*, 254–60; Anbinder, *Nativism and Slavery*, 215–19; McPherson, *Battle Cry of Freedom*, 153–58.

34. *Milwaukee Working Man* article reprinted in the Boston *Pilot*, July 26, 1856 (emphasis in the *Pilot*); *Irish-American*, December 6, 1856.

35. Boston *Pilot*, July 5, 1856. See also Boston *Pilot*, October 4, 1856; Anbinder, *Nativism and Slavery*, 187–92; Mulkern, *Know-Nothing Party*.

36. Anbinder, *Nativism and Slavery*, 220–33.

37. Kenny, *American Irish*, 118–21; Steven P. Erie, *Rainbow's End: Irish Americans and the Dilemmas of Urban Machine Politics, 1840–1985* (Berkeley: University of California Press, 1988), 26–27; Varon, *Disunion!*, 273–77.

38. Varon, *Disunion!*, 295–96; McPherson, *Battle Cry of Freedom*, 162–69; Karp, *Vast Southern Empire*, 6–7, 221–25.

39. Boston *Pilot*, March 21 and March 28, 1857; Karp, *Vast Southern Empire*, 183–84; Potter, *Impending Crisis*, 192–95; McPherson, *Battle Cry of Freedom*, 112–16; New York *Tablet*, June 13, July 21 (quote), August 21, 1857.

40. McPherson, *Battle Cry of Freedom*, 202–13 (Emerson quoted on p. 212); David S. Reynolds, *John Brown, Abolitionist: The Man Who Killed Slavery, Sparked the Civil War, and Seeded Civil Rights* (New York: Vintage, 2005), 296, 310–27, 343–47, and especially 360–69; Evan C. Carton, *Patriotic Treason: John Brown and the Soul of America* (New York: Free Press, 2006), 296–313, 321–23; Potter, *Impending Crisis*, 362–66, 376–80.

41. Peter B. Knupfer, "A Crisis in Conservatism: Northern Unionism and the Harpers Ferry Raid," in *His Soul Goes Marching On: Responses to John Brown and the Harpers Ferry Raid*, ed. Paul Finkelman (Charlottesville: University Press of Virginia, 1995), 119–48; Reynolds, *John Brown, Abolitionist*, 357–58; Carton, *Patriotic Treason*, 335; Boston *Pilot*, October 29, 1859; *Irish-American*, November 5, 1859.

42. *Irish-American*, November 5, 1859; Boston *Pilot*, October 29 and November 19, 1859.

43. Boston *Pilot*, December 3 and 10, 1859; Reynolds, *John Brown, Abolitionist*, 318; Joseph Barry, *The Strange Story of Harpers Ferry, with Legends of the Surrounding Country* (Martinsburg, WV: Thompson Brothers, 1903), 98; John-Erik Gilot, "Private Luke Quinn—The Unlikely Celebrity of Harpers Ferry," accessed June 15, 2021, https://emergingcivilwar.com/2018/06/16/private-luke-quinn-the-unlikely-celebrity-of-harpers-ferry/.

44. David Sim, *A Union Forever: The Irish Question and U.S. Foreign Relations in the Victorian Age* (Ithaca, NY: Cornell University Press, 2013), 77–83; New York *Tablet*, September 26 and October 2, 1857; David Brundage, *Irish Nationalists in America: The Politics of Exile, 1798-1998* (New York: Oxford University Press, 2016), 96–100.

45. *The Independent*, December 29, 1859; Henry Mayer, *All on Fire: William Lloyd Garrison and the Abolition of Slavery* (New York: W. W. Norton, 1998), 506.

46. Boston *Pilot*, January 21, 1860; *Irish-American*, January 21 and 28, 1860.

47. "A Columbia Irishman" to Editor of the *Irish-American*, February 4, 1860, printed in the *Irish-American*, February 18, 1860; *Irish-American*, January 28 and March 17, 1860; *The Independent*, December 29, 1859.

48. Potter, *Impending Crisis*, 405–15; McPherson, *Battle Cry of Freedom*, 213–16; Susannah Ural Bruce, *The Harp and the Eagle: Irish-American Volunteers and the Union*

Army, 1861–1865 (New York: New York University Press, 2006), 42–43; Christian G. Samito, *Becoming American Under Fire: Irish Americans, African Americans, and the Politics of Citizenship during the Civil War Era* (Ithaca, NY: Cornell University Press, 2009), 26. For Irish-American newspapers' support for Douglas, see *Irish Pictorial Weekly*, July 28 and September 1, 1860; "Cormac" to Editor of the *Irish-American*, February 11, 1860, printed in the *Irish-American*, February 18, 1860; Boston *Pilot*, September 29, 1860; *Irish-American*, May 26, 1860. For Lincoln's repudiation of nativism, see Foner, *Free Soil*, 232–36; Silverman, *Lincoln and the Immigrant*, passim.

49. James McPherson, *This Mighty Scourge: Perspectives on the Civil War* (New York: Oxford University Press, 2007), 9–11; Potter, *Impending Crisis*, 577–83; McPherson, *Battle Cry of Freedom*, 234–35, 257–59, and 273–84;

5. Irish Americans and the Union War

1. Ryan W. Keating, *Shades of Green: Irish Regiments, American Soldiers, and Local Communities in the Civil War Era* (New York: Fordham University Press, 2017), 10–11; Christian G. Samito, *Becoming American Under Fire: Irish Americans, African Americans, and the Politics of Citizenship during the Civil War Era* (Ithaca, NY: Cornell University Press, 2009), 27–28; Susannah Ural Bruce, *The Harp and the Eagle: Irish-American Volunteers in the Union Army, 1861–1865* (New York: New York University Press, 2006), 51–53; Ella Lonn, *Foreigners in the Union Army and Navy* (Baton Rouge: Louisiana State University Press, 1951), 42–43; Daniel MacNamara, *History of the Ninth Regiment, Massachusetts Volunteer Infantry, June 1861–June 1864*, with an introduction by Christian G. Samito (New York: Fordham University Press, 2000); Michael H. MacNamara, *The Irish Ninth in Bivouac and Battle; or, Virginia and Maryland Campaigns* (Boston: Lee and Shepard, 1867); Richard Demeter, *The Fighting 69th: A History* (Pasadena, CA: Cranford Press, 2002), 25–26; William L. Burton, *Melting Pot Soldiers: The Union's Ethnic Regiments* (New York: Fordham University Press, 1998), 112–60.

2. Bruce, *The Harp and the Eagle*, 3; Samito, *Becoming American*, 6–7.

3. James Zibro, "The Life of Paddy Yank: The Common Irish-American Soldier in the Union Army" (PhD diss., Catholic University of America, 2016), 20–21, 25 (quote), 99, 141–42, 191.

4. *Boston Journal* article reprinted in *Irish Pictorial Weekly*, April 27, 1861; Boston *Pilot*, July 20, 1861; Joseph M. Hernon, Jr., *Celts, Catholics, and Copperheads: Ireland Views the American Civil War* (Columbus: Ohio State University Press, 1968), 75–77; Samito, *Becoming American*, 27–29.

5. *Catholic Telegraph and Advocate*, January 19, January 26, March 9, March 16, March 30, and April 20, 1861; "A Western Catholic" to Editor of the *Catholic Telegraph and Advocate*, n/d, printed in the *Catholic Telegraph and Advocate*, April 13, 1861; *Philadelphia Herald and Visitor* article reprinted in the *Catholic Telegraph and Advocate*, May 11, 1861; John T. McGreevy, *Catholicism and American Freedom* (New York: W. W. Norton, 2003), 71–72; William B. Kurtz, *Excommunicated from the Union: How the Civil War Created a Separate Catholic America* (New York: Fordham University Press, 2016), 56–59; Benjamin J. Blied, *Catholics and the Civil War* (Milwaukee: 1945), 39–40; Archbishop

John Hughes to Bishop Patrick Lynch (Charleston, SC), August 23, 1861, printed in the *Catholic Telegraph and Advocate*, September 14, 1861.

6. William Dennis to John Dennis, October 15, 1861, SC14151, William Dennis Letters, New York State Library; *Irish Pictorial Weekly*, January 26 and April 20, 1861; "X.Y.Z." to Editor of the *Irish-American*, n/d, printed in the *Irish-American* May 25, 1861; *Cincinnati Catholic Telegraph and Advocate*, July 6, 1861.

7. Daly's speech quoted in D. P. Conyngham, *The Irish Brigade and Its Campaigns: With Some Account of the Corcoran Legion, and Sketches of the Principal Officers* (New York: William McSorley, 1867; repr., Gaithersburg, MD: Olde Soldier Books, n/d), 59–60; Harold Earl Hammond, *A Commoner's Judge: The Life and Times of Charles Patrick Daly* (Boston: Christopher Publishing House, 1954), 143–46.

8. Boston *Irish Pictorial Weekly*, January 5, February 16, and April 20, 1861; Keating, *Shades of Green*, 5, 244n.

9. Dublin *Nation*, October 11, 1862; Cian T. McMahon, *The Global Dimensions of Irish Identity: Race, Nation, and the Popular Press, 1840–1880* (Chapel Hill: University of North Carolina Press, 2015), 141; Dublin *Irishman*, May 4 and May 11, 1861; *Dundalk Democrat* article reprinted in the Boston *Pilot*, July 26, 1862; "Duhallow" to the Editor of the *Cork Examiner*, April 8, 1862, printed in the *Cork Examiner*, April 29, 1862; *Galway-American*, September 13, 1862.

10. *Galway-American*, April 19, 1862; Boston *Pilot*, August 30, 1862; Tom [Miller], Assistant Adjutant General, Irish Brigade to Patrick O'Donohue, October 26, 1862, James Shields Folder, Kenneth H. Powers Collection, United States Army Military History Institute, Carlisle, PA. (hereafter cited as Powers Collection, USAMHI) (emphasis in original). For native-born soldiers who held similar views, see Gary Gallagher, *The Union War* (Cambridge, MA: Harvard University Press, 2011), 70–73.

11. James McPherson, *Battle Cry of Freedom: The Civil War Era* (New York: Oxford University Press, 1988), 387–88; Howard Jones, *Union in Peril: The Crisis Over British Intervention in the Civil War* (Chapel Hill: University of North Carolina Press, 1992), 27–30; Amanda Foreman, *A World on Fire: An Epic History of Two Nations Divided* (New York: Penguin, 2010), 92–93.

12. *Irish-American*, June 1 and June 15, 1861; "Major" to Editor of the Boston *Pilot*, October 1862, printed in the Boston *Pilot*, October 18, 1862.

13. Norman B. Ferris, *The Trent Affair: A Diplomatic Crisis* (Knoxville: University of Tennessee Press, 1977); Jones, *Union in Peril*, 80–99; Foreman, *World on Fire*, 170–95; Resolution of the Philadelphia Ancient Order of Hibernians, December 18, 1861, printed in the *Catholic Telegraph and Advocate*, December 28, 1861; *Catholic Telegraph and Advocate*, January 8, 1862; Michael H. Leary to Nellie Desmond, December 19, 1861, Michael H. Leary Letters, Ms.1986.043, John J. Burns Library, Boston College (hereafter cited as Leary Letters, Burns Library); David Sim, *A Union Forever: The Irish Question and U.S. Foreign Relations in the Victorian Age* (Ithaca, NY: Cornell University Press, 2013), 86–87.

14. Duffy quoted in Hernon, *Celts, Catholics, and Copperheads*, 2; Robert Kee, *The Green Flag: A History of Irish Nationalism* (London: Weidenfield and Nicolson, 1972), 290–98, 313–15; David Brundage, *Irish Nationalists in America: The Politics of Exile, 1798–1998* (New York: Oxford University Press, 2016),100–101.

15. Boston *Pilot*, August 3, August 9, 1862; Samito, *Becoming American*, 120–25; William D'Arcy, *The Fenian Movement in the United States: 1858–1866* (Washington, D.C.: Catholic University of America Press, 1947); Thomas N. Brown, *Irish-American Nationalism, 1870–1890* (1966; repr., Westport, CT: Greenwood Press, 1980), 38–41.

16. *Irish-American*, July 26 and September 6, 1862; MacNamara, *History of the Ninth Regiment*, 74–75; *Galway American*, July 19, 1862.

17. *The Federal Scout*, March 11, 1862, quoted in Chandra Manning, *What This Cruel War Was Over: Soldiers, Slavery, and the Civil War* (New York: Random House, 2007), 73.

18. *New York Freeman's Journal*, August 31, 1861; McGreevy, *Catholicism and American Freedom*, 73–76; Mark E. Neely, Jr., *The Fate of Liberty: Abraham Lincoln and Civil Liberties* (New York: Oxford University Press, 1991); Patrick Dunny to Thomas Dunny, Esq., October 22, 1861, in "An Irishman Looks at Civil War," *Carloviana: Journal of the Old Carlow Society* (December 1967): 30; Dublin *Irishman*, June 15, 1861; Dublin *Daily News* article reprinted in the Boston *Pilot*, July 12, 1862.

19. *Catholic Telegraph and Advocate*, April 27, 1861; *Irish-American*, October 12, 1861; Boston *Pilot*, September 20, 1862; James McPherson, *Antietam: The Battle That Changed the Course of the Civil War* (New York: Oxford University Press, 2002), 27–40, 87–88; McPherson, *Battle Cry of Freedom*, 461–77; Bruce, *The Harp and the Eagle*, 85, 121–22.

20. Boston *Pilot*, September 29 and December 1, 1860; Mathew Brooks to Margaret Clark, January 1, 1861, T2700/3, Public Records Office of Northern Ireland.

21. *Irish Pictorial Weekly*, January 19, 1861; Cincinnati *Catholic Telegraph and Advocate*, February 2 and March 16, 1861; George M. Frederickson, *The Inner Civil War: Northern Intellectuals and the Crisis of the Union* (New York: Harper and Row, 1965), 57; Elizabeth R. Varon, *Disunion! The Coming of the Civil War, 1789–1859* (Chapel Hill: University of North Carolina Press, 2008), 340–41.

22. *Irish Pictorial Weekly*, January 26, 1861; Kevin Kenny, *The American Irish: A History* (New York: Pearson Education, 2000), 61; Dublin *Irishman*, May 4 and August 17, 1861.

23. Citizens of Boston [including Patrick Donahoe] to Governor John A. Andrew, n/d [Fall 1861], G01/Series 567X, Massachusetts Governor Executive Department letters, 1853–1893: 28th Regt. Infantry 1861–1864, Volume W32, Massachusetts State Archives (hereafter cited as 28th Regt. Infantry Files, Volume W32, MSA); Donahoe to Andrew, November 25, November 26, and December 10, 1861, 28th Regt. Infantry Files, Volume W32, MSA; *Irish-American*, October 12, 1861; *New York Freeman's Journal*, August 24, 1861; McGreevy, *Catholicism and American Freedom*, 68–71.

24. Damian Shiels, *The Irish in the American Civil War* (Dublin: History Press Ireland, 2013), 18–19; Bruce, *The Harp and the Eagle*, 83, 88–89; Conyngham, *Irish Brigade*, 97–98; Demeter, *The Fighting 69th*, 63–64.

25. James Shields to Charles Patrick Daly, February 10, 1862, Charles Patrick Daly Papers, Box 3, New York Public Library (hereafter cited as Daly Papers, Box 3, NYPL); Richard J. Purcell, "James Shields: Soldier and Statesman," *Irish Studies: A Quarterly Review* 21, no. 81 (March 1932): 85; Conyngham, *Irish Brigade*, 100; Bruce, *The Harp and the Eagle*, 88–89; Jennifer L. Weber, *Copperheads: The Rise and Fall of Lincoln's Opponents*

in the North (New York: Oxford University Press, 2006), 26; Charles F. Cooney, "Treason or Tyranny? The Great Senate Purge of '62," *Civil War Times Illustrated* 18 (1979): 30–31; McPherson, *Battle Cry of Freedom*, 457–60.

26. James Hall to Charles Patrick Daly, July 2, 1862, Daly Papers, Box 3, NYPL; Unidentified author to Editor of the *Irish-American*, June 28, 1862, printed in the *Irish-American*, July 12, 1862; Brigadier General Thomas Francis Meagher to President Abraham Lincoln, July 30, 1862, available at *Abraham Lincoln Papers at the Library of Congress*, Manuscript Division (Washington, D.C.: American Memory Project, [2000–2002]), accessed June 25, 2012, http://memory.loc.gov/ammem/alhtml/alhome.html; *Irish-American*, July 26, 1862; James A. Mulligan Diary, October 24, 1862, James A. Mulligan Papers, 1849–1900, Chicago History Museum (hereafter cited as Mulligan Diary, CHM); Lonn, *Foreigners in the Union Army and Navy*, 569–97.

27. Eric Foner, *The Fiery Trial: Abraham Lincoln and American Slavery* (New York: W. W. Norton, 2010), 192; Manning, *What This Cruel War Was Over*, 73–74; McPherson, *Battle Cry of Freedom*, 333–39, 496–97; Gallagher, *Union War*, 89–90; Charles Wagandt, *The Mighty Revolution: Negro Emancipation in Maryland, 1862–1864* (Baltimore: Johns Hopkins University Press, 1964), 117–18; Silvana R. Siddali, *From Property to Person: Slavery and the Confiscation Acts, 1861–1862* (Baton Rouge: Louisiana State University Press, 2005), 120–44.

28. *New York Freeman's Journal*, April 26, May 17, and July 12, 1862; James Shields to Charles Patrick Daly, August 8, 1862, Daly Papers, Box 3, NYPL; Gary Gallagher, ed., "A Civil War Watershed: The 1862 Richmond Campaign in Perspective," in *The Richmond Campaign of 1862: The Peninsula and the Seven Days* (Chapel Hill: University of North Carolina Press, 2000), 3–27; Andrew Birmingham to "Friend Murphy," July 14, 1862, in J. Noonan, Untitled Manuscript on the 69th New York Regiment, Powers Collection, USAMHI; Fr. Bernard O'Reilly to Charles Patrick Daly, July 28, 1862, Daly Papers, Box 3, NYPL; Mark Grimsley, *The Hard Hand of War: Union Military Policy Toward Southern Civilians, 1861–1865* (New York: Cambridge University Press, 1995), 127–28; Foner, *Fiery Trial*, 206–08.

29. *Irish-American*, October 11, 1862; Boston *Pilot*, October 18 and October 25, 1862; Weber, *Copperheads*, 77–78; Joel H. Silbey, *A Respectable Minority: The Democratic Party in the Civil War Era, 1860–1868* (New York: W. W. Norton, 1977), 80–83; Mark E. Neely, Jr., *Lincoln and the Democrats: The Politics of Opposition in the Civil War* (New York: Cambridge University Press, 2017), 120–21.

30. Dublin *Nation*, September 13 and November 8, 1862; Hernon, *Celts, Catholics, and Copperheads*, 75–76.

31. Burton, *Melting Pot Soldiers*, 124–25; Bruce, *The Harp and the Eagle*, 128–35; Samito, *Becoming American*, 127–28; George C. Rable, *Fredericksburg! Fredericksburg!* (Chapel Hill: University of North Carolina Press, 2002).

32. Chandra Manning, *Troubled Refuge: Struggling for Freedom in the Civil War* (New York: Alfred A. Knopf, 2016), 32–41; Foner, *Fiery Trial*, 169–71.

33. James Turner to his parents and sisters, May 20 and May 30 1861, SC12613, James B. Turner Papers, New York State Library (hereafter cited as Turner Papers, NYSL); Arthur O'Keefe to Michael and Mary O'Keefe, July 6, 1861, SC19231, O'Keefe Family Papers,

New York State Library; Kevin O'Brien, ed., *My Life in the Irish Brigade: The Civil War Memoirs of Private William McCarter, 116th Pennsylvania Infantry* (Campbell, CA: Savas, 1996), 3; Daniel Finn Diary, September 14, 1861, Civil War Miscellaneous Collection, USAMHI (hereafter cited as Finn Diary, CWMC, USAMHI); Manning, *What This Cruel War Was Over*, 49–50.

34. Michael Leary to Nellie Desmond, July 30 and August 16, 1861, Leary Letters, Burns Library; Leon F. Litwack, *Been in the Storm So Long: The Aftermath of Slavery* (New York: Alfred A. Knopf, 1979), 52–57 (quote on 53); Foner, *Fiery Trial*, 208.

35. Manning, *Troubled Refuge*, 176–89; Ira Berlin, Barbara J. Fields, Thavolia Glymph, Joseph P. Reidy, and Leslie Rowland, eds., *Freedom: A Documentary History of Emancipation, 1861–1867*, ser. I, vol. 1: *The Destruction of Slavery* (New York: Cambridge University Press, 1985), 11–13; Litwack, *In the Storm*, 55–63; Foner, *Fiery Trial*, 169–71; Siddali, *From Property to Person*, 81–82, 238–40; Ira Berlin, "Who Freed the Slaves," in *Union and Emancipation: Essays on Politics and Race in the Civil War Era*, ed. David W. Blight and Brooks D. Simpson (Kent, OH: Kent State University Press, 1997), 110–15; C. Peter Ripley, *Slaves and Freedmen in Civil War Louisiana* (Baton Rouge: Louisiana State University Press, 1976), 9–13; Grimsley, *Hard Hand of War*, 122–23.

36. "MAF" [Michael A. Finnerty] to Editor of the Boston *Pilot*, n/d, printed in the Boston *Pilot*, April 26, 1862; Timothy O'Leary et al. to Governor John Andrew, July 31, 1862, Go1/Series 567X, Massachusetts Governor Executive Department letters, 1853–1893, 9th Regt. Infantry 1861–1865: vol. 25, Massachusetts State Archives; Christian G. Samito, ed., *Commanding Boston's Irish Ninth: The Civil War Letters of Colonel Patrick R. Guiney, Ninth Massachusetts Volunteer Infantry* (New York: Fordham University Press, 1998); Benjamin Quarles, *The Negro in the Civil War* (New York: Russell and Russell, 1968), 78–92.

37. Daniel Finn Diary, May 28, 1862, CWMC, USAMHI.

38. Daniel Finn Diary June 1, June 9, June 27, and July 14, 1862, CWMC, USAMHI.

39. Manning, *What This Cruel War Was Over*, 67–68; Levi C. Brackett to Major Newton, March 27, 1862, 28th Regt. Infantry Files, Volume W32, MSA; Charles Chipman to Elizabeth Chipman, June 23, 1862, Charles D. Chipman Papers, Chipman Collection, USAMHI (hereafter cited as Chipman Papers, USAMHI); William J. K. Beaudot and Lance J. Herdegen, eds., *An Irishman in the Iron Brigade: The Civil War Memoirs of James P. Sullivan, Sergt., Company K, 6th Wisconsin Volunteers* (New York: Fordham University Press, 1993), 39–41; James Turner to "My Dear Little Sister Sarah," July 26, 1862, Turner Papers, NYSL; Thomas Cahill to Margaret Cahill, July 5, 1862, Transcription of letter in private collection of Charles Sibley, Hamden, CT, provided by Ryan Keating.

40. McPherson, *Battle Cry of Freedom*, 494–500; Manning, *What This Cruel War Was Over*, 83–102; Phillip Shaw Paludan, *A People's Contest: The Union and the Civil War, 1861–1865*, 2nd ed. (Lawrence: University of Kansas Press, 1996), 198–230; Foner, *Fiery Trial*, 230–31.

41. James Mulligan Diary, January 1, 1863, Mulligan Diary, CHM. See also the entry for February 10, 1863; "Murphy Maguire" to Editor of the Boston *Pilot*, January 17, 1863, printed in the Boston *Pilot*, February 7, 1863; James McPherson, *For Cause and Comrades: Why Men Fought in the Civil War* (New York: Oxford University Press, 1997),

120–23; Bruce, *The Harp and the Eagle*, 127–32, 138–40 (quote on 138); Manning, *What This Cruel War Was Over*, 87–88.

42. Zibro, "The Life of Paddy Yank," 145, 153–56.

43. "J. D." to Editor of the *Irish-American*, November 28, 1862, printed in the *Irish-American*, December 23, 1862; "J. D." to Editor of the *Irish-American*, December 11, 1862, printed in the *Irish-American*, December 20, 1862.

44. *Irish-American*, May 21, 1864; Conyngham, *Irish Brigade*, 561; "Gallowglass" to Editor of the *Irish-American*, n/d [shortly after Fredericksburg, December 1862], printed in the *Irish-American*, December 27, 1862; F. X. Martin, "The Normans: Arrival in Settlement (1169–1300)," in *The Course of Irish History*, ed. T. W. Moody and F. X. Martin, rev. and enl. edition (Cork: Mercier Press, 1984), 46.

45. *Irish-American*, May 21, 1864; Bruce, *The Harp and the Eagle*, 119; Stephen Sears, *Landscape Turned Red: The Battle of Antietam* (Boston: Houghton Mifflin, 2003), 243; Thomas Cahill to Father Hart, December 27, 1862, Transcription of letter in private collection of Charles Sibley, Hamden, CT, provided by Ryan Keating.

46. *Galway-American*, May 17, 1862; Dublin *Irishman*, October 11, 1862; *Dundalk Democrat* article reprinted in the Dublin *Irishman*, November 16, 1862; Toby Joyce, "The 'Galway-American,' 1862–1863: Part 1: James Roche and the American Civil War," *Journal of the Galway Archaeological and Historical Society* 47 (1995): 108; McMahon, *Global Dimensions*, 88; Hernon, *Celts, Catholics, and Copperheads*, 76–77.

47. Gallowglass to Editor of the *Irish-American*, August 16, 1862, printed in the *Irish-American*, August 23, 1862.

48. *New York Freeman's Journal*, July 12, 1862.

49. Gallagher, *Union War*, 46; Manning, *What This Cruel War Was Over*, 70–79.

6. Unionism and Emancipation on the Home Front and Battlefield

1. Chandra Manning, *What This Cruel War Was Over: Soldiers, Slavery, and the Civil War* (New York: Random House, 2007), 83–84.

2. Boston *Pilot*, August 16, 1862; Albon P. Man, Jr., "Labor Competition and the New York City Draft Riots of 1863," *Journal of Negro History* 36, no. 4 (October 1951): 377–79; Edward K. Spann, *Gotham at War: New York City, 1860–1865* (Wilmington, DE: Scholarly Resources, 2002), 87.

3. Ira Berlin, Joseph P. Reidy, and Leslie Rowland, eds., *Freedom: A Documentary History of Emancipation, 1861–1867*, ser. I, vol. 1: *The Destruction of Slavery* (New York: Cambridge University Press, 1985), 493–518; *Catholic Telegraph and Advocate*, July 23, 1862; Williston H. Lofton, "Northern Labor and the Negro during the Civil War," *Journal of Negro History* 34, no. 3 (July 1949): 258–60; Frank L. Klement, "Catholics as Copperheads during the Civil War," *The Catholic Historical Review* 80, no. 1 (January 1994): 39; James McPherson, *Battle Cry of Freedom: The Civil War Era* (New York: Oxford University Press, 1988), 507; Brian Kelly, introduction to *Labor, Free and Slave: Workingmen and the Anti-Slavery Movement in the United States*, by Bernard Mandel (1955; repr., Chicago: University of Illinois Press, 2007), xvli–xvlii; Sumner Eliot Matison, "The Labor Movement and the Negro during Reconstruction," *Journal of Negro History* 33, no. 4 (October 1948): 429–31; "Adelph" to Editor of *The Christian Recorder*, July 23, 1862, printed in *The*

Christian Recorder, August 2, 1862 (emphasis in original); *Catholic Telegraph and Advocate*, July 23, 1862; *Cincinnati Gazette*, July 16, 1862.

4. *Catholic Telegraph and Advocate*, July 23, 1862; Campbell Gibson and Kay Jung, *Historical Census Statistics on Population Totals by Race, 1790 to 1990, and by Hispanic Origin, 1970 to 1990, for the United States Regions, Divisions, and States*, Working Paper Series No. 76 (Population Division, U.S. Census Bureau: Washington, D.C., 2002), accessed March 6, 2012 http://www.census.gov/population/www/documentation/twps0076/twps0076.html; Ira Berlin, Steven F. Miller, Joseph P. Reidy, and Leslie Rowland, eds., *Freedom: A Documentary History of Emancipation, 1861–1867*, ser. I, vol. 2: *The Wartime Genesis of Free Labor: The Upper South* (New York: Cambridge University Press, 1993), 72, 630.

5. *Chicago Tribune*, July 11 and July 14, 1862; Craig Lee Kautz, "Fodder for Cannon: Immigrant Perceptions of the Civil War—The Old Northwest" (PhD diss., University of Nebraska, Lincoln, 1976), 107–12; James B. Swan, *Chicago's Irish Legion: The 90th Illinois Volunteers in the Civil War* (Carbondale: Southern Illinois University Press, 2009), 14; Soldiers of the 90th Illinois Volunteer Infantry Regiment to Governor Richard Yates, October 29, 1862, Administrative File, 90th Illinois Regiment, Record Group 301.018, Illinois State Archives (hereafter cited as 90th Illinois File, ISA).

6. New York *Freeman's Journal and Catholic Register*, August 2, 1862.

7. *Douglass' Monthly*, June 1862; Lofton, "Northern Labor and the Negro," 261; Edward K. Spann, "Union Green: The Irish Community and the Civil War," in *The New York Irish*, ed. Ronald H. Bayor and Timothy J. Meagher (Baltimore: Johns Hopkins University Press, 1996), 203-4; Florence E. Gibson, *Attitudes of the New York Irish Toward State and National Affairs, 1848–1892* (New York: Columbia University Press, 1951), 143–44; Phillip Shaw Paludan, *A People's Contest: The Union and the Civil War, 1861–1865*, 2nd ed. (Lawrence: University of Kansas Press, 1996), 182; *New York Times*, August 5, 1862; *New York Tribune* article reprinted in *Douglass' Monthly*, September 1862; *New York Evening Post*, August 5, 1862

8. *New York Times*, August 5 and August 9, 1862; *New York Evening Post*, August 5, 1862; *New York Tribune* article reprinted in *Douglass' Monthly*, September 1862.

9. *New York Evening Post*, August 5, 1862; *Douglass' Monthly*, September 1862; *New York Times*, August 5, 1862 and June 14, 1863; Man, "Labor Competition," 392–93.

10. *Freeman's Journal and Catholic Register*, August 16, 1862; Boston *Pilot*, August 16, 1862; Hughes quoted in Iver Bernstein, *The New York City Draft Riots: Their Significance for American Society and Politics in the Age of the Civil War* (New York: Oxford University Press, 1993), 112.

11. Kevin Kenny, *The American Irish: A History* (New York: Pearson Education, 2000), 125; New York *Daily Tribune*, August 8, 1862, quoted in Man, "Labor Competition," 388–92 (New York *Daily Tribune* quoted on p. 390); Bernstein, *New York City Draft Riots*, 110–12; Metropolitan *Record* article reprinted in the *Catholic Telegraph and Advocate*, October 8, 1862.

12. *New York Times*, September 25, 1862.

13. Bernstein, *New York City Draft Riots*, 6–7 and passim.

14. Susannah Ural Bruce, *The Harp and the Eagle: Irish-American Volunteers in the Union Army, 1861–1865* (New York: New York University Press, 2006), 173–76; Eugene

Murdock, *One Million Men: The Civil War Draft in the North* (Madison: University of Wisconsin Press, 1971), 6–7; Peter Levine, "Draft Evasion in the North during the Civil War," *Journal of American History* 67, no. 4 (March 1981): 816–34; Grace Palladino, *Another Civil War: Labor, Capital, and the State in the Anthracite Regions of Pennsylvania, 1840–1868* (Champaign: University of Illinois Press, 1990); Kevin Kenny, *Making Sense of the* Molly *Maguires* (New York: Oxford University Press, 1998), 87–94.

15. Bernstein, *New York City Draft Riots*, 18–23, 75–192; Adrian Cook, *Armies of the Streets: The New York City Draft Riots of 1863* (Lexington: University Press of Kentucky, 1974), 18–46; Seymour Walton Journal, Monday, July 13, 1863. Seymour Walton Journals, 1862–1866. Ms. fE5.W1766, Newberry Library, Chicago.

16. Bruce, *The Harp and the Eagle*, 179; *New York Times*, August 10, 1863; Bernstein, *New York City Draft Riots*, 27–31, 35–36.

17. Man, "Labor Competition," 397–402; Albon P. Man, Jr., "The Irish in New York in the Early Eighteen-Sixties," *Irish Historical Studies* 7, no. 126 (September 1950): 88–89; Bernstein, *New York City Draft Riots*, 118; Kenny, *American Irish*, 125; Boston *Pilot*, July 1, 1863; *Irish-American*, July 4, 1863; Ryan W. Keating, *Shades of Green: Irish Regiments, American Soldiers, and Local Communities in the Civil War Era* (New York: Fordham University Press, 2017), 144–45.

18. D. P. Conyngham, *The Irish Brigade and Its Campaigns* (New York: William McSorley, 1867), 547–48; Bernstein, *New York City Draft Riots*, 11; Cook, *Armies of the Streets*, 54, l28; *New York Times*, July 29, 1863; Bruce, *The Harp and the Eagle*, 180.

19. Roger Hunt, *Colonels in Blue: Union Army Colonels of the Civil War, New York* (Mechanicsburg, PA: Schiffler, 2003), 214; Cook, *Armies of the Street*, 100–101, 118–19; *New York Times*, July 8, 1867; *New York Tribune* article reprinted in the Dublin *Irishman*, August 1, 1863.

20. Brigadier General James Shields to Charles Patrick Daly, August 8, 1862, Box 3, Charles Patrick Daly Papers, New York Public Library (hereafter cited as Daly Papers, NYPL); James Turner, 63rd New York Infantry, to his family, July 19, 1862, SC12613, James B. Turner Papers. New York State Library; John O'Brien, 1st Connecticut Heavy Artillery, to Mary Walker Tennyson, February 9, 1863, John O'Brien Letters, Civil War Miscellaneous Collection, USAMHI (hereafter cited as O'Brien Letters, CWMC, USAMHI); Bruce, *The Harp and the Eagle*, 185; Christian G. Samito, *Becoming American Under Fire: Irish Americans, African Americans, and the Politics of Citizenship during the Civil War Era* (Ithaca, NY: Cornell University Press, 2009), 126; Manning, *What This Cruel War Was Over*, 265–266n.; McPherson, *Battle Cry of Freedom*, 600–11; Gary Gallagher, *The Union War* (Cambridge, MA: Harvard University Press, 2011), 72; Keating, *Shades of Green*, 132–54.

21. Resolution of the Officers of the 69th New York, July 13, 1863, printed in the Dublin *Irishman*, August 22, 1863; Bruce, *The Harp and the Eagle*, 44.

22. John O'Brien [4th CT Heavy Artillery] to Mary Walker Tennyson, July 14, 1863. O'Brien Letters, CWMC, USAMHI; Peter Welsh to Margaret Welsh, July 22 and August 2, 1863, in *Irish Green and Union Blue: The Civil War Letters of Peter Welsh*, ed. Lawrence Frederick Kohl with Margaret Cossé Richard (New York: Fordham University Press, 1996), 113, 185.

23. Brian Kelly, "Ambiguous Loyalties: The Boston Irish, Slavery, and the Civil War," *Historical Journal of Massachusetts* 24, no. 2 (1996): 165–204; Thomas O'Connor, *Civil War Boston: Home Front and Battlefield* (Boston: Northeastern University Press, 1997), 138–41; Michael Donlon [2nd U.S. Cavalry] to Patrick Donlon, August 19, 1863. Michael Donlon Letters, Civil War Miscellaneous Collection, United States Army Military History Institute; Edmund O'Dwyer, 23rd Illinois Infantry, to Thomas O'Dwyer, September 8, 1863, Edmund O'Dwyer Papers, Harrisburg Civil War Roundtable Collection, United States Army Military History Institute (hereafter cited as O'Dwyer Papers, HCWRC, USAMHI); Michael H. MacNamara, *The Irish Ninth in Bivouac and Battle; or, Virginia and Maryland Campaigns* (Boston: Lee and Shepard, 1867), 217; McPherson, *Battle Cry of Freedom*, 493–94, 590–99, 762–83.

24. Jennifer L. Weber, *Copperheads: The Rise and Fall of Lincoln's Opponents in the North* (New York: Oxford University Press, 2006), passim, but especially 4–6; Frank L. Klement, *The Copperheads in the Middle West* (Chicago: University of Chicago Press, 1960); Frank Klement, *The Limits of Dissent: Clement L. Vallandigham and the Civil War* (Lexington: The University Press of Kentucky, 1970); Strong quoted in Bruce, *The Harp and the Eagle*, 182–83; Manning, *What This Cruel War Was Over*, 117–18; Keating, *Shades of Gray*, 142–43, 148–54 (*Chicago Times* quoted on p. 149); *Cleveland Herald*, July 20, 1863; *New York Tablet* article reprinted in the *Cork Examiner*, August 7, 1863; Bishop of Buffalo quoted in Albon P. Man, Jr., "The Church and the New York Draft Riots of 1863," *Records of the American Catholic Historical Society of Philadelphia* 62, no. 1 (March 1965): 49.

25. This argument contrasts with Susannah Ural Bruce's interpretation of Irish-American support for the Union plummeting in 1863 because of immigrants' beliefs that the war was no longer serving their interests as Irishmen or Americans. See Bruce, *The Harp and the Eagle*, especially 190–232. The argument presented here is more in line with Christian Samito's emphasis on continued Irish-American support for the Union war. While Samito argues that Irish Americans' support for the war hinged on proving their loyalties to America and gaining the rights of citizenship, the present study contends that Irish-American Unionism was essentially transatlantic. See Samito, *Becoming American*, especially 132–33.

26. Kerby Miller, *Emigrants and Exiles: Ireland and the Irish Exodus to North America* (New York: Oxford University Press, 1985), 360; *New York Times*, April 4, 1863; James S. Donnelly, Jr., "The Irish Agricultural Depression of 1859–1864," *Irish Economic and Social History* 3 (1976): 33–54 (quote on p. 46); *Irish-American*, February 14, 1861, and April 4, 1863; Dublin *Freeman's Journal* article reprinted in the *Catholic Telegraph and Advocate*, March 19, 1862.

27. *New York Times*, May 25, 1862; "Address of the Executive Board of the Irish Relief Committee to the People of the United States," printed in the *New York Times*, April 4, 1863; David Sim, *A Union Forever: The Irish Question and U.S. Foreign Relations in the Victorian Age* (Ithaca, NY: Cornell University Press, 2013), 76; Conyngham, *Irish Brigade*, 385–87.

28. Bruce, *The Harp and the Eagle*, 136–59; William L. Burton, *Melting Pot Soldiers: The Union's Ethnic Regiments* (New York: Fordham University Press, 1998), 127–28; William B. Kurtz, *Excommunicated from the Union: How the Civil War Created a Separate*

Catholic America (New York: Fordham University Press, 2016), 108–12; McPherson, *Battle Cry of Freedom*, 685; *Irish-American*, April 18, 1863; Scrapbooks, vol. 3. Daly Papers, NYPL.

29. "An Irishman" to Editor of the *Irish-American*, n/d, printed in the *Irish-American*, March 7, 1863; "A Tipperaryman" to Editor of the *Irish-American*, March 11, 1863, printed in the *Irish-American*, March 20, 1863; William O'Meagher (37th NY) to Editor of the *Irish-American*, n/d printed in the *Irish-American*, May 2, 1863; Father William Corby to Editor of the *Irish-American*, May 23, 1863, printed in the *Irish-American*, June 6, 1863; "Irish Relief Committee" pamphlet, James P. McIvor Papers, New-York Historical Society (hereafter cited as McIvor Papers, NYHS); John Savage to Colonel James P. McIvor, 170th NY, April 7, 1863. McIvor Papers, NYHS; John H. Greene to Colonel James A. Mulligan, 23rd IL, June 5, 1863, Mulligan Papers, CHS; *Irish-American*, April 18, 1863; Damian Shiels, "Naming Over 800 Soldiers Who Supported the Poor of Ireland," *Irish American Civil War* blog, accessed July 15, 2021, https://irishamericancivilwar.com/2013/03/15/naming-over-800-union-soldiers-who-supported-the-poor-of-ireland/.

30. Joseph M. Hernon, Jr., *Celts, Catholics, and Copperheads: Ireland Views the American Civil War* (Columbus: Ohio State University Press, 1968), 22–28; Miller, *Emigrants and Exiles*, 359–61; Ella Lonn, *Foreigners in the Union Army and Navy* (Baton Rouge: Louisiana State University Press, 1951), 411–13, 424–25; *Western Star* article reprinted in the *New York Times*, August 20, 1863; Bruce, *The Harp and the Eagle*, 202–4; Dublin *Nation*, October 17, 1863; *Cork Examiner*, February 24 and March 21, 1863; Dublin *Irishman*, March 19, 1864.

31. Samito, *Becoming American*, 32; Bruce, *The Harp and the Eagle*, 54; Peter Welsh, 28th Massachusetts Infantry, to Margaret Welsh, February 3, 1863, in Kohl and Richard, *Irish Green and Union Blue*, 66; Edmund O'Dwyer, 23rd Illinois Infantry, to Ellen Dwyer Farley, December 20, 1863. O'Dwyer Papers, HCWRC, USAMHI.

32. New York *Herald*, April 8, 1863, reprinted in the *Galway American*, April 25, 1863; *Harper's Weekly*, May 23, 1863 quoted in Gallagher, *Union War*, 72–73; Jason H. Silverman, *Lincoln and the Immigrant* (Carbondale: Southern Illinois University Press, 2015), 113–17; *CG*, 38th Cong., 2nd Sess., Appendix, 1–2.

33. Boston *Pilot*, September 5 and September 9, 1863; John Hogan to Thomas O'Reilly, November 26, 1863, printed in the *Catholic Telegraph and Advocate*, December 23, 1863, and May 4, 1864; Heather Cox Richardson, *The Greatest Nation of the Earth: Republican Economic Policies during the Civil War* (Cambridge, MA: Harvard University Press, 1997), 160–68 (Lincoln quote on p. 164); Eric Foner, *The Fiery Trial: Abraham Lincoln and American Slavery* (New York: W. W. Norton, 2010), 260; Hernon, *Celts, Catholics, and Copperheads*, 23–27.

34. David Brundage, *Irish Nationalists in America: The Politics of Exile, 1798–1998* (New York: Oxford University Press, 2016), 101–2; Samito, *Becoming American*, 121, 257n; Bruce, *The Harp and the Eagle*, 80, 105, 192–93; Timothy Egan, *The Immortal Irishman: The Irish Revolutionary Who Became an American Hero* (Boston: Houghton Mifflin Harcourt, 2016); Sim, *A Union Forever*, 87; Patrick Steward and Bryan McGovern, *The Fenians: Irish Rebellion in the North Atlantic World, 1858–1876* (Knoxville: University of Tennessee Press, 2013), 24–49.

35. "D.P.C." to Editor of the *Irish-American*, September 23, 1863, printed in the *Irish-American*, October 10, 1863; Lt. Col. John E. Balfe, 35th IN to Governor O.P. Morton, August 19, 1863, Madison, IN, Bernard F. Mullen Papers, 35th Indiana Infantry Regiment, *Civil War Times Illustrated Collection*. United States Army Military History Institute; William Griffin, William FitzGerald and P. Byrne to Governor O. P. Morton, August 19, 1863, *CWTIC*, USAMHI; Felix Brannigan to his father in Ireland, n/d, 1863. Robert L. Brake Collection, USAMHI (emphasis in original); Cian T. McMahon, *The Global Dimensions of Irish Identity: Race, Nation, and the Popular Press, 1840–1880* (Chapel Hill: University of North Carolina Press, 2015), 141–42.

36. Samito, *Becoming American*, 121–22; Brundage, *Irish Nationalists in America*, 102; *Proceedings of the First National Convention of the Fenian Brotherhood*, held in Chicago, Illinois, November, 1863 (Philadelphia: James Gibbon, 1863), 28–29, 32, 35.

37. Col. Michael Corcoran to Judge Charles Patrick Daly, January 13, 1863, Daly Papers, Box 3, NYPL; James Mulligan Diary, January 16, February 12, and February 22, 1863. Mulligan Papers, CHS; "Fenian" to the Editor of the *Irish-American*, January 14, 1863, printed in the *Irish-American*, January 31, 1863; "P.O.S." to the Editor of the *Irish-American*, January 2, 1863, printed in the *Irish-American*, January 31, 1863; Conyngham, *The Irish Brigade*, 372–73; Major John Mahan to "Colonel Commanding," April 1863, 9th Regt. Infantry Files, MSA.

38. Darwin Hickley, 90th Illinois Infantry, to Adjutant General Allen C. Fuller, June 19, 1863, 90th Illinois File, ISA; Lieutenant John O'Brien, 1st Connecticut Heavy Artillery, to Mary Walker Tennyson, December 9, 1863, O'Brien Letters, CWMC, USAMHI; Keating, *Shades of Green*, 126–27; Zibro, "The Life of Paddy Yank," 144–45.

39. McPherson, *Battle Cry of Freedom*, 666–67; Manning, *What This Cruel War Was Over*, 114–22; Weber, *Copperheads*, 113–14, 118–22.

40. "Fenian" to Editor of the *Irish-American*, January 23, 1863, printed in the *Irish-American*, February 7, 1863; "P.J.D." to Editor of the Boston *Pilot*, January 17, 1863, printed in the Boston *Pilot*, February 7, 1863; Melanchten Smith to Adjutant General Allen C. Fuller, March 17, 1863, 90th Illinois File, ISA. For similar examples, see "Murphy Maguire," 7th Rhode Island Infantry, to Editor of the Boston *Pilot*, January 17, 1863, printed in the Boston *Pilot*, February 7, 1863; "Murphy Maguire," 7th Rhode Island Infantry, to Editor of the Boston *Pilot*, February 8, 1863, printed in the Boston *Pilot*, February 28, 1863; Christopher Byrne to Patrick Byrne, March 21, 1863 in Ruth-Ann Harris and Sally K. Sommers Smith, "The Eagle and the Harp: The Enterprising Byrne Brothers of County Monaghan," *Irish Studies Review* 18, no. 2 (2010): 178.

41. *New York Times*, April 19, 1863; Foner, *Fiery Trial*, 251; Captain Thomas K. Barrett to Editor of the *Chicago Times*, May 18, 1863, printed in the *Chicago Times*, May 25, 1863 (emphasis in *Chicago Times*); Captain Thomas K. Barrett to Adjutant General Allen C. Fuller, July 21, 1863, 90th Illinois File, ISA.

42. William J. K. Beaudot and Lance J. Herdegen, *An Irishman in the Iron Brigade: The Civil War Memoirs of James P. Sullivan, Sergt., Company K, 6th Wisconsin Volunteers* (New York: Fordham University Press, 1993), 83–84; John Dee, Personal War Sketch, *Personal War Sketches*, Arthur G. Biscoe Post 80, Grand Army of the Republic, Westborough History Center, Westborough, MA.

43. Peter Welsh to Margaret Welsh, February 3, 1863, in Kohl and Richardson, *Irish Green and Union Blue*, 66; MacNamara, *Irish Ninth in Bivouac and Battle*, 218; *Dublin Irishman*, June 25, 1864; Nicholas Flaherty Pension File, National Archives and Records Administration Building, Washington, D.C. (hereafter cited as NARA); First Lieutenant Nicholas Flaherty, 9th Massachusetts Infantry, to John L. Whiting, Esq., September 6, 1863, 9th Regt. Infantry Files, MSA (emphasis in original).

44. Ira Berlin, Joseph P. Reidy, and Leslie Rowland, eds., *Freedom: A Documentary History of Emancipation*, ser. II, *The Black Military Experience* (New York: Cambridge University Press, 1992), 12; Foner, *Fiery Trial*, 252; "Fenian," 164th New York Infantry, to Editor of the *Irish-American*, January 14, 1863, printed in the *Irish-American*, January 31, 1863; Gallagher, *Union War*, 111–13.

45. Manning, *What This Cruel War Was Over*, 196–98; Joseph T. Glatthaar, *Forged in Battle: The Civil War Alliance of Black Soldiers and White Officers* (New York: Free Press, 1990), 35–37, 265–66; Glatthaar, "'Glory,' the 54th Massachusetts Infantry, and Black Soldiers in the Civil War," *The History Teacher* 24 (August 1991): 478–79; Berlin et al., *Black Military Experience*, 19–20.

46. Colonel Thomas Wentworth Higginson, 1st South Carolina Volunteer Infantry (African Descent) to Governor John A. Andrew, January 19, 1863, Letter Book, 54th Massachusetts Volunteer Infantry Regiment, G01/Series 567X, Massachusetts Governor Executive Department letters, 1853–1893, 54th Regt. Infantry 1861–1863: vol. 21b, Massachusetts State Archives (hereafter cited as 54th MA Letterbook, MSA); Captain Bernard P. Murphy and Lieutenant P. D. O'Sullivan, 164th New York Infantry, to Governor John A. Andrew, April 2, 1863, 54th MA Letterbook, MSA. For further examples of soldiers from Irish-American regiments seeking commissions in black units, see Captain Patrick Black, 9th Massachusetts Infantry, to Governor John A. Andrew, November 12, 1863, 9th MA Letterbook, MSA; Captain Walter S. Bailey, 28th Massachusetts Infantry, to Major William Rogers, Massachusetts Assistant Adjutant General, July 10, 1865, 28th Regt. Infantry Files, vol. W32, MSA.

47. *Liberator*, December 7 and 14, 1860; First Lieutenant Nicholas Flaherty, 9th Massachusetts Infantry to John L. Whiting, Esq., September 6, 1863; Lieutenant William A. Plunkett et al., 9th Massachusetts Infantry to Governor John A. Andrew, January 3, 1864; Lieutenant William A. Plunkett, et al., 9th Massachusetts Infantry to Senator Henry Wilson, January 4, 1863, 9th Massachusetts Letterbook, MSA.

48. John Kingston [alias Jacob Moore] Pension File, NARA; Furlough Papers for John H. Kingston; Corporal John H. Kingston, 23rd Kentucky Infantry, to George L. Stearns, April 23, 1863; Corporal John H. Kingston, 23rd Kentucky Infantry, to Assistant Adjutant General Alfred Browne, May 28, 1863; Brigadier General R. H. Pierce to Governor John A. Andrew, August 12, 1863; Second Lieutenant John Kingston, 55th Massachusetts Infantry, to Colonel Nathaniel P. Hallowell, 55th Massachusetts Infantry, July 18, 1863; Colonel Nathaniel P. Hallowell, 55th Massachusetts Infantry, to Governor John A. Andrew, July 19, 1863, 55th Massachusetts Infantry Regiment Letter Book, G01/Series 567X, Massachusetts Governor Executive Department letters, 1853–1893, 55th Regt. Infantry 1862–1865: vol. 62. Massachusetts State Archives; Glatthaar, *Forged in Battle*, 108–20.

7. "All true Republicans": Irish-American Leaders and Emancipation

1. Gary Gallagher, *The Union War* (Cambridge, MA: Harvard University Press, 2011), 88–93; James McPherson, *Battle Cry of Freedom: The Civil War Era* (New York: Oxford University Press, 1988), 853–62; Eric Foner, *The Fiery Trial: Abraham Lincoln and American Slavery* (New York: W. W. Norton, 2010), 288–89.

2. Kevin Kenny, *The American Irish: A History* (New York: Pearson Education, 2000), 124–25; Benjamin J. Blied, *Catholics and the Civil War* (Milwaukee: 1945), 19–49; Madeline Hooke Rice, *American Catholic Opinion in the Slavery Controversy* (Gloucester, MA: Peter Smith, 1964), 86–109; Charles P. Connor, "The Northern Catholic Position on Slavery and the Civil War: Archbishop Hughes as a Test Case," *Records of the American Catholic Historical Society of Philadelphia* 96, no. 4 (1986): 37–48; Walter G. Sharrow, "John Hughes and a Catholic Response to Slavery in Antebellum America," *Journal of Negro History* 57, no. 3 (July 1972): 254–69.

3. William B. Kurtz, *Excommunicated from the Union: How the Civil War Created a Separate Catholic America* (New York: Fordham University Press, 2016), 34–40, 122–24; Joseph George, Jr., "'A Catholic Family Newspaper' Views the Lincoln Administration: John Mullaly's Copperhead Weekly," *Civil War History* 24, no. 2 (June 1978): 118–19; John T. McGreevy, *Catholicism and American Freedom: A History* (New York: W. W. Norton, 2003), 71–72.

4. *New York Times*, July 16, 1863; Dublin *Irishman*, August 1, 1863; Kurtz, *Excommunicated from the Union*, 112–13; *New York Tablet* article reprinted in the *Cork Examiner*, August 7, 1863; "Gotham" to Editor of the *Catholic Telegraph and Advocate*, July 25, 1863, printed in the *Catholic Telegraph and Advocate*, August 5, 1863; Albany *Atlas and Argus* article reprinted in the Dublin *Nation*, August 22, 1863; "Manhattan" to Editor of the *Cork Examiner*, July 22, 1863, printed in the *Cork Examiner*, August 7, 1863; *Catholic Telegraph and Advocate*, July 29, 1863; "Gotham" to Editor of the *Catholic Telegraph and Advocate*, n/d, printed in the *Catholic Telegraph and Advocate*, July 29, 1863.

5. Kurtz, *Excommunicated from the Union*, 68–88; Richard J. Purcell, "Missionaries from All Hallows (Dublin) to the United States, 1842–1865," *Records of the American Catholic Historical Society of Philadelphia* 34 (December 1942): 231; Regimental Descriptive Book, 23rd Illinois Infantry, Records of Volunteer Union Organizations, Civil War, RG 94: Records of the Adjutant General's Office, NARA; Starr quoted in Rev. James McGovern, ed., *The Life and Letters of Eliza Allen Starr* (Chicago: Lakeside Press, 1905), 183; James A. Mulligan Diary, January 1 and February 10, 1863. James A. Mulligan Papers, 1849–1900, Chicago History Museum (hereafter cited as Mulligan Diary, CHM).

6. James A. Mulligan Diary, February 12, 1863, Mulligan Papers, CHM; Mulligan quoted in *Catholic Telegraph and Advocate*, August 3, 1864; P. Casey, 23rd Illinois Volunteers, to Colonel James Mulligan, 23rd Illinois Volunteers, March 23, 1863, Mulligan Papers, CHM.

7. McGreevy, *Catholicism and American Freedom*, 82–84; Kurtz, *Excommunicated from the Union*, 98–99; *Catholic Telegraph and Advocate*, June 18, 1862. Until 1863, the newspaper was published as the *Catholic Telegraph and Advocate*. In its first 1864 edition, the title was shortened to the *Catholic Telegraph*. For brevity and clarity, only the *Catho-*

lic Telegraph is used in text. The newspaper's title on the date of publication is included in references.

8. New York *Freeman's Journal*, April 4, 1863; McGreevy, *Catholicism and American Freedom*, 73; *Catholic Telegraph and Advocate*, March 25 and April 8, 1863.

9. *Catholic Telegraph and Advocate*, April 8, April 22, and May 20, 1863 (emphasis in original); Kurtz, *Excommunicated from the Union*, 100–101.

10. "An Irish Catholic" to Editor of the *Catholic Telegraph and Advocate*, June 2, 1863, printed in the *Catholic Telegraph and Advocate*, June 10, 1863; Patrick Murphy to Editor of the *Catholic Telegraph and Advocate*, October 8, 1863, printed in the *Catholic Telegraph and Advocate*, October 28, 1863; *Catholic Telegraph and Advocate*, June 10, 1863; *Brownson's Review* article reprinted in the Dublin *Irishman*, August 29, 1863; McGreevy, *Catholicism and American Freedom*, 66–68, 84–85.

11. *Catholic Telegraph and Advocate*, September 23, 1863; John O'Meara to Editor of the *Catholic Telegraph and Advocate*, November 3, 1863, printed in the *Catholic Telegraph*, November 11, 1863; Thomas Farrell to Editor of the *Catholic Telegraph*, January 1864, printed in the *Catholic Telegraph*, January 20, 1864; "Josephus" to Editor of the *Catholic Telegraph*, January 21, 1865, printed in the *Catholic Telegraph*, February 1, 1865; *Catholic Telegraph*, December 21, 1864.

12. Frank L. Klement, "Catholics as Copperheads during the Civil War," *The Catholic Historical Review* 80, no. 1 (January 1994): 42–47 (*Democratic Herald* quoted on p. 47; emphasis in original); George, "'A Catholic Family Newspaper,'" 122–24; McGreevy, *Catholicism and American Freedom*, 68–69; Mary Augustine Kwitchen, *James Alphonsus McMaster: A Study in American Thought* (Washington, D.C.: Catholic University of America Press, 1949); New York *Freeman's Journal*, October 3, 1863; Boston *Pilot*, July 25, 1863.

13. Francis R. Walsh "Who Spoke for Boston's Irish? The Boston *Pilot* in the Nineteenth Century," *Journal of Ethnic Studies* 10, no. 3 (Fall 1982): 22; Boston *Pilot*, October 11, 1862, September 5, 1863, and April 22, 1865; Susannah Ural Bruce, *The Harp and the Eagle: Irish-American Volunteers in the Union Army, 1861–1865* (New York: New York University Press, 2006), 140–41; Robert Howard Lord, John E. Sexton, and Edward T. Harrington, *History of the Archdiocese of Boston; in the various stages of its development, 1641 to 1943* (Boston: Pilot Publishing, 1945), 706.

14. Boston *Pilot*, September 19 and October 17, 1863.

15. *Catholic Telegraph* article quoted in the Boston *Pilot*, December 17, 1864; Boston *Pilot*, August 13, 1862; D. Downing to Editor of the *Catholic Telegraph*, October 23, 1863, printed in the *Catholic Telegraph*, November 4, 1863.

16. *Universe* article quoted in "Gotham" to Editor of the *Catholic Telegraph*, February 18, 1864, printed in the *Catholic Telegraph*, February 24, 1864.

17. Jennifer L. Weber, *Copperheads: The Rise and Fall of Lincoln's Opponents in the North* (New York: Oxford University Press, 2006), 107; Albon P. Man, Jr., "Labor Competition and the New York City Draft Riots of 1863," *Journal of Negro History* 36, no. 4 (October 1951): 380–81; George, "'A Catholic Family Newspaper,'" 129–30.

18. *Catholic Telegraph and Advocate*, April 15, 1863.

19. *Catholic Telegraph and Advocate*, June 23, July 1, and July 15, 1863.

20. *Catholic Telegraph and Advocate*, July 15, 1863.
21. New York *Freeman's Journal*, August 15, 1863; Boston *Pilot*, August 1, 1863.
22. Cincinnati *Catholic Telegraph and Advocate*, September 22 and November 11, 1863 (emphasis in original); "J. H." to Editor of the *Catholic Telegraph*, January 10, 1864, printed in the *Catholic Telegraph*, January 20, 1864.
23. *Catholic Telegraph and Advocate*, September 9, 1863 (emphasis and extra punctuation in original); "Tennessean" to the Editor of the *Catholic Telegraph*, March 18, 1864, printed in the *Catholic Telegraph*, March 30, 1864; "An Observer" to the Editor of the *Catholic Telegraph*, March 22, 1864, printed in the *Catholic Telegraph*, March 30, 1864; "Matha" to Editor of the *Catholic Telegraph and Advocate*, July 24, 1863, printed in the *Catholic Telegraph and Advocate*, July 29, 1863; "Gotham" to Editor of the *Catholic Telegraph*, March 11, 1864, printed in the *Catholic Telegraph*, March 16, 1864.
24. *Catholic Telegraph and Advocate*, November 11, 1863 (emphasis in original), and July 27, 1864; McPherson, *Battle Cry of Freedom*, 766–67.
25. David T. Gleeson, *The Green and the Grey: The Irish in the Confederate States of America* (Chapel Hill: University of North Carolina Press, 2016), 118–24; Dublin *Nation* article reprinted in the Boston *Pilot*, January 23, 1864.
26. Damian Shiels, *The Irish in the American Civil War* (Dublin: History Press Ireland, 2013), 143–47; Bruce, *The Harp and the Eagle*, 196–98, 205; Joseph M. Hernon, Jr., *Celts, Catholics, and Copperheads: Ireland Views the American Civil War* (Columbus: Ohio State University Press, 1968), 30–32; *New York Times*, July 10 and August 12, 1864; *Irish-American*, February 13, February 20, March 19, and April 2, 1864.
27. Dublin *Irishman*, September 17, 1864; *Cork Examiner*, April 25, 1863; *Galway-American*, November 14, 1863, and February 27, 1864; West quoted in Bruce, *The Harp and the Eagle*, 199; Hernon, *Celts, Catholics, and Copperheads*, 32–34.
28. Patrick Maher to Lawrence O'Brien, January 7, 1864, Transcription of letter in private collection of Charles Sibley, Hamden, CT, provided by Ryan Keating; Thomas Hamilton Murray, *History of the Ninth Regiment, Connecticut Volunteer Infantry, the 'Irish Regiment,' in the War of the Rebellion, 1861–1865* (New Haven, CT: Price, Lee and Adkins, 1903); Joseph T. Glatthaar, *The March to the Sea and Beyond: Sherman's Troops in the Savannah and Carolinas Campaign* (Baton Rouge: Louisiana State University Press, 1985), 63–64, 126–28; Chandra Manning, *What This Cruel War Was Over: Soldiers, Slavery, and the Civil War* (New York: Random House, 2007), 187; Dublin *Irishman*, February 4, 1865; "Garryowen" to Editor of the of the *Irish-American* reprinted in the Dublin *Irishman*, November 26, 1864.
29. Bruce, *The Harp and the Eagle*, 59; John D. Hayes and Doris D. Maguire, "Charles Graham Halpine: Life and Adventures of Miles O'Reilly," *New-York Historical Society Quarterly* 51, no. 4 (1967): 327–28; Chandra Manning, *Troubled Refuge: Struggling for Freedom in the Civil War* (New York: Alfred A. Knopf, 2016), 86–91; Douglas R. Egerton, *Thunder at the Gates: The Black Civil War Regiments that Redeemed America* (New York: Basic Books, 2016), 90, 98–100.
30. Hayes and Maguire, "Charles Graham Halpine," 334–35 (quote on p. 335); James McPherson, *For Cause and Comrades: Why Men Fought in the Civil War* (New York: Oxford University Press, 1997), 173; D. P. Conyngham, *The Irish Brigade and Its Cam-*

paigns: With Some Account of the Corcoran Legion, and Sketches of the Principal Officers (New York: William McSorley, 1867; repr., Gaithersburg, MD: Olde Soldier Books, n/d), 424–37; Boston *Pilot*, January 30, 1864; Cincinnati *Catholic Telegraph*, April 20, 1864; *Irish-American*, April 16, 1864; Dublin *Irishman*, May 14, 1864.

31. Bruce, *The Harp and the Eagle*, 207–13; McPherson, *Battle Cry of Freedom*, 751–73 (Greeley quoted on p. 762).

32. Hernon, *Celts, Catholics, and Copperheads*, 14, 19, 21–22, 34; Bruce, *The Harp and the Eagle*, 200; Robert Kee, *The Green Flag: A History of Irish Nationalism* (New York: Penguin, 1972), 103; *Irish People*, November 19, 1864.

33. Hernon, *Celts, Catholics, and Copperheads*, 74–77; Dublin *Nation*, November 8, 1862; *Cork Examiner*, August 15, October 15, and October 27, 1863; *Irish People*, December 3, 1864.

34. *Daniel O'Connell and the Committee of the Irish Repeal Association of Cincinnati* (Cincinnati: Catholic Telegraph Office, 1863). Samuel J. May Anti-Slavery Collection, Cornell University Library, accessed May 14, 2012, http://ebook.library.cornell.edu; *Catholic Telegraph and Advocate*, August 5 and 12, 1863.

35. New York *Freeman's Journal*, August 22, 1863; Boston *Pilot*, September 5, 1863 (emphasis in original).

36. Edmund O'Dwyer to Thomas O'Dwyer, September 8, 1863, Edmund O'Dwyer Papers, Harrisburg Civil War Roundtable Collection, United States Army Military History Institute (hereafter cited as O'Dwyer Papers, HCWRC, USAMHI); James M. McPherson, "'Spend Much Time in Reading the Daily Papers': The Press and Army Morale in the Civil War," in *This Mighty Scourge: Perspectives on the Civil War* (New York: Oxford University Press, 2007); Cian T. McMahon, *The Global Dimensions of Irish Identity: Race, Nation, and the Popular Press, 1840–1880* (Chapel Hill: University of North Carolina Press, 2015), 134–35; John Hogan to Dr. Thomas O'Reilly, November 26, 1863, printed in the *Catholic Telegraph and Advocate*, December 23, 1863; Thomas O'Reilly to Editor of the *Missouri Democrat*, n/d, reprinted in the *Catholic Telegraph and Advocate*, December 23, 1863.

37. *New York Times*, June 17, 1887; A Democratic Workingman, "To the laboring men of New York" (New York: n/p, July 18, 1863), *Lincolnia LB-2187*, Abraham Lincoln Presidential Library, Springfield, IL (hereafter cited as ALPL); *Chicago Tribune*, August 19, 1863.

38. Dublin *Irishman*, October 8, 1864.

39. Rory T. Cornish, "An Irish Republican Abroad: Thomas Francis Meagher in the United States, 1852–1865," in *Thomas Francis Meagher: The Making of an Irish American*, ed. Cornish and John M. Hearne (Dublin: Irish Academic Press, 2005), 139–62; Paul R. Wylie, *The Irish General: Thomas Francis Meagher* (Norman: University of Oklahoma Press, 2007), 117–79; Timothy Egan, *The Immortal Irishman: The Irish Revolutionary Who Became an American Hero* (Boston: Houghton Mifflin Harcourt, 2016), 196–97, 233–34; Bruce, *The Harp and the Eagle*, 156–60.

40. Bruce, *The Harp and the Eagle*, 158–59; Conyngham, *Irish Brigade*, 424–30; Boston *Pilot*, January 30, 1864; Dublin *Irishman*, May 14, 1864; Egan, *Immortal Irishman*, 257–59.

41. Thomas Francis Meagher, *Letters on Our National Struggle* (New York: Loyal Publication Society, 1863), accessed May 16, 2012, http://www.archive.org/stream/lettersonournatioomeag#page/n3/mode/2up; McMahon, *Global Dimensions*, 134–35; First Lieutenant Thomas F. Wildes to Colonel James A. Mulligan, December 14, 1863, quoted in Bruce, *The Harp and the Eagle*, 216–17.

42. Thomas Francis Meagher to Editor of the Dublin *Citizen*, September 26, 1863, in *Letters on Our National Struggle*, 3; Thomas Francis Meagher to Editor of the Dublin *Irishman*, September 5, 1863 in *Letters on Our National Struggle*, 11.

43. Thomas Francis Meagher to Editor of the Dublin *Citizen*, September 26, 1863, in *Letters on Our National Struggle*, 5.

44. Thomas Francis Meagher to Editor of the Dublin *Irishman*, September 5, 1863, in *Letters on Our National Struggle*, 14; Thomas Francis Meagher to Editor of the Dublin *Citizen*, September 26, 1863, in *Letters on Our National Struggle*, 5–6. On the use of Mexico as a warning against internal discord during Reconstruction, see Gregory P. Downs, "The Mexicanization of American Politics: The United States' Transnational Path from Civil War to Stabilization," *American Historical Review* 117, no. 2 (April 2012): 387–409.

45. Thomas Francis Meagher to J. J. Janney, Secretary and Treasurer Union Committee, Columbus, Ohio, September 23, 1863, printed in the *Irish-American*, September 26, 1863; *New York Times*, October 9, 1864; *Irish-American*, November 12, 1864; Bruce, *The Harp and the Eagle*, 155–60; Hernon, *Celts, Catholics, and Copperhead*, 93–108; Dublin *Irishman*, January 9, 1864; "Gotham" to Editor of the *Catholic Telegraph and Advocate*, November 21, 1863, printed in the *Catholic Telegraph and Advocate*, November 25, 1863; *Catholic Telegraph and Advocate*, November 16, 1864; Boston *Pilot*, May 7, 1864.

46. Edmund O'Dwyer, 23rd Illinois Infantry, to Ellen Dwyer Farley, December 20, 1863, O'Dwyer Papers, HCWRC, USAMHI; "Graiguenemanna" to Editor of the *Catholic Telegraph and Advocate*, August 29, 1864, printed in the *Catholic Telegraph and Advocate*, September 7, 1864; "Mac" to Editors of the *Irish-American*, September 4, 1864, printed in the *Irish-American*, September 24, 1864.

47. Manning, *What This Cruel War Was Over*, 181–212; Gregory P. Downs, *After Appomattox: Military Occupation and the Ends of War* (Cambridge, MA: Harvard University Press, 2015).

48. James L. Crouthamel, *Bennett's New York Herald and the Rise of the Popular Press* (Syracuse: Syracuse University Press, 1989), 112–37; *Herald* quoted in the *Catholic Telegraph*, April 20, 1864.

49. Colonel Thomas Cahill, 9th Connecticut Volunteers, to Margaret Cahill, July 5, 1862; Colonel Thomas Cahill, 9th Connecticut Volunteers, to Father Hart, December 27, 1862. Transcription of letters from private collection of Charles Sibley, Hamden, CT, provided by Ryan Keating; "D." to Editor of the *Catholic Telegraph and Advocate*, May 14, 1864, printed in the *Catholic Telegraph and Advocate*, May 18, 1864.

Conclusion: Irish America and Ireland after the Civil War

1. Kevin Kenny, *The American Irish: A History* (New York: Pearson Education, 2000), 131–38; Kerby A. Miller, *Emigrants and Exiles: Ireland and the Irish Exodus to North America* (New York: Oxford University Press, 1985), 346–53.

2. Kenny, *American Irish*, 141–48; Miller, *Emigrants and Exiles*, 353–59.

3. Miller, *Emigrants and Exiles*, 492 (quote), 495–97; Kenny, *American Irish*, 149–54; Hasia Diner, *Erin's Daughters: Irish Immigrant Women in the Nineteenth Century* (Baltimore: Johns Hopkins University Press, 1983), 68–80; David Noel Doyle, *Native Rights and National Empires—The Structure, Divisions, and Attitudes of the Catholic Minority in the Decade of Expansion, 1890–1901* (New York: Arno Press, 1976), 48–63.

4. Kenny, *American Irish*, 159; Steven P. Erie, *Rainbow's End: Irish Americans and the Dilemmas of Urban Machine Politics, 1840–1985* (Berkeley: University of California Press, 1988), 36; Lucy E. Salyer, "Reconstructing the Immigrant: The Naturalization Act of 1870 in Global Perspective," *Journal of the Civil War Era* 11, no. 3 (September 2021): 382–86, 389–93; Christian G. Samito, *Becoming American Under Fire: Irish Americans, African Americans, and the Politics of Citizenship during the Civil War Era* (Ithaca, NY: Cornell University Press, 2009), 172–216; David Sim, *A Union Forever: The Irish Question and U.S. Foreign Relations in the Victorian Age* (Ithaca, NY: Cornell University Press, 2013), 97–127.

5. Kenny, *American Irish*, 158–63; Erie, *Rainbow's End*, 25–66; Edward M. Levine, *The Irish and Irish Politicians: A Study in Social and Cultural Alienation* (South Bend: University of Notre Dame Press, 1966), 36–37; Jack Beatty, *The Rascal King: The Life and Times of James Michael Curley (1874–1958)* (Reading, MA: Addison-Wesley, 1992), 19, 31–33, 74–80.

6. Susannah Ural Bruce, *The Harp and the Eagle: Irish-American Volunteers in the Union Army, 1861–1865* (New York: New York University Press, 2006), 257–62.

7. David Brundage, *Irish Nationalists in America: The Politics of Exile, 1798–1998* (New York: Oxford University Press, 2016), 103; Patrick Steward and Bryan McGovern, *The Fenians: Irish Rebellion in the North Atlantic World, 1858–1876* (Knoxville: University of Tennessee Press, 2013), 80–83; Bruce, *The Harp and the Eagle*, 239–41; Miller, *Emigrants and Exiles*, 335–36.

8. Steward and McGovern, *Fenians*, 112–40, 199–205; Brundage, *Irish Nationalists in America*, 104–6; Sim, *Union Forever*, 88–95; Bruce, *The Harp and the Eagle*, 242–43; Salyer, "Naturalization Act of 1870," 386–87.

9. Miller, *Emigrants and Exiles*, 343, 441–42; Kenny, *American Irish*, 173; Brundage, *Irish Nationalists in America*, 106–7.

10. Kenny, *American Irish*, 173–79; Brundage, *Irish Nationalists in America*, 111–26; Miller, *Emigrants and Exiles*, 441–47; Thomas N. Brown, *Irish American Nationalism, 1870–1890* (1966; Westport, CT: Greenwood Press, 1980), 85–98.

11. Kenny, *American Irish*, 194–96; Brundage, *Irish Nationalists in America*, 146–50.

12. Kenny, *American Irish*, 196–99; Brundage, *Irish Nationalists in America*, 154–57.

13. De Valera quoted in Kevin Kenny, "'Freedom and Unity': Lincoln in Irish Political Discourse," in *The Global Lincoln*, ed. Richard Carwardine and Jay Sexton (New York: Oxford University Press, 2011), 164; Brundage, *Irish Nationalists in America*, 165–67; Peter Hart, *Mick: The Real Michael Collins* (New York: Penguin, 2007), 395–99.

14. Brundage, *Irish Nationalists in America*, 172–83.

15. Dublin *Freeman's Journal*, July 15, 1924; Brundage, *Irish Nationalists in America*, 175–76; Ely Janis, *A Greater Ireland: The Land League and Transatlantic Nationalism in Gilded Age America* (Madison: University of Wisconsin Press, 2015), passim.

16. Cian T. McMahon, *The Global Dimensions of Irish Identity: Race, Nation, and the Popular Press, 1840–1880* (Chapel Hill: University of North Carolina Press, 2015); James P. Rodechko, "An Irish-American Journalist and Catholicism: Patrick Ford of the *Irish World*," *Church History* 39, no. 4 (December, 1970): 524–25; Brundage, *Irish Nationalists in America*, 119–20.

17. Kenny, *American Irish*, 174–79; Brundage, *Irish Nationalists in America*, 119–22; McMahon, *Global Dimensions*, 172–73.

Bibliography

PRIMARY SOURCES

Manuscript Collections

Abraham Lincoln Presidential Library and Museum, Springfield, Illinois
A Democratic Workingman, "To the laboring men of New York." New York: n/p, July 18, 1863. *Lincolnia LB-2187.*
A Democratic Workingman, "Dan'l O'Connell on Democracy." New York: Sinclair Tousey, October 13, 1863. *Lincolnia LB-2176.*
Boston Public Library, Rare Books and Manuscripts Division
Anti-Slavery Collection.
Chicago History Museum, Chicago, Illinois
James A. Mulligan Papers, 1849–1900.
Illinois State Archives, Springfield, Illinois
Administrative File, 90th Illinois Regiment. Record Group 301.018.
John J. Burns Library, Archives and Manuscripts Department, Boston College
Michael H. Leary Letters, 1861–1863, Ms. 1986.043.
Massachusetts State Archives, Boston, Massachusetts
G01/Series 567X, Massachusetts Governor Executive Department letters, 1853–1893
9th Regt. Infantry 1861–1864, vol. 25.
28th Regt. Infantry 1861–1864, vol. W32.
54th Regt. Infantry 1861–1863: vol. 21b.
55th Regt. Infantry 1862–1865: vol. 62.
National Archives and Records Administration, Washington, D.C.
Record Group 94: Records of the Adjutant General's Office, Book Records of Union Military Organization
Christopher Byrne Pension File.
Christopher Plunkett Pension File.
Daniel Finn Pension File.
Daniel G. MacNamara Pension File.
James Mulligan Pension File.
John Kelly Pension File.
John Kingston Pension File.
Michael Donlon Pension File.
Michael Meehan Pension File.
Michael O'Brien Pension Files.
Nicholas Flaherty Pension File.

Peter Welsh Pension File.
Regimental Descriptive Book, 9th Massachusetts Infantry Regiment.
Regimental Descriptive Book, 23rd Illinois Infantry Regiment.
National Library of Ireland, Dublin, Ireland
John Eliot Cairnes Papers, Ms. 8964.
Lalor Family Letters, Ms. 8567.
Letters to Daniel O'Connell, 1840–1846, Ms. 13, 649.
Letters to John M. Kelly, Dublin, Ms. 10, 511
Memoir of Maj. Gen. Thomas Francis Meagher; with Diary, Correspondence, Speeches, etc. Compiled and edited by Frederick Kearney. New York: n/p, 1869, Ms. 9728.
Typescript copies of letters by Maj. Gen. James Shields, U.S.A., 1858, 1873–75, P. 5329.
New York Historical Society, New York City
James P. McIvor Papers.
New York Public Library, Manuscript Division, New York City
Charles Patrick Daly Papers.
New York State Library, Albany, New York
James B. Turner Papers, SC12613.
O'Keefe Family Papers, SC19231.
William Dennis Letters, SC14151.
William Ward Letter, SC19458.
Newbury Library, Chicago, Illinois
Seymour Walton Journals, 1862–1866, Ms. fE5. W1766.
Private Collection of Charles Sibley, Hamden, CT
Thomas Cahill Letters.
Public Records Office of Northern Ireland, Belfast, Northern Ireland
Byrne Letters, D3531.
Mathew Brooks Letter, T2700/3.
McElderry Papers, T2414.
O'Hanlon Letters, D885.
United States Army Military History Institute, Carlisle, Pennsylvania
Charles Chipman Papers.
Civil War Miscellaneous Collection
Daniel Finn Diary.
John Dillon Papers.
John O'Brien Letters.
John O'Conell Memoir, 1861–1866.
Michael Donlon Letters.
Michael O'Brien Letters.
Civil War Times Illustrated Collection
Bernard F. Mullen Papers.
Harrisburg Civil War Roundtable Collection
Edmund O'Dwyer Papers.
Kenneth H. Powers Collection
James Shields Folder.

J. Noonan Papers.
Mathew Murphy Letters.
Robert L. Brake Collection
Daniel G. Crotty Memoir, typed manuscript.
Felix Brannigan Letter.
69th Pennsylvania Papers.
United States Government Publications
Library of Congress, Manuscript Division
Abraham Lincoln Papers. Washington, D.C.: American Memory Project, 2000–02, http://memory.loc.gov/ammem/alhtml/alhome.html.
United States Congress. *Congressional Globe.*
31st Congress. 1st Session.
33rd Congress. 1st Session.
38th Congress. 1st Session.
United States War Department. *War of the Rebellion: A Compilation of the Official Records of the Union and Confederate Armies.* Washington, US Government Printing Office, 1889–1901.
Westborough History Center, Westborough, Massachusetts
Personal War Sketch Book, Arthur G. Biscoe Post 80, Grand Army of the Republic.

Newspapers

Catholic Mirror (Baltimore), 1854
Catholic Telegraph and Advocate (Cincinnati), 1847–1854, 1861–1865
Charleston Mercury (SC), 1847, 1854
Chicago Tribune, 1855–1865
Christian Recorder (Philadelphia), 1862–65
Citizen (New York), 1854
Cork Examiner, 1845–1850, 1861–1865
Daily Delta (New Orleans), 1845–1847
Daily Enquirer (Cincinnati), 1854–55
Douglass' Monthly (Rochester, NY), 1861–1863
Frederick Douglass' Paper (Rochester, NY), 1851–54
Freeman's Journal and Catholic Register (New York), 1861–1865
Galway-American, 1862–1863
Galway Vindicator and Connaught Advertiser, 1845–1847, 1854, 1861–1863
Irish-American (New York), 1849–1865
Irishman (Dublin), 1861–1865
Irish Pictorial Weekly (Boston), 1859–1861
Liberator (Boston), 1845–1860
Nation (Dublin), 1845–54, 1861–1865
National Anti-Slavery Standard (New York), 1847, 1849–1850, 1854
National Era (Washington, D.C.), 1847–1848, 1850–1859
New York Tablet, 1857–1858

New York Times, 1861–1865
North Star (Rochester, NY), 1847–1850
Pilot (Boston), 1847–1865
Vindicator (Belfast), 1847

Published Primary Sources

Barry, Joseph. *The Strange Story of Harpers Ferry, with Legends of the Surrounding Country*. Martinsburg, WV: Thompson Brothers, 1903.

Berlin, Ira, Barbara J. Fields, Thavolia Glymph, Joseph P. Reidy, and Leslie S. Rowland, eds. *Freedom: A Documentary History of Emancipation, 1861–1867*. Series I, vol. 1: *The Destruction of Slavery*. New York: Cambridge University Press, 1985.

Berlin, Ira, Joseph P. Reidy, and Leslie S. Rowland, eds. *Freedom: A Documentary History of Emancipation, 1861–1867*. Series II: *The Black Military Experience*. New York: Cambridge University Press, 1982.

Berlin, Ira, Steven F. Miller, Joseph P. Reidy, and Leslie Rowland, eds., *Freedom: A Documentary History of Emancipation, 1861–1867*. Series I, vol. 2: *The Wartime Genesis of Free Labor: The Upper South*. New York: Cambridge University Press, 1993.

The Boston Riot, July 14, 1863: A Plain Statement of Facts, by a Plain Man. Boston, 1863.

The Boston Slave Riot, and Trial of Anthony Burns. Boston: Fetridge and Company, 1854.

Conyngham, D. P. *The Irish Brigade and Its Campaigns: With Some Account of the Corcoran Legion, and Sketches of the Principal Officers*. New York: William McSorley, 1867. Reprint, Gaithersburg, MD: Olde Soldier Books, n/d.

Corcoran, Michael. *The Captivity of General Corcoran, Being the Only Authentic and Reliable Narrative of the Trials and Sufferings Endured during Twelve Months' Imprisonment in Richmond and Other Southern Cities*. Philadelphia: Barclay, 1864.

Dublin Anti-Slavery Society. *To Irish Emigrants who are going to the United States of America*. Dublin: R. D. Webb, n/d.

Duffy, Charles Gavan. *Young Ireland: A Fragment of Irish History, 1840–50*. London: T. Fisher Unwin, 1896.

Dunny, Patrick. "An Irishman Looks at Civil War." *Carloviana: Journal of the Old Carlow Society* (December 1967): 30.

Faust, Drew Gilpin, ed. *The Ideology of Slavery: Proslavery Thought in the Antebellum South, 1830–1860*. Baton Rouge: Louisiana State University Press, 1981.

Ferrie, Joseph P. *Yankees Now: Immigrants in the Antebellum United States, 1840–1860*. New York: Oxford University Press, 1999.

Fitzhugh, George. *Cannibals All! Or, Slaves Without Masters*. Edited by C. Vann Woodward. 1857. Reprint, Cambridge, MA: Harvard University Press, 1960.

Foner, Philip S., ed., *The Life and Writings of Frederick Douglass*, vol. 1. New York: International Publishers, 1952.

Forbes, Robert F. *An Interesting Memoir of the Jamestown Voyage to Ireland*. Boston: James B. Cullen, 1890.

Gibson, Campbell, and Kay Jung. *Historical Census Statistics on Population Totals by Race, 1790 to 1990, and by Hispanic Origin, 1970 to 1990, for the United States Regions,*

Divisions, and States. Working Paper Series No. 56. Population Division, U.S. Census Bureau, Washington, D.C., 2002.
Grant, James. *Impressions of Ireland and the Irish*. Philadelphia: G. B. Zieber, 1845.
Halpine, Charles Graham. *The Life and Adventures, Songs, Services, and Speeches of Private Miles O'Reilly, Pseud. (47th Regiment, New York Volunteers)*. New York: Carleton, 1864.
Haughton, Samuel. *Memoir of James Haughton, with Extracts from His Private and Published Letters, by His Son, Samuel Haughton*. Dublin: E. Ponsoby, 1877.
Higginson, Thomas Wentworth. *Army Life in a Black Regiment*. Boston: Fields, Osgood, 1870.
———. *Cheerful Yesterdays*. Boston: Houghton Mifflin, 1898.
Kohl, Lawrence Frederick, with Margaret Cossé Richard, eds. *Irish Green and Union Blue: The Civil War Letters of Peter Welsh*. New York: Fordham University Press, 1996.
MacNamara, Daniel. *History of the Ninth Regiment, Massachusetts Volunteer Infantry, June 1861–June 1864*, with an introduction by Christian G. Samito. Boston: E. B. Stillings, 1899. Reprint, New York: Fordham University Press, 2000.
MacNamara, Michael H. *The Irish Ninth in Bivouac and Battle; Or, Virginia and Maryland Campaigns*. Boston: Lee and Shepard, 1867.
McCarter, William. *My Life in the Irish Brigade: The Civil War Memoirs of Private William McCarter, 116th Pennsylvania Infantry*. Edited by Kevin E. O'Brien. Campbell, CA: Savas, 1996.
McGovern, Rev. James, ed. *The Life and Letters of Eliza Allen Starr*. Chicago: Lakeside Press, 1905.
Meagher, Thomas F. *Letters on Our National Struggle*. New York: Loyal Publication Society, 1864.
Mitchel, John. *Jail Journal; or, Five Years in British Prisons*. New York: Office of the "Citizen," 1854. Reprint, New York: Woodstock Books, 1996.
———. *The Last Conquest of Ireland (Perhaps)*. Edited by Patrick Maume. Dublin: University College Dublin Press, 2005.
Mitchell, D. W. *Ten Years Residence in the United States*. London: Smith, Elder, and Co., 1862.
Mooney, Thomas. *A History of Ireland, from Its First Settlement to the Present Time*. Boston: Self-published, 1845.
O'Connell, Daniel. *Daniel O'Connell upon American Slavery: With Other Irish Testimonies*. New York: American Anti-Slavery Society, 1860.
———. *The Irish Patriot: Daniel O'Connell's Legacy to Irish Americans*. Philadelphia: Printed for Gratuitous Distribution, n/d.
O'Donovan, Jeremiah. *A Brief Account of the Author's Interview with His Countrymen, and the Parts of the Emerald Isle Whence They Emigrated, Together with a Direct Reference to Their Present Location in the Land of Their Adoption, during His Travels through Various States of the Union in 1854 and 1855*. Pittsburgh: Published by the author, 1864.
Parker, Theodore. *The Material Condition of the People of Massachusetts*. Boston: Published by the Fraternity, 1860.

Proceedings of the First National Convention of the Fenian Brotherhood. Philadelphia: James Gibbon, 1863.

Samito, Christian G., ed. *Commanding Boston's Irish Ninth: The Civil War Letters of Colonel Patrick R. Guiney, Ninth Massachusetts Volunteer Infantry.* New York: Fordham University Press, 1998.

Society of Friends, Ireland. *Transactions of the Central Relief Committee of the Society of Friends during the Famine in Ireland, in 1846 and 1847.* Dublin: Hodges and Smith, 1852.

Beaudot, William J. K., and Lance J. Herdegen, eds. *An Irishman in the Iron Brigade: The Civil War Memoirs of James P. Sullivan, Sergt., Company K, 6th Wisconsin Volunteers.* New York: Fordham University Press, 1993.

Tappan, Lewis. *The Fugitive Slave Bill: Its History and Unconstitutionality; With an Account of the Seizure and Enslavement of James Hamlet, and His Subsequent Restoration to Liberty.* New York: American Anti-Slavery Society, 1850.

Taylor, Clare, ed. *British and American Abolitionists: An Episode in Transatlantic Understanding.* Edinburgh: Edinburgh University Press, 1974.

Weiss, John, ed. *Life and Correspondence of Theodore Parker, Minister of the Twenty-Eighth Congregational Society, Boston*, vol. 1. New York: Appleton, 1864.

SECONDARY SOURCES

Anbinder, Tyler. *Five Points: The 19th-Century New York City Neighborhood That Invented Tap Dance, Stole Elections, and Became the World's Most Notorious Slum.* New York: Plume, 2002.

——— . *Nativism and Slavery: The Northern Know-Nothings and the Politics of the 1850s.* New York: Oxford University Press, 1992.

——— . "Which Poor Man's Fight? Immigrants and the Federal Conscription of 1863." *Civil War History* 52, no. 4 (December 2006): 344–72.

Arenson, Adam. *The Great Heart of the Republic: St. Louis and the Cultural Civil War.* Cambridge, MA: Harvard University Press, 2011.

Armitage, David, et al. "Interchange: Nationalism and Internationalism in the Era of the Civil War." *Journal of American History* 98 (September 2011): 455–89.

Arnesen, Eric. "Whiteness and the Historians Imagination," *International Labor and Working-Class History* 60 (Fall 2001): 3–32.

Athearn, Robert G. *Thomas Francis Meagher: An Irish Revolutionary in America.* Boulder: University of Colorado Press, 1949.

Baker, Jean H. *Affairs of Party: The Political Culture of Northern Democrats in the Mid-Nineteenth Century.* New York: Fordham University Press, 1998.

Ballard, Michael B. *Vicksburg: The Campaign That Opened the Mississippi River.* Chapel Hill: University of North Carolina Press, 2004.

Barker, Gordon S. *The Imperfect Revolution: Anthony Burns and the Landscape of Race in Antebellum America.* Kent: Kent State University Press, 2010.

Bartlett, Thomas, and Keith Jeffery, eds. *A Military History of Ireland.* New York: Cambridge University Press, 1996.

Baum, Dale. *The Civil War Party System: The Case of Massachusetts, 1848–1876*. Chapel Hill: University of North Carolina Press, 1984.

———. "Know-Nothingism and the Republican Majority in Massachusetts: The Political Realignment of the 1850s." *Journal of American History* 64, no. 4 (1978): 959–86.

Beatty, Jack. *The Rascal King: The Life and Times of James Michael Curley (1874–1958)*. Reading, MA: Addison-Wesley, 1992.

Bender, Thomas. *A Nation Among Nations: America's Place in World History*. New York: Hill and Wang, 2006.

Berlin, Ira. "Who Freed the Slaves." In *Union and Emancipation: Essays on Politics and Race in the Civil War Era*, edited by David W. Blight and Brooks D. Simpson. Kent, OH: Kent State University Press, 1997.

Bernstein, Iver. *The New York City Draft Riots: Their Significance for American Society and Politics in the Age of the Civil War*. New York: Oxford University Press, 1993.

Billington, Ray Allen. *The Protestant Crusade, 1800–1860*. Chicago: Quadrangle Books, 1938.

Blied, Benjamin J. *Catholics and the Civil War*. Milwaukee: 1945.

Bric, Maurice J. "Daniel O'Connell and the Debate on Anti-Slavery, 1820–50." In *History and the Public Sphere: Essays in Honour of John A. Murphy*, edited by Tom Dunne and Laurence M. Geary. Cork: Cork University Press, 2005.

Brooke, John L. *"There Is a North": Fugitive Slaves, Political Crisis, and Cultural Transformation in the Coming of the Civil War*. Amherst: University of Massachusetts Press, 2019.

Brown, Christopher Leslie. *Moral Capital: Foundations of British Abolitionism*. Chapel Hill: University of North Carolina Press, 2006.

Brown, Thomas N. *Irish-American Nationalism, 1870–1890*. 1966; reprint, Westport, CT: Greenwood Press, 1980.

Bruce, Susannah Ural. *The Harp and the Eagle: Irish-American Volunteers and the Union Army, 1861–1865*. New York: New York University Press, 2006.

Brundage, David. *Irish Nationalists in America: The Politics of Exile, 1798–1998*. New York: Oxford University Press, 2016.

Burchell, R. A. *The San Francisco Irish, 1848–1880*. Berkeley: University of California Press, 1980.

Burton, William L. *Melting Pot Soldiers: The Union's Ethnic Regiments*. New York: Fordham University Press, 1998.

Campbell, Stanley W. *The Slave Catchers: Enforcement of the Fugitive Slave Law, 1850–1860*. Chapel Hill: University of North Carolina Press, 1970.

Carton, Evan C. *Patriotic Treason: John Brown and the Soul of America*. New York: Free Press, 2006.

Carwardine, Richard, and Jay Sexton, eds. *The Global Lincoln*. New York: Oxford University Press, 2011.

Chaffin, Tom. *Giant's Causeway: Frederick Douglass's Irish Odyssey and the Making of an American Visionary*. Charlottesville: University of Virginia Press, 2014.

Cimbala, Paul A., and Randall M. Miller, eds. *Union Soldiers and the Northern Home Front: Wartime Experiences, Postwar Adjustments*. New York: Fordham University Press, 2002.

Clark, Dennis. *The Irish in Philadelphia: Ten Generations of Urban Experience.* Philadelphia: Temple University Press, 1973.
Clark Efford, Allison. "Civil War–Era Immigration and the Imperial United States," *Journal of the Civil War Era* 10, no. 2 (June 2020): 233–53.
Click, Patricia C. *Time Full of Trial: The Roanoke Island Freedman's Colony, 1862–1867.* Chapel Hill: University of North Carolina Press, 2001.
Comerford, R. V. *The Fenians in Context: Irish Politics and Society, 1848–82.* Dublin: Wolfhound Press, 1985.
Connor, Charles P. "The Northern Catholic Position on Slavery and the Civil War: Archbishop Hughes as a Test Case." *Records of the American Catholic Historical Society of Philadelphia* 96, no. 4 (1986): 37–48.
Cook, Adrian. *Armies of the Streets: The New York City Draft Riots of 1863.* Lexington: University Press of Kentucky, 1974.
Cooney, Charles F. "Treason or Tyranny? The Great Senate Purge of '62." *Civil War Times Illustrated* 18 (1979): 30–31.
Cornish, Rory T. "An Irish Republican Abroad: Thomas Francis Meagher in the United States, 1852–1865." In *Thomas Francis Meagher: The Making of an Irish American*, edited by Cornish and John M. Hearne. Dublin: Irish Academic Press, 2005.
Costello, Francis. "The Deer Island Graves, Boston: The Irish Famine and Irish-American Tradition." In *The Meaning of the Famine*, edited by Patrick O'Sullivan. London: Leicester University Press, 1997.
Cox, Lawanda. *Lincoln and Black Freedom: A Study in Presidential Leadership.* Columbia: University of South Carolina Press, 1981.
Craven, Avery O. *The Growth of Southern Nationalism, 1848–1861.* Baton Rouge: Louisiana State University Press, 1953.
Cullop, Charles P. "An Unequal Duel: Union Recruiting in Ireland, 1863–1864." *Civil War History* 13 (June 1967): 101–13.
Cunliffe, Marcus. *Chattel and Wage Slavery: The Anglo-American Context.* Athens: University of Georgia Press, 1979.
D'Arcy, William. *The Fenian Movement in the United States: 1858–1866.* Washington, D.C.: Catholic University of America Press, 1947.
Davis, Richard. *The Young Ireland Movement.* Totowa, NJ: Barnes and Noble, 1987.
Demeter, Richard. *The Fighting 69th: A History.* Pasadena, CA: Cranford Press, 2002.
Dillon, William. *Life of John Mitchel.* London: K. Paul, Trench, 1888.
Dolan, Jay. *The Immigrant Church: New York's Irish and German Catholics, 1815–1865.* Baltimore: John Hopkins University Press, 1975.
Donald, David Herbert. *Charles Sumner and the Coming of the Civil War.* New York: Alfred A. Knopf, 1960.
Donnelly, James S., Jr. *The Great Irish Potato Famine.* Gloucestershire: Sutton Publishing, 2001.
Downs, Gregory P. "The Mexicanization of American Politics: The United States' Transnational Path from Civil War to Stabilization." *American Historical Review* 117, no. 2 (April 2012): 387–409.
Doyle, David Noel. "The Irish as Urban Pioneers in the United States, 1850–1870." *Journal of American Ethnic History* 10, no. 1–2 (Fall 1990–Winter 1991): 36–59.

———. *Native Rights and National Empires—The Structure, Divisions, and Attitudes of the Catholic Minority in the Decade of Expansion, 1890–1901.* New York: Arno Press, 1976.

Doyle, Don H. *The Cause of All Nations: An International History of the American Civil War.* New York: Basic Books, 2015.

Egan, Timothy. *The Immortal Irishman: The Irish Revolutionary Who Became an American Hero.* Boston: Houghton Mifflin Harcourt, 2016.

Egerton, Douglas R. "Rethinking Atlantic Historiography in a Postcolonial Era: The Civil War in a Global Perspective." *Journal of the Civil War Era* 1 (March 2011): 79–95.

———. *Thunder at the Gates: The Black Civil War Regiments That Redeemed America.* New York: Basic Books, 2016.

Eichorn, Niels. *Liberty and Slavery: European Separatists, Southern Secession, and the American Civil War.* Baton Rouge: Louisiana State University Press, 2019.

Ernst, Robert. *Immigrant Life in New York City, 1825–1863.* New York: King's Crown Press, 1949.

Fabrikant, Robert. "Emancipation and the Proclamation: Of Contrabands, Congress, and Lincoln." *Howard Law Journal* 49 (Winter 2006): 313.

Faust, Drew Gilpin. *This Republic of Suffering: Death and the American Civil War.* New York: Alfred A. Knopf, 2008.

Ferris, Norman B. *Desperate Diplomacy: William H. Seward's Foreign Policy, 1861.* Knoxville: University of Tennessee Press, 1976.

———. *The Trent Affair: A Diplomatic Crisis.* Knoxville: University of Tennessee Press, 1977.

Fields, Barbara J. "Whiteness, Racism, and Identity." *International Labor and Working-Class History* 60 (Fall 2001): 48–56.

Finkelman, Paul. "Garrison's Constitution: The Covenant with Death and How It Was Made." *Prologue* 32, no. 4 (2000).

Fleche, Andre M. *The Revolution of 1861: The American Civil War in the Age of Nationalist Conflict.* Chapel Hill: University of North Carolina Press, 2012.

Fogarty, Gerald P. "Public Patriotism and Private Politics: The Tradition of American Catholicism." *U.S. Catholic Historian* 4 (1984): 1–48.

Foner, Eric, ed. "Abolitionism and the Labor Movement in Antebellum America." In *Politics and Ideology in the Age of the Civil War.* New York: Oxford University Press, 1980.

———. *The Fiery Trial: Abraham Lincoln and American Slavery.* New York: W. W. Norton, 2010.

———. *Free Soil, Free Labor, Free Men: The Ideology of the Republican Party.* Rev. ed. 1970; reprint, New York: Oxford University Press, 1995.

———, ed. "Lincoln and Colonization." In *Our Lincoln: New Perspectives on Lincoln and His World.* New York: W. W. Norton, 2008.

Foreman, Amanda. *A World on Fire: An Epic History of Two Nations Divided.* New York: Penguin, 2010.

Formisano, Ronald P. *The Birth of Mass Political Parties: Michigan, 1827–1860.* Princeton, NJ: Princeton University Press, 1971.

Foster, Roy F. *Modern Ireland: 1600–1972.* New York: Viking, 1988.

Franklin, John Hope. *The Emancipation Proclamation*. Garden City, NY: Doubleday, 1963.
Frawley, Sister Mary Alphonsine, S.S.J. *Patrick Donahoe*. Washington, D.C.: Catholic University of America Press, 1946.
Frederickson, George M. *The Inner Civil War: Northern Intellectuals and the Crisis of the Union*. New York: Harper and Row, 1965.
Gallagher, Gary, ed. "A Civil War Watershed: The 1862 Richmond Campaign in Perspective." In *The Richmond Campaign of 1862: The Peninsula and the Seven Days*. Chapel Hill: University of North Carolina Press, 2000.
———. *The Union War*. Cambridge, MA: Harvard University Press, 2011.
Geary, James W. *We Need Men: The Union Draft in the Civil War*. Dekalb: Northern Illinois University Press, 1991.
Genevese, Eugene. *The World the Slaveholders Made: Two Essays in Interpretation*. New York: Pantheon, 1969.
Geoghegan, Patrick. *Liberator: The Life and Death of Daniel O'Connell*. Dublin: Gill and Macmillan, 2010.
George, Joseph, Jr. "'A Catholic Family Newspaper' Views the Lincoln Administration: John Mullaly's Copperhead Weekly." *Civil War History* 24, no. 2 (June 1978): 112–32.
Gibson, Florence E. *The Attitudes of the New York Irish Toward State and National Affairs, 1848–1892*. New York: Columbia University Press, 1951.
Gienapp, William. "The Crime Against Sumner: The Caning of Charles Sumner and the Rise of the Republican Party." *Civil War History* 25 (1979): 218–45.
———. "Nativism and the Creation of a Republican Majority in the North before the Civil War." *Journal of American History* 72, no. 3 (1985): 529–59.
———. *The Origins of the Republican Party, 1852–1856*. New York: Oxford University Press, 1987.
Glatthaar, Joseph T. *Forged in Battle: The Civil War Alliance of Black Soldiers and White Officers*. New York: Free Press, 1990.
———. "'Glory,' the 54th Massachusetts Infantry, and Black Soldiers in the Civil War." *The History Teacher* 24 (August 1991): 478–79.
———. *The March to the Sea and Beyond: Sherman's Troops in the Savannah and Carolinas Campaign*. Baton Rouge: Louisiana State University Press, 1985.
Gleeson, David T. *The Irish in the South, 1815–1877*. Chapel Hill: University of North Carolina Press, 2001.
———. "Securing the 'Interests' of the South: John Mitchel, A. G. Magrath, and the Reopening of the Transatlantic Slave Trade." *American Nineteenth-Century History* 11, no. 3 (2010): 279–98.
Glickstein, Jonathan. *American Exceptionalism, American Anxiety: Wages, Competition, and Degraded Labor in the Antebellum United States*. Charlottesville: University of Virginia Press, 2002.
———. "'Poverty Is Not Slavery': American Abolitionists and the Competitive Labor Market." In *Antislavery Reconsidered: New Perspectives on the Abolitionists*, edited by Lewis Perry and Michael Fellman. Baton Rouge: Louisiana State University Press, 1979.

Goodbody, Rob. *A Suitable Channel: Quaker Relief in the Great Famine*. Bray, Ireland: Pale Publishing, 1995.

Grimsley, Mark. *The Hard Hand of War: Union Military Policy Toward Southern Civilians, 1861–1865*. New York: Cambridge University Press, 1995.

Gutman, Herbert. *The Black Family in Slavery and Freedom, 1790–1925*. New York: Pantheon, 1976.

Handlin, Oscar. *Boston's Immigrants: A Study in Acculturation*. Rev. and enl. ed. 1941; reprint, Cambridge, MA: Harvard University Press, 1959.

Harding, Vincent. *There Is a River: The Black Struggle for Freedom in America*. New York: Harcourt Brace Jovanovich, 1981.

Harris, Leslie M. *In the Shadow of Slavery: African Americans in New York City, 1626–1863*. Chicago: University of Chicago Press, 2003.

Harris, Ruth-Ann, and Sally K. Sommers Smith. "The Eagle and the Harp: The Enterprising Byrne Brothers of County Monaghan." *Irish Studies Review* 18, no. 2 (2010): 173–83.

Harrison, Richard S. *Richard Davis Webb: Dublin Quaker Printer (1805–72)*. Cork: Red Barn Publishing, 1993.

Hayes, John D., and Doris D. Maguire. "Charles Graham Halpine: Life and Adventures of Miles O'Reilly." *New-York Historical Society Quarterly* 51, no. 4 (1967): 326–44.

Hernon, Joseph M., Jr., *Celts, Catholics, and Copperheads: Ireland Views the American Civil War*. Columbus: Ohio State University Press, 1968.

Higham, John. *Strangers in the Land: Patterns of American Nativism, 1860–1925*. 2nd ed. New Brunswick, NJ: Rutgers University Press, 1992.

Hirota, Hidetaka. "Nativism, Citizenship, and the Deportation of Paupers in Massachusetts, 1837–1883." PhD diss., Boston College, 2012.

Holt, Michael F. *Forging a Majority: The Formation of the Republican Party in Pittsburgh, 1848–1860*. New Haven, CT: Yale University Press, 1969.

———. *The Political Crisis of the 1850s*. New York: Wiley, 1978.

———. *The Rise and Fall of the American Whig Party: Jacksonian Politics and the Onset of the Civil War*. New York: Oxford University Press, 1999.

Holt, Thomas. *Black Over White: Negro Political Leadership in South Carolina during Reconstruction*. Urbana: University of Illinois Press, 1977.

Hunt, Roger. *Colonels in Blue: Union Army Colonels of the Civil War, New York*. Mechanicsburg, PA: Schiffler, 2003.

Huston, James. "Interpreting the Causation Sequence: The Meaning of the Events Leading to the Civil War." *Reviews in American History* 34 (September 2006): 324–31.

Ignatiev, Noel. *How the Irish Became White*. New York: Routledge, 1995.

Jackson, Alvin. *Ireland, 1798–1998: Politics and War*. Malden, MA: Blackwell, 1999.

Janis, Ely. *A Greater Ireland: The Land League and Transatlantic Nationalism in Gilded Age America*. Madison: University of Wisconsin Press, 2015.

Jenkins, Brian. *Fenians and Anglo-American Relations during Reconstruction*. Ithaca, NY: Cornell University Press, 1969.

Johnson, Ronald, and Ousmane K. Power-Greene, eds. *In Search of Liberty: African American Internationalism in the Nineteenth-Century Atlantic World*. Athens: University of Georgia Press, 2021.

Johnson, Walter. *Soul by Soul: Life Inside the Antebellum Slave Market*. Cambridge, MA: Harvard University Press, 1999.

Jones, Howard. *Abraham Lincoln and a New Birth of Freedom: The Union and Slavery in the Diplomacy of the Civil War*. Lincoln: University of Nebraska Press, 1999.

———. *Union in Peril: The Crisis Over British Intervention in the Civil War*. Chapel Hill: University of North Carolina Press, 1992.

Jones, Paul. *The Irish Brigade*. Gaithersburg, MD: Olde Soldier Books, 1969.

Karamanski, Theodore. *Rally Round the Flag: Chicago and the Civil War*. New York: Rowman and Littlefield, 2006.

Kautz, Craig Lee. "Fodder for Cannon: Immigrant Perceptions of the Civil War—The Old Northwest." PhD diss., University of Nebraska, Lincoln, 1976.

Kearney, H. F. "Father Mathew: Apostle of Modernisation." In *Studies in Irish History Presented to R. Dudley Edwards*, edited by Art Cosgrave and Donal McCartney. Dublin: University College, Dublin, 1979.

Keating, Ryan W. *Shades of Green: Irish Regiments, American Soldiers, and Local Communities in the Civil War Era*. New York: Fordham University Press, 2017.

Kee, Robert. *The Green Flag: A History of Irish Nationalism*. New York: Penguin, 1972.

Kelly, Brian. "Ambiguous Loyalties: The Boston Irish, Slavery, and the Civil War." *Historical Journal of Massachusetts* 24, no. 2 (1996): 165–204.

Kenny, Kevin. *The American Irish: A History*. New York: Pearson Education, 2000.

———. "American-Irish Nationalism." In *Making the Irish American: History and Heritage of the Irish in the United States*, edited by J. J. Lee and Marion R. Casey. New York: New York University Press, 2006.

———. "'Freedom and Unity': Lincoln in Irish Political Discourse." In *The Global Lincoln*, edited by Richard Carwardine and Jay Sexton. New York: Oxford University Press, 2011.

———, ed. *Ireland and the British Empire: The Oxford History of the British Empire Companion Series*. New York: Oxford University Press, 2004.

———. *Making Sense of the Molly Maguires*. New York: Oxford University Press, 1998.

———. "Nativism, Labor, and Slavery: The Political Odyssey of Benjamin Bannan, 1850–1860." *Pennsylvania Magazine of History and Biography* 118, no. 4 (October 1994): 325–61.

Kerrigan, Colm. *Father Mathew and the Irish Temperance Movement, 1838–1849*. Cork: Cork University Press, 1992.

———. "Irish Temperance and US Antislavery: Father Mathew and the Abolitionists." *History Workshop* 31 (Spring 1991): 105–19.

Keyes, Michael. *Funding the Nation: Money and Nationalist Politics in Nineteenth-Century Ireland*. Dublin: Gill and Macmillan, 2011.

Kinealy, Christine. *Daniel O'Connell and the American Anti-Slavery Movement*. London: Pickering and Chatto, 2011.

———. *A Death-Dealing Famine: The Great Hunger in Ireland*. Chicago: Pluto Press, 1997.

———. *The Great Irish Famine: Impact, Ideology, and Rebellion*. New York: Palgrave, 2002.

———. "The Liberator: Daniel O'Connell and Anti-Slavery." *History Today* 57, no. 12 (December 2007).
Klement, Frank L. *The Limits of Dissent: Clement L. Vallandigham and the Civil War.* Lexington: University Press of Kentucky, 1970.
———. "Catholics as Copperheads during the Civil War." *Catholic Historical Review* 80, no. 1 (January 1944): 36–57.
Kleppner, Paul. *The Third Electoral System, 1853–1892: Parties, Voters, and Political Cultures.* Chapel Hill: University of North Carolina Press, 1979.
Kolchin, Peter. "Whiteness Studies: The New History of Race in America." *Journal of American History* 89, no. 1 (2002): 154–73.
Knupfer, Peter B. "A Crisis in Conservatism: Northern Unionism and the Harpers Ferry Raid." In *His Soul Goes Marching On: Responses to John Brown and the Harpers Ferry Raid*, edited by Paul Finkelman. Charlottesville: University Press of Virginia, 1995.
———. *Union as It Is: Constitutional Unionism and Sectional Compromise, 1787–1861.* Chapel Hill: University of North Carolina Press, 1991.
Krieg, Joann P. *Whitman and the Irish.* Iowa City: University of Iowa City Press, 2000.
Kurtz, William B. *Excommunicated from the Union: How the Civil War Created a Separate Catholic America.* New York: Fordham University Press, 2016.
Kwitchen, Mary Augustine. *James Alphonsus McMaster: A Study in American Thought.* Washington, D.C.: Catholic University of America Press, 1949.
Laderman, Gary. *The Sacred Remains: American Attitudes Toward Death, 1799–1883.* New Haven, CT: Yale University Press, 1996.
Laurie, Bruce. *Beyond Garrison: Antislavery and Social Reform.* New York: Cambridge University Press, 2005.
Legg, Marie-Louise. *Newspapers and Nationalism: The Irish Provincial Press, 1850–1892.* Dublin: Four Courts Press, 1999.
Levine, Bruce. *Half Slave and Half Free: The Roots of Civil War.* Rev. ed. 1992; reprint, New York: Hill and Wang, 2002.
Levine, Peter. "Draft Evasion in the North during the Civil War." *Journal of American History* 67, no. 4 (March 1981): 816–34.
Linderman, Gerald. *Embattled Courage: The Experience of Combat in the American Civil War.* New York: Free Press, 1987.
Litwack, Leon F. *Been in the Storm So Long: The Aftermath of Slavery.* New York: Alfred A. Knopf, 1979.
———. *North of Slavery: The Negro in the Free States, 1790–1860.* Chicago: University of Chicago Press, 1961.
Lofton, Willis H. "Northern Labor and the Negro during the Civil War." *Journal of Negro History* 34, no. 3 (July 1949): 251–73.
Lonn, Ella. *Foreigners in the Union Army and Navy.* Baton Rouge: Louisiana State University Press, 1951.
Mageean, Deirdre M. "Emigration from Irish Ports." *Journal of American Ethnic History* 13, no. 1 (1993): 6–30.
Man, Albon P., Jr. "The Irish in New York in the Early Eighteen-Sixties." *Irish Historical Studies* 7, no. 126 (September 1950): 87–108.

———. "Labor Competition and the New York City Draft Riots of 1863." *Journal of Negro History* 36, no. 4 (October 1951): 375–405.
Mandel, Bernard. *Labor, Free and Slave: Workingmen and the Anti-Slavery Movement in the United States*. New York, 1955. Reprint, Chicago: University of Illinois Press, 2007.
Manning, Chandra. *Troubled Refuge: Struggling for Freedom in the Civil War*. New York: Alfred A. Knopf, 2016.
———. *What This Cruel War Was Over: Soldiers, Slavery, and the Civil War*. New York: Random House, 2007.
Masur, Kate. "'A Rare Phenomenon of Philological Vegetation': The Word 'Contraband' and the Meanings of Emancipation in the United States." *Journal of American History* 93 (March 2007): 1050–84.
Matison, Sumner Eliot. "The Labor Movement and the Negro during Reconstruction." *Journal of Negro History* 33, no. 4 (October 1948): 426–68.
May, Robert E., ed. *The Union and the Confederacy and the Atlantic Rim*. West Lafayette, IN: Purdue University Press, 1995.
Mayer, Henry. *All on Fire: William Lloyd Garrison and the Abolition of Slavery*. New York: W. W. Norton, 1998.
McDaniel, W. Caleb, and Bethany L. Johnson. "New Approaches to Internationalizing the History of the Civil War Era: An Introduction." *Journal of the Civil War Era* 2, no. 2 (June 2012): 145–50.
———. *The Problem of Democracy in the Age of Slavery: Garrisonian Abolitionists and Transatlantic Reform*. Baton Rouge: Louisiana State University Press, 2013.
———. "Repealing Unions: American Abolitionists, Irish Repeal, and the Origins of Garrisonian Disunionism." *Journal of the Early American Republic* 28, no. 2 (Summer 2008): 243–69.
McFeely, William S. *Yankee Stepfather: General O. O. Howard and the Freedmen*. New Haven, CT: Yale University Press, 1968.
McGee, Owen. "'God Save Ireland': Manchester Martyr Demonstrations in Dublin, 1867–1916." *Eire-Ireland: A Journal of Irish Studies* 46, no. 3–4 (September 2001): 39–66.
McGovern, Brian. *John Mitchel: Irish Nationalist, Southern Secessionist*. Knoxville: University of Tennessee Press, 2009.
McGreevy, John T. *Catholicism and American Freedom: A History*. New York: W. W. Norton, 2003.
McKivigan, John R. *Forgotten Firebrand: James Redpath and the Making of Nineteenth-Century America*. Ithaca, NY: Cornell University Press, 1998.
McMahon, Cian T. "Did the Irish 'Become White'? Global Migration and National Identity, 1842–1877." PhD diss., Carnegie Mellon University, 2010.
———. *The Global Dimensions of Irish Identity: Race, Nation, and the Popular Press, 1840–1880*. Chapel Hill: University of North Carolina Press, 2015.
———. "Ireland and the Birth of the Irish-American Press, 1842–61." *American Periodicals: A Journal of History and Criticism* 19, no. 1 (2009): 5–20.
McPherson, James M. *Abraham Lincoln and the Second American Revolution*. New York: Oxford University Press, 1991.

———. *Antietam: The Battle That Changed the Course of the Civil War*. New York: Oxford University Press, 2002.
———. *Battle Cry of Freedom: The Civil War Era*. New York: Oxford University Press, 1988.
———. *For Cause and Comrades: Why Men Fought in the Civil War*. New York: Oxford University Press, 1997.
———. *The Struggle for Equality: Abolitionists and the Negro in the Civil War and Reconstruction*. Princeton, NJ: Princeton University Press, 1964.
———. *This Mighty Scourge: Perspectives on the Civil War*. New York: Oxford University Press, 2007.
———. "Who Freed the Slaves." *Proceedings of the American Philosophical Society* 139, no. 1 (March 1995): 1–10.
Miller, Floyd J. *The Search for a Black Nationality: Black Emigration and Colonization 1787–1863*. Urbana: University of Illinois Press, 1975.
Miller, Kerby A. *Emigrants and Exiles: Ireland and the Irish Exodus to North America*. New York: Oxford University Press, 1985.
———. "Revenge for Skibbereen: Irish Emigration and the Meaning of the Great Famine." In *The Great Famine and the Irish Diaspora in America*, edited by Arthur Gribben. Amherst: University of Massachusetts Press, 1998.
Mitchell, Brian. *The Paddy Camps: The Irish of Lowell, 1821–1861*. Urbana: University of Illinois Press, 1998.
Mitchell, Reid. *The Vacant Chair: The Northern Soldier Leaves Home*. New York: Oxford University Press, 1993.
Morris, Thomas D. *Free Men All: The Personal Liberty Laws of the North, 1780–1861*. Baltimore: Johns Hopkins University Press, 1974.
Mulkern, John. *The Know-Nothing Party in Massachusetts: The Rise and Fall of a People's Movement*. Boston: Northeastern University Press, 1990.
———. "Scandal Behind the Convent Walls: The Know-Nothing Nunnery Committee of 1855." *Historical Journal of Massachusetts* 11 (1983): 22–34.
Murdock, Eugene C. *One Million Men: The Civil War Draft in the North*. Madison: University of Wisconsin Press, 1971.
Murphy, Angela F. *American Slavery, Irish Freedom: Abolition, Immigrant Citizenship, and the Transatlantic Movement for Irish Repeal*. Baton Rouge: Louisiana State University Press, 2010.
———. "Daniel O'Connell and the 'American Eagle' in 1845: Slavery, Diplomacy, Nativism, and the Collapse of America's First Irish Nationalist Movement." *Journal of American Ethnic History* 26, no. 2 (2007): 3–26.
Neely, Mark E., Jr. *The Fate of Liberty: Abraham Lincoln and Civil Liberties*. New York: Oxford University Press, 1991.
Nelson, Bruce. "'Come Out of Such a Land, You Irishmen': Daniel O'Connell, American Slavery, and the Making of the 'Irish Race.'" *Éire-Ireland* 42 (2007): 58–81.
———. *Irish Nationalists and the Making of the Irish Race*. Princeton, NJ: Princeton University Press, 2012.
———. "My Countrymen Are All Mankind." *Field Day Review* 4 (2008): 260–73.

Nowlan, Kevin B. "The Origins of the Press in Ireland." In *Communications and Community in Ireland*, edited by Brian Farrell. Dublin: Mercier Press, 1984.
Oates, Stephen B. *To Purge This Land with Blood: A Biography of John Brown*. 2nd ed. Amherst: University of Massachusetts Press, 1984.
O'Connell, Maurice R. "O'Connell, Young Ireland, and Negro Slavery: An Exercise in Romantic Nationalism." *Thought* 64, no. 253 (1989): 130–36.
O'Connor, Thomas H. *The Boston Irish: A Political History*. Boston: Northeastern University Press, 1995.
———. *Civil War Boston: Home Front and Battlefield*. Boston: Northeastern University Press, 1997.
Oickle, Alvin F. *Disaster in Lawrence: The Fall of the Pemberton Mill*. Charleston, SC: History Press, 2008.
Oldham, Ellen M. "Irish Support of the Abolitionist Movement." *Boston Public Library Quarterly* 10 (1958): 175–87.
Osofsky, Gilbert. "Abolitionists, Irish Immigrants, and the Dilemmas of Romantic Nationalism." *American Historical Review* 80, no. 4 (1975): 889–912.
Palladino, Grace. *Another Civil War: Labor, Capital, and the State in the Anthracite Regions of Pennsylvania, 1840–1868*. Champaign: University of Illinois Press, 1990.
Paludan, Phillip Shaw. *A People's Contest: The Union and the Civil War, 1861–1865*. 2nd ed. Lawrence: University of Kansas Press, 1996.
Pessen, Edward. *Jacksonian America: Society, Personality, and Politics*. Rev. ed. 1969; reprint, Chicago: University of Illinois Press, 1998.
Potter, David. *The Impending Crisis: 1848–1861*. New York: Harper and Row, 1976.
Potter, George. *To the Golden Door: The Story of the Irish in Ireland and America*. Boston: Little, Brown, 1960.
Puleo, Stephen. *Voyage of Mercy: The USS* Jamestown, *the Irish Famine, and the Remarkable Story of America's First Humanitarian Mission*. New York: St. Martin's Press, 2020.
Purcell, Richard J. "James Shields: Soldier and Statesman." *Studies: An Irish Quarterly Review* 21, no. 81 (March 1932): 73–87.
———. "Missionaries from All Hallows (Dublin) to the United States, 1842–1865." *Records of the American Catholic Historical Society of Philadelphia* 34 (December 1942): 204–49.
Quarles, Benjamin. *Black Abolitionists*. New York: Oxford University Press, 1969.
———. *The Negro in the Civil War*. New York: Russell and Russell, 1968.
Quinn, John F. "Expecting the Impossible? Abolitionists' Appeals to the Irish in Antebellum America." *New England Quarterly* 82, no. 4 (December 2009): 667–710.
———. *Father Mathew's Crusade: Temperance in Nineteenth-Century Ireland and Irish America*. Boston: University of Massachusetts Press, 2002.
———. "'The Nation's Guest?': The Battle between Catholics and Abolitionists to Manage Father Theobald Mathew's American Tour, 1849–1851." *U.S. Catholic Historian* 22, no. 3 (Summer 2004): 19–40.
———. "'Three Cheers for the Abolitionist Pope!': American Reaction to Gregory XVI's Condemnation of the Slave Trade, 1840–1860." *Catholic Historical Review* 90, no. 1 (January 2004): 67–93.

Rable, George C. *Fredericksburg! Fredericksburg!* Chapel Hill: University of North Carolina Press, 2002.
Rawson, Michael. *Eden on the Charles: The Making of Boston.* Cambridge, MA: Harvard University Press, 2010.
Reilly, Matthew C., and Jerome Handler. "Contesting White Slavery in the Caribbean: Enslaved Africans and European Indentured Servants in Seventeenth-Century Barbados." *New West Indian Guide* 91 (2017): 30–55.
Reynolds, David S. *John Brown, Abolitionist: The Man Who Killed Slavery, Sparked the Civil War, and Seeded Civil Rights.* New York: Vintage, 2005.
Riach, Douglas C. "Daniel O'Connell and American Anti-Slavery." *Irish Historical Studies* 20, no. 77 (March 1976): 3–25.
———. "Ireland and the Campaign Against American Slavery, 1830–1860." PhD diss., University of Edinburgh, 1975.
———. "Richard Davis Webb and Antislavery in Ireland." In *Antislavery Reconsidered: New Perspectives on the Abolitionists*, edited by Lewis Perry and Michael Fellman. Baton Rouge: Louisiana State University Press, 1979.
Rice, Madeline Hooke. *American Catholic Opinion in the Slavery Controversy.* Gloucester, MA: Peter Smith, 1964.
Richardson, Heather Cox. *The Greatest Nation of the Earth: Republican Economic Policies during the Civil War.* Cambridge, MA: Harvard University Press, 1997.
Ripley, C. Peter. *Slaves and Freedmen in Civil War Louisiana.* Baton Rouge: Louisiana State University Press, 1976.
Rodechko, James P. "An Irish-American Journalist and Catholicism: Patrick Ford of the *Irish World*." *Church History* 39, no. 4 (December 1970): 524–40.
Rodgers, Nini. *Ireland, Slavery, and Anti-Slavery: 1612–1865.* New York: Palgrave Macmillan, 2007.
Roediger, David R. *The Wages of Whiteness: Race and the Making of the American Working Class.* Rev ed. New York: Verso, 2000.
Rubin, Jay. "Black Nativism: The European Immigrant in Negro Thought, 1830–1860." *Phylon* 39, no. 3 (1978): 193–202.
Rugemer, Edward. *The Problem of Emancipation: The Caribbean Roots of the American Civil War.* Baton Rouge: Louisiana State University Press, 2008.
Salyer, Lucy E. "Reconstructing the Immigrant: The Naturalization Act of 1870 in Global Perspective." *Journal of the Civil War Era* 11, no. 3 (September 2021): 382–405.
Samito, Christian G. *Becoming American under Fire: Irish Americans, African Americans, and the Politics of Citizenship during the Civil War Era.* Ithaca, NY: Cornell University Press, 2009.
Schecter, Barnet. *The Devil's Own Work: The Civil War Draft Riots and the Fight to Reconstruct America.* New York: Walker, 2005.
Sears, Stephen W. *Landscape Turned Red: The Battle of Antietam.* Boston: Houghton Mifflin, 2003.
Sewell, Richard H. *Ballots for Freedom: Antislavery Politics in the United States, 1837–1860.* New York: Oxford University Press, 1976.
Sharrow, Walter G. "John Hughes and a Catholic Response to Slavery in Antebellum America." *Journal of Negro History* 57, no. 3 (1972): 254–69.

Sheehan-Dean, Aaron, ed. "The Blue and the Gray in Black and White: Assessing the Scholarship on Civil War Soldiers." In *The View from the Ground: Experiences of Civil War Soldiers*. Lexington: University Press of Kentucky, 2007.

———. *Reckoning with Rebellion: War and Sovereignty in the Nineteenth Century*. Gainesville: University Press of Florida, 2020.

Shiels, Damien. *The Irish in the American Civil War*. Dublin: History Press Ireland, 2013.

Siddali, Silvana R. *From Property to Person: Slavery and the Confiscation Acts, 1861–1862*. Baton Rouge: Louisiana State University Press, 2005.

Silbey, Joel. "The Civil War Synthesis in American Political History." *Civil War History* 10 (1964): 130–40.

———. *A Respectable Minority: The Democratic Party in the Civil War Era, 1860–1868*. New York: W. W. Norton, 1977.

Silverman, Jason. *Lincoln and the Immigrant*. Carbondale: Southern Illinois University Press, 2015.

Sim, David. *A Union Forever: The Irish Question and U.S. Foreign Relations in the Victorian Age*. Ithaca, NY: Cornell University Press, 2013.

Sinha, Manisha. *The Counterrevolution of Slavery: Politics and Ideology in Antebellum South Carolina*. Chapel Hill: University of North Carolina Press, 2000.

———. *The Slave's Cause: A History of Abolition*. New Haven, CT: Yale University Press, 2016.

Smith, John David, ed. *Black Soldiers in Blue: African American Troops in the Civil War Era*. Chapel Hill: University of North Carolina Press, 2002.

Spann, Edward K. "Union Green: The Irish Community and the Civil War." In *The New York Irish*, edited by Ronald H. Bayor and Timothy J. Meagher. Baltimore: Johns Hopkins University Press, 1996.

Stewart, James Brewer. *Holy Warriors: The Abolitionists and American Slavery*. Rev. ed. New York: Hill and Wang, 1997.

———. *Wendell Phillips: Liberty's Hero*. Baton Rouge: Louisiana State University Press, 1986.

Swan, James B. *Chicago's Irish Legion: The 90th Illinois Volunteers in the Civil War*. Carbondale: Southern Illinois University Press, 2009.

Sweeney, Fionnghuala. "'The Republic of Letters': Frederick Douglass, Ireland, and the Irish Narratives." In *New Directions in Irish-American History*, edited by Kevin Kenny. Madison: University of Wisconsin Press, 2003.

Tager, Jack. *Boston Riots: Three Centuries of Social Violence*. Boston: Northeastern University Press, 2001.

Taylor, Amy Murrell. "Following the Paths of the Civil War's Refugees from Slavery." *Journal of the Civil War Era* 10, no. 2 (June 2020): 148–59.

Toomey, Michael. "'Saving the South with All My Might': John Mitchel, Champion of Southern Nationalism." In *Thomas Francis Meagher: The Making of an Irish American*, edited by John M. Hearne and Rory T. Cornish. Dublin: Irish Academic Press, 2005.

Townend, Paul A. *Father Mathew, Temperance, and Irish Identity*. Portland, OR: Irish Academic Press, 2002.

Tuchinsky, Adam. *Horace Greeley's New-York Tribune: Civil War–Era Socialism and the Crisis of Free Labor*. Ithaca, NY: Cornell University Press, 2009.
Tyrell, Ian R. *Sobering Up: From Temperance to Prohibition in Antebellum America, 1800–1860*. Westport, CT: Greenwood Press, 1979.
Ural, Susannah J., ed. "'Ye Sons of Green Erin Assemble': Northern Irish American Catholics and the Union War Effort, 1861–1865." In *Civil War Citizens: Race, Ethnicity, and Identity in America's Bloodiest Conflict*. New York: New York University Press, 2010.
Varon, Elizabeth R. *Disunion! The Coming of the Civil War, 1789–1859*. Chapel Hill: University of North Carolina Press, 2008.
Von Frank, Albert J. *The Trials of Anthony Burns: Freedom and Slavery in Emerson's Boston*. Cambridge, MA: Harvard University Press, 1998.
Wagandt, Charles. *The Mighty Revolution: Negro Emancipation in Maryland, 1862–1864*. Baltimore: Johns Hopkins University Press, 1964.
Wallenstein, Peter. "Incendiaries All: Southern Politics and the Harpers Ferry Raid." In *His Soul Goes Marching On: Responses to John Brown and the Harpers Ferry Raid*, edited by Paul Finkelman. Charlottesville: University Press of Virginia, 1995.
Walsh, Francis R. "The Boston *Pilot* Reports the Civil War." *Historical Journal of Massachusetts* 8 (1981): 5–16.
———. "Who Spoke for Boston's Irish? The Boston *Pilot* in the Nineteenth Century." *Journal of Ethnic Studies* 10, no. 3 (Fall 1982): 21–36.
Walsh, Victor A. "A Fanatic Heart: The Cause of Irish-American Nationalism in Pittsburgh during the Gilded Age." *Journal of Social History*, no. 15 (1981): 187–204.
Way, Peter. *Common Labour: Workers and the Digging of North American Canals, 1780–1860*. New York: Cambridge University Press, 1993.
Weber, Jennifer L. *Copperheads: The Rise and Fall of Lincoln's Opponents in the North*. New York: Oxford University Press, 2006.
Wilentz, Sean. *Chants Democratic: New York City and the Rise of the American Working Class, 1788–1850*. New York: Oxford University Press, 1994.
Wilson, David A. *United Irishmen, United States: Immigrant Radicals in the Early Republic*. Ithaca, NY: Cornell University Press, 1998.
Wittke, Carl. *The Irish in America*. Baton Rouge: Louisiana State University Press, 1956.
Woodworth, Steven E. *This Great Struggle: America's Civil War*. New York: Rowman and Littlefield, 2011.
Wubben, Hubert H. "Dennis A. Mahoney and the *Dubuque Herald*, 1860–1863." *Iowa Journal of History* 56 (October 1958): 289–320.
Wylie, Paul R. *The Irish General: Thomas Francis Meagher*. Norman: University of Oklahoma Press, 2007.
Zibro, James. "The Life of Paddy Yank: The Common Irish-American Soldier in the Union Army." PhD diss., Catholic University of America Press, 2016.

Index

6th Wisconsin Regiment, 195
7th Rhode Island Regiment, 161
9th Connecticut Regiment, 160, 164, 221, 235
9th Massachusetts Regiment, 12–13, 138, 144, 146, 157, 159, 181, 189, 192, 199, 249–50; and desertion, 162–63; organization of, 134
10th Ohio Regiment, 159, 208
11th New York Regiment, 178
15th Maine Regiment, 142
17th Wisconsin Regiment, 146
20th Maine Regiment, 220
23rd Illinois Regiment, 152, 161, 187, 191, 207, 230
23rd Kentucky Regiment, 199
24th Connecticut Regiment, 221
28th Massachusetts Regiment, 160, 180, 186, 196
29th Wisconsin Regiment, 192
34th New York Regiment, 157
35th Indiana Regiment, 190
47th New York Regiment, 223
50th Massachusetts Regiment, 195
54th Massachusetts Regiment, 13, 222
69th New York Regiment, 134, 146–47, 153, 179, 189, 224, 229; as Union's most famous Irish-American unit, 222
90th Illinois Regiment (Irish Legion), 172, 192, 194–95
116th Pennsylvania Regiment, 157
164th New York Regiment, 191, 197–98
1848 Irish rebellion, 42–43, 49, 72–73

abolitionism, 15, 20; appeals to Irish immigrants, 5, 9, 16, 42–45, 47–49, 54, 56, 63; and disunion, 7, 118–19, 148–49, 165–66, 213; and famine relief, 35–37; and Father Mathew, 75–78; in Ireland, 2–5, 17, 21–24; Irish Americans opposed to, 11–12, 21, 32, 38, 40, 42, 46, 57–58, 61–62, 66, 77, 80, 83–101, 106–7, 129, 152–54, 159, 176, 211, 227, 232, 237, 239; and nativism, 100, 111, 133; opposition to in Ireland, 7–8, 19, 26, 30–33, 40–41, 55, 89–90, 93, 106, 111, 226, 237; ties to Great Britain, 7–8, 59–60, 141, 150
Act of Union (1801), 15, 17, 60, 65, 68, 73
African Americans: compared to Irish, 55–56, 100; Irish American racism toward, 13, 118, 157–58, 171–73, 176–77; support of famine relief, 34
Alien and Sedition Acts (1798), 128
Allen, Annie, 21
Allen, Richard, 17, 19–20, 36, 44
American Anti-Slavery Society (AASS), 22, 60, 75
American Party, 113, 117, 121–23. *See also* Know-Nothings
Andrew, John A., Governor, 197–200
Anglophobia, 53–54, 58–60, 63–64, 136, 141, 144–45, 165, 190
anti-Catholicism: and abolitionism, 22, 89, 112, 127; in Ireland, 19, 21–22; Irish American efforts to combat, 139, 205; of Know-Nothings, 111, 113–17; and New York City Draft Riots, 206; and Republican Party, 147; and Whig Party, 68
Australia, 5

Barrett, Thomas, Captain, 195
Batchelder, James, 87–88

Battle of Antietam, 154–55, 162, 164, 168
Battle of Bull Run (1861), 145, 147
Battle of Chancellorsville, 162, 168, 192
Battle of Fort Sumter, 132, 134, 138–39, 142, 150, 156
Battle of Fort Wagner, 13
Battle of Fredericksburg, 155, 162, 164, 168, 175, 178, 191
Battle of Gettysburg, 180, 193, 201, 216
Battle of Vicksburg, 160, 162, 180, 193, 195, 201, 216
Beecher, Henry Ward, Reverend, 94, 119, 127
Belfast, 2, 22–23, 47, 71, 184, 221
Beman, Amos G., 57
Bennett, James Gordon, 234
Boerly, Thomas, 127, 130
Boston, 122, 157, 200; and famine relief, 34, 71; and Father Cahill, 140; Father Mathew in, 75, 78; Irish immigrants in, 11–13, 53, 61, 65, 72, 86–89, 99, 103, 134, 138, 146, 148, 152, 162, 181, 186, 196, 198, 211, 217, 220, 242, 249
Boston Pilot, 51, 72, 103, 149, 159, 224, 233; Anglophobia of, 60; on the Catholic Church and slavery, 212–13, 216–17; criticism of caning of Sumner, 120; criticism of John Mitchel, 94–95; criticizes conscription, 205; and Father Mathew, 74, 79, 81; as leading Irish American newspaper, 211, 249; as official archdiocesan paper, 11–12; opposition to abolitionism, 47, 58–59, 77, 82, 84–90, 98, 105, 112, 118–19, 121–22, 125–28, 143, 148, 150, 154, 161, 211–12, 227; opposition to nativism, 89, 122–23, 128–29, 155; support for Union cause, 125, 138, 143, 145, 147, 173, 212
Brannigan, Felix, 190
Brenan, Joseph, 102, 104
Broderick, Captain, 32
Brooklyn riots, 172–75
Brooks, Preston, 117, 119–20
Brown, John, 101, 117, 132, 199; raid on Harpers Ferry, 126–29

Buchanan, James, 110
Burns, Anthony, 13, 115, 134, 158, 162; capture and reenslavement of, 87–90
Burnside, Ambrose, General, 162
Butler, Andrew, 69
Butler, Benjamin, General, 156
Butler, Thaddeus, Reverend, 207–8

Cahill, Daniel W., Reverend, 103, 140–42
Cahill, Thomas, Colonel, 160, 164, 235, 237–38
Calhoun, John C., 60
Campbell, John, 61
Canada, 5, 86–87, 189, 218, 243
Carroll, Hugh, 130
Cass, Thomas, 88
Catholic Church, 12; influence on Irish immigrants, 54; opposition to reform movements, 4; patriotism of, 138–39, 182; priests as Union army chaplains, 206–8; sisters as Union nurses, 207; views on slavery, 83–87, 205–13, 217
Catholic emancipation in Ireland, 32, 68
Catholic Telegraph and Advocate (Cincinnati), 11–12, 51, 144, 205–6, 224, 232–33, 235; on Cincinnati riots, 170–71; criticism of abolitionism, 149; support for emancipation, 208–18, 226–27; support for Union cause, 138, 140
Chapman, Maria Weston, 21–22, 24
Charlestown Convent Burning (1834), 128
Chase, Salmon P., 115–16
Chicago, 57; 1863 Fenian Convention, 190; Irish immigrants in, 3, 11, 50, 106, 116, 181, 207
Cincinnati: 1862 riots, 170–72; Irish immigrants in, 3, 11, 116, 128, 138–39, 148, 171–72, 208; and Irish Repeal, 31, 226
Citizen (New York): anticlericalism of, 95; and Irish-American nationalism, 52, 91; John Mitchel as editor of, 52; proslavery views of, 52, 91, 95–96; support for Union cause, 89, 230–32
Clan na Gael, 244–45
Clements, Edward, 31

INDEX

Collins, Michael, 247
Columbian Artillery, 88
Compromise of 1850, 67, 83–84
Conyngham, David P., 190, 222
Copperheads, 176, 181, 193
Corby, William, Reverend, 185
Corcoran, Michael, General, 134, 146, 191
Corcoran's Irish Legion, 146, 163, 189, 191, 194, 230
Cork, 54, 74; abolitionism in, 21, 23, 25, 47; and famine relief, 22, 71; Frederick Douglass in, 2, 23, 25; and Irish emigration, 45, 221
Cork Examiner: on American famine relief efforts, 34–35; and Father Mathew, 75, 77; on Irish suffering, 53, 69; support for abolitionism, 23, 25, 46; support for Confederacy, 141–42, 155, 186, 226
Crosby, George, 71
Curley, James Michael, 242
Curley, Michael, 242
Curti, Merle, 34, 70

Dallas, George M., 40
Daly, Charles Patrick, Judge, 140, 151–53, 184, 191, 223
Davis, Thomas, 28–29, 32, 37
Dee, John, 195–96
Democratic Party, 226, 235; anti-war faction, 176, 185; Irish American support for, 4–5, 54, 68, 70, 100–1, 108, 113, 116–22, 124–27, 131–32, 151, 241; opposition to emancipation, 155, 168
Dennis, William, 139
de Valera, Éamon, 246–47
Devoy, James, 244–48
Devoy, John, 244
Dillon, John Blake, 31
Doheny, Michael, 95–96, 128
Donahoe, Patrick, 81, 121, 123, 145; background, 84; criticism of John Mitchel, 94–95; criticism of slavery, 47, 77, 83, 85, 87; opposition to abolitionism, 58–59, 78, 85–86, 90, 98, 118, 127–29, 205, 211–12; support for Union cause, 138, 150, 206
Donlon, Michael, 180
Douglas, Stephen A., 79, 93, 108, 131
Douglass, Frederick, 45, 77, 93, 114, 161, 199, 250; on Irish poverty, 55–56; tour of Ireland, 2, 21–26
Dred Scott v. Sandford, 124–25
Dublin, 12, 84, 99, 222; and abolitionism, 20–21, 45, 47, 92, 226; Frederick Douglass in, 2, 23–25, 56; and famine relief, 35, 58, 65, 71; and Irish immigration, 73, 107, 207, 220–21; and Irish nationalism, 38, 72, 128, 144–45, 189, 243–48; and Irish repeal, 17, 26, 28, 65; and support for Union, 229
Dublin Anti-Slavery Society, 45–46
Duffy, Charles Gavin, 28–29, 144
Dunny, Patrick, 147
Dyer, Thomas, 116

emancipation in British West Indies (1833), 6, 59–60
Emancipation Proclamation, 174; Irish American criticism of, 5, 161–68, 181, 194, 207, 212; Irish American support for, 193–96, 202–3, 205, 213; preliminary proclamation, 154–55
England, 29; and abolitionism, 11, 23, 60, 94, 127–28, 143, 150; and immigration, 4, 7; Irish criticism of, 19, 58–60, 122, 141–42, 149, 218; and Irish nationalism, 189–91, 220; and Irish Repeal, 17, 28; and the United States, 31, 141, 144. *See also* Great Britain

Farrell, Thomas, 210
Faulkner, C. J., 89
Fenian Brotherhood, 165, 184, 221, 229; 1863 Chicago Convention, 190–91; 1866 invasion of Canada, 243; efforts to liberate Ireland, 243–44; and McManus funeral, 144–45; origins of, 128–29; in Union army, 10, 145, 169, 182, 188–91, 194, 225–26, 238, 243

Fillmore, Millard, 122–23
Finn, Daniel, 157, 159–60
Finnerty, Michael, Lieutenant, 159
First Confiscation Act, 158
Fitzpatrick, John, Bishop, 34
Flaherty, Nicholas, 12–13, 196–97
Flynn, Patrick, 194
Foner, Eric, 152
Ford, Patrick, 245, 248–50
Francis, John, 23
free labor: as championed by Rev. Edward Purcell, 217–18, 229; economy of North, 8, 103–4, 113; Irish-American criticism of, 100–2, 105–6, 110–11, 132, 166
Frémont, John C., 119, 122–23
Friends of Irish Freedom (FOIF), 246
Fugitive Slave Law, 45, 67, 83–87, 89–90, 153

Gallagher, Gary W., 147
Galway, 71, 249; Frederick Douglass in, 2; Irish emigration from, 220–21, 242
Galway-American: support for emancipation, 165; support of Union cause, 141, 165, 186, 221, 225
Gardner, Henry J., Governor, 115
Garrison, William Lloyd, 11, 36, 47, 56, 78, 93, 249; and Father Mathew, 75–77; support for disunion, 73–74, 82; support for Irish Repeal, 27, 54, 60; transatlantic ties to Ireland, 12, 22–23, 27, 44
German Americans, 99, 112, 116, 122–23, 177, 194, 217
Grant, James, 25
Grant, Ulysses, General, 195, 224–25
Great Britain, 122; and abolitionism, 59, 63, 101, 149, 154; Act of Union with Ireland (1801), 17; and Irish nationalism, 3, 19–20, 27, 73, 132, 204, 244, 247; and the United States, 29–30, 143, 148. *See also* England
Great Irish Potato Famine, 2, 9, 16, 19, 22, 53, 134; American relief efforts, 2, 7, 9, 33–36, 42, 54, 69–71, 99, 183–85, 191, 237; effect on Irish immigration, 50; and Irish American identity, 49
Greeley, Horace, 18, 127, 154, 174, 218, 225
Guiney, Patrick R., Colonel, 159

Halpine, Charles Graham, 222
Hanlon, Patrick, 54
Haughton, James, 93, 229; abolitionism of, 39–41, 44–45, 48, 57, 61–62, 67, 76, 88, 91–92, 95, 97; criticism of Irish Americans over slavery, 114; as leading Irish reformer, 20; opposition to slaveholders' Repeal contributions, 27–28, 35–36, 38, 40, 46, 58; support for Young Ireland, 38
Hayes, Benjamin, Private, 200
Herbert, Philemon, 120–21
Hibernian Anti-Slavery Society (HASS), 229; abolitionism of, 3, 7, 12, 16, 23, 26, 42, 44–47, 55, 61; and famine relief, 36; as middle-class Protestant movement, 17, 19, 21–22; support for Irish Repeal, 19
Hickley, Darwin, 192
Higginson, Thomas Wentworth, 88, 198
Hogan, John, Reverend, 227
Hughes, John, Archbishop, 95, 145, 147, 174; opposition to abolitionism, 83, 86; reaction to draft riots, 206; support for Union cause, 139, 205

Ireland, Mary, 22, 24
Irish Americans: after the Civil War, 239–42, 248–50; and Anglophobia, 59–60, 143–44; and anti-Catholicism, 21, 68, 89, 111–16, 181; antislavery appeals to, 57–58, 63; and Catholic Church, 4, 12, 18, 50, 54, 83, 85–87, 112, 117, 138–39, 182; compared to African Americans, 55–56, 58; criticism of Lincoln and war, 147, 154–55, 185, 197; criticism of North's free labor economy, 100–1, 103, 106, 110, 170, 173, 181; critique of antislavery, 8–10, 100–1, 108, 111, 135,

148–55, 166–68, 170–71, 174, 188, 201, 213–14, 227, 231; and Democratic Party, 120–21, 124–26, 131–32; desertion, 193; and fugitive slaves, 67, 84, 87, 89–90; and Great Irish Potato Famine, 34–35, 51, 53–54, 185; and Irish nationalism, 128, 144–45, 189, 245–46, 248; and nativism, 100, 112–14, 118, 123; and New York City Draft Riots, 169, 175, 177, 179–80, 206; opposition to abolitionism and antislavery, 2, 12, 21, 30, 41, 43, 47–49, 59, 61–63, 76–78, 80, 89, 98, 100, 111, 114, 119, 132–33, 148, 154–55, 165, 195, 211, 226, 234, 237; opposition to slavery, 5, 47, 83–84, 94, 96–97; racism against African Americans, 5, 13, 57, 172–75; reasons for enlisting in Union army, 137–40, 146; serving in USCT regiments, 197–201; in the South, 99; support for Democratic Party, 69–70; support for emancipation, 2, 13, 195–97, 203–5, 209, 213, 227–29, 231–32, 234–35, 249–50; in a transatlantic perspective, 2–9, 11, 98, 128, 139, 170; unionism, 8–10, 65–70, 72–74, 76, 81–82, 84, 87, 89–90, 94, 97, 101, 123, 126, 133–40, 144, 148, 150, 152, 155–56, 164–66, 169, 185–86, 188, 190, 193, 197, 199, 201–4, 229, 233–34, 237–39, 243–44, 249; view of United States as ally of Ireland, 1, 9, 65–66, 68, 70, 73, 82–84, 94, 100, 132–33, 146–47, 238

Irish Brigade, 153, 157, 160, 163–64, 178, 180, 196, 223; at Battle of Antietam, 164; at Battle of Fredericksburg, 155, 162; and famine relief, 185–86; General Thomas Francis Meagher as leader of, 145, 150, 189, 224–25, 229–30, 233; and Irish nationalism, 190; recruitment efforts for, 150–52, 184

Irish Confederation, 11, 37–40, 43, 58, 63, 92

Irish immigration to the United States: before the war, 15, 41, 43–44, 48–50, 62, 65, 106, 112–13; during Civil War, 44, 48–49, 141, 169, 182, 186–88, 191, 201, 219; immigration-as-exile motif, 4, 49, 52, 59, 62–63, 91, 140, 143, 183; postwar, 239

Irishman (Dublin): criticism of abolitionism, 107, 150; support for Fenian Brotherhood, 190; support for Union cause, 141, 165, 186, 220, 224–25, 229–30; and Thomas Meagher, 232

Irish Relief Society, 1, 183–85

Irish Repeal movement, 29, 229; and abolitionism, 15–18, 24–25, 27–28, 30–33, 38–39, 42, 48, 58, 63, 76, 99; American support for, 18, 26, 28, 31–32, 34, 37, 47–48, 54, 60, 65, 72–73, 76, 143, 226, 228; and Catholic Church, 19; and Great Irish Potato Famine, 37; origins of, 17; popularity of, 17, 20, 26, 68

Irish Republican Brotherhood (IRB), 10, 128, 145, 189, 243–44, 246

Irish War of Independence (1919–21), 246

Jennings, Isabel, 21

Kansas-Nebraska Act (1854), 93, 97–98, 108–10, 117–19, 121–24, 127, 131

Keating, Thomas, 120

Keenan, Patrick, 172–73, 175

Kelly, Richard, 172

Kennedy, Patrick, 105

Kenyon, John, Reverend, 38–39, 58

King James Bible, public schools' use of, 115

Kingston, John (Jacob Moore), 199–201

Knights of St. Patrick, 1, 184

Know-Nothings, 100–1, 107, 112, 120, 130, 132, 154; and 1856 election, 121–23; origins of, 111–13; ties to antislavery politics, 113–17

labor competition critique of emancipation, 170–74

Lalor, William, 107

Lambert, John, 86
Lawrence, Amos, 34, 127
Lawrence (Massachusetts), 107
Leary, Michael, 144, 157–58
Lee, Robert E., General, 128, 148, 162, 168, 243
Liberator, 249
Liberator (Boston): abolitionism of, 25; efforts to recruit Irish Americans to antislavery, 11, 57; and Father Mathew, 76; on Irish poverty, 55–56; letters from Irish abolitionists, 27, 36, 61–62
Limerick, 2, 21, 23–24, 45, 47, 71
Lincoln, Abraham, 143, 151, 225, 230; donates to famine relief, 71; and Emancipation Proclamation, 154, 161–63, 208, 212; encourages wartime immigration, 187–88; Gettysburg Address, 247; Irish-American criticism of, 13, 132, 148–49, 153, 206–7; Irish-American support for, 233; opposition to Know-Nothings, 116–17, 131
LNRA (Loyal National Repeal Association), 11, 17–18, 20, 26–27, 30–32, 37–38, 48, 58, 63
Lynch, Patrick, 77, 83, 102, 118, 121, 127

MacNamara, James, 199
MacNamara, Michael, 181, 196, 199
Madden, R. R., Doctor, 39
Mahan, John, Major, 192
Maher, Patrick, 221
Mannix, Mary, 24
Martin, John, 219
Mathew, Father Theobald, 47, 67, 97, 140; temperance campaigns of, 24, 74; tour of United States, 74–80
McCarter, William, Private, 157
McCarthy, Timothy, 54, 103
McClellan, George B., General, 1, 148, 154, 162, 185, 187
McClure, James, 88
McCluskey, John, Colonel, 142
McDermott, Hugh, 146

McElderry, William, 96
McGee, Thomas D'Arcy: and Father Mathew, 77; opposition to abolitionism, 92, 107; praise of the United States, 39–40; and Young Ireland, 52–53, 59, 62
McManus, Terrence Bellew, 144–45
McMaster, James Alphonsus, 172; criticism of abolitionism, 150, 153, 166, 208–9, 211
McPherson, James, 83
McWhirk, George, 114
Meagher, Thomas Francis, 3, 52, 91, 95, 178, 186, 192, 221; joins Fenians, 189; recruitment of Irish Americans for Union army, 145–46, 150–52; support for emancipation, 229–34
Meehan, Michael, 195
Meehan, Patrick, 127, 130, 184
Metropolitan Record (New York): as archdiocesan newspaper, 147; opposition to emancipation, 174, 205–6, 210–11, 214, 217; opposition to war, 184, 211
Milwaukee, 139
Missouri Compromise, 82, 93, 108
Mitchel, John, 37, 54, 59, 62, 99, 104; "Alabama plantation" letter, 93–98; *Jail Journal*, 52–53; opposition to tying Repeal to abolitionism, 28; portrayal of famine as genocide, 53; support for American slavery, 52, 89, 91, 94, 219
Moore, Jacob, 199–201
Mullaly, John, 205, 210, 214, 217
Mullen, Bernard, Colonel, 189–90
Mulligan, James A., Colonel, 152, 161, 191–92, 207–8
Murphy, Angela, 26, 30, 47
Murphy, Patrick, 210

Nation (Dublin): and antislavery movement, 18, 44–46, 76, 91; criticism of Daniel O'Connell, 31, 37; and famine relief, 34; and Father Mathew, 77; on Irish immigrants in the United States, 102, 104; and Irish nationalism, 20, 29; and Irish relations with the United

States, 35, 38, 40, 70; opposition to abolitionism, 32, 38, 41, 43, 58–60, 82, 226; as paper of Young Ireland, 1, 17, 28; support for Confederacy, 141–42, 155, 186, 219, 226

National Anti-Slavery Standard (New York), 92; controversy over slaveholder contributions to famine relief, 36; on efforts to recruit Irish Americans to antislavery, 11, 57; and Father Mathew, 76; on Irish poverty, 55

National Era (Washington, D.C.): and Father Mathew, 75; on Irish American opposition to abolitionism, 59; and nativism, 114, 116

nativism, 64; and antislavery politics, 111–17, 127–28; and Republican Party, 122–23, 131, 135, 188. *See also* Know-Nothings

Naturalization Act of 1870, 241

Nell, William C., 57

Nelson, Bruce, 41

New York City, 82, 174, 244; Catholic patriotism in, 139; and famine relief, 71, 184, 187; and Father Mathew, 74–75, 78; Irish immigrants in, 3, 11–12, 47, 50, 52, 58–59, 61, 81, 90, 94–96, 99, 106, 108, 129, 146, 148, 169, 172, 177, 186, 206, 209–10, 214, 219, 222, 230, 232, 246, 249; and Irish nationalism, 64–65, 72–73, 129; and Irish Repeal, 34

New York City Draft Riots, 5, 10, 169, 175–77, 179–82, 184, 200–1, 203, 216, 224

New York City's Academy of Music, 1–3, 186

New York Freeman's Journal, 11–12, 51; criticism of abolitionism, 47, 150, 153, 166, 173–74, 208–9, 211, 216, 227; criticism of war, 147; racism of, 172, 177

New York Irish-American, 11; criticism of abolitionism, 61, 76–77, 82, 107, 118–19, 121, 126–27, 130, 143, 154, 164, 232; criticism of slavery, 77; and disunion, 81; and famine relief, 184–85; and Father Mathew, 79; and Irish-American racism, 194, 197; Irish American readership of, 102; Irish nationalism of, 12, 51, 190; Irish readership of, 69–70; links Republicans to nativism, 122–23; and James Shields, 152; and support for Union cause, 139–40, 163, 165, 191, 222, 224

Nugent, Robert, Colonel, 177–79

O'Brien, Henry, 177–79
O'Brien, John, 180, 192
O'Brien, Lawrence, Captain, 221
O'Brien, William Smith, 39, 147
O'Connell: Daniel, 1843 letter condemning American slavery, 61, 226–28; Daniel, abolitionism of, 3, 15–19, 24–28, 30, 46–48, 63, 75–76, 78, 83, 86, 209, 226–29; Daniel, "American eagle" speech, 30–34, 37, 48, 190; Daniel, and Catholic emancipation in Ireland, 68; Daniel, as leader of Repeal movement, 15, 17, 26, 28–29, 37–38, 47, 60, 63, 65, 68, 73, 143; John, 18, 27, 31
O'Dwyer, Edmund, 181, 187, 227, 233
O'Gorman, Richard, 1–2, 154, 183–85, 214
O'Higgins, William, Reverend, 208
O'Keefe, Arthur, 157
O'Mahony, John, General, 128, 189, 225, 244
O'Meara, John, 210
O'Neill, John, General, 244
Opdyke, George, 184
Order of the Star-Spangled Banner (OSSB), 112–13. *See also* Know-Nothings
O'Reilly, Bernard, Reverend, 153
O'Reilly, Thomas, 228
O'Reilly, Ulrica, Sister, 206

Parker, Theodore, 22, 89, 118–19; links Catholicism to slavery, 22
Parnell, Charles Stewart, 245
Peninsula Campaign (1862), 153, 159

Philadelphia, 121; famine relief efforts in, 34, 71; Irish immigrants in, 50, 61–62, 99, 129, 139, 147–48, 210
Phillips, Wendell, 76, 89, 164, 250
Pillsbury, Parker, 92
Pittsburgh, 139
Plunkett, Christopher, 199
Polk, James K., 29
poverty: in Ireland, 9, 19, 55, 63, 66, 75, 111, 113, 137, 150, 214, 248; among Irish Americans, 75, 105–6, 113, 137, 214; of Irish compared to African American slavery, 49, 56, 58, 63, 105–6
Powers, James, 129–30
Purcell, Edward, Reverend: on Irish American labor, 171, 214–15, 218–19, 221; support for emancipation, 205, 208–12, 214, 216–17, 221, 224, 226–28; support for Union cause, 138
Purcell, John, Archbishop, 208–10

Queen's Proclamation of Neutrality, 143
Quinn (U.S. Marine), 127

Redpath, James, 250
Reilly, Thomas, 73
Remond, Charles Lenox, 22, 47
Republican Party, 111, 121, 175, 187; accused of anti-Catholicism, 147; accused of nativism, 100, 116, 122–23, 131–32, 135–36, 154, 229–30, 237; encourages immigration, 188; and free labor, 214, 216; Irish-American criticism of, 13, 101, 123–24, 154; opposition to slavery, 121–22, 124, 126–27, 148–50, 153–54, 231, 237
Roche, James, 165, 221
Roman Catholicism. *See* Catholic Church
Rossa, Jeremiah O'Donovan, 221
Russell, Henry, 36
Russell, John, Lord, 33, 51

Sadlier, Dennis and James, 205–6
San Francisco, 3, 106, 144, 233
Savage, John, 52, 184
Scott, Richard, 31

Second Confiscation Act, 153, 158
Seward, William Henry, 18, 79, 90, 127
Shields, James, General, 151–53, 158, 167
Sims, Thomas, 86, 90
slavery: British opposition to, 15, 43, 59, 61; and Catholicism, 38, 84, 86–87, 114, 204–5, 207–11, 213, 216; and disunion, 65, 74, 82, 119, 127, 134, 149, 153–54, 194, 241; Frederick Douglass on, 55–56; expansion of, 9, 60, 66–67, 81, 83, 92–93, 98, 100, 108–9, 111–12, 117, 122, 124, 126, 130–32; and Father Mathew, 75–81; and free labor, 103, 105; fugitive slaves, 87–90, 135, 159–60; Irish opposition to, 17–19, 22–23, 26–28, 30–33, 35–36, 39–40, 45, 47–48, 63, 227–28; and Irish Repeal, 58, 99; Irish-American views on, 2–11, 13, 42, 46, 49, 57, 64, 78, 83, 88, 90–91, 94–98, 102, 107, 112–13, 118–19, 152, 155, 163, 182, 213–18, 221, 229, 232, 234–35, 237–39, 249; and nativism, 113–14, 123; and Union cause, 156, 158, 161, 163–66, 170–71, 175, 177, 193, 196–97, 200–3, 212, 226, 231, 233–34
Smyth, P. J., 165
Stephens, James, 128, 145, 189, 225–26, 244
St. Patrick's Day, 34, 71, 128
Sullivan, James P., 139, 141, 149, 160, 195–96
Sumner, Charles, 90–91, 117; caning of, 119–21
Sweney, Thomas, 88

Taney, Roger, 124
Tappan, Lewis, 85, 87
Taylor, John, 88
Thomas, Lorenzo, Adjutant General, 195
Thompson, George, 60–62, 143
Trent Affair, 144, 166
Turner, James (Gallowglass), 157, 163–65
Tyler, John, 60

Ulster Protestants, 44
United States Colored Troops (USCT), 195; Irish American service in, 197–201
Ural, Susannah J., 6

Vallandigham, Clement, 193
Van Buren, Martin, 18
Van Diemen's Land, 52

Walker, William, 125–26, 172
Walsh, Mike, 108–10, 124
Webb, Maria, 45
Webb, Richard Davis, 229; abolitionism of, 17, 24, 59; antislavery outreach to Irish immigrants, 45; compares Irish poor to slaves, 55; criticism of James Haughton, 92; on Ireland, 21; opposition to aid from American slaveholders, 35–36
Welsh, Peter, 180, 186–87, 196

Wilson, Henry, 115
Wood, Fernando, 170
Wright, Henry C., 35, 57, 61

Young Ireland: in 1848 rebellion, 42, 72–73; criticism of Mitchel's pro-slavery views, 95–96; criticism of O'Connell, 29–32, 37–38; as exiles, 43, 49, 51–52, 59, 63–64, 183–84; as exiles in the United States, 43, 49, 51–53, 58–59, 64, 91, 104, 219; and famine relief, 70; and Irish nationalism, 16–17, 33, 63, 128, 222; opposition to abolitionism, 28, 31–32, 40–41, 58–59, 62, 91–92, 94, 154, 226

Ian Delahanty is an associate professor of history at Springfield College, where he teaches classes in American history, the Civil War era, American immigration history, and public history.

RECONSTRUCTING AMERICA
Andrew L. Slap, series editor

Hans L. Trefousse, *Impeachment of a President: Andrew Johnson, the Blacks, and Reconstruction.*

Richard Paul Fuke, *Imperfect Equality: African Americans and the Confines of White Ideology in Post-Emancipation Maryland.*

Ruth Currie-McDaniel, *Carpetbagger of Conscience: A Biography of John Emory Bryant.*

Paul A. Cimbala and Randall M. Miller, eds., *The Freedmen's Bureau and Reconstruction: Reconsiderations.*

Herman Belz, *A New Birth of Freedom: The Republican Party and Freedmen's Rights, 1861 to 1866.*

Robert Michael Goldman, *"A Free Ballot and a Fair Count": The Department of Justice and the Enforcement of Voting Rights in the South, 1877–1893.*

Ruth Douglas Currie, ed., *Emma Spaulding Bryant: Civil War Bride, Carpetbagger's Wife, Ardent Feminist—Letters, 1860–1900.*

Robert Francis Engs, *Freedom's First Generation: Black Hampton, Virginia, 1861–1890.*

Robert F. Kaczorowski, *The Politics of Judicial Interpretation: The Federal Courts, Department of Justice, and Civil Rights, 1866–1876.*

John Syrett, *The Civil War Confiscation Acts: Failing to Reconstruct the South.*

Michael Les Benedict, *Preserving the Constitution: Essays on Politics and the Constitution in the Reconstruction Era.*

Andrew L. Slap, *The Doom of Reconstruction: The Liberal Republicans in the Civil War Era.*

Edmund L. Drago, *Confederate Phoenix: Rebel Children and Their Families in South Carolina.*

Mary Farmer-Kaiser, *Freedwomen and the Freedmen's Bureau: Race, Gender, and Public Policy in the Age of Emancipation.*

Paul A. Cimbala and Randall Miller, eds., *The Great Task Remaining Before Us: Reconstruction as America's Continuing Civil War.*

John A. Casey Jr., *New Men: Reconstructing the Image of the Veteran in Late-Nineteenth-Century American Literature and Culture.*

Hilary Green, *Educational Reconstruction: African American Schools in the Urban South, 1865–1890.*

Christopher B. Bean, *Too Great a Burden to Bear: The Struggle and Failure of the Freedmen's Bureau in Texas.*

David E. Goldberg, *The Retreats of Reconstruction: Race, Leisure, and the Politics of Segregation at the New Jersey Shore, 1865–1920.*

David Prior, ed., *Reconstruction in a Globalizing World.*

Jewel L. Spangler and Frank Towers, eds., *Remaking North American Sovereignty: State Transformation in the 1860s.*

Adam H. Domby and Simon Lewis, eds., *Freedoms Gained and Lost: Reconstruction and Its Meanings 150 Years Later.*

David Prior, ed., *Reconstruction and Empire: The Legacies of Abolition and Union Victory for an Imperial Age.*

Sandra M. Gustafson and Robert S. Levine, eds., *Reimagining the Republic: Race, Citizenship, and Nation in the Literary Work of Albion W. Tourgée.* Foreword by Carolyn L. Karcher.

Brian Schoen, Jewel L. Spangler, and Frank Towers, eds., *Continent in Crisis: The U.S. Civil War in North America.*

Raymond James Krohn, *Abolitionist Twilights: History, Meaning, and the Fate of Racial Egalitarianism, 1865–1909.*

Hilary N. Green and Andrew L. Slap, eds., *The Civil War and the Summer of 2020*.

Ian Delahanty, *Embracing Emancipation: A Transatlantic History of Irish Americans, Slavery, and the American Union, 1840–1865*.

www.ingramcontent.com/pod-product-compliance
Ingram Content Group UK Ltd.
Pitfield, Milton Keynes, MK11 3LW, UK
UKHW041810220225
455401UK00003B/28